T0338161

2016 Stonewall Honor Book for Nonfiction
American Library Association

2015 Gold Award for Nonfiction/LGBT
Foreword Review's INDIEFAB Book of the Year Award

"A riveting page-turner that keeps on giving . . . seamlessly enriched by attention to time and place. A must read for scholars and general readers alike."
   —***Western Historical Review***

"Highly recommended."
   —***Midwest Book Review, Wisconsin Book Watch***

"Extraordinary feat of detective work. One of the most fascinating characters ever to make Portland home."
   —***Oregon Historical Quarterly***

"A compelling inquiry into the life of one of early Oregon's most courageous individuals. Michael Helquist's meticulous research and clear writing illuminates Marie Equi's extraordinary life in a way that shows the continued relevance of her activism, and the persistence of the many causes for which she fought."
   —**Eric Alan, Music, Arts, and Culture host for NPR affiliate KLCC-FM**

"A stirring biography and history that is meticulously researched, passionately and eloquently rendered and is just a great read."
   —**James Anderson, author, *The Never-Open Desert Diner*, 2015**

"A richly detailed and enthralling book. Helquist vividly narrates how this passionate, keen, and caring woman dared to live openly as a lesbian and to fight fiercely for social justice, as a physician, suffragist, abortionist, Wobbly, anti-imperialist, and self-named 'Queen of the Bolsheviks'—enjoy!"
   —**Nancy Krieger, PhD, Harvard T.H. Chan School of Public Health**

"Michael Helquist has written a marvelous biography of Marie Equi. . . . She contributed to the well-being of so many as a doctor, a supporter of workers especially those in the IWW, an advocate of woman suffrage, and an opponent of World War I, for which she paid dearly when she was incarcerated at San Quentin. She was an 'out' lesbian at a time when few were. In this well-written, accessible biography of so extraordinary a personage Helquist has made a splendid contribution to both feminist and lesbian history."
   —**Bettina Aptheker, Professor, Feminist Studies Department, University of California, Santa Cruz**

Marie Equi

Radical Politics and Outlaw Passions

MICHAEL HELQUIST

Oregon State University Press Corvallis

Library of Congress Cataloging-in-Publication Data

Helquist, Michael, 1949–, author.
Marie Equi : radical politics and outlaw passions / Michael Helquist.
  p. ; cm.
  Includes bibliographical references and index.
  ISBN 978-0-87071-595-2 (original trade pbk. : alk. paper) – ISBN 978-0-87071-815-1 (e-book)
  I. Title.
  [DNLM: 1. Equi, Marie, 1872-1952. 2. Physicians, Women–Oregon–Biography.
  3. Feminism–history–Oregon. 4. History, 19th Century–Oregon. 5. History,
  20th Century–Oregon. 6. Homosexuality, Female–Oregon–Biography.
  7. Politics–Oregon–Biography.   WZ 100]
  610.92–dc23
  [B]

                                        2015021431

∞ This paper meets the requirements of ANSI/NISO Z39.48-1992
(Permanence of Paper).

Oregon State University Press
121 The Valley Library
Corvallis OR 97331-4501
541-737-3166 • fax 541-737-3170
www.osupress.oregonstate.edu

To Dale, with awe and appreciation

Contents

Acknowledgments

Writing history requires a trek through the highs and lows of inspiration, discipline, and perseverance in pursuit of a story and its meaning. To have company along the way lightens the load, informs the journey, and rallies the spirit. I am indebted to everyone who advised and supported me throughout several years.

The work of historians Tom Cook and George Painter of the Gay Lesbian Archives of the Pacific Northwest (GLAPN) first introduced me to the life of Dr. Marie Equi, one of Portland's early woman doctors, political radicals, and lesbians. Next, the oral histories of Equi's contemporaries, including her daughter, by Sandy Polishuk, Susan Dobrof, and Nancy Krieger intrigued me with the possibility of a book-length biography. Krieger's discovery of the US Department of Justice's file on Equi and her journal article on Equi's history encouraged me to scour dozens of personal and institutional archives, newspaper reports, church records, and court documents. I am grateful to each of these scholars for their early work. Special thanks to Sandy Polishuk for sharing her trove of Equi materials.

Historical biographies happen because curious, dedicated librarians and archivists accommodate one more project and one more researcher who seeks their insight and hopes for their passion. Sara Piasecki, former head of the Historical Archives & Collections at Oregon Health & Science University, and Karen Peterson, former archivist of that collection, provided more assistance than I knew to request. Others essential to my research include Brian Johnson and Diana Banning at the City of Portland Archives and Records Center; Paul Albert Cyr, curator of the special collections of the New Bedford Free Public Library; library director Geoff Wexler and Shawna Gandy, Susan Seyl, and Richard Engeman of the Oregon Historical Society Research Library; Erika Gottfried, Tamiment Library at New York University; Lorna Elliott at The Dalles/Wasco County Public Library; and Sally Schwartz of the National Archives & Records Administration (NARA).

My appreciation also goes to the Oregon State Archives, Multnomah County Library, the Special Collections & University Archives at the University of Oregon, Wasco County Historical Society, California State Archives, the San Francisco Public Library, The Lilly Library of Indiana University,

NARA offices in San Bruno, California, and Seattle; and the Department of Manuscripts of the National Library of Ireland.

Relatives and contemporaries of Marie Equi provided valuable insight, including Heather Lukes, Margaret Lahargoue, Jeanine Gordon, George Wright, Margaret D., and Arthur Champlin Spencer. I also appreciate the insights of Philip Klindt about Dr. Belle Cooper Rinehart. For our exhaustive search of court records and newspapers regarding the Harriet Speckart inheritance dispute, I salute Karen Able, a Speckart family descendent. In addition, I am indebted to George Delbert and Marie Cyphers Smith for their recollections of Equi's homestead outside The Dalles, Oregon, and to Bette Sinclair for the tour of Equi's house in Portland.

Portions of this project previously appeared in different forms, thanks to the encouragement of Eliza Canty-Jones, editor, *Oregon Historical Quarterly*; Karen Sundheim, manager, James C. Hormel Gay & Lesbian Center at the San Francisco Public Library; Terrence Kissack, former director, and Gerard Koskovich, cofounder, GLBT Historical Society in San Francisco; Sara Piasecki and Karen Peterson, Oregon Health & Science University; colleagues at the Pacific Northwest History Conference, and the editors of the Oregon Encyclopedia Project.

This project has been more rewarding for the collaboration and encouragement of historians Kimberly Jensen, Janice Dilg, Sandy Polishuk, Susan Stryker, Kim Klausner, Michael Munk, Rosalyn Baxandall, Rickie Solinger, Barbara Fisher, and Dona Munker.

The enthusiasm and guidance I received from the staff of the Oregon State University Press have been exemplary. I am particularly thankful to Mary Elizabeth Braun, acquisitions editor, for her wisdom, insight, and patience. I am proud that Marie Equi's biography is part of the OSU Press catalog. I also thank the two anonymous reviewers for wading through an unwieldy manuscript. My sincere thanks to manuscript readers Tom Cook, Paul Cyr, Ken Grosserode, John Lundell, Deb Janes, Jo Ellen Keever, Terence Kissack, Kim Klausner, Richard Osmon, George Painter, Karen Peterson, and Bill Rivers.

Special thanks to William Woods, Richard Osmon, Jamie Guyn, Thomas Duke, Lenore McDonald, Jarie Bolander, Will Valentine, and Cynthia Sasaki. I am grateful to my parents and family for their encouragement. Most of all, Dale Danley, my husband, has persevered for more than a decade with day-to-day and into-the-night collaboration, willing to engage in endless talk, dozens of revisions, and untold hours of technical assistance. I believe Marie Equi would toast his dedication as well—with expensive whiskey.

Preface

Front-page reports of the pitched battle to the north were the talk of Portland on the rainy morning of November 6, 1916. Six men were slain and dozens more wounded in the lumber town of Everett, Washington, during a bloody free-speech skirmish. Once Dr. Marie Equi heard about the five young labor radicals killed and the others stricken, she dropped everything and rushed to provide medical care for the wounded protesters.[1]

Sheriff's deputies had ambushed members of the Industrial Workers of the World—*Wobblies*, as they were called—who had tried to defend the Everett mill workers objecting to a 20 percent pay cut. The Wobblies were caught in a deluge of gunfire. Stunned by their casualties, they retreated to Seattle where they were charged with complicity in murder. Equi stopped first at the jail and then proceeded to the city hospital in the company of Elizabeth Gurley Flynn, the radical labor leader revered as the "Rebel Girl." The bedridden men hooted and cheered when they saw Equi. "Good ole Doc, we *knew* you'd come to us," several told her. Equi tended the wounded and castigated the authorities for failing to provide adequate medical care. At the resulting trial, she testified about the condition of the injured and then went on to rally support for the defendants implicated in what became known as the Everett Massacre.[2]

"We knew you'd come to us." Equi responded to the Everett conflict as a matter of course. It was how she understood her place in the world. She valued loyalty and risked imprisonment to protest injustice against the disadvantaged, the outsiders, and the outcasts of society. At the same time, Equi tolerated no insult to her working-class background, her choice of female companions, or her political beliefs. She was a strong, determined, freethinking woman, and those who crossed her met with fierce opposition. In her most resolute stance, she asserted her right to free speech when the law of the land claimed she had none.

And yet Equi was neither a strident advocate nor a rigid ideologue. Her politics were personal, fluid, and eclectic. She operated with a straightforward sense of right and wrong, aligning herself with causes and groups when they matched her beliefs and experiences. After first promoting Progressive Era

reform—woman suffrage, eight-hour workdays, and civic improvements—
she became radicalized by the blows of police clubs and embraced anarchism
as the means to obtain economic and social justice. She championed the
goals of the IWW and espoused an overthrow of an economic system with
its rampant inequities. She became an early advocate of occupational health,
joining women strikers exploited by low pay and sordid working conditions.
She marched so often with unemployed men that the media referred to them
as her "army." She refused to abide by restrictions on women's access to abortion and birth control, and she spent time in jail to defend their rights. During
the World War I era, she decried the corporate war profiteering of the global
conflict, and federal agents labelled her one of the most dangerous radicals in
the United States.[3]

Equi lived openly as a lesbian, although she was not known to have publicly proclaimed or affirmed her sexual identity. At a time when so few women
risked public exposure of their same-sex preferences, Equi chose to do as she
pleased, caring little if she became a social outcast as a result.

Historian Karen Blair noted in 2001 that "all too little" research and writing
had been undertaken about Pacific Northwest women engaged in politics,
radicalism, and sexual issues. More recently, Kimberly Jensen assessed the
same terrain and found encouraging progress in studies of women's role in
politics. Yet, accounts of radical women in the Pacific Northwest in the late
nineteenth and early twentieth centuries still comprise a mere handful. Labor
radicalism roiled through the region, and the tumult was hardly the domain of
men alone.[4]

Biographies of lesbians of the Pacific Northwest during this period are
even scarcer, and the situation in Northern California is similar. Susan Stryker
and Jim Van Buskirk were hard-pressed in their review of lesbian and gay lives
in the San Francisco Bay Area to find more than a few references to lesbians in
the region prior to World War I. For these reasons the life story of Equi, along
with her intimate companions, is crucial to understanding the role of lesbians
in the history of the Pacific Northwest and Northern California.[5]

Few role models existed to guide Equi as she sought an intimate relationship with another woman, and she mustered considerable courage and resolve
to live as a transgressive sexual outsider. Through circumstance and scandal,
she placed loving lesbian relationships before the public in Oregon and much
of the Pacific Northwest for the first time at the end of the nineteenth century and again in the early twentieth century. She was among the first known

lesbians to adopt a child legally in the region and the first woman whose same-sex preferences figured in two cases before the Ninth Circuit Court of Appeals and one before the US Supreme Court. She lived up to the description of a correspondent during her imprisonment, who described her as "unusually out of the ordinary."[6]

Equi's commitment to medicine and her patients for nearly thirty years represents one of her greatest achievements. To her patients, friends, and comrades alike, she was simply "Doc." She earned her medical degree at a time when working-class women, if they felt they must pursue a professional career, were expected to become nurses. In 1903, she became one of the first sixty women physicians in Oregon.[7] Her ease with working-class patients and among laborers who worked the farms, factories, and forests made her distinctive among other doctors in the Pacific Northwest. Her willingness to help women with birth control and abortion when both were illegal set her further apart from many of her colleagues. But Equi's commitment to medical care combined with her generosity appeared to mitigate the criticism and disapproval directed her way. Although government officials uniformly castigated her as a dangerous and degenerate radical, more dispassionate observers recognized her overriding good will and humanity.

One of the initial challenges of this project has been documenting and understanding Equi's life given the loss of her journals, many of her personal papers, and memorabilia, most of which were apparently discarded after her death in 1952. No formal oral histories of her exist, and no recordings of her many talks have been located. Historians often encounter this difficulty in researching women's lives at a time when their experiences and contributions were less valued. But Equi appeared less committed than several of her contemporaries—Emma Goldman, Margaret Sanger, and Elizabeth Gurley Flynn, for example—to leaving recollections and writings for her legacy. As it turned out, discovery of other primary sources helped document Equi's life and revealed further her considerable historical footprint.

Extensive oral histories conducted in the 1980s by Portland historians—until recently held mostly in private collections—with Equi's daughter, nurse, attorney, medical colleagues, and political allies provide a richer, more detailed view of Equi's relationships and political involvements than previously reported. Additional documents in a dozen archives—located in university libraries, court records, probate files, historic newspapers, registers of deeds, the National Library of Ireland, and sacramental records stored at the Equi family church in New Bedford, Massachusetts—contributed to a more complete and nuanced understanding of her life and times. In one particularly helpful repository—the National Archives and Records Administration located in San Bruno, California—the court records of a trial involving her longtime companion Harriet Speckart include Equi's testimony about her early medical career, her budding lesbian relationship, and the sex-and-money scandal that appeared on the front pages of the *Sunday Oregonian* newspaper.[8]

Ironically, the federal agency that sought to silence Equi became the largest repository of materials that give voice to her political thinking, radical acts, and personal relationships. Through an extensive surveillance operation, US Department of Justice agents reported on Equi's day-to-day movements in the period prior to her sedition trial and during her imprisonment. More than eight hundred pages were preserved and archived. While any document filed by an undercover agent is problematic given the potential for bias, inaccuracies, and outright misrepresentation, Equi's files often present information in her voice that can be confirmed with other sources.[9]

Equi also generated a considerable amount of local, regional, and occasionally national newspaper coverage—more than three hundred articles over a forty-year span beginning with her arrival in Oregon in 1892. These reports of her civic reform work, political protests, legal battles, love affairs, and social appearances—along with several interviews—yielded a more complete account of political motivations and activities. Similar to reports filed by federal agents, newspaper articles must be judged for accuracy. In several instances, the newspaper's bias reveals how Equi was presented to the public and reflects the political and cultural environment of her time.[10]

In the final tally, what Equi chose to do with her life revealed much of what she valued, perhaps as well as lost journals might have indicated. Her direct involvement with the political turmoil and social transformation in America a century ago reflects how one woman lived her life on the edge of public opprobrium. She risked being one of the most feared and hated women in the Pacific Northwest—almost an outcast for her radicalism and lesbianism—to remain true to her belief in social and economic justice. She earned her reputation as a remarkable woman during exceptional times. How she engaged the struggles of her day with courage and compassion makes Equi's life story important to anyone interested in the issues then and concerned about similar injustice today.

1
A Crazy Patchwork

I found her always sincerely repentant for any misdemeanor, and striving to gain under difficulties a self-control that she saw others exhibit.
—Mary E. Austin, New Bedford High School teacher

All her life people tried to make sense of Marie Equi. To her father she was "overly enthusiastic about anything she set her mind." Her high school teachers found her either a "very earnest scholar" or an "exceptionally unruly, headstrong girl." At age twenty-one a small-town newspaper touted her "A Queen Today" for the public horsewhipping she inflicted upon a scoundrel of a minister. The US Army commended her medical care for earthquake-stricken San Franciscans in 1906 but later vilified her politics as a threat to the nation. Other radical women described her as a "crushed falcon" needing care and comfort or a "stormy petrel" foretelling trouble. And once, during a dark, questioning period in her life, a friend assured Equi that she was "perfectly sane, though perhaps unusually out of the ordinary."[1]

Equi once remarked on an aspect of character she shared with everyone else. "Aren't we a crazy patchwork of ancestral and environal expressions?" she wrote. Her own particular patchwork—one that led to radical activism—stitched Old World ancestry with a large working-class family in a high-minded, wealthy Massachusetts city in the latter half of the nineteenth century.[2]

Giovanni Equi, Marie's father, jostled onto a steamship with three hundred others for a month-long transatlantic voyage when he was twelve years old. He had spent his childhood in Fornaci di Barga near the walled city of Lucca in Tuscany, where his ancestors had lived for generations. The Equi clan was believed to reach back to medieval, perhaps ancient, times, and the family took pride in its lineage and homeland. But Giovanni left behind his parents and grandparents, brothers and sisters—most of whom he would never see again—for the chance of opportunity and prosperity in America. In May 1853, after seemingly endless days on the passenger ship *Gondar*, Giovanni and his cousin Luigi rushed the gangplank for the docks of New York, a burgeoning city of a half million people.

Several days later, they boarded a steamship for New Bedford, Massachusetts, situated below the flexing arm of Cape Cod on Buzzards Bay.[3]

New Bedford thrived as the whaling capital of the world when Giovanni Equi arrived. The city's harbor bristled with the masts of three hundred whaling ships that drew ten thousand sailors and landmen from ports worldwide. Hundreds of casks of whale oil were unloaded almost every day. The whale trade grossed $30 million annually for the city, making it one of the wealthiest in the nation. Everything about New Bedford seemed to thrum with the arriving and departing ships—the smell of the oil on the docks, the sailors carousing on Johnny Cake Hill, and the riches tallied in the dockside counting houses. The fine public buildings near the harbor and the turreted mansions with manicured gardens along the outer County Road dazzled newcomers. Two years before Giovanni arrived, Herman Melville extolled the city's beauty with its "long avenues of green and gold" with maples shading the cobbled streets.[4]

Here Giovanni joined his older brother, Dominico, a stonemason who had settled in the city during the 1840s. Dominico purchased property and built a house along Second Avenue near the waterfront where he, Giovanni, and, later, their two brothers lived. Giovanni learned masonry, anglicized his name to John, and settled into his new life.[5]

The whaling trade brought sailors and laborers from ports around the world, and New Bedford's twenty-one thousand residents represented one of the most diverse populations in America. But the Equi brothers and a handful of others were the only Italians in the city. A dozen years later when John started looking for a wife, he found few eligible women from his homeland. But while Italian emigration to America remained a trickle at the time, the Irish flooded the country seeking relief from famine. More than 20 percent of Ireland's population—approximately 1.7 million people—came to America between 1840 and 1860. They were the lucky ones. More than one million back home died from starvation following the devastating potato blight and the neglect of the British government. Among the thousands of "famine immigrants" who made New Bedford their home, John Equi found his wife.[6]

Sarah Mullins, Marie's mother, was born in 1849 in County Tyrone, one of the original nine counties of the ancient Celtic kingdom of Ulster. She missed the worst of the famine and the scourge of cholera that terrorized families in her early years. Sarah's parents—Thomas Mullins and Catherine McGreevy—were fiercely opposed to Britain's rule over Ireland, and Marie believed her grandparents bestowed a kind of ancestral fervor for independence. In 1858 when Sarah was nine, her father had already died, and she and

Members of Marie Equi's family in New Bedford, Massachusetts, about 1905. Mother Sarah Mullins Equi (seated, far left) and father John Equi (seated, middle); sister Kate Equi Vanni (seated, far right), James C. Gay (standing, far left) beside sister Sophie Equi Gay, Anthony Loftus (standing, right) and sister Flora Equi Loftus (standing, far right). Oregon Historical Society, bb013183.

her mother fled the country for America. Little is known of her early years in New Bedford, but she and her mother settled in the city as the United States sank into its own whirlpool of strife leading to the Civil War. Sarah's future husband, John Equi, is not known to have fought in the war, but he, too, had experienced a land of conflict in a pre-unified Italy. A year after the Civil War ended, in April 1866, twenty-five-year-old John Equi married Sarah Mullins, age seventeen, in a Catholic service. The young couple settled in the family compound on Second Street.[7]

Six years later, on April 7, 1872, Marie Diana Equi was born at home. She was John and Sarah's fifth child and fifth daughter. The next week she was baptized in the St. Lawrence, Martyr Catholic Church, a massive Gothic structure with a soaring bell tower. Marie later described her father as a non-practicing Catholic, but he had helped lay the foundation of St. Lawrence and regarded it as the family church. Thereafter, the Equis celebrated all their baptisms, confirmations, and marriages under the oak-framed, vaulted ceiling amid a profusion of red, green, and black marble.[8]

Sarah Equi gave birth to six more children—another girl and five boys—bringing the total to eleven over a sixteen-year period. The size of the Equi family was not unusual among immigrant Irish and Italian Catholics, although a wide variety of birth control devices were available in general stores and pharmacies during the 1860s and 1870s. Marie and her siblings were far removed from the notion of a protected childhood free of chores and early employment. Her early years revolved around her mother's several pregnancies, care of her younger siblings, and housework. She later recalled how much she hated doing the family laundry.[9]

Before she was ten years old, Marie witnessed firsthand the limits of medical science. An older sister succumbed to what was called "paralysis of the brain," a brother died from croup, and another from diphtheria. Three of her young cousins also died. The deaths in the Equi households were typical in New Bedford and nationwide at a time when tuberculosis, cholera, and a slew of other maladies posed a constant threat.[10]

Marie remembered her early years fondly, and she worshipped her father for his good spirits and easy manner. Slim and angular with a moustache and goatee, John Equi at six feet tall towered over other men. He was a dependable provider and a skilled tradesman, and, although well liked and caring, Marie later confided to friends that her father sometimes flew into drunken rages so frightening that her mother hid the children.[11]

During Marie's childhood, New Bedford shifted from dependence on whaling to the massive industrialization that had begun its sweep across the country. Petroleum was discovered in northwest Pennsylvania in 1859, and whaling soon lost its dominance on the market. Extracting oil from the land was cheaper, safer, and yielded greater profits than hunting whales on the open seas thousands of miles away. The city's capitalists transitioned to modern manufacturing, specifically in textile production, and exploited new steam power technology to dominate the market for fine cotton fabrics. New Bedford and its Wamsutta brand soon became known nationally for high-quality shirting, muslin, and bleached sheeting. By 1871, the Wamsutta Mills hunkered down on five acres at the north end of the waterfront while the Potomska Mills secured the south end. In the years to follow, dozens of other mills crowded between, and the thicket of ship masts so familiar to Marie's parents gave way to a crowded stand of smokestacks.[12]

The "better families" of New Bedford seldom ventured near the waterfront district that served as a neighborhood haunt for Marie and her siblings.

The Equis' neighbors were the working-class families who toiled in the mills, on the docks, and at the factories. Workers flooded in from other parts of New England and Canada. Highly skilled operators from England demanded a guaranteed ten-hour workday, better working conditions, and guarantees of no wage cuts. Marie recalled that when she was young her father invited hungry strikers to family meals, and she heard all about their grievances.[13]

Although Marie later described her family as working class and struggling, her parents managed to acquire real estate a year after her birth. New Bedford's population had increased by more than 20 percent during the 1870s, and the city expanded beyond the waterfront district and west of County Road with its grand mansions. In this new western district, John and Sarah Equi purchased an undeveloped lot and spent the next few years constructing a small apartment building. Five years later John Equi and his siblings inherited the family house from their recently deceased brother, Dominico, and John purchased the property from the others. At the time, only 49 percent of the adult male population in the country managed to own real estate, yet Marie's father, working as a stonemason, claimed two lots.[14]

When Marie was eight years old, her family relocated to their new West End house on James Street. Their neighborhood was in a demographic jumble of a district that included wealthy whaling-era families, recently rich textile barons, and working-class Irish. In this mix Marie's Italian-Irish family struggled to find a niche. They represented New Bedford's largest immigrant population, the Irish, as well as the least prevalent, the Italians. In 1880 only eleven Italians over the age of eleven lived in the city's six wards. The Irish ostracized the Equis because they were Italian and everyone else resented them as famine Irish, or so it seemed to Marie as a girl. John Equi may have eased the ill will with his amiable nature, which was so obliging that he altered the spelling of the family surname to "Aque" to match how locals pronounced it.[15] *

In later years, Marie referred to a childhood bout of tuberculosis so severe that her parents sent her to Florida to live with family friends. By age ten she had returned to the city and enrolled in Middle Street Grammar, a tough and turbulent school, overcrowded with more than 450 students housed in a poorly maintained building. Hallways were used as classrooms, and every spring thaw, the girls' outdoor yard was ankle-deep in mud with only a narrow wood plank to play upon. Despite the deficiencies at Middle Street, New

---

* Equi's father and most of his children retained the "Aque" spelling for all of their lives. Equi changed hers to the original spelling as an adult. For the sake of clarity, the Equi spelling is used throughout this narrative.

Bedford boasted a well-regarded school system led by a progressive superintendent who emphasized cognitive skills rather than rote memorization, rigid discipline, and examinations. Under this regimen, Marie excelled during the next four years in several subjects, especially Reading, US History, and English. One instructor found it a pleasure to teach her because she loved to study so much. "I always found her a very earnest pupil," she wrote, even if other teachers thought Marie was impulsive and a troublemaker. Marie persevered and graduated from grammar school in the spring of 1886.[16]

During her studies at New Bedford High School, Marie formed a close relationship with one of her teachers, Mary E. Austin, who listened to her hopes and troubles. Austin thought her young student's devotion to studying mitigated her lack of self-control and frequent misbehavior. She judged Marie an "excellent scholar" with whom she enjoyed "long earnest talks" away from the classroom. Austin explained later that she came to understand how much Marie regretted her acting out and tried to achieve the self-control she saw others exhibit. Austin may have been the first adult to understand the personal struggle that dogged Marie for years.[17]

Although devoted to her studies, circumstances forced Marie to drop out of high school after her first year to work in the city's textile mills. She was fortunate to complete even that much study as working-class parents seldom kept their children—sons or daughters—in school beyond the required age. Her parents still had three children at home under the age of twelve, and perhaps they could not afford to keep her out of the workforce. Yet a few months before Marie left school, John and Sarah Equi purchased additional real estate—an empty lot near their house.[18]

Marie joined nineteen hundred other teenage girls and women who labored in the city's factories. Given her age, education, and background, she may have worked as a weaver responsible for monitoring the movement of yarn into looms. She would have had little time to dwell on how much she missed her studies. Weavers had to stop the looms and manually replace the bobbins more than one hundred times a day. For their tiring work and long hours—usually twelve- and sometimes fourteen-hour shifts—they earned ninety cents a day, worked five days a week, and earned a total far from a living wage. Inside the factories, men, women, and children endured the whirring, spinning din of the machines that vibrated the floor boards and seemed to shake the building. Workers suffered from headaches and ear-ringing for hours after their shifts. The windows were kept closed—often nailed shut—to ensure humidity for more pliable cotton threads, and the resulting heat was

Children who worked in the textile mills of New Bedford, Massachusetts, in the 1880s at a time of few legal restrictions on childhood labor. Library of Congress, LC-DIG-nclc-02250.

oppressive. Workrooms became so hazy with lint that operators coughed throughout their shifts and sometimes vomited small cotton balls after a day's work. Already susceptible to a recurrence of tuberculosis, Marie later talked of the labored breathing and pain in her lungs that followed her workdays.[19]

Marie witnessed children working at jobs that would have been dangerous for adults. Although Massachusetts had set limits on child labor in 1888, children younger than fourteen were allowed to work a half-day and then attend school for the remaining half. Yet the restrictions still left the city's youngsters representing 8 percent of the workforce. Marie also toiled with women who looked as if they had never been girls. One ex-mill worker recalled, "The souls of these mill girls seemed starved and looked from their hungry eyes, as if searching for mental food."[20]

After two years of millwork, Marie might easily have despaired of a brighter future, but a high school companion, Betsey Bell Holcomb, intervened with a bold plan to get Marie accepted in an all-girls school to pursue her studies. The two appeared to have little in common. Marie was a fourteen-year-old first-year student from a large Catholic immigrant family while Betsey, at seventeen, was in her senior year, the oldest of five children from a prominent and well-off Unitarian family. Betsey's father began his career clerking in the family grocery store, and, in time, he became owner of one prosperous business, directed another, served on the city's board of trade, and became a member of the local Elks fraternal club. Despite all their differences,

Betsey was impressed with Marie's intelligence, spirit, and passion for learning that matched her own. For Marie, Betsey was an attractive woman with a self-assuredness she longed to possess.[21]

The same year that Marie left high school for the mill, Betsey graduated and enrolled at Wellesley College, an elite school northwest of Boston that offered one of the best educations available to a young woman at the time. The Wellesley campus boasted its own lake lined with azaleas and rhododendrons. College Hall, where many of the students slept and studied, featured parlors filled with artwork, a dining room with Wedgwood service, a library with ten thousand volumes, and modern laboratories. Betsey appeared to be a popular student, and her schoolmates nicknamed her "Bessie," a name she adopted for the rest of her life. She completed her first year and returned for a second.[22]

If Bessie enjoyed a schoolgirl crush with Marie, the Wellesley community would have welcomed it. In the late nineteenth century, many all-women colleges explicitly supported students who became emotionally or physically engaged with one another. Female faculty members often became role models with their own relationships, often living as couples on campus. During Bessie's study at Wellesley, Katherine Lee Bates, an English literature instructor who later served as chair of the English department, began an intimate relationship with Katharine Coman, a faculty member and later chair of the economics department. Such arrangements were dubbed "Wellesley marriages"—a localized version of the more commonly recognized "Boston marriages" that involved two wealthy or professional women who established a household together without the help of men. Women could engage in these pairings seeking intimate companionship without acknowledging any sexual conduct, and their associations were considered "romantic friendships." These women, who would readily be considered lesbians today, enjoyed the twilight years of an accepting, tolerant environment before new theories of sexuality led to a more complex, less accepting atmosphere.[23]

During her summer break in New Bedford after her second year at college, Bessie took charge of Marie's plight with a Christian zeal for social good shared by many of her Wellesley peers. The students deferred marriage and families to delve into the overwhelming needs of immigrants and laborers, often volunteering in settlement houses and tenement slums. Bessie's interests remained closer to home: she intended to free Marie from the dangerous, mind-numbing millwork and find a way for her to continue her studies.[24]

At first Bessie proposed that Marie undertake a work-study arrangement at Wellesley. College administrators suggested instead that Marie apply to

Northfield Seminary for Young Ladies. With only two weeks remaining before the start of the academic year, Bessie sent an urgent letter to the Northfield principal urging him to admit Marie. She explained that her friend suffered "as hard a blow as could have fallen upon the girl" when she was obliged to leave school. With the certainty that "God's will is in my plan," she vowed to send one hundred dollars of her own savings plus later payments from her allowance to cover Marie's tuition for one year. She depleted her savings, but she was willing to do so, she wrote, "Because I desire to see her develop into a true Christian woman." Bessie's generosity was surprising, and her parents' concurrence even more so. Beyond the first year, she hoped Marie would earn a scholarship, work her way through Northfield, and then gain another scholarship for advanced study.[25]

After eleven days of hope and worry, admission forms from Northfield arrived, and Bessie rushed to complete them. She described Marie's traits as "impulsiveness, generosity, kindness of heart, genuine religious feeling, and earnestness." She wrote that Marie desired most of all to be "a noble, helpful, and well-educated woman." Bessie also obtained recommendations from her own father, from Marie's grammar and high school teachers, and from the Equi family doctor. Northfield was a Protestant institution, and Bessie adroitly emphasized Marie's "strong Protestant tendencies" rather than mentioning her Catholic upbringing. Her efforts won the day, and, in September 1889, Marie entered Northfield's preparatory department at the junior level.[26]

Northfield was a picture postcard of a town located in north central Massachusetts near the borders of Vermont and New Hampshire, about 150 miles from New Bedford. Dwight Lyman Moody, a shoe salesman turned successful Christian revivalist, founded Northfield Seminary in 1879 to educate impoverished but talented girls from around the world. The institution was famous for enrolling Choctaw and Sioux students and for graduating a former slave. Marie took residence in Hillside House, a dormitory with gabled roofs, shuttered windows, and covered wooden porches.[27]

Northfield Seminary proved a good fit for Marie. With so many students from different backgrounds, she was no longer an outsider. Every day she donned the school uniform—a long-sleeved black dress with a large black bow tied at the neck and black shoes. She undertook her studies without worry about money or family responsibilities, and her final examination scores far exceeded her entry marks. She performed well in Essay and Bible Studies, ranked high in deportment, and developed an intense religious devotion. Inside her Bible, she wrote her "Motto for '89," a fervent declaration to be "everything good and pure for Christ's sake." She prayed that the Lord would give her the strength to conquer her trials and to "lean on him" in her troubles.[28]

Yet after one year at Northfield, Bessie's plans for Marie stalled. No scholarship was forthcoming, and Bessie was unable to finance another year of study on her own. In December 1890, Marie left the school and returned to dim prospects in New Bedford. At nineteen, she was at a loss. Living at her parents' house was not an option, and she had no money of her own. One older sister had married and another was engaged, but Marie had already rebuffed one suitor and marriage held no interest for her.[29]

John Equi intervened on his daughter's behalf and arranged for her to stay with relatives in Tuscany. At Fornaci di Barga, "the great furnace of Barga," situated halfway up the hillside overlooking the Serchio Valley in Lucca Province, Marie lived with one of her uncles and helped tend his terraced vineyards and olive groves. She became fluent in Italian, and, she later told friends and family, she studied at the University of Pisa. At some point, however, she quarreled with her uncle and then returned to the United States in July 1892 on the ship *Werra*. She cleared customs at the newly opened station at Ellis Island, and, according to a story she enjoyed telling, she arrived in New York with no money and only a banana to sustain her. A well-to-do couple paid her fare to New Bedford.[30]

Marie found her hometown more dense, urban, and industrial. The population pushed to over forty thousand with more than two-thirds being first and second generation immigrants. Sailors from Cape Verde and the Azores had outfitted many of the old whalers—"floating shipwrecks," they were dubbed—and shuttled passengers between New Bedford and their home islands. With another nine textile mills in operation, the city had become more intensely industrialized. Electrification of the municipal streetcars had begun, and telephones were in common use. Change was underway, yet Marie's prospects remained much the same as before. She was a young woman adrift with nothing but millwork awaiting her.

Bessie was no longer in New Bedford or at college. After her exceptional efforts to get Marie into a school, she had dropped out of Wellesley in the middle of her junior year. She was the oldest child, but social custom prevented her from someday managing the family business. She apparently wanted more than to wait for gentlemen callers to offer her a future. Instead she embarked on an adventure in the Far West, one that Marie would soon join.[31]

2
Horsewhip in Hand

She is a queen today.
The Dalles Weekly Chronicle, The Dalles, Oregon

While Marie Equi floundered in the East, Bessie Holcomb embarked on one of the boldest journeys a nineteenth-century single woman could take. She left behind her family, her social standing, and her Wellesley education to venture forth as a New Woman, independent and ready to determine her own future. In the fall of 1891, Holcomb braved a three-thousand-mile rail trip to the outer reaches of the Far West, where she intended to stake her claim to an Oregon homestead.

Oregon fever first gripped the nation in the early 1840s with visions of abundant land, rich soil, and fresh air that enticed farmers from their worn-out fields, factory workers from the din of their days, young bucks seeking a quick fortune, and others weary of cramped city life. Railroad companies and land developers flooded the East and Midwest with advertisements of bustling main streets and good jobs for the taking. They targeted the adventurous and the desperate, those ready to embrace the new or escape the old in the bountiful Oregon Country. At the time, the United States and Great Britain shared ownership of the vast territory in a tenuous arrangement, but the US federal government worked hand-in-glove with railroad titans to secure a lock on the vast expanse with a strong American presence. They understood that settlers with land holdings would help ensure government and corporate control in the new communities. The US Congress added incentives by dangling virtually free acreage to prospective homesteaders. The strategies worked, and the British ceded the vast expanse below the current Canadian border in 1846.[1]

Congress passed the Oregon Donation Land Act in 1850 to steer more settlers to the Pacific Northwest, and within five years homesteaders claimed two-and-a-half-million acres. More inducements followed. The Homestead Act of 1862 entitled any citizen—man or woman, whether married or single—to one hundred and sixty acres after cultivating at least five acres and living on the land for five years. This five-and-five proposition offered women a degree of land-based independence never before available, and hundreds of Eastern and Midwestern women eagerly accepted. As the 1890s closed, women represented 12 to 15 percent of all homesteaders in the West.[2]

By 1891, travelers from the East Coast, like Bessie Holcomb, embarked on a five-to-seven day trip to reach the West on the transcontinental route. They traveled to Chicago by way of the Union Pacific Overland route with a range of accommodations: Pullman Palace sleepers, tourist sleepers, or free reclining chairs. From Chicago they crossed the Mississippi River, rolled into Omaha, and then pushed across the Nebraska plains where gritty dust and soot settled everywhere in the cars. Meal stops were brief at one-café outposts, and passengers suspected their leftovers awaited passengers on the next train. At the Utah border, those bound for Oregon left the mainline route and took the Oregon Short Line across the new state of Idaho. They rumbled through broad stretches of plateaus, mountains, and forests before sidling along the banks of the legendary, muscular Columbia River to reach The Dalles in north central Oregon. Most of the Short Line passengers continued farther west for another eighty-five miles to Portland, on the opposite side of the Cascade Mountains, but a few stopped at the small river city with the odd-sounding name. Locals could tell them that early French fur trappers were reminded of a smooth stone called *dalle* back home when they saw the basalt rock that shaped the Columbia River narrows. The river course became known as *The Dalles of the Columbia*, and the name of the outpost was later anglicized to rhyme with "the pals."[3]

New arrivals in The Dalles in the late autumn of 1891 anticipated shade trees, church steeples, and a three-story brick opera house. Instead, they found a half-burnt town ruined by a devastating blaze that lay waste twenty blocks a few months earlier. Holcomb had taken leave of a proud, 250-year-old city touted as one of the wealthiest in the country with a population of forty-five thousand. At The Dalles she beheld a virtually unknown fifty-year-old river city with only three thousand residents. But the blackened remains were slowly giving way to new sidewalks and rebuilt homes and stores, and she decided to stay.[4]

Holcomb was a latecomer in the rush for Oregon homesteads. Early settlers had already crossed the Cascade Mountains to claim the state's best farmland: the Willamette Valley and the fertile acres in the southwest part of the state. Her options lay east of the Cascades, and she chose the mid-Columbia region with The Dalles as its center of commerce. The city sat on a basaltic tableland formed by an ancient lava flow. Across the Columbia River to the north in Washington State, the cliffs rose some fifty feet high above the riverbank before yielding to rolling hills. But on the Oregon side, the shoreline gently sloped upward a half mile from the river toward recessed cliffs, creating a half-bowl appearance. The rail station, ferry landing, hotels, churches, and shops, as well as most of the dwellings, clustered in this enclave below the rimrock bluff. To the west of town the land stretched a few miles to the foothills of the Cascades, and in this area near Chenowith Creek, Holcomb staked her claim. She purchased the rights to 122 acres from a previous settler and paid sixteen dollars in filing fees. Her new homestead stretched high and back from the river, hugging the sloping terrain below the basalt cliffs and extending over the bluff. Bunch grass and sagebrush covered the lower acres along with a scattering of red bark pines and scraggly scrub oaks. With basalt outcroppings scattered across the land, Holcomb's homestead was typical of the rough and rocky stretches that remained for late settlers. The land was suitable only for grazing, but she lacked the resources to manage stock. Cultivating some of the land would have to do.[5]

From the top of the bluff Holcomb enjoyed a sweeping view of the snow-covered peaks of Mount Hood and Mount Adams with the broad Columbia below reflecting the silvery blue, or sometimes, gunmetal gray of the sky. The stretch along the river once hosted thousands of Chinookan-speaking native peoples who gathered for the largest annual trade fair of the region. Much of the commerce centered on the abundant run of salmon, so plentiful that they seemed to darken the river near the thunderous roar of rapids to the east.[6]

The law allowed up to six months before homesteaders were required to live on their land, and Holcomb stayed in town the first winter, which saw temperatures cold enough for chunks of ice to bob in the river. In the spring she took residence on the homestead and planted vegetables and grapes in a two-acre garden, one that had been cleared by "grubbing the sage" as it was called. A nearby spring supplied water that she carried by bucket to the garden and house. She may have refurbished an existing structure on her land with volunteer or hired help, but, in any event, by April she completed her house, all twelve by thirty feet of it.[7]

Homesteading could be a lonely and frustrating endeavor, and a good many discouraged settlers defaulted on their claims. One single woman, who worked her acres in Eastern Oregon during the early 1900s, lamented the beginning homesteader's never-ending chores, the privations, loneliness, and desperation. For many the separation from family and friends became unbearable, and they suffered through long periods of isolation. Holcomb had neighbors who lived down the hill and several others to the west, but she lacked personal contact with her family or a close friend to help her through the hard times. Either by her initiative or at Equi's request, Holcomb soon enjoyed the company of another woman.[8]

On September 10, 1892, the *Times-Mountaineer*, one of the local newspapers, announced a new arrival from Massachusetts: "Miss Aque, of New Bedford, is in the city and will spend the winter months with her friend, Bessie Holcomb." The notice had to please Equi. She was twenty years old with no high school diploma, little or no money, and scant work experience, but her appearance in the West was treated as an occasion of interest.[9]

Equi knew a dry climate would be better for her tuberculosis-damaged lungs, and the chance to live out West could not have come at a better time. She stepped off the train when The Dalles glowed in the late summer with flowers still in bloom, daytime temperatures favored the eighties, and evening hours carried a welcome chill. The beauty of the high desert and the commanding presence of the Columbia impressed most visitors, and Equi later remarked that the wide-open spaces of the West captured her heart.[10]

Equi adjusted to the rhythms of small-town life in The Dalles—the twice-daily "fast-mail" train, the market days when wagons bounced into town with produce and grains, and the winds that swept through from the Columbia River Gorge, either the warm *Chinook* or the cooling *zephyr*. She became familiar with the East-of-the-Cascades character of the people—their hardiness and practicality honed by living close to the land in an arid climate and making do with available resources. At the homestead, she tended the garden, gathered water from the stream, and helped manage Holcomb's outpost in the West.[11]

Holcomb may have been exceptionally generous when she intervened on Equi's behalf in New Bedford, but for her to share close quarters on an isolated property three thousand miles from Massachusetts suggested something more. She knew from her Wellesley experience that two women could be committed to each other and live together in a reasonable fashion. Equi may have understood this as well, or, she may have simply jumped at the chance to be with a woman she cared for so much. But rural Oregon was new cultural territory for Equi and Holcomb, and they could not assume that people in The Dalles shared the sentiments of privileged Eastern society and

Marie Equi in her early twenties, when she homesteaded with Bessie Holcomb outside The Dalles, Oregon along the Columbia River. Oregon Historical Society, bb013181.

its elite women's colleges. Social norms in the rural West reflected a desire for Eastern-style propriety that often collided with the demands of working the land. Women were expected to cope with the vagaries of farm and ranch life and to apply however much independence and single-mindedness was necessary.[12]

Equi and Holcomb's living arrangement was uncommon but not unheard of among the hundreds of young single women who settled in the West. Few people doubted that the homesteaders needed all the help they could muster. Yet Equi's appearance in town inevitably triggered curiosity and gossip. She and Holcomb were two unrelated women living together who were too young to be spinsters but old enough to be married.

Settlers from the East often remained outsiders in western towns, but Holcomb's teaching position at the Wasco Independent Academy, a prestigious private school in town, helped ease her entry into local circles. She had been an ideal candidate for the Academy. At age twenty-four she was not a child-teacher like the girls of sixteen who began their careers to pay their way through high school. She was town-mannered, educated at an Eastern college, and from a family of means. She was a good fit for the class-conscious Academy directors, who readily hired her to teach part-time beginning with the fall term. Later that summer the board president and superintendent, the Reverend O. D. Taylor, offered her a full-time position with a corresponding increase in pay. On that basis Holcomb undertook the most common occupation for single women homesteaders. But the arrangement with Reverend Taylor would not hold, and it would propel Equi into a dustup in the center of town that garnered headlines throughout the West.[13]

The wealthy families of The Dalles had founded the Academy in 1880 and erected a handsome, two-story building with a bell tower high on the slope overlooking the center of town. More than two hundred pupils enrolled for the primary grades through high school and college preparatory, and the school's graduates included attorneys, physicians, and a US Congressman. The school was respectable in every way, except, oddly, in its choice of superintendent, the Reverend Taylor. He was an ambitious, wily character whose misadventures and fraudulent schemes had bedeviled The Dalles for years. In 1881 the First Baptist Church had welcomed him as their pastor, but he envisioned more than preaching the glory of God. Five years later, he and his wife acquired eight hundred mostly barren acres on the Washington State side of the Columbia River directly across from The Dalles. Taylor then leveraged the purchase into a land fraud scheme common in the West—he promoted and sold lots in an imaginary city to gullible investors.[14]

Throughout 1891 and 1892, Taylor traveled the East Coast touting the city parks, broad boulevards, and booming industries of what he called *Grand Dalles*, a civic concoction that supposedly rivaled all other cities in Eastern Washington and Oregon. He extolled the grandeur of the bridge that spanned the Columbia River and the superior rail line with direct service to Portland. His maps and circulars depicted lush city blocks, fine civic buildings, and prosperous businesses, including a boot and shoe factory with jobs for five hundred workers. But anyone who had visited The Dalles knew the truth: there was no bridge or rail line and, for that matter, no Grand Dalles beyond a few shacks and a soon-to-be-abandoned factory. As the *New York Times* proclaimed, "Unless the Grand Dalles has changed remarkably within ten months, it is a particularly barren and inaccessible spot."[15]

Taylor exploited speculators as well as hard-pressed folks—widows, elderly couples, and young families—looking for a more promising life in the West. Critics joked that Taylor worked both sides of the river, hustling real estate on the north and preaching Christ on the south. The *Times-Mountaineer* railed against Taylor's deceptions and described his schemes as "one of the most fraudulent land booms ever originated in the northwest." Land development and resource allocation already roiled western politics, and Taylor's attempts to launch a competitive city across the river threatened the economic standing of The Dalles and Eastern Oregon. His mistreatment of common folks riled locals, including Marie Equi, and ultimately led to his comeuppance.[16]

At the time Equi settled in The Dalles, an edgy, sometimes violent restlessness stalked the country. One episode was closely followed in the nation's newspapers. A stalled labor dispute at the Carnegie Steel Company in Homestead, Pennsylvania, erupted in violence, leaving seven workers and three company agents dead in the summer of 1892. The governor dispatched seven thousand troops into the town of twelve thousand. They stayed three months, long enough to strain strikers' resolve and exhaust their funds. Within this tense standoff, two anarchists, Alexander Berkman and Emma Goldman, plotted to kill the company's manager, Henry Clay Frick, whose refusal to negotiate with the strikers had triggered the violence. But Berkman bungled the assault by failing to kill Frick after firing three shots and stabbing him four times. Berkman was sentenced to twenty-two years in prison for the attempted assassination, but Goldman escaped charges. Newspapers nationwide covered the conflict, and the reports may have been Equi's first introduction to Goldman, who later shaped Equi's own radical beliefs.

Throughout the winter of 1892–1893, the national economy sustained multiple blows, which unsettled the public even more. The country's gold reserve plummeted, and railroad stocks sank after lavish spending on the transcontinental lines. The US Treasury struggled to stabilize the currency, and investors feared economic collapse. During the first six months of 1893, nearly two hundred national banks failed. The panic was on, and the stock market crashed in July, losing 35 percent of its value. Bankruptcies claimed seventy-four railroad companies, including the Union Pacific and the Northern Pacific, both crucial to Pacific Northwest commerce. When the Union Pacific slid into receivership, the company pulled its railway shops out of The Dalles and moved them to Portland. Three hundred men lost their jobs or were forced to relocate, reducing the city's population by a third. The local economy slumped, banks and shops failed, and everyone longed for relief.[17]

Reverend O. D. Taylor, superintendent of
the Wasco Academy in The Dalles, Oregon,
was horsewhipped in the center of town in
1893 by an indignant Marie Equi. Source
and date uncertain.

In the late spring of 1893, Holcomb presided over graduation ceremonies at the Academy, and circumstances seemed almost normal. But by that summer she had still not received the full salary promised her by Reverend Taylor. At first the superintendent denied her claim, and then he ignored her entreaties altogether. By midsummer Holcomb and Equi could endure no more.

The morning of July 21, 1893, started out hot and then soared to "bake-oven," as locals described the temperature spikes. It was a day to stay out of the heat, not tussle in the street. But Equi and Holcomb strode into Taylor's real estate office downtown and demanded the one hundred dollar overdue payment. In a huff he refused and ushered them to the street with a threat to level charges against them. The two women were incensed. Holcomb wanted to wield an umbrella against her former boss, but Equi's blood was up and she insisted on a rawhide whip instead. Perhaps Holcomb wished her companion had shown greater restraint, or, instead, felt pleased that Equi had so readily defended her interests. But, from that point, she later told a reporter, "The affair turned out as it did."[18]

That afternoon Equi stalked back and forth outside the superintendent's office, located in the French & Company bank building at the corner of Second and Washington Streets. She shouted threats to horsewhip him if he stepped outside. She paced for more than an hour, swirling the dust around her full skirt in the sweltering heat. People hurried to see what ruckus stirred the town center, worried there might be a run on the bank. Women lifted their dresses and stepped carefully along the wooden sidewalk wary of jutting nails. Men and boys pushed into the streets, jumping over stacked poles ready for new telephone wires. The onlookers were relieved to hear of Equi's complaint, and then many cheered and added their own catcalls to the uproar. When Equi appeared to retreat from the scene, Taylor tried to slip unnoticed into the crowd. But he resembled former US President Ulysses S. Grant with a bushy beard and serious demeanor, and he could not easily escape unnoticed. Equi intercepted him in front of the coroner's office, a block south of the bank, and whacked his shoulder with the whip, prompting him to curse her, grab her wrists, and force her to drop her weapon. She later complained that her antagonist hit her in the breast. Men on the block rushed to her aid, pulled Taylor away, and restrained him while she rained blows thick and fast on his back. The throng grew to several hundred as word of the thrashing spread. Taylor escaped and ran farther south on Washington Street, but the skirmish continued. Men on the next block held him and delivered a few punches of their own before letting Equi renew her attack. Finally, Taylor wrenched free and escaped by way of the road leading to the top of the bluff.[19]

The county sheriff had been alerted to the uproar, and he intercepted Equi and escorted her to the courthouse. She was accompanied by Holcomb and Belle Cooper Rinehart, wife of the mayor of The Dalles, who later said she tagged along out of curiosity. The judge dismissed the assault and battery charges but placed Equi under a $250 bond to keep the peace. A local druggist served as her bailsman, and the three women repaired to the office of Rinehart's husband. Equi was bedraggled and spent from the ruckus, her skirt and shirtwaist torn and dirty. She recovered by the evening and then retreated with Holcomb to the homestead. A downpour soon broke the intense heat and marked the close of Equi's tumultuous entry into Oregon's public life.[20]

The incident on Washington Street became a sensation, and the dailies jumped on the story. "O.D. Taylor Chastised" headlined the *Chronicle,* but it depicted the minister as a surprised victim of a horsewhip-yielding "young lady of Italian descent," who possessed "remarkable vigor." Taylor was a stockholder in the company that owned the paper, and his relationship likely influenced its coverage. The report described the schoolteacher and her companion as "friends of long standing" with an "ardent affection between them." It also suggested that "the singular infatuation between them" had caused a near total estrangement of Holcomb from her family. An unnamed source suggested that her wealthy father had refused to provide a home for Equi as a result of their relationship. The paper granted that as homesteaders the two women were "much admired for their pluck" even if the day's reflection of it could not be applauded. In conclusion, the *Chronicle* saluted Equi: "She is queen today."[21]

The rival paper, the *Times-Mountaineer,* accused Taylor of shirking his obligation to pay Holcomb her full salary, and it suggested the humiliation of a public horsewhipping by a petite girl was just desserts for the scoundrel. As for the character of the two women, the newspaper judged Holcomb "a scholarly and highly accomplished young lady . . . held in high estimation in this community." Equi was described as "very much attached to her (companion), and her friendship amounts to adoration."[22]

The next day a *Times-Mountaineer* reporter interviewed Equi and Holcomb in their modest home for a feature article that became one of the first public accounts of women living together as a same-sex couple in the West. The two women remarked on the several bouquets of flowers sent by admirers as well as the fabric delivered to Equi for a new dress. Holcomb impressed the newsman with her "pleasant countenance," and Equi presented a "sanguine, joyous temperament" with a "jovial disposition." He wrote that Equi was an eager, interesting conversationalist with a "discriminating use of words." She explained that she was aggravated that Taylor had duped so many people in town, and she offered no apology for her assault. Holcomb, in turn, denied the allegation of a rift with her family. The reporter commented that the two women intended to remain "indissoluble friends whom nothing can separate." With the affair concluded, Equi and Holcomb declared they wished nothing more than "to be left alone" in their isolated home.[23]

People in The Dalles appeared titillated by the horsewhipping. Many probably judged the assault as unladylike and inappropriate, but few publicly expressed alarm over the incident. Equi on her own might have received a less sanguine reception for her public display, but she benefited from her association with Holcomb. Besides, the horsewhipping seemed to provide a diversion from the daily reports of economic disruption and fiscal pain. The story continued to reverberate, and the *Times Mountaineer* boosted its printing by an additional one hundred copies to meet the demand. Oregon's largest circulation newspaper, the *Morning Oregonian* in Portland, carried the story as did the *San Francisco Examiner* ("Flogged by a Woman" ran its headline) and even the *New York Times*.[24]

During the following week, the local papers found new tidbits for their readers. Merchants sold 250 raffles at one dollar each for the rawhide used in the whipping and awarded the proceeds to Holcomb. The *Chronicle* noted that "a scurrilous report reflecting upon the character" of the two homesteaders had been circulated in town by an "unconscionable liar," who was quickly silenced by more respectable citizens. The report nevertheless suggested that at least a few observers believed the homesteaders' relationship involved more than a romantic friendship.[25]

Civic leaders and the newspaper editors were none too eager to entertain the possibility that two respectable women, especially a teacher, conducted what many would consider an improper relationship in their midst. But the hint of lesbianism in the anonymous report had to concern Equi and Holcomb. The previous summer local and state newspapers had covered the shocking story of a murder that thrust lesbianism into public discourse. Nineteen-year-old Alice Mitchell had slashed the throat of seventeen-year-old Freda Ward—a young woman she loved and wanted to marry—on the streets of Memphis, Tennessee. A medical journal was quick to describe "sexual perversion" and the "abnormally developed sexual life" of an individual emotionally and sexually drawn to the same sex. Newspapers conjectured whether nonconforming behavior among girls and women—ranging from tomboy pursuits to career-seeking women avoiding marriage—suggested sexual perversion and mental illness. A sole doctor expressed a minority opinion that passionate love by one woman for another was not an indication of insanity. Finally, Mitchell asserted some control of her case. She pleaded insanity, and the judge committed her to an asylum.

The Mitchell sensation and its aftermath helped mark the beginning of the end for public acceptance of romantic friendships, and it further linked lesbians and homosexual men with mental illness and criminal behavior in the public mind. Yet, in Equi's case, the acclaim she received for punishing Taylor may have empowered her to live more openly as a lesbian and may have emboldened her to challenge social injustice in the years ahead.[26]

Just as the novelty of the horsewhipping began to fade, Reverend Taylor returned to the front pages. The deputy sheriff of Multnomah County—the jurisdiction for the Portland area—arrested Taylor for larceny and embezzlement of $50,000 from the real estate firm he founded. Taylor's attorney, the former US Senator and US Attorney General George H. Williams, helped his client dodge the charges on a technicality, but Taylor's transactions and schemes kept him embroiled in court cases for years.[27]

In time the public's attention returned to the economic downturn. During the two weeks following the street scuffle, four Portland banks closed. Pendleton, an Eastern Oregon city, found itself swamped with a "blanket brigade" of unemployed men who were "dead broke." Then the troubles hit Wasco Independent Academy. In August 1893, the board of directors announced there would be no new school term. The much-loved school had graduated its last class, and Holcomb was without a job. During the hard times that followed, she offered private classes in a room above a downtown department store.[28]

After the horsewhipping incident, Equi developed a lasting relationship with Belle Cooper Rinehart, the woman who had accompanied her to the courthouse after the horsewhipping. Their association was curious given the difference in their social standing. Rinehart was thirty-one years old, a mother of four young sons, and the wife of Willard E. Rinehart, a highly respected physician as well as mayor. She was a handsome woman, intelligent, assertive, and self-reliant. She and her family lived in a grand three-story house with gable windows and open porches above the bluff. Yet Equi later recalled how she and Rinehart had often enjoyed springtime walks among the rock lilies in the woods outside town. The older woman sometimes visited the homesteaders, and she entertained Equi at her own home. When Equi stopped there, she often hid notes of endearment. In one missive Rinehart found, she wrote, "My idol, with heart of gold and feet of clay." Equi's infatuation did not appear to disrupt her relationship with Holcomb, but it reflected a pattern in her later life of romantic longings for other independent-minded women.[29]

Tragedy struck Rinehart in the autumn of 1893 when her husband died of complications from appendicitis, leaving her to raise their four young sons. She decided to support her family by becoming a doctor herself, and she left her sons with her parents while she enrolled in medical school first at Willamette University in Salem, Oregon, and then at the University of Oregon in Portland.[30]

The professional paths taken by Holcomb and Rinehart probably influenced Equi's choice for her own future. Holcomb attained a degree of independence as a teacher, but she lost her position to an unscrupulous employer and a sinking economy. Rinehart had been a teacher herself when she was single, but, with four sons to support, she chose medicine, and the higher income of a physician, for her new career. Although nursing was a more common pursuit for women in the 1890s—especially working-class women like Equi—it held the same disadvantages as teaching with lower wages and dependency on an employer. For someone of Equi's strong will and temperament, the chance to be her own boss had to be appealing. She would have also understood that being a sexual outsider left her vulnerable to disapproval and discrimination. Becoming a physician bestowed her with social and economic protections that accompanied the professional classes. In addition, Equi knew from her own family's experience about the critical need for medical care for poor and working-class families. As a physician, she could contribute to others' well-being and become independent and financially secure. With these and perhaps other factors influencing her, Equi started studying for medical school entry examinations. Her decision to do so became the most important development of her sojourn in the West.[31]

Little more is known of Equi and Holcomb's stay in The Dalles. However, in August 1896 one of the dailies reported that the two women escaped the one hundred–degree temperatures for a trip down the cool Columbia River Gorge. They boarded the sternwheeler *Regulator* for a morning excursion into the bracing river spray, the rugged cliffs on either side of them. In the Gorge, Equi and Holcomb found the lush, green Oregon so heavily advertised to prospective settlers. The air was moist and heavy with a damp, mossy scent, and the ground absorbed their steps in a spongy grip.[32]

Just before Christmas in 1896, Bessie Holcomb filed her intent to make final proof on her homestead claim. She had fulfilled the five-year and five-acre requirements, and the patent to the homestead was granted. Her claim was among more than two million acres transferred in Oregon under the Homestead Act from 1890 to 1900. She and Equi had succeeded where thousands of homesteaders in Oregon—especially in the arid eastern part of the state—had failed. They had persisted not only to "prove up" their land claim but to "prove out" as independent, unmarried women sufficient to the challenge and who contributed to the economic development of the West.[33]

As Equi and Holcomb prepared to leave The Dalles, the economy began to right itself. A twenty-year construction project—a navigation lock west of town—opened the river for the first time to direct and convenient transport, creating a boon for river commerce. The future looked brighter in The Dalles than it had for five years, but the two homesteaders undertook a new course that would disrupt their relationship and, for Equi, attract far more acclaim and notoriety than her tussle in the street with the reverend. On March 22, 1897, the two women from New Bedford shuttered their below-the-rimrock house and left their homestead behind.[34]

3
The Audacity to Succeed

Female doctors are failures! It is a fact there are from six to eight ounces
less brain matter in the female, which shows how handicapped she is.
Dr. R. Beverly Cole, Dean, University of California Medical Department

Marie Equi and Bessie Holcomb chose San Francisco—the *Queen of the Pacific* and the *Paris of the West*, as it was known—for their new home. In the spring of 1897, Equi was twenty-five years old and more certain of her future course. San Francisco offered three well-regarded medical schools, and she hoped for admittance to at least one of them. Holcomb, at twenty-nine, had proved herself as a teacher and a homesteader. Now she was eager to pursue her interest in landscape painting. After years of living on the land with few career opportunities, the West Coast's largest city drew the two companions to its storied hills and a new world of promise.

On their way to San Francisco, Equi and Holcomb stopped in Portland where Belle Cooper Rinehart was about to graduate from medical school and return to The Dalles to establish her practice. Then they departed from the recently completed Union Station on Southern Pacific's *California Express* for the forty-hour trip to their new home. As the train rolled through the Willamette Valley south of Portland, the two companions viewed the lush farmland claimed by the first homesteaders to the state and then the dense forests that stretched into California. The springtime colors contrasted brightly with the subtle gray-greens and yellow-browns east of the Cascades. The next day, small towns slipped by until they reached the northern extension of San Francisco Bay at Carquinez Strait, where a ferry, long enough to accommodate all the cars, crossed the deep-water channel. A few hours later they reached the Oakland Mole, an immense wooden causeway that jutted into the bay toward San Francisco, giving passengers a direct connection to ferry slips for the final leg of the journey. Late afternoon sunlight streamed from behind the twenty-story skyscrapers in San Francisco, and the slender, graceful clock tower of the Ferry Building, set to open later in the year, beckoned the travelers.[1]

San Francisco was a great splurge of a city at the end of the nineteenth century, modern and cosmopolitan with a palpable excitement in the air. The city embraced its early Gold Rush reputation—full of extravagant, raucous, and licentious carryings-on—even as it celebrated its status as the undisputed capital of commerce, finance, and the arts of the West Coast and beyond. New arrivals joined the rush of city life as soon as they left the docks and stepped onto Market Street, the main boulevard for business and transport. Cable cars ground to a stop at the Ferry Building ready to collect and disperse passengers down the street or into the neighborhoods. Horse-drawn wagons and hand-carts rumbled over the cobblestones, and bicyclists and pedestrians dodged the jumble of traffic as best they could. Runners shouted the best deals at nearby hotels, and newsboys hawked the latest editions.[2]

San Francisco had fired the public imagination ever since the Gold Rush and few Americans lacked an impression of the city. But the most remarkable aspect of San Francisco at the end of the century was its incredible growth. A mere fifty years earlier a handful of white settlers took refuge from ocean fog and sand-laden winds and hunkered down in cabins at the edge of San Francisco Bay. Until the discovery of gold in 1848 triggered a massive migra-tion to Northern California, the settlers' outpost failed to register among the one hundred most populous cities in the nation. But when Equi and Holcomb arrived in 1897, San Francisco ranked as the eighth largest in the country. Viewed from prominent hilltops, the spread of the city was striking. More than 340,000 people inhabited houses and apartment buildings that spread over formerly bare sand dunes like an incoming tide that never retreated.[3]

Equi and Holcomb took rooms on Market Street in the seven-story Donohoe Building, one of the better addresses a dozen blocks from the Ferry Building. The department store Weinstock & Lubin filled the street level of the building with all the fashions that never reached The Dalles. The Donohoe sat on one of the triangular blocks created by Market Street's diagonal slash through two different street grids, and in the middle of the triangular block spread the Bay City Market, crammed with fruit and vegetable stalls, a sau-sage factory, and specialty vendors. Two blocks farther west on Market Street stood City Hall, completed after only twenty-seven years of construction. Its ungainly, slender dome was easily outclassed by the elegant Hall of Records nearby. A block south of Market on Seventh Street, Italian craftsmen labored on the federal courthouse that would figure prominently in Equi's future.[4]

Within this big-city tumult, Equi needed to find a job. To pay her rent and save for tuition, she took a cashier position at Miss Tillie Taylor's restaurant,

The Donohoe Building
on Market Street in San
Francisco was the first
residence in the city for
Marie Equi and Bessie
Holcomb. San Francisco
History Center, San
Francisco Public Library.

a small operation on Post Street not far from San Francisco's Union Square.
The elite Olympic Club and a synagogue faced Miss Taylor's restaurant, and
the new City of Paris department store nearby was the talk of the town. With
her new job, she joined the 20 percent of American women at the time who
delayed marriage—or avoided it altogether—and entered the workforce.
Holcomb relied on her savings, or assistance from her parents, and undertook
painting rather than becoming one of the city's well-paid teachers. Her work
attracted attention in local art circles, and she exhibited at the Mark Hopkins
Institute and at the Mechanics Institute Fair. Years later, in 1905, Holcomb
was included in a newspaper write-up titled "New Names in Art that Show
Promise." Both newcomers typified the emerging New Woman who stepped
away from traditional roles and economic restraints, but Equi's aspirations
to become a doctor bucked the norms even among working women. Only 6
percent of all physicians in the country were female.[5]

Marie Equi was not the first in her family to settle in San Francisco.
Her father's younger brother Joseph had left New Bedford when news of the
Gold Rush still tantalized easterners. He settled first in Sonoma in Northern
California and prospered with a produce business during the 1870s, and

then relocated his family and business to San Francisco's Mission District. Equi's aunt Fortuna, her husband, Paolino Galli, and their four children also made a home in the city several blocks west of City Hall, where they managed a fruit and vegetable stand. Equi's move to San Francisco may have occasioned her first meeting with her California relatives, but her reputation had preceded her. Four years earlier, the widely read *San Francisco Examiner* carried an account of her horsewhipping a Baptist minister in a small Oregon town.[6]

Equi and Holcomb found that many more single women roomed together in San Francisco for the sake of economy and companionship, and their arrangement was unlikely to prompt much comment. (Their bond held firm, and in March 1898 Holcomb honored Equi's help proving the homestead claim by deeding her a half share of the property.)[7] But overall little is known about San Francisco's social environment for women seeking intimate company with other women during the late 1890s. Equi's outgoing nature may have eased the entry for them into a new social circle, and Holcomb, too, would have probably befriended women, lesbians among them, interested in art. The public's understanding of homosexuality in the late nineteenth century was limited for the most part to newspaper reports of sensational affairs. Accounts of same-sex activity during the city's early decades relate mostly to Gold Rush–era men cavorting together in campfire dances and skits. Occasional stories of men and women passing as the opposite sex suggest that variations in sexual behavior were introduced early into San Francisco's culture. In later decades, the men who caroused in the city's no-holds-barred dives on Pacific Avenue contributed to the city's reputation as Sodom by the Sea.[8]

The appearance of Oscar Wilde in San Francisco in 1882 had sparked great interest and titillation for more mainstream society. Wilde was a twenty-eight-year-old Irish aesthete from London, a celebrity known for his refined tastes, effeminate garb, and theatrical prowess. When he lectured on art and decoration, he did so dressed in his signature velvet coat, lace cuffs, short breeches, and long stockings. At his other American stops, Wilde's audience reportedly included "pallid young men with banged hair." For many Americans, Wilde's tour and the newspaper coverage of it was their first, substantial exposure to homosexuals, and it shaped their opinions of alternative, outsider sexuality. Then, in 1895, the American public had vilified Wilde as a degenerate reprobate after he was convicted and sentenced to prison for having sex with a younger aristocratic man. The incident forced Americans to recognize that same-sex activity extended beyond the lower classes, although they could dismiss it still as a proclivity of distant European elites.[9]

Most applicants to medical school gained entry by presenting a high school or college diploma, a teacher's certificate, or proof of prior acceptance from another college. But for individuals like Equi who never completed high school, the successful completion of an entry exam was the only option. Passing an English exam had been the sole requirement in years past, but criteria steadily became stiffer. A few years after Equi's application, San Francisco's medical schools removed the entry exam as an option and required a minimum of a high school education. A few required two years of college as well.[10]

The increasing demands on applicants reflected a major, long-term transformation of American medical education toward more professionalism. A great many doctors, represented by the American Medical Association (AMA), wanted to bolster the public's regard for their profession by increasing competency among practitioners. They hoped their support for stricter entry requirements would block unqualified applicants and, not coincidentally, reduce competition and increase their own incomes. In time many of the private medical colleges became affiliated with universities and adopted those institutions' higher standards for admission and training.[11]

In the midst of these fluctuations, Equi's plans for medical school were well timed. She gained entry when requisites were within her reach, and she began coursework when the quality of instruction was steadily improving. Her trajectory was remarkable. Ten years after dropping out of high school at age seventeen, she was on her way to becoming a professional. Equi's determination and audacity transcended the limits of her working-class roots and carried her to the steps of a medical college.

Just fifty years earlier in 1849, Elizabeth Blackwell became the first woman to graduate from an American medical school. Her achievement marked the start of women's arduous and protracted struggle to enter a profession other than teaching. Initially female applicants were so regularly refused entry to medical colleges that they resorted to institutions founded for women alone. Once state universities started to admit women to their medical departments in the 1870s, however, the number of their female students soared. By 1880 women graduates in medical practice increased tenfold to nearly 2,500. By the time of Equi's first year of study, nearly 7,400 women practiced medicine nationwide. Ironically, she began her studies when women were at the peak of enrollment. Within a few more years, their numbers began a long-term decline caused by the closing of women's schools, increasing costs of education, more demanding entrance requirements, and ongoing gender discrimination.[12]

In October of 1899, Equi enrolled at the College of Physicians and Surgeons, one of San Francisco's three schools of regular medicine, meaning allopathic and not alternative. Founded in 1896, "P&S," as it was widely known, was San Francisco's newest medical college. A local dentist and entrepreneur had founded the school and made it a successful venture, partly by charging each faculty member $500 for a full professorship. For their part, first-year students paid at least $115 for matriculation, tuition, and anatomy lectures. The fees were too steep for Equi, and Holcomb helped her with tuition.[13]

The three-story P&S building featured well-furnished lecture rooms, specialty laboratories, and dissecting rooms. Located at Fourteenth and Valencia Streets in the Mission District, the college boasted a convenient location opposite the Southern Pacific Hospital and near the City and County Hospital, prized for the clinical experience it offered students. P&S was coeducational at its founding, and two to three women were registered in each year's freshman class. In the mostly male environment, women students found allies where they could, and Marie Equi was fortunate to befriend Mary Ellen Parker, a younger woman who had spent much of her life in the eastern Sierra town of Bridgeport, California. Her father was a Scottish immigrant and a successful attorney, and her mother was a homemaker and a devout Roman Catholic of Irish descent. Parker earned a teaching certificate in Ogden, Utah, before starting her medical studies in San Francisco. She was more reserved than Equi but, according to her relatives, she was every bit as intelligent, opinionated, and strong willed. In their first year Equi and Parker studied the full range of sciences in addition to pharmacology and physiology. Their instructors were all men since the few women professors at P&S taught courses not open to first-year students—gynecology, abdominal surgery, and medicine. But Equi became acquainted with a few of the women faculty and impressed them enough to be invited to intern with them in the years ahead.[14]

With the end of the fall term, students might have engaged in the national debate raging over America's military conduct after its victory in the Spanish American War of 1898. The US had injected itself into the colonial insurrections of Cuba and The Philippines against Spain, the old colonial power of the Americas, and the nation's leaders positioned San Francisco as the lead city for a new American empire. Business titans were all too willing to cooperate. They envisioned San Francisco dominating Pacific Basin trade much as it already did on the West Coast.[15]

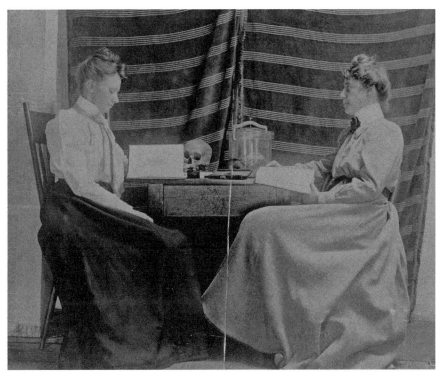

Mary Ellen Parker (left) and Marie Equi (right) were medical school classmates and companions at three different colleges in four years. Courtesy of The Lilly Library, Indiana University, Bloomington, Indiana.

The American public rallied to the independence movements, yet intense economic and geopolitical interests powered the country's involvement in further hostilities. After the end of the war with Spain, the US triggered another conflict with Filipino insurgents who refused to trade the yoke of colonial Spain for the shackles of industrial America. The betrayal of the freedom-seeking Filipinos and the increasing American war casualties troubled the public back home. Soldiers' letters about sweeping through whole villages and leaving no one alive stoked public doubts even more. The Anti-Imperialist League, with thirty thousand members nationwide, railed against the war and the new spirit of militarism. The league was no ragtag group of dissidents—its supporters included Mark Twain, Samuel Gompers of the American Federation of Labor, the industrialist Andrew Carnegie, and social activist Jane Addams. Even former presidents William Henry Harrison and Grover Cleveland signed up as members. But the anti-imperialists were overwhelmed by rampant yellow journalism that stirred war fever and the prospect of windfall profits for American businesses.

The Affiliated Colleges (later the University of California San Francisco) among the swirling sand of a remote section of San Francisco, circa 1898. Marie Equi attended one year of medical school here. San Francisco History Center, San Francisco Public Library.

We can only speculate whether Equi shared the antiwar activity and distrust of America's industrial claims for the end-of-century wars, but the sentiments extended into the twentieth century and later commanded her full attention.[16]

In early 1900 Equi and Holcomb reduced their expenses and relocated to a large apartment building on Franklin Street near City Hall. They rented rooms from a young German-American telegraph operator and his wife, and Mary Ellen Parker took an apartment one block away. Saint Ignatius College and Church dominated their new neighborhood, filling one complete block, and attracting visitors with the majestic sound from the 5,300 pipes of its new organ.[17]

Equi and Parker completed their first year of study at P&S, and then in the autumn of 1900 they transferred to the new campus of the University of California Medical Department, located on a distant, fog-swept hill overlooking Golden Gate Park. The medical department had begun as Toland Medical College, one of the city's first proprietary schools. Like other private medical schools in the West, Toland was established by a strong-willed man of medicine, Dr. Hugh Toland, who positioned his investment for every advantage. After several years of prospering, however, the college floundered amid faculty rivalries. In 1873 Toland offered the operation to the regents of the state university, and Toland Medical became a professional school of the University of California in 1873. As a result of the merger, the new department adopted the university's open admission policy for women, making it the first coeducational medical school in the state.[18]

Yet women students found little welcome at the university's medical school. In the 1890s, Helen M. Doyle recounted that both professors and male students treated women students as "an experiment and something of a joke." The professor of obstetrics and gynecology liked to disparage women as having "six to eight ounces less brain power" than men. When Doyle graduated, a female classmate received the highest marks of any graduate in the previous ten years.[19]

Equi's new campus with three main buildings offered few amenities, and it was linked to the city by a single trolley line. But Equi and Parker began once again to fit into a new academic community. Their sophomore year was a time to study the scientific basis of medicine before delving into aspects of clinical care, and course work included anatomy with a focus on dissection, organic chemistry, and an introduction to embryology. In the year 1900, students also observed the real-life interplay of medicine, public health, and politics when an outbreak of bubonic plague took hold in San Francisco. City and state leaders disputed and discredited the reports of plague—all in the interest of protecting commerce and civic reputation—until the prevalence of the scourge became too obvious to hide.[20]

Something went awry for Equi during her second year of study. Under ideal circumstances, sophomores immersed themselves in the academic culture of the institution and forged bonds with peers and professors, who would be their colleagues after graduation. But Equi completed the semesters only to transfer yet again to a third school. This time she chose to leave San Francisco and the state altogether for reasons that were perhaps more personal than academic. She could obtain no better medical training in the West than what was available in San Francisco, and another transfer required establishing herself with new professors and a new student body. That may have been the point. Given the harassment of women students and Equi's quick temper, her relations at the school may have soured, but her changed relationship with Bessie Holcomb may have been a factor as well.

Holcomb's steady presence in Equi's life from New Bedford to San Francisco had given her a secure base as she set her career path and matured as a woman. They had enjoyed the flush of intimacy that defined their homestead years and the sense of adventure from settling into San Francisco, but, in 1901, after nearly ten years of companionship, their interests diverged. Equi had drawn close to Parker, and Holcomb had begun a new relationship as well—this time with a man. She had taken a job as a stenographer for the Wagner Leather Company, an outfit in the Financial District that sold shoe leathers, skirtings, and harnesses. There she started dating her boss, the firm's senior manager, Alexander J. Cook. Holcomb was in her early thirties, and she was apparently drawn to a more conventional life with a husband and children. Within three years she and Cook married and made their home in San Francisco.[21]

As Equi prepared to leave the Bay Area in 1901, tinderbox politics threatened the nation. On September 6, Leon Czolgosz, a factory worker and a son of Polish immigrants, shot and gravely wounded President William McKinley at the world's fair in Buffalo, New York. Once police apprehended Czolgosz, he proclaimed his adherence to the radical views of anarchist Emma Goldman, whom he had heard speak in Chicago four days earlier. Police arrested Goldman and charged her with inciting the attempted assassination, even though she had met Czolgosz just once and briefly. The "guilt-by-lecture" accusation did not hold, and Goldman was eventually released. But the antipathy toward anarchists in the country became more intense and pervasive after the president died of his wounds. Czolgosz was eventually tried, convicted of murder in the first degree, and executed by electrocution. Theodore Roosevelt assumed the presidency, and the fevered antagonism toward radical activists ebbed, at least for a while.[22]

Equi is not known to have engaged in politics during her San Francisco years. Woman suffrage might have commanded her attention, but California's right-to-vote campaign slumped after a stinging defeat in 1896 and had yet to rebound. As Equi took her leave of California, San Francisco remained a touchstone, the place where she had persevered and set her course toward a life as an independent professional woman.

4
Doctor and Suffragist

Marie D. Equi: A Fearless Champion of Freedom for Women
Abigail Scott Duniway, Oregon's woman suffrage pioneer

This time Marie Equi chose Portland—the cool, green metropolis of the Pacific Northwest. She arrived in 1901 at the cusp of Portland's boom times. An influx of twenty-five thousand newcomers boosted the population to ninety thousand over a three-year period. In another ten years, the number would double and make the city one of the fastest growing in the nation. Civic leaders envisioned a regional powerhouse and a commercial gateway to Pacific nations. At a time of high civic spirits, Equi passed through Union Station with a new companion, Mary Ellen Parker, and a letter of admittance to her third medical school.[1]

Portland offered the only study of regular medicine north of San Francisco. In 1867, Willamette University organized the first lectures in medicine in Oregon, and the university provided the state's sole medical education for twenty years. But, in an example of the intensely bitter academic rivalries that bedeviled medical colleges at the time, four defiant professors bolted the department ten years later and established a rival in 1887: the University of Oregon Medical Department. Equi chose this new school to complete her studies. She and Parker enrolled in September 1901 and joined ninety other students in a three-story building with soaring gables and peaks on the outskirts of the downtown district. In their class of ten students, Equi and Parker were two of five women, an unusual male and female equity for a medical school. Yet the university had welcomed women since its founding, and, in 1901, the fourteen female students in all the departments represented 15 percent of the student body.[2]

The third year of medical school marked a shift toward the actual practice of medicine, and, in Portland, students undertook clinical work at Good Samaritan Hospital, located across the street from the school. Equi wasn't known to fault her new school, but the medical department fared poorly in what became known as the Flexner Report, an evaluation facilitated by the American Medical Association. Given its scant resources, limited library holdings, and lack of full-time professors, the reviewers concluded the department lacked a credible reason to exist. As might be imagined, university faculty and administrators took exception to the findings and sparred with the AMA for several years.[3]

Despite their greater numbers, female medical students in Oregon suffered hostility from male faculty and students. At Willamette University, Mary B. Purvine complained in her memoirs of "a terrible existence" as the only woman in a class of four men who made her the butt of their vulgar and abusive jokes. In other schools the harassment discouraged many women from completing their studies or from entering the profession after they graduated. However, a number of women managed to negotiate their student years with less confrontation. Esther Pohl Lovejoy described a more harmonious time with the mostly male student body at the University of Oregon when she attended in the early 1890s. But she was also dating one of the male students at the time and that association probably shielded her. Equi, on the other hand, was a single woman associated with another woman, and both her assertiveness and her sexuality probably factored into the treatment she received. She later confided that the harassment often led her to throw herself on her bed by the end of the day.[4]

Equi and Parker had become close companions, and they shared an apartment a few blocks from the university. At one point, they sat for a portrait photograph together, facing each other with a human skull and stacks of books artfully placed on a table between them. Equi struck a reflective, confident pose while Parker appeared tentative and self-conscious. But they developed a good rapport and forged a bond that lasted for years. Equi later joked that during their school years in Portland they would dissect cadavers in the morning and then toss back drinks in the afternoon to get a free lunch. When away from her studies, Equi worked part-time as a nurse to pay her tuition, and, in the summer, she provided medical care for a company in the gold mining region outside Bridgeport, California, Parker's hometown.[5]

In their studies and reading, Equi and Parker were probably exposed to the increasingly popular theories of European psychologists regarding sexual identities and behaviors, including homosexuality. How they described or identified their own same-sex relationship is not known. But they continued to room together in an arrangement that saved on rent, provided mutual support, and, possibly, led to romance and sex.

Just as Equi completed her four years of study, a respected Oregon physician tried to block her graduation. Dr. Belle Cooper Rinehart pleaded with the dean of the medical school, Dr. Simeon E. Josephi, to withhold a diploma

Marie Equi (fourth from left) and Mary Ellen Parker (fourth from right, rear) in medical school dissection class, circa 1900-1903. Courtesy of The Lilly Library, Indiana University, Bloomington, Indiana.

from Equi, saying she was unfit to practice medicine. Rinehart was the same woman whom Equi had befriended following the horsewhipping incident ten years earlier in The Dalles. Yet in 1903 Rinehart made a special trip from The Dalles to derail Equi's career. According to reports filed years later, she told the dean that Equi had a violent temper and had once threatened her companion, Bessie Holcomb, during an argument. Whether Rinehart was also motivated by issues in her own relationship with Equi is not known. The dean was well aware of Equi's temper as faculty members had complained that she used "very bad language" over the telephone. Equi's short fuse became well known in later years, and there's little doubt that it flared earlier as well. But Rinehart's complaint failed to persuade the dean, who might have found it odd that with the very low percentage of women doctors one would turn against another to such an extent. He knew Equi had completed her coursework satisfactorily. He was certainly aware of disagreeable traits among other established physicians, and, perhaps, he was reminded of his own strong-willed, contentious past when he abandoned the faculty of Willamette University to establish the department he now led.[6]

As it happened, Equi's particular mix of anger and sense of justice landed her in the *Oregonian* a few weeks before her graduation. The paper reported an incident in which Equi slapped a male student after he belittled her as a "fool." During a classroom dispute over a proposed student fee to support campus football—a sport open only to men at the time—she objected to the discriminatory nature of the payment. Seventy years before the federal law known as Title IX guaranteed equity in athletics for women, Equi argued that women received no direct benefit from the fee yet they would be required to pay dues in order to vote in student body elections. Equi never took kindly to insult or mistreatment, no matter the stature of the offender. She explained to the newspaper that she also objected to the preferential treatment given male students in all facets of student life.[7]

Sixteen years after dropping out of high school to work in a textile mill, Equi gathered with other seniors for graduation ceremonies held at Portland High School. They settled into the assembly hall filled with friends and family while a string orchestra played Tchaikovsky's *Chant sans paroles.* In his address to the graduates, Dr. K. A. J. Mackenzie encouraged the students to undertake postgraduate work at hospitals on the East Coast or in Europe, if possible, and then to settle in a well-to-do rural district before trying to establish themselves in the city. He earned a round of applause for his final advice: "Don't settle in a place that is too healthy."[8]

Equi's journey from a factory job in Massachusetts to a profession in Oregon demanded fortitude and resilience, and her achievement was all the greater given her background. In 1900 only 17 percent of all women physicians were native-born children of one or more immigrant parents. In Oregon she was among the first sixty women to graduate from a state medical school. Yet an additional hurdle remained—a medical license. Before 1895 anyone with a medical school degree could easily obtain a license to practice medicine in Oregon. By 1903, however, the state board of medical examiners required a written test of all new graduates and of any physician recently moved to the state. On April 9, 1903, Marie Equi and Mary Ellen Parker passed the examination and received their licenses, joining the ranks of the first professional women practicing in the Pacific Northwest.[9]

New doctors did not necessarily feel prepared for patient care as soon as the ink dried on their licenses, and by 1904 about 50 percent of them in the United States undertook hospital internships for advanced and supervised training. Those who could not obtain or afford positions on the East Coast or in Europe sought openings at local hospitals, and a few relied on preceptorships with experienced physicians in private practice. In Portland, however, women graduates found few opportunities for either kind of work.[10]

Equi and Parker secured their internships in San Francisco instead. Equi worked for six months with Dr. Florence Nightingale Ward, a respected surgeon and national leader in homeopathic medicine. Ward had graduated from San Francisco's Hahnemann Medical College of the Pacific, the center of homeopathic education in the West, before taking advanced study in gynecological surgery at hospitals in New York and in Europe. She returned to San Francisco and established what was later described as the largest practice of a woman physician west of Chicago. As an apprentice to Ward, Equi became familiar with the most advanced surgical procedures. She also learned to provide care in the homeopathic tradition of extensive physician-patient communication, limited invasive procedures, and use of small doses of substances to prompt the body's normal healing processes. On a collegial level, Equi observed in Ward an independent, determined woman who achieved considerable success without compromising her principles.[11]

Equi was fortunate to seek her homeopathic training at a time when the gap between regular medicine and homeopathy had narrowed, the open war from 1850 to 1880 between the two disciplines having subsided. By supplementing her training with homeopathic practices, Equi enhanced her competitive advantage in the medical marketplace on the West Coast. In Portland, as well as in San Francisco, medical practitioners included physicians licensed in regular medicine, and others who based their services in homeopathy, physiomedical treatments, Chinese medicine, and midwifery. Entrepreneurs who offered patent medicines and supplements rounded out the competition.[12]

Over the next few years, Equi returned to San Francisco for ongoing advanced study, and worked with Dr. Sophie B. Kobicke, one of the few specialists in the city who understood the new and complicated procedures associated with bladder and kidney surgery. During her stints in the city, Equi kept a rigorous schedule with shifts three days a week at the public hospital clinic on Mission Street and another three days at Cooper Medical College where she assisted gynecologist George B. Summers with operations.[13]

With a mix of courage and pragmatism, Equi and Parker left San Francisco in November 1903 to establish practices in Pendleton, Oregon, a town of six thousand people, situated 230 miles east of Portland in the northeastern section of the state. They apparently took heed of Dr. Mackenzie's advice at their graduation ceremony to start working in a rural district to learn how to manage a practice.

Pendleton stretched along the south bank of the Umatilla River as it rushed westward through rolling hills of sagebrush and grasses from its headwaters in the snow-capped Blue Mountains. With the coming of the railroads in the early 1880s, Pendleton boomed as a commercial hub for the farmers and ranchers of the region. By rail and river, Eastern Oregon's wheat, livestock, wool, and fruit were carried to the markets in Portland and beyond. The trade helped establish Pendleton as the fourth largest city in the state by the early 1900s. Residents boasted of running water, electricity, telephone service, and paved roads. They took pride in its opera house, its business college, the downtown Italianate commercial brick buildings, and the Queen Anne houses in the southside neighborhoods. But the city was hardly a benign outpost. With more than thirty saloons and at least a dozen brothels, Pendleton was the good-times favorite among the region's cowboys, ranch hands, and out-of-towners.[14]

Physicians were always in short supply in Central and Eastern Oregon, and Pendleton touted two draws for prospective practitioners: the Sisters of St. Francis opened St. Anthony's Hospital in 1903 and the federal government hired doctors to provide medical care to the Cayuse, Umatilla, and Walla Walla peoples at the nearby Umatilla Indian Reservation.[15]

Equi and Parker registered with Umatilla County authorities on November 2, 1903, and established their office as well as their lodging in the ornate stone and brick Judd Building downtown. They joined eleven established doctors, all men, with offices in town.[16]

Physicians working in Oregon's high desert and plains dealt with challenges far different from those found in cities. They often traveled for hours by horseback or buggy to reach patients at distant ranches and homesteads. Once they arrived, the doctors frequently found that prospective patients mistrusted what they considered New Medicine, preferring their own folk remedies instead. Fred deWolfe, a local chronicler who became a statewide journalist, later wrote of Equi's unstinted courage and dedication on the range. According to his account, Equi rode on horseback in the countryside providing medical care to Indians and cowboys.

Medical care for the local tribes was a complicated affair, and the degree to which Equi actually provided treatment is uncertain. By the early 1900s the Indian population had been decimated by diseases of the white men, and their own doctors were unable to cure many of the new maladies, resulting in a loss of tribal status for them. Indians on the reservation often had little choice but to accept medical care from white doctors, though it could be equally ineffective. Equi was not among the contract doctors serving the reservation, and native peoples living off the reservation were unlikely to summon her for medical care. But circumstances were fluid, and she may have assisted them on occasion. In any event, the accounts of Equi's doctoring in the remote stretches of Umatilla County burnished her reputation.[17]

Equi's general practice thrived, and she later recalled that she had all the work she could handle. Ten years earlier a local paper, the *Pendleton Tribune*, had covered the story of the young woman who horsewhipped a Baptist minister in The Dalles, but if people in town connected the story to Equi, no accounts appeared of undue interest about the two new women doctors setting up practice and living together.[18]

Unlike Equi, Parker found little success in Pendleton with her own practice, and she attracted few patients seeking treatment for her eye, ear, nose, and throat specialty. After several months of effort, she decided to seek opportunity elsewhere. Equi chose loyalty to her companion over her own more promising start, and she and Parker returned to Portland.[19]

Equi appeared to relocate with relative ease, but her moves also reflected the demands on women practitioners at the time. Like most female doctors, she sought the best choices among the few possibilities. In Portland she and Parker took a fifth-floor office in the nine-storied Oregonian Building, the city's first skyscraper, located at Sixth and Alder Streets in the core of the downtown district. Erected in 1892 in the grand Richardson-Romanesque style with a sculpted stone exterior, the building featured a 203-foot clock tower that served as a civic timepiece. The building offered all the modern conveniences—electricity, artesian water, and elevators—making it the most popular commercial address in the city. The two women shared an office large enough to accommodate a waiting room and two examining areas outfitted with the typical equipment of the day: a table or reclining chair for the patient, a cabinet for pharmaceuticals, brass scales, and the means to sterilize instruments. They posted their examining room hours—ten to noon in the morning and two to five in the afternoon with evening hours reserved for visiting patients in their homes. And, once again, Equi and Parker rented an apartment together, this time on Jefferson Street, several blocks from the city's center. Overall business was booming in Portland, and apparently the two new doctors prospered enough to afford their new surroundings. They settled into familiar city rhythms—the horse-drawn sprinklers that dampened dust on downtown streets, the Southern Pacific locomotives still steaming along Fourth Street—with every reason to expect a bright future.[20]

Women doctors remained a novelty, even in a state like Oregon that licensed nearly twice the national percentage of female practitioners. The greater numbers in the state probably reflected the early acceptance of female students in the medical schools. A niche for women existed in Portland's medical world, but many people thought the mix of new medicine with its emphasis on precise causes for specific diseases and the New Woman ready to treat their maladies was too much too soon. Most women physicians in the late nineteenth and early twentieth centuries specialized in treating women and children. Like Equi, many had witnessed the difficulties of childbirth and the scourge of childhood diseases in their own families. They welcomed the opportunity to improve women's conditions and provide sound care to children, but other women resented the constraint on their professional aims. Male doctors, after all, felt no compunction to establish practices mostly for male clients. But women doctors were a hardy bunch by and large, and many accepted what was available even as they pushed against the barriers. Obstetrics posed a different problem. New women doctors seeking to specialize in obstetrics tried to sidestep lingering resentments over physicians who wanted to usurp the traditional role of midwives. They avoided any suggestion that they were better trained than midwives, and one doctor negotiated this uncertain terrain by making her reputation in surgery so that she could "enter obstetrics through a surgical door . . . with skill and distinction."[21]

Equi readily established her general medicine practice in Portland in 1905 with an emphasis on obstetrics and gynecology as well as maternal and childhood health. The internship in San Francisco had helped her develop a reputation as a skilled diagnostician, and her background in New Bedford gave her a natural rapport with Portland's working-class and immigrant populations. In the year Equi started seeing patients, nearly eight hundred people died of tuberculosis in the state. Typhoid fever claimed a death rate of 25 percent, and measles scored the greatest prevalence with more than eight hundred cases reported in Portland alone. Children all too often contracted diphtheria, the same malady that claimed Equi's younger brother during her childhood. No effective remedy was available then, but Equi and her colleagues relied on an antitoxin for treatment.[22]

Equi's expertise encompassed more than the infectious diseases of the day. In February 1905 she lectured on "Nervousness in Children" before Portland's Home Training Association, and an account of her talk was published in the *Oregonian*. She described the common symptoms of nervousness and then linked the condition to a combination of heredity and environment. She emphasized that such children were "painfully aware of faults," and she advised caretakers to avoid harsh criticism, to help the child learn self-control, and to guide the use of nervous energy. Her prescriptions seemed to draw on her own experience as a schoolgirl in New Bedford, and they suggest an interpretation of her own early behavior.[23]

Once established with an office and home, Equi and Parker renewed their involvement with the Portland and Multnomah County Medical Society and the Oregon Medical Society. Although the state organization first accepted women in 1877, the local society excluded women until 1902, a full eighteen years after its founding. Two years later Equi and Parker were also admitted, and women doctors then totaled more than a dozen. Women welcomed the recognition from the medical associations, but they also formed their own alliance, the Medical Club of Portland, in 1900 to support each other more directly. Among the members, Equi formed several close relationships that continued for decades.[24]

Portland's ongoing commercial and residential growth was only one of the big stories in Oregon when Equi began her medical practice in the city. Beginning in 1902, the state's male electorate approved so many "direct democracy" reforms that pundits and reformers across the nation hailed the Oregon System as a harbinger of civic and political transformation. Before the enactment of the sweeping changes, citizens had no direct means to place measures on the ballot, repeal laws, recall elected officials, or elect their US senators directly. Most importantly, women lacked the fundamental facet of citizenship: the right to vote.[25]

Oregon's innovations reflected a new force in the nation's body politic—a political vision and undertaking called Progressivism—that expressed a yearning for social change and a widespread discontent with the intrusions of corporate interests into American politics. Progressives hoped to forge a new political paradigm free of domination by corporate power brokers and guided by a robust exercise of citizen engagement. In this movement Marie Equi found her initial footing as an activist.

Progressives lobbied the federal government and local municipalities to adopt policies and undertake programs to improve society and protect the public. They pushed for a more enlightened social order that shielded women and children from abuses on the job, expanded voting rights, and regulated consumer goods. And they urged reforms in the civil service system to steer control away from political hacks. During the first two decades of the new century, Progressives' efforts steadily loosened the grip of the industrial and corporate elite over the workforce and of the political party bosses over the political process. But the reform-minded advocates also embraced measures of social control that proved to be intrusive and problematic.[26]

Women ready for social and political change were especially drawn to the Progressive agenda, and at first they focused on public health measures and protection of those most vulnerable to injustice and unhealthy environments. They supported civic housekeeping, a broad array of initiatives to sweep corruption from local government and help single women, unwed mothers, and families struggling with unemployment and poor health. Once they engaged in essentially political activism, women became increasingly convinced their success in the civic realm depended on securing the right to vote.[27]

Equi started her career in Portland during the early, frothy days of the Progressive and feminist fervor in the city. She was familiar with political strife—from workers' strikes in New Bedford and protests by the unemployed in The Dalles to longshoreman shutting down San Francisco's waterfront. But not until she secured her own livelihood was she known to engage in struggles for civic reform and economic justice.

The work of Oregon's relentless and indomitable woman suffrage leader, Abigail Scott Duniway, drew Equi to the push for the right to vote. She was nearly forty years younger than "Mrs. Duniway," as everyone referred to her, and their life experiences were vastly different. But Equi found in the older woman an accomplished, self-made advocate with a fiery temperament and a big-hearted embrace of life. For the first time perhaps, she was in close association with a woman whose traits and passion mirrored her own. Duniway came to appreciate Equi's commitment as well and later wrote of her, "Marie D. Equi, a fearless champion of freedom for women."[28]

For more than thirty years, Duniway had carried the suffrage message across Oregon, and no road was too rutted or muddied, no public gathering too small or hostile to disrupt her mission. She was as comfortable with businessmen, attorneys, and doctors as she was with farmers, ranch hands, and housewives, and she marshaled her own considerable experiences to engage audiences with a mix of feminist advocacy, frontier lore, and strident barbs at opponents. Her rough-hewn manner, defensiveness, and stubbornness often alienated other suffragists and weakened her campaigns, but she believed she knew best and her critics found her perseverance difficult to ignore. Those who knew her well understood the influence of her background on her personal and political behavior.[29]

Abigail Jane "Jenny" Scott, the future Mrs. Duniway, was an often sickly girl of seventeen when her father uprooted the family from their Illinois farm in 1852 for a glimmering hope of something better in the West. Jenny had spent five months in "an apology for an academy" in which she "never did, could or would study." She distrusted authority, resisted discipline other than her own, and re-sented the farm work expected of her. For the trip West, Jenny's father appointed her chronicler of their trek, a task she initially resisted. Later she used her frontier experiences to pen Oregon's first commercially published novel, *Captain Gray's Company*, in 1859. In Oregon, Jenny married Benjamin Duniway and became a farm wife with six children. When an injury permanently disabled her husband, she alone supported the family by both teaching and opening a millinery shop. The business venture exposed her to dozens of women burdened by a legal sys-tem that favored men and left wives responsible for their husband's debts. Their plight convinced her that women needed the vote to exercise their citizenship but especially to wield the power necessary to change their circumstances.[30]

In 1870 Duniway organized Oregon's first state suffrage association. The following year she persuaded Susan B. Anthony, the national suffrage leader, to join her on a campaign tour throughout the state, creating a bond between the two leaders that lasted three decades before unraveling. Starting in 1872, Duniway led one attempt after another to wrest the right to vote from Oregon's male electorate. She rallied Oregon's suffragists for one more try in 1906.[31]

Equi joined the Oregon Equal Suffrage Association, the organization led by Duniway, to secure the vote. She learned at the start that Duniway insisted on a "still hunt" strategy, a low-key effort with no rallies and little public orga-nizing. The longtime leader believed in recruiting influential men and women to the suffrage cause without stirring the passions of the general electorate or the known opponents. Her methods riled the directors of the National American Women Suffrage Association (NAWSA), the country's primary right-to-vote organization. They preferred a "hurrah campaign" filled with public lectures, canvassing, endorsements, and parades. Susan B. Anthony, the venerated president of NAWSA, had concluded years earlier that Oregon would never close the deal on suffrage with Duniway in command. Circum-stances had changed for the one-time friends once NAWSA leaders sought to exert their influence in state campaigns. Duniway's insistence on a more subtle approach no longer meshed with what Anthony had in mind, and the resulting struggles between state and national leaders injected fractious, often bitter, infighting into local efforts. The conflicts were to be expected as strong, driven leaders were needed for the massive undertaking of changing laws in all the states. And, more to the point, no particular campaign strategy had proven successful across the board, leaving battles over strategy inevitable.[32]

In 1905, circumstances favored NAWSA's campaign strategy when Port-land hosted the first world's fair in the Pacific Northwest. These grand events were still all the rage in the country after earlier extravaganzas in Chicago, Buffalo, and St. Louis. Americans flocked to see industrial and scientific marvels, towers of elaborately arranged agricultural goods, and the best fine arts the host city could muster. Portland's event, the Lewis and Clark Exposition, marked the centennial of the American exploration of the Oregon Country, and it positioned the city as a destination for settlers and a prime prospect for investors.[33]

The fair drew exhibits from twenty-one nations and most of the states to the Guilds Lake area on the outer-reaches of northwest Portland. Each built its own pavilion on the fairgrounds, and Oregon erected an imposing Forestry Building with enormous fir tree trunks still clad with bark. It was quickly dubbed "the biggest log cabin in the world." The exposition was wildly successful and drew more than one and a half million visitors who were thrilled to see the first automobile built in Oregon, Infant Incubators where six babies were nurtured to gain strength, and the motor-driven blimp piloted by eighteen-year-old Lincoln Beachey in the first lighter-than-air flight in the Pacific Northwest.[34]

Portland's physicians rallied to welcome fairgoers. Equi, Esther Pohl, and other doctors served on the bureau of information committee to greet visiting doctors, and the medical society helped host the annual meeting of the American Medical Association. But most of Equi's attention focused on the first NAWSA convention to be held in the West.[35]

Suffragists had wanted to take a greater role in the planning of the exposition, but male directors of the operation blocked any significant engagement. Not to be dismissed altogether, feminists staged the annual NAWSA convention during the exposition. Nationally known suffrage leaders—Susan B. Anthony, Carrie Chapman Catt, and Anna Howard Shaw—arrived with hundreds of delegates intent upon winning the vote in Oregon the following year.[36]

The suffragists gathered at the First Congregational Church, a massive Venetian Gothic structure in downtown Portland designed to resemble the Old South Church in Boston. Yellow bunting, roses, and lilies framed the stage, and in front of the podium more flowers formed the word PROGRESS. Delegates sporting yellow ribbons—the color chosen for the suffrage campaign—were delighted with the hospitality of Oregonians, and optimism prevailed that the state would jumpstart the stalled national suffrage movement. Anna Howard Shaw, a licensed physician, ordained minister, and the new NAWSA president, stirred the audience as she refuted claims that suffrage

Woman Suffrage Day at the Lewis and Clark Exposition, June 30, 1905, Portland, Oregon. Abigail Scott Duniway and Susan B. Anthony (fourth and fifth women from left in front row). The woman standing behind Susan B. Anthony, to the left in a lapel jacket, appears to be Marie Equi. Oregon Historical Society, bb013170.

would distract women from their duties as mothers and housewives. She was widely acclaimed as a brilliant, persuasive public speaker who lived and breathed the suffrage cause. But she struggled to manage the usual challenges for an underfinanced and understaffed advocacy organization riven with quarrelsome factions and impeded by cultural norms and political interests. Behind the scenes in Portland, NAWSA field workers tried to undercut Mrs. Duniway's influence by establishing a rival organization. At the convention the national leaders offered to finance another Oregon campaign as long as they, and not Duniway, managed it. The conflict ensured a statewide effort with a festering dispute just below the surface.[37]

On the last day of the convention, Equi launched a short-lived campaign to be appointed to Portland's new post of public market inspector. She described women as particularly suited for the job, and few doubted that the filthy conditions in the city's markets required a strong hand. Equi won the support of NAWSA and that of the Oregon Equal Suffrage Association, and the *Oregonian* declared that Equi had "the strongest endorsement of any candidate." She appeared poised for her first public office. But Portland's new reform-minded mayor, Harry Lane, and the city's board of health had already chosen Sarah Evans, the president of the Portland Women's Club, for the post. Even before she was passed over, Equi pulled back from consideration. She sent a terse note to the mayor declaring she no longer wanted the job. She objected to the manner in which he had summarily dismissed the previous board of health members, including one of her woman doctor friends, and she charged the salary was woefully inadequate.[38]

On the same day the morning paper reported Equi's turnabout on the post, a sensational story placed her in the midst of an apparent homicide. Mrs. Minnie Van Dran, a high-society personality and a personal friend of Equi's, died after drinking ginger ale spiked with prussic acid. Investigators ruled out suicide, and Portlanders were abuzz for weeks with news of the investigation. Mrs. Van Dran was forty-one years old and the daughter of a prominent Albany, Oregon family. Her husband, Kasper Van Dran, was the proprietor of a Washington Street saloon in downtown Portland. In an unusual intervention, the *Oregonian* asked Mary Ellen Parker to determine the contents of the soda bottle. She and Equi found enough prussic acid to poison at least two hundred people. They also assisted with the autopsy and testified before the coroner's jury. The police cleared the victim's husband and sister, but they never solved the murder.[39]

The newspaper coverage of Equi's role in the public market dispute followed by her assistance with a murder investigation of a friend—a mix of her political beliefs, personal life, and professional conduct—typified and shaped what Portlanders learned of her as she came to greater public attention. In the next eighteen months, however, first impressions would mean little as Equi garnered more public acclaim and notoriety than anyone would have imagined.

5
To the Rescue with the Oregon Doctor Train

Dr. Marie Equi: One of the most conspicuous examples of self-sacrifice in a desire to aid the suffering that has been seen in Portland.
Oregon Daily Journal

In November 1905, when Portlanders still glowed with the success of their world's fair, Marie Equi encountered a woman who captured her imagination and swept her into a longtime intimate relationship. She fell in love with the refined and well-educated Harriet Speckart, heiress to a fortune. The two women first met at The Hill, a high-class residential hotel in Portland, where Equi and Mary Ellen Parker had begun residing earlier that year. Speckart, age twenty-two, her younger brother, Joseph, age seventeen, and her mother, Mrs. Henrietta Speckart, had also settled into rooms at the hotel.[1]

At first, Equi and Parker exchanged pleasantries with Speckart, her mother, and brother as they crossed paths to and from the hotel dining room. During the next few weeks, Equi spoke more frequently and privately with the younger woman, enough for Speckart to confide her deep longing to be free of her mother's strict oversight. Equi and Parker commiserated with Speckart and drew her into a friendship that increased her desire to live independently. More importantly, Equi's exuberance and charm delighted and captivated Speckart. Equi was ten years older and successful in her profession. She was intelligent and determined, and she loved a good time. In turn, Equi became increasingly enamored with the beautiful woman with long, blond tresses and a sweet, reserved, and unaffected temperament. She may have been intrigued by the prospect of a romance in which for the first time she was the older, more confident, and more experienced woman.

Equi and Speckart concealed their budding attraction from Mrs. Speckart as best they could. Equi was casual and cordial with her love interest's mother, and, on occasion, partnered with her in card games. Behind the drawing room decorum, however, romance and passion flourished until Mrs.

Speckart noticed her daughter's flush of excitement in the company of her new doctor friend. She later described how appalled and panicked she felt over her daughter's swooning for another woman. She immediately suspected that Equi was a gold digger after the family's wealth. She tried and failed to discourage her daughter from seeing Equi again. Mrs. Speckart became so concerned with the affair that she abruptly gathered her family and departed Portland for San Diego in mid-December 1905. She told others she desperately hoped her daughter would come to her senses once separated from what she believed was Equi's unhealthy, manipulating influence.[2]

The Speckarts' wealth came from investments in breweries and real estate. When Harriet Speckart's father, Adolph Speckart, died in 1893, he bequeathed his extensive estate to his wife and two children. Following her husband's death, Mrs. Speckart traveled with her children to Germany to visit relatives, and Harriet and Joseph continued their education at private schools. Mrs. Speckart became accustomed to determining all matters that concerned her children, well past the time when her daughter came of age. In 1901, the Speckarts had returned to the United States and settled in San Diego for several years.[3]

Speckart missed Equi terribly and wrote to her every day from southern California, often slipping wildflowers into the envelope. She confided to a favorite aunt in Germany that "my doctor" wrote her almost as often. Her confidences to her aunt fairly glowed with the thrill of her new romance, and she expressed little reticence in disclosing her love for another woman. For Christmas, she wrote her aunt that Equi had sent a book of poems by Robert Browning and Elizabeth Barrett Browning and a gold chain with a heart-shaped amethyst. She later apologized to her aunt for not writing more frequently and explained, ". . . with people in love one has to have patience." She blithely added, "It is a pity that Momma does not like her also." Speckart seemed enlivened by the new possibilities in her life. She arranged to take piano lessons, and she hoped to learn Italian to converse with Equi in another language. On one occasion, Speckart responded to her aunt's inquiry about marriage. "Yes, I am very happy single, especially now that I have Dr. Equi. I need no more, she loves me the same as I love her."[4]

Equi wrote Speckart that her own busy days helped her endure their separation. She later recalled, "I was at the hospital from eight in the morning until noon, and I had a good practice at the time and was in my office from two until six every evening and after the evening hours I was called out and didn't have a minute to myself." Yet she managed to arrange a reunion with Speckart in San Diego by declining to represent Oregon at the national suffrage convention scheduled for Baltimore that year. In late February 1906, Equi took passage from Portland on the steamer *Columbia* bound for San Francisco where she intended to take another course in surgery and clinical work. During her weeks in the Bay Area, she wrote Speckart that she would stay with a "lady friend," perhaps Bessie Holcomb. Two years earlier during a visit to San Francisco, Equi returned to Holcomb her own half-interest in their homestead property. The gesture may have been in appreciation for Holcomb's help with tuition payments or as a belated wedding gift. Holcomb had married her employer, Alexander J. Cook, in 1903, two years after Equi departed for Portland. Equi finished her medical stint in March and continued to San Diego, where she and Speckart devised a plan for reuniting in Portland.[5]

By not attending the NAWSA gathering in Baltimore, Equi missed the last opportunity to see Susan B. Anthony alive. The venerable suffragist was taken ill while returning from the convention to her home in Rochester, New York, and she never recovered. Just hours before her death on March 13, 1906, at age eighty-six, Anthony confided her greatest regret to her longtime suffrage ally and chosen successor, Anna Howard Shaw: "To think I have had more than sixty years of hard struggle for a little liberty, and then to die without it seems so cruel."[6]

During her final days Anthony worried about the outcome of Oregon's suffrage vote and complained of the campaign expenses in the state. Her passing emboldened NAWSA leaders to commit more resources to the Oregon effort. Nine top officers and strategists departed for Oregon for the last two months of the campaign. They were heartened to find more than forty active suffrage clubs in the state with dozens of campaign committees and five thousand volunteers. The operation had become the well-coordinated, statewide effort that the "nationals" had long insisted was essential for victory. Their tactical opponent, Abigail Scott Duniway, resented the noisy commotion of the campaign, but she rallied local suffragists and delivered a rousing talk on the night before a national calamity halted all campaign plans.[7]

On the following day, April 18, the *Oregonian* published too early in the morning to cover the biggest story of the new century. Instead, Portlanders read the grim account of three African-American men lynched by a mob in Springfield, Missouri, and they followed the plight of two hundred thousand Italians left homeless and destitute after the eruption of Mount Vesuvius. Yet by midmorning, no one paid attention to anything but what news they could get from San Francisco. An operator of the local Postal Telegraph Company had suspected trouble as he completed his night shift. Just after five o'clock in the morning, his connection with San Francisco went dead. He queried the operator in Ashland, the southern Oregon exchange for north-south transmissions, but Ashland had been severed from the Bay Area as well. Eighteen minutes later the Sacramento office relayed the news from Chicago that San Francisco had been struck by the worst earthquake in California history, causing massive devastation and death.[8]

During the next several hours, word of San Francisco's earthquake traveled by word-of-mouth as Portlanders awoke. Telephones were rare in the city, and anxious throngs crowded telegraph offices and pleaded to send messages to loved ones in the Bay Area. But too few lines were open to accommodate their requests. The city's commerce slumped, and the *Oregonian* noted, "The horror of it all turned men's minds from business." The disaster hit Portlanders hard across the board. As far back as the California Gold Rush of 1849, people in the state had been linked with their neighbors to the south. Able-bodied men had deserted Oregon towns to seek their fortunes in the gold trade, and farmers left behind thrived by providing provisions to the flood of gold-seekers in the Bay Area. By 1906, a great many Portlanders were San Francisco natives or had married into San Francisco families. Dozens of local businesses had begun in the Bay Area, and several civic leaders started their careers there. All these associations led to a pall of anxiety settling over Portland. Equi was in the thick of the worry with no word of her many relatives, friends, and medical school colleagues in the stricken city. She could rely only on the newspapers' daily listing of those located or lost to the disaster.[9]

The great San Francisco earthquake and fire of 1906 remained the greatest natural disaster in the country for nearly one hundred years. The tragedy caused thirty-four hundred fatalities, left more than two hundred thousand people homeless, and leveled much of the nation's ninth largest city. San Franciscans needed a massive amount of relief—food, clothing, medications, and housing—but no federal agency or private charity was equipped to respond to a crisis of that magnitude.[10]

As firestorms raged through the stricken city, communities nationwide rallied to help the disaster victims, but the people of Portland were the first to organize a comprehensive relief effort. The Rose City had the advantage of proximity—it was the closest large city after Los Angeles—and it had a direct rail connection to San Francisco. Portlanders also possessed the means to contribute both cash and supplies. Besides, business and civic leaders recognized the disaster as a threat and an opportunity. They feared the interruption of trade with San Francisco, and they relished the chance to demonstrate their big city status. Beyond resources, goodwill, and self-interest, Portlanders brought to the relief campaign decades of experience with civic betterment work, much of it planned and implemented by women through clubs and various social welfare organizations. Their experiences and the alliances they had formed positioned them to mount Portland's most extensive humanitarian effort ever.[11]

By midmorning of the day after the disaster, the wives and daughters of Portland's business leaders formed the Women's Relief Committee for the California Sufferers, and they scrambled to gather supplies and medical personnel to send to the disaster zone. Their goals were remarkably ambitious: to equip a medical contingent for departure in twelve hours, collect bedding and clothing for thousands of San Franciscans, and organize for the ten thousand refugees expected to arrive in Portland within days. In short order, the committee secured a baggage car from Southern Pacific and a passenger car from the Pullman Company, and they canvassed wholesalers door-to-door for medicines, medical equipment, food, and clothing.[12]

To recruit doctors and nurses, the committee chose Dr. Kenneth Alexander J. Mackenzie, a leading surgeon and professor of clinical medicine at the University of Oregon Medical Department. At age forty-seven Mackenzie was well positioned for the assignment due to his service as the chief surgeon for the Oregon Railway and Navigation Company, the local operator of the Southern Pacific line. Mackenzie sought doctors and nurses at the city hospitals, offering them nothing but the chance to serve on a two-week mission. Although he warned volunteers they would endure hardship and face exposure to contagious disease and civil unrest, Mackenzie easily met his quota of doctors and nurses and turned away others.[13]

Equi was quick to volunteer, and she was the only woman doctor on the Oregon relief mission. Just three years out of medical school, she might have seemed an unlikely choice, but having a woman physician supervise and lodge with the nurses made sense. Mackenzie also knew Equi firsthand. She had taken two years of his anatomy classes, and she had worked with him at the hospital. Most importantly, she was willing.

In just ten hours the relief committee garnered twenty tons of supplies— chloroform, ether, disinfectants, hot water bottles, splints, and gauze—as well as the few medications available such as morphine, digitalis, and strychnine. The forty-two doctors and nurses of the mission gathered at Union Depot for

Portland doctors and nurses pose at Union Station on April 19, 1906 before traveling to provide medical care to earthquake-stricken San Franciscans. Marie Equi at the far right. *Oregonian*, Portland, April 20, 1906.

the 8:45 evening departure. Equi was accompanied to the sendoff by Mary Ellen Parker. All the volunteers were dressed in proper traveling attire—the women in floor-length dresses and coats with broad, swooping hats and the men in suits and bowlers. Except for the red crosses pinned to their sleeves, they appeared to be en route to a convention or the opera season in San Francisco. The Southern Pacific cars, soon dubbed the *Doctor Train* by the local press, steamed away from the station on schedule, crossed the river, and rolled into the night.[14]

With the mission underway, Mackenzie took no chances with the city's reputation or his own. He presented Equi and the others with a written loyalty oath that placed the mission under "the orders, authority and discipline of the Government of the United States as prevailing under martial law in the City of San Francisco." (Although the Bay City was never placed under martial law, almost everyone at the time believed it had been). None of the volunteers objected and everyone signed.[15]

The medical corps received few accounts of the disaster while they traveled. The fires continued to rage as they left Portland, so hot that San Franciscans dodged cobblestones popping from the street and watched whole buildings incinerate in seconds. Sixty miles north of San Francisco the relief team first viewed earthquake damage when they rolled past flattened farm houses. At ten miles from the city the heavy stench of smoke was unavoidable. United States Army officers met the doctor train once it eased into the Oakland Mole near the foot of Seventh Street today. From there Equi and the other medics boarded a military steamer to cross the bay. Only that morning, three days after the earthquake, had the fires been stopped. In the early light of the day, the city lay blackened by fire with thirty thousand buildings and nearly five hundred city blocks destroyed, including the area of today's Financial District,

Civic Center, much of South of Market, and fiery intrusions into the Mission District and along the edge of the Western Addition.[16]

The steamer pushed west past San Francisco's waterfront and approached the fog-bound Presidio, the US Army base at the northern tip of the peninsula. There the medics reported to military officers of the army's general hospital. The Oregon corps found the base functioning remarkably well given the damage to the hospital, power plant, and supply depot. Almost immediately, the army had accepted injured and panicked civilians fleeing the firestorms in the city. Their first evening in San Francisco, Equi, Mackenzie, and the others were integrated into the army's relief operations, each assigned to specific duties under the command of a military medical officer. A dozen of the young male Oregon doctors undertook the basic grunt work of public health—digging trenches and setting up latrines—at two refugee camps. Whatever visions they held of heroic service in the adventure of a lifetime were quickly dashed in the ditches. Lieutenant Colonel George H. Torney, the officer in charge of enforcing strict sanitation measures in the city, directed Mackenzie to establish a contagious disease hospital near the Presidio. Mackenzie anticipated a surge of infectious diseases—measles, chickenpox, scarlet fever, diphtheria, and mumps—but no epidemic swept the city. Mackenzie told a reporter that the efficient, if disagreeable, work of the sanitary corps saved San Francisco from the "worst scenario."[17]

Equi and the Portland nurses began their duties at the Presidio's hospital, a three-hundred-bed facility built in 1898. They worked with a dozen army doctors and forty army corps nurses unaccustomed to treating civilians, and they struggled to handle more than 350 refugees. Most patients presented with intestinal problems, sprains, or burns brought about by stress, shock, and the sudden exposure to outdoor living. But for many the physical ailments disguised the psychological impact of losing loved ones, homes, and livelihoods.[18]

The army charged Equi and her contingent of nurses with obstetrics care, and their unit became known as the "Oregon ward." The design of the army hospital permitted nurses as well as patients to get fresh air in wide corridors, called galleries, open on one side and glassed on the other. But Equi and the nurses worked long days, often with only snatches of sleep, and rarely had time to enjoy the view of ships coursing through the Golden Gate.

Newspaper reporters from Portland were eager to file stories from San Francisco, and they found in Equi a ready source of copy. A week after her arrival she recounted how the disaster seemed to have had no ill effects on the twenty-three newborns delivered at the Oregon ward. The infants were thought to be the first born in a military hospital in the United States, and Equi declared them among the healthiest she had encountered in a long time. A few days later, a fire broke out near the ward in the early morning hours, and Oregonians read about Equi's rescue of the patients. She raced to them with a wheelchair, wrapped each mother and infant with a blanket, eased them into the chair, and wheeled them out of danger. Equi described the quiet, stoic demeanor of the two dozen mothers with an eloquence seldom found in the newspaper.

> All the agonies and tortures those poor mothers had suffered be-
> fore they had been brought to the hospital had so deadened their
> senses, so numbed their minds, that they faced the fire horror with
> a spirit of calmest resignation and without fear. They had already
> suffered too much to suffer more.[19]

The *Oregon Daily Journal* featured another piece titled "Dr. Marie D. Equi Seizes a Motor Car." In that account, Equi left the Presidio hospital one day for a trip into the city, but she was later unable to arrange a return. Carriages and horses were hard to come by, and automobiles were rare in the city, especially after the army had appropriated so many for emergency transport. Equi hailed to a stop one gentleman being driven about by his chauffeur and directed the driver to take her to the hospital. When he refused, she appealed to a nearby soldier who ordered the owner and the driver to accommodate her. Equi settled herself nicely on the cushioned seats and cheerily waved to onlookers as she rolled away.[20]

For all the difficulties of disaster duty, Equi thrived at her post. She managed her duties well and experienced no problems under army command. She also enjoyed the company of another single, professional woman, Gail Laughlin, who had managed to pay her own way on the doctor train from Portland. At age thirty-seven she was a talented lecturer and organizer from Maine who left her New York law practice to work fulltime on woman suffrage with NAWSA. She then helped organize the Oregon campaign and lectured throughout the state. At the time of the earthquake, Laughlin had no medical training to warrant her trip to San Francisco. Her interests appeared to lay closer to the heart. Her intimate companion, Dr. Marguerite (Mary) A. Sperry, lived in San Francisco, and Laughlin's only way to confirm Sperry's well-being was to travel there. She was much relieved to find Sperry safe. On their third night in the

The San Francisco earthquake and fire of 1906 caused an estimated 3,400 deaths and left 200,000 homeless in the greatest natural calamity in the US before Hurricane Katrina in 2005. Library of Congress LC-USZ62-128020.

stricken city, Equi and Laughlin walked to the damaged Ferry Building from the Presidio grounds and listened to the military band. The sky was dark with no city glow since gaslights were not permitted. Laughlin later recalled they were unable to walk on the sidewalks because they remained too hot from the fire. "Any description of San Francisco is beyond words," Laughlin later told the *Oregonian*. "It was hard for us to get over the feeling that we were not walking among the ruins of some ancient city that had been dead for a thousand years." She remarked on the orderliness in the city with people being so generous and helpful to one another. Laughlin soon returned to Portland to resume her suffrage work, and, after the campaign, established a law practice first in Denver and then in San Francisco. Laughlin lived with Dr. Sperry in a lesbian relationship until Sperry's death in 1919 and later served in the Maine state legislature.[21]

San Franciscans who took refuge in the hospitals and camps voiced so much appreciation for the work of the Oregon medics that the volunteers felt blindsided by the fierce criticism several local physicians lobbed their way. Less than two weeks after the Oregonians arrived, a San Francisco doctor disrupted an emergency meeting of five hundred local practitioners with a demand that the Oregon corps leave the city at once. He complained that they were unneeded and unwanted and that their very presence threatened the livelihoods of local doctors.[22]

Dr. Mackenzie attended the meeting and bristled at the charges, especially since he had tried to ease the relocation of local doctors to other states and had pledged one hundred dollars of his own money to a fund for their benefit. Equi was also present for the proceedings, and the San Francisco physician who filed the complaint, Dr. Henry Kugeler, had been a professor of hers at the University of California. She told a reporter afterward that the resolution was meant for all outside physicians not just those from Oregon. Nevertheless, she noted that the resolution "nearly precipitated a riot." She castigated the California physicians for first criticizing outsiders and then asking for help obtaining medical books, supplies, and instruments to restart their businesses. "You never saw such a disorganized band of men in your life," she complained. "They were unfit for work and were helpless to meet the situation. Without outside assistance the terrors of the situation would have been multiplied many-fold."[23]

Mackenzie and Equi misread the frustration that fueled the rebuke. The motion was eventually tabled, but the resolution made sense. The Oregon medics had rallied without being invited, and they departed Portland too quickly to be informed that the California governor had advised doctors and nurses not to rush into the state. Hundreds of local providers feared for their livelihood with their offices and equipment destroyed. They had already lost clients —the wealthy ones sought refuge outside the city and the poor enjoyed free medical care at makeshift clinics and hospitals.[24]

The sting of the criticism was lightened by effusive praise from elected officials and army officers. California Governor George C. Pardee thanked Oregon for its rapid response in sending aid and personnel to his state. He singled out Equi and Mackenzie for doing so much "at a time when we were practically helpless." San Francisco Mayor Eugene Schmitz recognized the "magnificent spirit of philanthropy" shown by so many Oregonians. The commanding officer at the General Hospital presented Equi with a medal and a commendation on behalf of the US Army. The citation read, "Your manifestation of executive ability has been marked, and the conduct and services of the corps of nurses under your charge has been uniformly satisfactory in every degree." According to a Portland newspaper, Equi was only the second woman physician detailed for service at a US General Hospital.[25]

With the conclusion of their two-week commitment, the Oregon volunteers prepared to leave. Under a mandate from President Theodore Roosevelt, the American Red Cross took charge of relief operations as its first major disaster relief operation. The Oregon physicians relinquished their posts, and the doctor train departed Oakland for Portland on May 5. Equi, however, extended her stay an extra week, probably to view the full damage and to visit her relatives and friends.[26]

Eighteen days after the earthquake struck, a resurgent city began to take shape. The Ferry Building and much of the Mission District were once again lit with electricity. Nearly all the trolley lines operated, but a ride along Market Street revealed how massive a reconstruction effort faced the city. Empty, charred steel frames stood block after block amid vast piles of debris on ragged, cracked sidewalks. Many of Equi's personal landmarks in the city had vanished in the firestorms, including her first residence on Market Street, her second home and the nearby St. Ignatius church, her first medical school, and the county hospital where she had interned.

San Francisco was not completely devastated, and most residents survived both the earthquake and fire with minimal losses or harm, including Equi's relatives, colleagues, and friends. Her professional associates were unharmed, but they mourned the extensive damage to the newly built Hahnemann Hospital, completed just eight days before the earthquake. Bessie Holcomb, her husband, and their one-year-old son survived the disaster as well, and their home on Divisadero Street remained intact. However, firestorms in the city's waterfront district destroyed her husband's leather goods business.[27]

Equi returned home and found Portlanders justly proud of their humanitarian work. In a few weeks, they had collected more than $250,000 in cash for earthquake sufferers. Citizens stepped forward to provide assistance on a scale the government was unable to muster. Unlike several California cities, Portland accepted Bay Area refugees without fear or precautions against "the wrong kind" flooding into the city, and more than five thousand people stopped in Portland. Residents provided them with food, clothing, and medical care.[28]

Although disaster news no longer filled the front pages of Portland newspapers, the *Evening Telegram* heralded Equi's arrival and touted her as "one of the hitherto unsung heroines of the San Francisco disaster." Equi deflected the praise to Mackenzie's leadership and to the exceptional service of the nurses under her care. She suggested that their names "should be emblazoned on a roll of honor so that all might know of what sort of stuff our Oregon daughters are made." In her absence the local papers had doted on Equi and her relief work with nearly twenty articles in as many days, more than for any relief doctor other than Mackenzie. The *Oregon Daily Journal* ran an effusive piece that anointed Equi as "one of the most conspicuous examples of self-sacrifice in

[a] desire to aid the suffering that has been seen in Portland." The article also touted Equi for giving up a successful practice to work nonstop amid "all kinds of danger."[29]

The newspapers' extensive coverage of Equi reflected more than appreciation for her humanitarianism. Her distinction as the only woman doctor on the mission made Equi good copy for the Oregon reporters working in San Francisco. She also knew how to tell a good story, and she understood how to engage reporters and provide them with ready content. But the relief mission occurred in the midst of heated public debate over women's role in society, and women were pushing for the right to vote in the upcoming Oregon primary. A majority of male voters repeatedly balked at the idea of women taking charge of their lives and engaging matters in the public sphere. By touting the courage and service of one professional woman, the press and civic leaders appeared supportive of women even while they continued to resist their full voting rights. Nevertheless, the public acclaim had to be deeply satisfying to Equi. Thirteen years earlier a newspaper had proclaimed her *Queen for Today* for her righteous justice on the streets of The Dalles. Now as a result of her relief work, people in Oregon as well as many in California read of her generosity, compassion, and good humor as well as her clinical and management skills. In her newly adopted city, Equi could feel less an outsider—if only for a while.

6
Love (Almost) in the Open

She loves me the same as I love her.
Harriet Speckart
We are just friends, bosom companions.
Marie Equi

Nothing inflames a new romance like disapproval or a forced separation. Marie Equi and Harriet Speckart endured both—the first from the suspicious, controlling Mrs. Speckart and the second by the disaster that struck San Francisco and the Bay Area. Through it all Equi's and Speckart's desire for each other deepened and their resolve to be together strengthened. As circumstances played out, disapproval of their commitment triggered a scandal rife with charges of sexual impropriety, attempted theft of an inheritance, and an eerie power wielded by Equi.

During their San Diego tryst in March 1906, Equi and Speckart devised a plan for the latter's return to Portland. Speckart told her mother that she must seek treatment there for the tuberculosis and dropsy that her "Doc" had diagnosed. Their ruse worked except that Mrs. Speckart insisted on accompanying her daughter. The Speckarts had to wait out the embargo on passenger rail travel following the San Francisco calamity, but finally in mid-May, they traveled from San Diego to Portland where Equi and Speckart were reunited. Even then they found little peace. Mrs. Speckart continued to quarrel with her daughter, ostensibly over the inheritance. Below the surface roiled a bitter mother-daughter relationship entangled with Mrs. Speckart's dismay and loathing of Harriet's lesbian affections.[1]

Within weeks the dissension among the Speckarts—now including young Joseph Speckart as well—erupted into an unseemly affair splashed on the front page of the widely read *Sunday Oregonian*. "Quarrel Among Speckart Heirs, Family at Outs, Daughter Leaves Mother" the piece trumpeted. The lengthy account described a disputed inheritance, a daughter's revolt against her mother and brother, and allegations that Dr. Marie Equi had manipulated the younger woman's affections to plunder the family wealth. Oregonians sipped their morning coffees while poring over details of the Speckart troubles, the terms of the inheritance, and Mrs. Speckart's attempt to keep her twenty-three-year-old daughter from receiving her fair share. The story may have titillated readers with the tale of a daughter's defiance and of the supposed immoral persuasion, if not outright seduction, of a young, innocent woman by an older professional woman. The irony that Oregon's recent heroine-to-the-rescue was now cast as a possibly degenerate gold digger could not have been lost on many readers.[2]

Harriet Speckart's supposed vulnerability fit nicely with the prevailing notion that women, especially young women, needed protection from unhealthy influences. But her wealth placed her outside the stereotype of the usual target population. Most Progressives sought to assist or protect *women adrift,* the single girls and young women seeking employment in cities without benefit of family or husbands. A well-to-do woman like Speckart was expected to manage her own way. At the same time, her insistence on obtaining her inheritance and conducting her romantic life as she saw fit reflected the emergence of independent women who sought their rights to citizenship, including full standing in the judicial system.[3]

The *Oregonian* piece delivered a primer on the tangled affairs of the Speckarts. Harriet's father, Adolph Speckart, had been a wealthy businessman and investor with part-ownership of breweries in Montana, Washington, and Oregon as well as mines in California, real estate, and an extensive portfolio of stocks and bonds. He died in 1893 in Butte, Montana, and left an estate of nearly $250,000 to his widow and their two children. Each was bequeathed one-third of the estate with Mrs. Speckart holding the children's shares until they reached the age of majority (age eighteen in Montana for females). Although Mrs. Speckart was named executrix in her husband's will, she never fully administered the estate. Whether her failure to do so resulted from procrastination, faulty legal advice, or outright fraud became a primary facet of the dispute. She certainly appeared negligent in not disbursing her children's inheritances when they came of age, her daughter in 1901 and her son in 1905. Harriet, in fact, did not learn of the bequest until May 1906, and that belated disclosure especially angered her. By that time she and her brother were due an amount that would make them millionaires today.[4]

For readers of the *Oregonian,* a regional connection made the Speckart story even more engaging. Mrs. Speckart was related by marriage to the brewery titan Leopold Schmidt, who owned the Olympia Brewing Company of Tumwater, Washington, along with holdings in Oregon. With this in mind,

Harriet Speckart rejected the entreaties of her mother, Mrs. Henrietta Speckart, and of her brother, Joseph, to abandon her love affair with Marie Equi. Oregon Historical Society, bb013184.

Portlanders pondered Mrs. Speckart's fear that her daughter would disregard family interests and squander her share of the estate. She was so concerned that she sought to become her daughter's legal guardian to control her access to the funds. Speckart's grievances were cast as those of a privileged young woman who chafed against the limits her mother set on her finances and social life. Joseph Speckart, it appeared, was concerned about his inheritance as well, but he chose to join forces with his mother. What pitted them against Speckart was her relationship with Equi.[5]

Mrs. Speckart complained to the *Oregonian* that Equi had "alienated the affections" of Harriet so much that her daughter no longer cared about her family. She admitted to resenting her daughter's new emotional attachment, and she had told others at their hotel that "the friendship must cease." These same residents reported that Speckart had become "great chums" with Equi, Dr. Mary Ellen Parker, and Mrs. Marie Daggett, a friend of theirs who worked for the Multnomah County Juvenile Court. The four women were said to have formed "a clique which could not be broken up." The *Oregonian* tiptoed around the implications of the close bond between Equi and Speckart, but follow-up stories and reports in other papers portrayed Equi as a predator wielding an unhealthy psychological sway over the younger woman.[6]

The *Oregonian* story highlighted a supposed brawl between Equi and Joseph Speckart that followed an argument between the Speckart siblings over a cache of letters from Equi that Joseph had grabbed from his sister. Speckart became distraught when her brother refused to return the correspondence, and she telephoned Equi for help. When Equi arrived at the family's apartment, she flew into a rage, according to the newspaper, when Joseph refused to release the letters. Equi reportedly threatened his life and shook him by the throat. He broke free and escaped out the window and onto a fire escape. Mrs. Speckart tried to intervene, but Equi reportedly pushed her into a chair. The article concluded with Speckart departing The Hill altogether and leaving the city with the three other members of the clique for a weekend at Seaside, the Oregon coast resort. The Speckart affair continued to play out in the Portland dailies in the days ahead, but the Sunday scandal piece set the first impressions of what became a drawn-out battle.[7]

News of the Speckarts' feud and Equi's role in it carried beyond Oregon's borders with features in the *Seattle Post-Intelligencer* and the *Morning Olympian* in Olympia, Washington. In the latter account, Mrs. Speckart's attorney said the letters in question revealed attempts to grasp control of the Speckart wealth. The *San Francisco Call* forged into new territory with its front-page screamer, "Heiress Victim of Hypnotist, Rich Oregon Girl Is in Power of Woman Physician." The article reminded readers of Equi's role in the Oregon relief mission to the city, and then claimed she had threatened suicide after her "peculiar relations" with Speckart were exposed.[8]

Equi refuted the accusations after her stay at the coast. "Yes, I read all that stuff in the papers," she told a reporter, "but didn't pay any attention to it. It is nonsense. The charges are so ridiculous that I don't care to discuss them seriously." But she added that Speckart had never been a patient of hers and that she had only befriended her after learning she was being mistreated by her family. She scoffed at the suggestion that her letters revealed a criminal intent to acquire the family's wealth. "They cannot show a line in which the girl asked for money for me, nor in which I asked the girl for money," she said. "I pay my own bills and do not need any Speckart money to help me along." Mary Ellen Parker confirmed Equi's story, "Why, neither Dr. Equi nor I want Miss Speckart's money." When they met the young woman, she said, "We didn't know whether she was worth five cents or $500,000."[9]

Parker offered her own explanation of Speckart's attraction to Equi. "The girl took a particular liking to Dr. Equi because the latter was so buoyant and joyful and strong. You know how a strong person impresses one who is weak physically. The girl has been so hedged about and suppressed by her mother that she has become timid and needed a good, strong friend to sustain her inner troubles." Parker recognized, of course, the infatuation between the two women, but she deflected attention from their intimate relations to a more practical association and highlighted Equi's good intentions.[10]

Equi dismissed the alleged skirmish with the Speckarts. She said she had solicited the help of the district attorney once she received Harriet's call and then waited at the Speckarts' room for the police. She claimed they threatened her, but she denied attacking Harriet's mother or brother. The actual events are uncertain, yet Equi seldom took insult or accusation calmly.

The police arrived and retrieved the letters from Joseph, and later the district attorney returned them to Equi. "How ridiculous to claim that there was evidence of any incriminating character in those letters," Equi told a reporter. "If there had been any, don't you think District Attorney Manning would have indicted me, instead of turning the letters over to me? Bosh and nonsense."[11]

Equi's letters to Speckart may not have been incriminating, but they brimmed with endearments and intimacies, according to a *Portland Evening Telegram* report. An unattributed source to the paper suggested the letters "burn with a love as fervid as the billet-doux of any Don Juan." Equi had ample opportunity to indulge in passionate flourishes—Joseph Speckart later reported that she had written more than one hundred letters to his sister during the four months they were apart.[12]

Equi was astute to engage the district attorney and request police assistance as a means to secure the letters. She effectively cleared her name by claiming an official review of what she had written. Yet more rumors and allegations flew. One suggested Equi promised the district attorney to not see or correspond with Speckart again, and that she instead concealed letters in books at the public library for Speckart to retrieve. Equi had to have found the whole affair infuriating and threatening to her privacy and reputation. The actual content of her letters to Speckart are not known, but she may very well have expressed her fervent love and sexual desire for her. She had every reason to keep them from public view. But the skirmish over her correspondence served as prelude for the legal battle to come. With the letters secured, Equi recast her relationship in more socially acceptable terms. "She has come to me with her troubles," she told a reporter, "and we have been very much together since the trouble began." She said, "We are just friends, bosom companions." In fact, Equi had begun the longest intimate relationship of her life.[13]

Charges and denials proliferated throughout the following week. At one point Leopold Schmidt, the brewery magnate, hired the Thiele Detective Service to uncover anything derogatory or criminal about Equi that might be used against her. After an exhaustive search, the operatives discovered nothing of merit.[14]

In light of the scandal, much of the praise and renown for Equi's courage and generosity in the San Francisco relief mission probably faded. If nothing else, Portlanders were confronted with a more nuanced impression of her that would become more pronounced in the years ahead. From a larger perspective, the scandal exploited public fears of what might befall a woman like Speckart who asserted her independence. The dispute also rattled the sensibilities of those who wanted to protect the social order, one in which daughters did not threaten or malign their mothers or get swept away in forbidden romances.

The Speckart sensation became the second widely published account of a lesbian relationship in Oregon, and, perhaps , in the Pacific Northwest, with Equi's companionship with Bessie Holcomb being the first. Both incidents occurred within a larger context of a perceived injustice or threat, but it was the prospect of intimacy between two women that appeared to propel and lodge the stories into public discourse. Each occasion involved respectable and professional women who could not be dismissed as unfortunate lower-class immigrants or unsavory types from disreputable districts. Equi's intimate affairs—thrust into public view—forced Portlanders to recognize that same-sex relations prevailed at all levels of society.

The Speckart Affair, as it came to be known, distracted the public from the woman suffrage measure about to be decided by Oregon's male voters in the June election. Other suffragists might have regretted that the controversy embroiled two independent women just as the campaign tried to assuage fears of women's changing roles in society. But NAWSA leaders could sympathize with Equi's circumstances given their own domestic arrangements. Anna Howard Shaw, the current president, Carrie Chapman Catt, the former president, Frances Willard, president of the Women's Christian Temperance Union, and Alice Stone Blackwell, the editor of *Woman's Journal*—all engaged in romantic and sexual relations with lesbian lovers. They, however, managed to keep their intimate affairs out of the papers.[15]

In some quarters, suffragists were regularly taunted as aggressive, short-haired, *mannish* women who did not like men. Few suffrage leaders directly challenged the lesbian slurs, but they often tried to avoid looking the part, being careful how they dressed and presented themselves. Oregon's suffrage leader, Abigail Scott Duniway, took it upon herself to counter the depiction of suffragists as *unsexed women* bent on wielding power and triggering a war between the sexes. Presumably she wanted to assure male voters that suffragists did indeed like and love men but she used a homophobic assault to do it. [16]

In 1899, Duniway delivered a stormy talk at the annual suffrage convention in Grand Rapids, Michigan. She proclaimed, "Show me a woman who doesn't like men, and I will show you a sour-souled, vinegar-visaged specimen of unfortunate femininity, who owes the world an apology for living in it at all." Warming to her subject, she added, "The very best thing she could do for her country . . . would be to steal away and die, in the company of the man who doesn't like women." Duniway's antipathy for NAWSA leaders—many of them lesbians who opposed her political strategies—perhaps fueled her vitriolic remarks. Her speech was not filed away in convention proceedings, seldom to be seen again. She included it in her autobiography, *Pathbreaking*, published in 1914. At some point Equi probably learned of Duniway's sentiments and her reaction is not known, but the remarks reflected the disapproval and disdain that Equi and other lesbians encountered even among their allies.[17]

Oregon's campaign had already stalled during the mobilization for earthquake relief, and afterward it struggled to regain momentum. By mid-May 1906, suffragists no longer beamed with confidence as they tried to persuade and argue their way to victory. The Oregon Equal Suffrage Association, the group that Equi aligned herself with, railed against upper-class women who poured money into opposition efforts. These antisuffragists rejected the notion that women voters would improve politics, government, and society. A wealthy and influential cadre of them feared losing the special place they believed most women enjoyed. They objected to the prospect of being burdened by voting, jury duty, and the expectation of holding office. And they questioned whether lower-class women, if granted the vote, would defer to the better judgment of the elite.[18]

Suffragists worried as well that the liquor interests—the brewers and liquor store operators—would once again swing Oregon's voters against them. With good reason, the liquor men feared enfranchised women would usher in an era of prohibition. Suffrage leaders struggled to finesse the prohibition issue, and the prospect, or threat, of outlawing alcohol complicated their efforts in Oregon. They contended with the Women's Christian Temperance Union as well as Progressives who supported adoption of prohibition. The issue provided no safe haven—suffragists figured they would alienate potential supporters no matter what position they took. In truth, many suffragists considered alcohol control a lesser concern.[19]

The national suffrage organization worried that an Oregon victory was slipping away, and they rushed more organizers and speakers to the state. Anna Howard Shaw, NAWSA's president, returned to the state determined to jumpstart the stalled campaign and help Oregon lead other West Coast states into suffrage. Following her return from quake-damaged San Francisco, attorney Gail Laughlin solicited support from labor organizations and from Oregon's Socialist Party to turn out the working-class vote. Her outreach was especially important since NAWSA generally treated working-class voters and immigrants as a low priority.[20]

Equi was new to suffrage politics, but she garnered attention as an up-and-coming professional woman with Progressive instincts. The newspapers occasionally noted her contributions and leadership, but mostly her work in this, her first political endeavor, was similar to that of hundreds of other Oregon women who toiled in the campaign. Speckart, however, was much impressed with her companion's efforts. She wrote to an aunt that her Doc worked on the *woman question* nonstop "with all her might."[21]

"The women of the world have their eyes on Oregon," suffragist Alice Stone Blackwell told a reporter in May 1906, but on Election Day the men of Oregon gave them reason to look away. Suffrage lost by more than ten thousand votes out of eighty-four thousand cast. Portland and Multnomah County, with the highest populations in the state, soundly defeated the measure, and all Willamette Valley counties, except Lane County, the home of the University of Oregon, rejected suffrage as well. The loss proved a devastating setback for Oregon's right-to-vote advocates, and the outcome shadowed them for years.[22]

Members of NAWSA blamed the liquor trade and fears of prohibition for the suffrage loss. They dodged other factors, such as their lackluster appeal to laborers antagonized by corporate exploitation. And they weren't eager to acknowledge that their media-intensive hurrah campaign had met the same fate as Abigail Scott Duniway's earlier, quieter tactics. Duniway, for her part, castigated the nationals for their noisy demonstrations that she felt had doomed Oregon's chances. Yet the experience in other western states that won the vote prior to 1906—Colorado in 1893 and Idaho in 1896—suggested that a vigorous upfront campaign with work by local suffrage clubs, collaboration with political parties, and public meetings stood the best chance of victory in the West. From an historical perspective, the conflict over suffrage strategy anticipated the era of modern marketing and communications in political campaigns.[23]

By early June 1906, the Speckart dispute had devolved into seemingly endless litigation. Equi stood by Harriet throughout that summer, accompanying her to court hearings in Portland and Olympia, until she received word that her own mother had become ill with a critical kidney condition.[24]

Fourteen years earlier, Equi had despaired of making a life for herself in New Bedford, but she returned as a well-educated, professional woman whose relief work in San Francisco had earned her accolades from governors, mayors, and generals. Her circumstances had shifted considerably compared to those of siblings, most of whom remained in their hometown with their families. Of her three brothers, one worked as a carpenter, another as a glasscutter, and the youngest as an operator at one of the textile mills. Her three sisters were married with children and managed their households. Her parents still lived in their Tremont Street home in the working-class neighborhood where she had spent her teenage years, and her father continued to work as a mason. Changes in the old whaling city were more dramatic. The population had swelled by 50 percent to a total of eighty thousand with more than 40 percent of residents foreign-born. The Irish still held the lead overall, but the number of Portuguese arrivals had soared. Italian-born immigrants, now at close to 350, finally edged up to one percent of the population. Portuguese and Cape Verdean men held onto the vestiges of whale fishery, but smokestacks from more than a dozen new textile mills cluttered the shores of the Acushnet River. Much of the workforce now looked to the mills for their livelihoods. Much more than Portland or San Francisco, New Bedford had acquired the look, the smell, and the culture of a heavily industrialized city.[25] [26]

Equi cared for her mother for six months until, in February 1907, Sarah Equi died at age fifty-eight. The family gathered for a memorial Mass at their parish church followed by a burial at St. Mary's Catholic cemetery, the traditional burial ground for the Irish of New Bedford. Shortly thereafter, Equi returned to Oregon.[27]

Back in Portland, Equi appeared to have taken in stride any fallout from the Speckart affair. If anything she was more assertive about her relationship with Speckart.

In June 1907, with the city bedecked everywhere with roses, she and Speckart participated in Portland's biggest celebration of the year: the first Rose Carnival and Fiesta. The day before the parade, local gardeners donated tens of thousands of roses to decorate floats in the official festival colors—pink, rose, and green. On Saturday, June 22, a few scattering clouds gave way to sunshine for the grand floral parade.

Equi and Speckart, dressed in their finery, joined hundreds of other Portlanders who competed for awards in the parade. They took their position in the category of "Carriage and Pair"—a four-wheeled carriage pulled by two horses—with two other entries. They rode a loop through the downtown, all the time enjoying the cheers of more than one hundred thousand onlookers thronged on the sidewalks. Later that day the judges announced winners among the various entries and awarded Equi and Speckart second place and a fifty-dollar prize. What better outcome for their day together—and their public display of companionship—than recognition and applause?[28]

7
A Criminal Practice

She did most of it for nothing 'cuz working-class women needed it.
If they could, they paid. If not, not.
Lew Levy, member, Industrial Workers of the World

No one knows when Marie Equi decided to break the law as part of her general medical practice. On the surface, there was little reason to suspect that hers was different from those of other physicians. She maintained her office in respectable downtown buildings. She participated in meetings of the local medical societies, and she developed generally good relations with colleagues. By all appearances, she was a member in good standing with the local medical establishment, except that, at some point during her first ten years practicing in Portland, she started providing abortions.[1] She joined a band of licensed physicians who risked prosecution and loss of their licenses, or, more likely, damage to their reputations, to help women end their pregnancies.

In the latter half of the nineteenth century and the early decades of the twentieth, abortion became an increasingly public concern that entangled physicians, the courts, the clergy, and politicians in a thicket of moral, legal, and economic dilemmas. The complexities began decades earlier when the American Medical Association (AMA) collaborated with government and civic authorities to outlaw abortion. The AMA spoke for regular physicians rather than practitioners of alternative healing, and it sought to enhance the status, professional domain, and financial well-being of its members at a time when medical science offered few diagnostic and clinical tools. A primary strategy for the association was to eliminate the competition of midwives who had assisted women with childbirth, including abortion, for as long as anyone could remember. The AMA worked state by state to outlaw abortion to drive midwives from medical care and to establish regular doctors as the sole source of medical care.[2]

The AMA was not alone in seeking to stigmatize abortion and punish providers. Civic boosters, business interests, and politicians readily joined the efforts to regulate morality. Many figured that well-ordered, proper communities attracted more settlers, commerce, and investments. Church leaders, in turn, supported restrictions purported to bolster moral behavior. The campaign drew on the fear of many Americans that immigrant births, combined with access to abortion, would overwhelm the declining Anglo-Saxon birthrate. The AMA's efforts achieved remarkable success. By 1900, "virtually every jurisdiction" in the United States had banned abortion. But the laws codified new definitions of criminal abortion that complicated enforcement and ultimately helped physicians like Equi provide her abortion services.[3]

One of the most contentious aspects of the abortion bans was confusion and disagreement about when life began. Traditional beliefs asserted that the moment arrived once a woman detected a quickening or movement of the fetus—generally between the fourth and sixth month of pregnancy. Before quickening occurred, women relied on midwives to help remove what they considered a blockage to their menstrual cycle. They undertook these procedures as straightforward interventions that held little moral or legal weight, and they did so without interference by the state. The new laws, however, prohibited abortive acts at every stage of pregnancy, even before quickening. Yet many women and their doctors continued to endorse the traditional beliefs, and their views often complicated abortion prosecutions.[4]

Another stumbling block for prosecutors lay embedded in many of the abortion bans. A provision required the state to prove that a practitioner intended to end the life of a child. In the private setting of a patient's home or a practitioner's office, only the participants knew the pregnant woman's circumstances, the nature of her request, and the practitioner's response. If challenged by law officers after an abortion occurred—and especially if the woman died during the procedure—providers could claim the patient presented conditions unrelated to pregnancy.[5]

Many of the state bans included what became known in the legal arena as the therapeutic exception, an allowance for the practitioner to assist with an abortion if the woman's life was threatened. The therapeutic exception was a reasonable, well-intentioned, and potentially life-saving option, but it created a "legal loophole," in the words of one historian, for abortions to proceed even without the danger of death. Doctors might invoke the therapeutic exception to justify an abortion because they believed women ought to control their own reproduction. Or they might invoke physical, psychological, or even financial difficulties that their patients presented. For example, a physician might decide that pregnancy resulting from rape merited an abortion or that an additional birth might exacerbate the dire financial straits of a family. Practitioners might also interpret the therapeutic exception loosely enough to end a pregnancy as a favor to friends and business associates or to gain referrals when no risk to health was apparent.[6]

These uncertainties with law and medicine prevailed when Equi established her medical practice in Portland in 1905. Oregon's abortion ban had held sway for over fifty years by then, starting in 1854 when the territorial legislature followed the lead of twenty-one other states and territories and criminalized abortion. Ten years later (and after statehood) Oregon legislators revised the law to reflect more modern scientific understanding. They removed the quickening doctrine and added the therapeutic exception. They declared intent to do harm a necessary condition of guilt, and they specifically referred to a child—rather than a fetus—although the legal definition of when life began remained unresolved. The destruction of a child became a manslaughter offense, and the punishment for harming the child or the mother was set at one to fifteen years in prison. Anyone who procured an abortion could be held liable, but the pregnant woman was not.[7]

During these early decades when abortion was a crime, women who approached physicians for an abortion usually received one of three responses. A small number of doctors honored the requests and performed the procedure without a fuss. Many more physicians refused any help whatsoever. One of these—a doctor from Walla Walla, Washington—bemoaned the choices women made. He wrote to the journal *Northwest Medicine* that he advised single, pregnant women to get married, to take refuge in a foundling asylum if necessary, or to abide by their wedding vows if married. He was appalled to learn from a survey that only twenty-one of ninety-seven of his patients did as they were told. Perhaps the largest number of doctors referred patients to colleagues whom they trusted for their expertise and discretion.[8]

Women unable to afford physicians' fees sought help from unlicensed, entrepreneurial practitioners who operated at maternity hospitals or menstrual clinics. There they might receive competent care, but the more commercial nature of the facility increased women's risks of exposure and damage to their reputations. The poor and most disadvantaged women often relied on hack operators in back rooms along Portland's waterfront or in the North End district. Or they might resort to instruments, such as rubber catheters, to induce abortions themselves. When hope faded and shame soared, the most distressed turned to suicide.[9]

Laws seldom have much impact without enforcement, but authorities in Portland waited nearly twenty years before taking the city's first abortion case to court. In November 1873 the *Oregonian* reported the indictment of C. G. Glass for manslaughter following the death of a nineteen-year-old single woman, Mary E. Hardman, after an abortion performed the previous month. The conduct and outcome of the case and of the ones to follow helped establish the perception of risk for doctors like Equi, who later chose to violate the law.[10]

Glass advertised his practice as "The Eclectic Dispensary" for treatment of "chronic and private diseases" of men and women. At his downtown office, he served young men who had "weakened and injured their constitutions by secret habits" and women who were "dragging out a life of misery" due to "diseases peculiar to their sex." He also promoted the sale of *Female Regulatory Pills*. His services and transactions represented the kind of alternative operation that the local medical society wanted to banish from the city.[11]

In the ensuing trial, Glass testified that Hardman was already several months pregnant when he first examined her, but he found that she was "carrying a dead child." He asserted that she had admitted to earlier seeking assistance of a midwife and to ingesting oil of tansy, a plant believed to induce abortions. He gave the ill woman lodging—after accepting the considerable sum of $250 for his services—but she died soon thereafter, he said, of bilious intermittent fever. His diagnosis was contested by two regular physicians who believed the woman had succumbed due to inflammation and hemorrhage associated with an abortion. After a three-day trial in the Multnomah County Circuit Court, the jury retreated to consider Glass's intent, the viability of Hardman's pregnancy, and the cause of death. After two-and-a-half hours of deliberation, the jury found Glass guilty, and the judge sentenced him to five years in the state penitentiary. Portland's first abortion trial ended with a conviction, but the outcome proved more an exception than the rule for prosecutions in the decades ahead.[12]

By the time Equi obtained her medical license in 1903, only three practitioners had been convicted of providing abortions. Prosecutors found that insufficient evidence peculiar to abortion charges and the ambiguities of the abortion law made convictions difficult to obtain. On one occasion, in 1899, the therapeutic exception came into play when a doctor testified that his patient had so badly injured herself in an attempted abortion that he had to perform the operation to save her life. He was found guilty in a first trial, but the judge permitted a second trial only to have the charges withdrawn by the woman. The few guilty verdicts during the thirty years could not have deterred many providers, and newly licensed physicians like Equi might easily have decided that the risks were tolerable compared to the desperation of their patients.[13]

Equi started her practice in Portland in 1905, however, just as a surge in Progressive Era fervor for social reform and control triggered a spike in abortion prosecutions with nine trials undertaken within three years. She had thrust herself into the thick of the Progressive movement in common cause with other reformers, but she could not abide the restrictions on abortion that her colleagues now championed. Many believed easy access to abortion threatened the social order by alleviating unintended consequences of premarital sex and by separating intercourse from reproduction. Their concerns were exacerbated in April 1907 when Portland police arrested Dr. Charles Herbert T. Atwood on charges of an illegal procedure conducted on a sixteen-year-old woman. The *Oregonian* described the arrest as "the first of a crusade" against physicians who performed criminal operations."[14]

Atwood was an unremarkable fifty-three-year-old married man with three adult children who had settled in Portland's Woodstock district a few years earlier. He practiced from offices in the downtown Lewis Building on Fourth Street. "Dr. Atwood, female disease cases, private hospital" one of his newspaper notices read. The advertisement attracted Willard B. Holdiman, a forty-year-old married man with two children who impregnated Hattie Fee, the daughter of his housekeeper. Holdiman arranged for Atwood to perform an abortion on Fee. When she suffered complications, she sought help from the Travelers' Aid Society, a Progressive Era organization dedicated to diverting young women from moral threats in the city. Lola G. Baldwin, director of the agency, would later become the nation's first policewoman. Baldwin prepared the charges against Holdiman for statutory rape and against Atwood for abortion.[15]

Onlookers packed the courtroom of Judge Calvin Gantenbein of the Multnomah County Circuit Court the first day of Atwood's trial. The city's leading attorneys and physicians jockeyed for bench space, and contingents from the Salvation Army, Travelers' Aid, and the Boys and Girls Society stood where they could. From the start, the trial exposed the difficulty of obtaining a conviction. Atwood denied any criminal intent, and he claimed to have administered only legal medicines. He then declared that Fee was not pregnant when she visited him. He sowed further doubt when he questioned why Fee's mother had not supported the charges, although the woman had reason to be hesitant to testify against Holdiman, her employer. Atwood's nineteen-year-old office assistant testified that she had seen nothing unprofessional during Fee's visit. The prosecution's case relied on Fee's testimony alone. The judge cleared the courtroom before she "sobbed out her story," according to a newspaper report, while Atwood shielded his eyes with his hand. Fee described her sickness and distress after the operation, but her pitiful tale did not resolve questions about Atwood's intent. The jurors failed to reach a verdict, and the judge acknowledged the "perplexing issues" in the case before he dismissed them. The district attorney secured a retrial date, but the case was ultimately dismissed once both he and the judge decided Oregon's laws were insufficient to prove manslaughter.[16]

Spurred by the Atwood case, Portland's medical society leaders vowed to identify and prosecute "the many able but unscrupulous physicians" who broke the law and disgraced the profession. Dr. Alan Welch Smith, secretary for the society, complained that a clique of doctors dared to advertise their "unholy vocation" and then boasted how much money they pocketed.

The *Oregonian* reported that "legitimate physicians" had known for some time that at least a dozen of their colleagues performed abortions, yet few rank and file doctors chose to report the suspects. Many doctors possessed the surgical skills to end pregnancies without complications, and they protected the clinical prerogatives they felt were integral to the practice of medicine.

Doctors also coped with real financial concerns. Many served families whose business they wanted to retain, even if it meant performing an abortion or referring their patient to a colleague who was more willing to oblige. In doing so, they assisted and protected their middle-class and wealthier patients who could afford their services.[17]

Portland's antiabortion campaign was off to an inauspicious start. If anything, Atwood's trial broadcast the prevalence of abortions while the dismissal exposed the limits of the law. Hattie Fee, her family, and, presumably, the wife and children of the alleged rapist had suffered the most during the juggernaut of investigations, prosecution, and newspaper exposure that laid bare their lives and damaged their reputations.[18]

An especially egregious incident the following year, in 1908, stirred Portland's Progressive establishment further. Mayor Harry Lane and the city's board of health had recently elected Dr. Esther Pohl (later Pohl Lovejoy), a prominent suffragist, as the new city health officer to implement public health reforms critical to the mayor's Progressive agenda. In February Pohl reported to the board of health that Golda W. Rowland, a twenty-five-year-old schoolteacher from Washington State, had died from an abortion performed at a suspect establishment, the X-Radium Institute, in downtown Portland. The odd name of the facility apparently reflected the public's interest in the use of X-ray technology in American hospitals and the relatively recent discovery of radium. According to newspaper reports, Ernest Heymans, the proprietor of the institute, forged the signature of a Portland physician on Rowland's death certificate. The doctor denied the claim, and the scandal devolved into countercharges and further accounts of questionable proceedings. The county coroner apparently had neglected his duty to report criminal activity in an effort to protect the family's name, and a consulting physician had falsely listed endocarditis as the cause of death. The disclosures disturbed Portlanders, and there were more to come.[19]

Dr. William Eisen, a physician who had worked at the institute, claimed in a newspaper article that "infants, prematurely born" had been "incinerated in a furnace," and he indicated that other physicians performed abortions at the facility. The disclosures prompted health officer Pohl to lament, "Think of a poor, unfortunate girl, dying among a crowd of grafters, such as Heymans and his assistants." She believed such crimes were numerous in the city and were easily concealed. The same day that Pohl reported the incident, Heymans sold his interest in the clinic and fled the city. One newspaper suggested that local physicians had helped him elude the police to prevent disclosure of their identities. Four days later the police closed the institute.[20]

The moral implications of the case prompted ministers and priests to take to their pulpits. J. Whitcomb Brougher, the pastor of Portland's First Baptist Church, spoke of the Rowland "murder" before an overflow audience. "The case in question is 'specially startling only in the fact that it has been made public," he said. He deplored that many women felt driven to death rather than endure the disgrace of their condition, and he exhorted Portlanders to rid the city of abortion providers, who he called a "generation of vipers." Not all clergy were as outspoken. A representative of the Roman Catholic Archdiocese advised a concerned committee that Archbishop Alexander Christie would not permit his priests to speak about the matter. It was the policy of the church, he said, to conduct their endeavors quietly.[21]

Once again, a conviction eluded the authorities, and John Manning, the Multnomah County District Attorney, denied responsibility for the outcome. "I have been through the courts many times with these cases and have never been able to score a conviction, much as the courts and I have tried," he told one newspaper. He complained that Oregon had a statute against manslaughter, not abortion. "But manslaughter is the taking of life. Life must be present before it can be destroyed. In nearly every case of abortion there is no taking of life, according to the legal and medical authorities."[22]

In the speeches, sermons, and newspaper reports during these high-profile cases, abortion was invariably described as a uniformly dangerous procedure provided by reprobates and sought mostly by single women who had strayed or had been abused. The various officials assumed that the public shared their sentiments, but private talk among women, with spouses or lovers, and between doctors and patients dealt with everyday realities in which abortion was understood to be a usually safe operation performed by licensed and skilled physicians, midwives, or by women themselves. They knew that married women obtained abortions as frequently as single women and that unwanted pregnancies were less associated with "immoral" behavior than claimed. The discrepancy between public pronouncements and these quiet confidences obscured a real understanding of abortion and of women's demand for it.[23]

By 1915 the surge of Progressive Era abortion trials had ended due to prosecutors' and medical leaders' waning interest, the emerging birth control debate, and the double scourges of World War I and the 1918 Influenza Pandemic. Overall Portland prosecutors achieved a 30 percent conviction rate for the twenty-seven abortion trials conducted between 1873 and 1920, a record similar to that of other cities. The small number of trials and even fewer convictions proved to be little deterrence for either women seeking abortions or to providers helping them. Most doctors, in fact, enabled the practice of abortion, directly or indirectly, by invoking the therapeutic exception, referring patients to willing providers, offering medical care following abortions, or by not reporting colleagues who performed abortions. For these reasons, women in the early 1900s in Portland obtained an estimated six thousand or more abortions annually from a dozen or more practitioners. Yet the illegality, possible investigations, and threat of public humiliation hovered over most women who sought to make their own reproductive decisions.[24]

Equi never appeared in the *Oregonian* for her abortion work, and no records suggest she was prosecuted for helping end pregnancies. She was one of the skilled regular physicians who helped women with abortions without legal trouble for anyone involved. She maintained a general practice—not opting for abortion services only—and she adopted a holistic approach to women's health that included access to birth control information. Similar to most other physicians, she did not leave accounts of her assistance with abortions, but her

Dr. Marie Equi, a skilled and discreet abortion provider, never faced legal action for her work. Oregon Historical Society, bb002610.

actions reflected her priorities. Several of Equi's contemporaries attested to her distinction as the only Portland physician of her time known to incorporate abortion services into a larger commitment to women's reproductive rights.[25]

Of the two dozen licensed physicians known to perform abortions in Portland, two were women well known to Equi. Maude Van Alstyne and Alys

Bixby Griff were also graduates of the University of Oregon Medical Department, and both overlapped their time on campus with her. Van Alstyne established her practice in downtown Portland's Broadway Building, a ten-story structure with a white pressed brick exterior that boasted an opulent, marble lobby with chandeliers. The location served her clients well. They could as easily be stopping at the clothing stores, drug store, or dentist offices inside. Van Alstyne, described by a colleague, as a "dour and aloof" woman, managed a small operation and apparently avoided any difficulties with the police.[26]

Alys Bixby Griff became Equi's great friend and confidant. She was a dynamic and engaging woman whose personality and presence commanded attention wherever she went. Following a pattern familiar to other physicians who provided abortions, Griff focused at first on diseases of women, but ten years into her practice she shifted to full-time abortion work. The demand had become apparent with six to eight women at a time crowding her office, according to her assistant. With their experience, Van Alstyne and Griff could have confirmed that the procedure itself was relatively uncomplicated and safe when performed early in pregnancies by a skilled practitioner. They might also have oriented Equi to the practice and business of abortion.[27]

Dr. Alys Bixby Griff switched her general medicine practice to full-time abortion work to meet the significant demand in Portland.OHSU Historical Collections & Archives, Portland, Oregon.

Abortion could be a lucrative specialty depending on the practitioner's ability and reputation. Fees were usually based on the progression of the pregnancy, often beginning at twenty-five dollars. Women paid more—sometimes considerably more—for late-term procedures that required additional time and posed greater risks of hemorrhage and infection. Jessie Laird Brodie, a Portland physician who started her practice in the mid-1920s, believed the abortions Equi performed were "D & C," meaning dilation and curettage, the most common form of medical abortion and a standard gynecological procedure. Laird believed Equi provided the service in her office and that she lacked many anesthetics that were then available only at hospitals. Equi was thought to charge poor women fifteen to twenty dollars and rich women fifty dollars for the service.[28]

According to Equi's contemporaries, she performed abortions for a wide range of clients—her regular patients, poor, working-class, and immigrant women, political activists, and the wealthy clients referred to her. Equi became cherished among politically radical men and women in the Pacific Northwest for her willingness to help with abortions. Lew Levy, a radical comrade, extolled her work, recalling, "She did most of it for nothing . . . 'cuz working-class women needed it." And, he added, "If they could, they paid, if not, not."[29] The labor activist and journalist Julia Ruuttila thought Equi performed abortions with the best of intentions. "She believed that women should have the right of choice, and should not be forced to bear a child . . . if they didn't want that child or couldn't take care of it." [30]

Another confidant, Margaret D., a woman who Equi had delivered as a newborn and who later became her nurse, recalled that Equi told her that many Portland doctors referred their clients for abortions because they trusted her. She also recalled Equi's quips. When Margaret and her girlfriends visited Equi's practice in the 1920s, she said, "We'd stop in her office and she'd always slip us a couple of dollars and she'd tell us, 'Now if you girls get in trouble, you come to me.'"[31]

Equi developed a reputation for her abortion work that lingered even after she closed her practice. Dr. Jessie Laird Brodie recalled that women doctors of her day—starting in the 1920s—were often stigmatized by male colleagues. "The main problem we had was that if you were a woman physician and lived in this area, they'd say you did abortions like Marie Equi." She added, "It seemed to put you under suspicion right away." Brodie may have been speaking more for herself, but she believed most doctors were unwilling to risk their licenses or reputations by agreeing to help end pregnancies. The perception of illegal procedures was enough in itself, she believed, to damage a doctor's livelihood and standing in the community. "No legitimate doctor felt he could do it, but then a number discarded that protection and went ahead and did abortions," Brodie said. "They felt so strongly about it, and I think Marie Equi was one of that type."[32]

Equi apparently negotiated the abortion controversy without undue concern. She bucked the demands of medical leaders, Progressive stalwarts, prosecutors, and the clergy and focused instead on the needs of her patients. She was well accustomed to the disapproval of others for her willingness to speak her mind, for her lesbianism, and as a result of her political activism. She seldom met the expectations for proper female or professional behavior, and she brushed aside directives about what clinical services to provide her patients. She lived as an outsider herself and, as a result, perhaps had more empathy for women held morally and sexually irresponsible for seeking abortions. She operated as a *physician of conscience,* a description employed by historian Carol Joffe for abortion providers who respected their patients' interests above all else.[33]

Equi never let disapproval for her abortion work keep her from actively participating in the business of the local medical society, and she kept her membership active throughout her career. In 1909 she and her colleagues rallied around a breakthrough discovery that saved lives and shaped the future of medical research. It started that fall in the German laboratory of Dr. Paul Ehrlich. His team of bacteriologists discovered an arsenic compound, *number 606,* which effectively treated and sometimes cured syphilis. The scientists declared number 606 a magic bullet to target a scourge of mankind and, by 1910, it was on the market as Salvarsan—a remarkably quick course from the laboratory to clinical use. The scientific rationale that led to the discovery of Salvarsan helped create the new field of chemotherapy, and it soon became the most widely prescribed drug in the world. Physicians in the Pacific Northwest obtained Salvarsan soon after its release, and reports of clinical outcomes filled regional medical journals. Equi administered Salvarsan to her patients, and she reported her findings at a meeting of the medical society. She reported injecting the drug intramuscularly with good results, and she strongly advised "bed treatment" as well.[34]

Most physicians steered clear of the newspapers, believing exposure would diminish their stature with the public. Equi believed the opposite, and she readily provided good copy to advance a cause or her own interests. In the midst of controversies she appeared in the newspapers more often than most, if not all, other doctors in the Pacific Northwest. In 1911 alone, Equi received several column inches when she rattled one of Portland's social welfare institutions with charges of mismanagement and dangerous disregard for those in its care. She and a friend, Dr. Mary MacLachlan, had been rebuffed when they tried to assist an eighteen-year-old unmarried woman who had just given birth to a child she had no means of supporting. They took the infant to Portland's Baby Home, a private outfit that received state funding and donations from many of Portland's elite families. The director of the home refused to accept the infant without formal proof of relinquishment by the mother accompanied by payment in advance for three months care. Equi assured the director that the mother had indeed given the child over to her care, but she bristled at the notion of prepayment, saying it was out of the question and an affront to decency.[35]

Equi took her objections to the Medical Club of Portland, the local association of women physicians, which promptly endorsed her position. The Oregonian soon carried the story with an account by Equi of the many problems at the institution—the failure to isolate infants with infectious diseases, the lack of trained staff, and insufficient medical care overall. The previous September, City Health Officer Dr. C. H. Wheeler concluded that four babies had died within one week due to improper feeding at the Baby Home. Other doctors had complained among themselves about the facility, but no other private practice physicians had come forward publicly until Equi and MacLachlan spoke out. The Baby Home requested and won exoneration from the charges by the local juvenile court once the mother involved provided a formal release for her infant.[36]

On another occasion Equi's reputation as an outsider led to an association with a cross-dresser arrested in a "white slavery" incident. In September 1912, Portland police arrested twenty-eight-year-old Harry Allen of Seattle for transporting a woman across state lines for immoral purposes. Equi was reported to have visited Allen in jail. During the police interrogation, Allen claimed he was innocent, and that he was, in fact, a woman whose birth name was Nan Pickerell. He also declared that he was "married" to his female companion, who had willingly traveled to Oregon with him.[37]

Although western newspapers occasionally carried reports of cross-dressing men and women, the police and the public were uncertain what to make of Allen. Was he a man as he presented himself, a woman who wanted to dress as a man, a woman who refused to wear feminine attire, or a woman forced by circumstances to seek the better paying jobs reserved for men? Few people were conversant with the psychological nuances of cross-dressing and the subtleties of an individual's gender and sexuality identification. At the time of his arrest, Allen explained that he had "always wanted to be one of the boys" and had dressed in men's clothing for the last dozen years. He described having a "boyish manner" as a child that remained and that his current "long stride and basso voice" were now natural. Although Portland Police suspected Allen of using a "disguise" for criminal purposes, the "white slavery" charge was dropped once his sex was discovered.[38]

The Harry Allen affair prompted Portlanders to consider the phenomenon of cross-dressing, but they could treat it as a curiosity far removed from their lives. Another year would pass before the world of sexual outsiders intruded too closely to dismiss. For many observers, Equi's association with a cross-dresser may have placed her at greater distance from the rest of society, but she remained a doctor willing to treat an individual others avoided. As with abortion, she followed her own sense of medical and moral responsibilities.

8
A Period of Balance

She lives in a sphere which I approve, all gifted women, who made
something of themselves, can do something, and are somebody.
Harriet Speckart

For a five-year span beginning in 1907, Marie Equi enjoyed a kind of balance in
her life uncommon to many activists and professionals. She made a home with
her new companion, Harriet Speckart. She kept her medical practice strong
and growing, and she thrust herself into campaigns for direct democracy and
government reforms. Unlike the majority of early twentieth century women
with fewer opportunities, she found a way to be romantically involved, professionally engaged, and politically active. But what appeared balanced for her
might easily have been precarious for others.

After her romance with Speckart disrupted The Hill hotel in late 1905,
Equi decamped with Mary Ellen Parker to the nearby Elton Court Residence,
an elegant five-story hotel on Yamhill Street that offered guests generous quarters and a fine dining room. The new lodging reflected her successful practice
and her wish for top-of-the-line accommodations. Soon thereafter, Speckart
settled in with Equi, and they made their first home together. Then, as if to
flaunt their reputation as the clique of The Hill, the three women welcomed
Mrs. Marie Daggett to Elton Court.[1]

Equi kept company with a wide range of women friends—other physicians, suffragists, social workers, and activists. Her outgoing nature, strong
opinions, and readiness to provide a good story drew others into her circle, and
her income permitted her to entertain with dinners and outings. Her name occasionally appeared in the society pages as a symphony patron, a horse-show
enthusiast, and a tourist at resort hotels on the Oregon coast.[2]

Speckart was enthralled with the excitement of a new life away from her
family and in an environment where she could be an independent, modern
woman. She wrote to an aunt in Germany that Equi lived "in a sphere which I
approve, all gifted women, who made something of themselves, can do something, and are somebody. No small talk and social nothingness, everything is

discussed and with the whole soul, it makes life spicy." Although unidentified in the letter, these "gifted women" probably included other lesbians. Once the dailies insinuated Equi and Speckart's lesbian relationship, other lesbians would have recognized their similar interests. Portland already attracted single, independent women with the promise of employment as the city's economy surged in the wake of the world's fair. Feminists journeyed to the city to help with the suffrage campaign, and Equi actively expanded her circle of female friends. She often acted as a one-woman welcome party for celebrated women speakers who stopped in the Rose City, so much so that birth control advocate Margaret Sanger remarked upon her open-arm receptions. She wrote years later of Equi, "Upon arrival she captures every well-known woman who comes to Portland." With a mix of circumstance, attraction, and personal effort, Equi's circle became a precursor of the larger, self-identified lesbian subcultures that flourished in American cities several years later.[3]

In 1908 Equi and Parker relocated their practices to the classier Medical Building, Portland's newest office tower. The six-story, buff-brick structure on Alder Street became the prestigious professional hub in town with the city's top doctors and dentists and the local medical society as tenants. Equi was successful enough to keep her office there for five years until she was no longer welcome.[4]

A year after Equi and Speckart began living together, Parker decided to seek something different in her life, and, in 1908, she left her practice and the city. For nearly ten years she and Equi had been constant companions, supporting each other through medical school, post-graduate study, and the uncertainties of new medical careers. But Parker's practice had not thrived earlier in Pendleton, and she may have had similar difficulties in Portland. Or the changed interpersonal dynamic with Equi's affections focused on Speckart may have prompted her move. She returned to her hometown, Bridgeport, California, where her parents still lived, and, for reasons unknown, she did not establish a medical practice in California. Her experience was not unlike that of other women physicians who, after striving to obtain their licenses, found they were unable to make a career of it or were unwilling to endure the required sacrifices. The total number of women physicians in the United States reached its peak about the time Parker left medicine with nine thousand in practice, about 6 percent of all doctors.[5]

Parker understood a life in medicine, however, and she stayed close to it by marrying James T. White, a county doctor. The newlyweds traveled throughout Europe for several years and then settled in Oakland, California, where, in August 1911, she gave birth to their only child, William Anthony.

Tragically, her new life as a doctor's wife ended abruptly seven months later when her husband died at age forty-five. She never remarried, and she relied on her parents for help raising her son. She and Equi remained friends for many more years.[6]

Shortly after Parker's departure, Equi and Speckart relocated to Portland's newest hotel, the seven-story, finely appointed Nortonia at Eleventh and Stark Streets. Deluxe English walnut furnishings greeted visitors in the lobby, and patrons feasted in a grand dining room accompanied by an orchestra every evening. On an expansive roof garden, guests enjoyed cocktails, music, and dancing. Speckart was tickled with her new residence, and she sent picture postcards of the Nortonia to her relatives. On one card depicting the dining room, she penciled an "x" on a table along the wall to indicate where she sat. She and Equi took their table knowing the regulars likely gossiped about them, but they lived as they wished and remained at the Nortonia for three years.[7]

For a woman little exposed to money matters in her early years, Speckart found her new life mired in a financial swamp of disputed family assets and poorly managed accounts. But she showed little reluctance to battle her relatives with righteous determination. The crux of her position was clear and to the point. Mrs. Speckart had denied her daughter her rightful inheritance for a full five years after she came of age, and she had neglected administration of the estate so much that a true account of Harriet's share was hopelessly lost in a maze of stocks, realty, and loans. As the legal maneuvers and court appearances multiplied, the Speckarts—daughter, mother, and brother—staked out their positions and refused to compromise.[8]

Two days before Harriet Speckart rode with Equi in Portland's Rose Fiesta parade in July 1907, her attorney filed a petition in the superior court of Olympia, Washington, charging her mother and uncle with conspiracy to withhold her inheritance and accusing them of fraud and deceit. She objected to an earlier ruling that established jurisdiction in Washington State instead of Montana where her father's will was filed, and she demanded immediate release of the inheritance due her. She also argued for removal of her uncle, Leopold Schmidt, the estate administrator. She had good reason to object to Schmidt's role—he had tried to subvert her father's wishes and arrange for her to receive just one-half of her inheritance.[9]

In September 1907 Speckart sat with Equi in the Olympia courtroom as her uncle requested dismissal of her petition. Three months later the judge ruled against Speckart, but she appealed to the Washington State Supreme

Court, and, in December, all seven judges agreed she had "ample grounds to complain." They stripped Schmidt of his estate administration, and overturned the state's assumption of jurisdiction. They criticized Mrs. Speckart for her failure to close the estate years ago, but they did not order a distribution of assets. Harriet Speckart had scored a victory, but she was back to pressing her case for a full accounting and an equitable share of the estate.[10]

The case clouded much of Equi and Speckart's early relationship, binding them in a mutual struggle but also subjecting them to its constant discord. Together they negotiated the bias and inequality women faced in the judicial system. As Speckart found, female plaintiffs were often denied legal standing in court, or, when they did gain access, their concerns were stereotyped or dismissed. She dealt with this treatment mostly in the lower courts, but on all levels she had to assert her rights of citizenship and object to charges that she no longer had her wits about her. Although Equi's role in the proceedings was limited, her relations with Speckart remained a factor with accusations that she had exerted an immoral, unnatural influence.

When Speckart filed further grievances in the federal district court in Tacoma in 1908, the judge chastised her for a greediness that could deprive her mother and uncle of "their last penny" if her petition was granted. He allowed that her mother had neglected her administrative duty, but he found no evidence of "slothfulness, imprudence, nor dishonesty." Then he shifted the blame. Harriet Speckart, he found, was neither "heartless, nor avaricious," but her "unnatural conduct" in pursuing the case was due to the "baneful influence of a meddlesome person who dominates her by the exertion of a mysterious psychological power." His claim resurrected Mrs. Speckart's allegations from two years earlier when she portrayed Equi as a malevolent and suspicious force in her daughter's life. The judge concluded that Speckart had become the tool of someone who lacked legal standing in the case, and he ruled that her petition lacked equity. He then dismissed the case.[11]

When Speckart appealed the latest judgment to the Ninth Circuit Court of Appeals in San Francisco, the judges reversed the district finding and found that she did indeed have standing and that there was insufficient evidence to indicate an inability to exercise free will or manage her own property. However, the judges allowed that Mrs. Speckart's negligence with the distribution might have resulted from concerns over her daughter's "strange friendship which they deplored." The court implicitly accepted disapproval of homosexuality as reasonable cause for neglect of legal responsibility. For Equi, Speckart's case was the first of two occasions in which her personal morality and same-sex preference were implicated before the court of appeals.[12]

The appeals court gave Speckart her greatest victory after more than five years of litigation and affirmed her right to her inheritance, but did she ever get it? Two-and-a-half years earlier, in July 1909, Mrs. Speckart admitted under oath that she held property, stock, and money that belonged to her daughter, and the judge ordered her to deposit more than $60,000 with the court registry. From this amount Speckart was due to receive $50,000 along with another $6,000 for allowances as well as stock shares in the family breweries valued at more than $43,000. Speckart received the money and the stocks worth nearly $100,000, a sum comparable on an inflation basis to $2.5 million today.[13]

Harriet Speckart had become a wealthy woman, and she began to diversify her holdings with a purchase in 1910 of property in southwest Portland for $4,750. The following year she sold the lot for $5,600, making a tidy profit, reflecting the city's booming economy.[14]

The Speckart case continued, inexplicably, until 1922 when the district court of Washington issued a final decree, clearing the court registry of all the assets it held during the family's dispute. It ordered a distribution to Speckart of $12,000 in cash, and more than $16,000 in stock certificates. Observers at the time suggested Speckart might have obtained more money—and spent less on attorneys—if she had settled the matter earlier.[15]

The legal wrangling, begun in 1906, stirred so much hurt and rancor that Speckart never repaired relations with her mother. Mrs. Speckart returned to Germany in 1912 to spend her remaining years with relatives. Before departing, she signed her last will and testament and bequeathed ten dollars to her daughter. After her mother died in 1915, Speckart contested the probate proceedings, but the will was upheld.[16]

Speckart was never a political activist, but her pursuit of justice in the courts reflected the spirit of the times with women demanding their rights and, when they could, taking legal action to secure them. Her litigation flew in the face of norms for proper womanly behavior at a time when prejudice against women was entrenched in the legal system and law profession. While Speckart pursued her case in 1910, only 558 women practiced law in the country compared with more than 9,000 women physicians. Even if acting in her own self-interest, Speckart advanced women's rights by standing her ground and forcing the courts to recognize her as an independent female plaintiff. The extent and nature of Equi's role in pursuing the case is undocumented, but she probably helped fuel Speckart's sense of injustice with her own anger over being vilified in the press and in courts of law.[17]

The election year of 1912 rocked the state and the nation. In Oregon women mounted the sixth campaign to win the right to vote, and Equi thrust herself into the effort more experienced in Progressive causes. In the previous six years since the last suffrage campaign, Equi helped advance the reformist agenda that dominated state politics. She supported reform candidates and pushed to obtain public financing for the University of Oregon. She supported prison reform and opposed capital punishment. But no issue for her surpassed women's right to vote.[18]

The suffrage loss in 1906 had enervated Oregon suffragists, and membership in the state suffrage organization plummeted. In both 1908 and 1910, Abigail Scott Duniway soldiered on with hapless campaigns, but each failed miserably. In 1910 she resorted to a plan that would grant suffrage only to female homeowners who paid property taxes, thus sparking a storm of protest from Progressives and labor activists.[19]

By 1912 the dynamics for women's right to vote in Oregon had shifted. Suffragists to the north and south had already secured the vote—Washington in 1910 and California in 1911. Oregon became the laggard on the West Coast, and local suffragists appealed to state pride to close the gap. A new generation of mostly younger women recoiled from the long-running conflict between Duniway and the national suffrage leaders over campaign tactics. Instead, they launched a multifaceted, everything-goes approach with nearly two dozen organizations operating independently with "neither head nor tail," according to local leader Esther Pohl Lovejoy. No single organization led the effort, and no one individual determined strategy. They let loose every outreach and dissemination strategy available in an early twentieth-century campaign—an organized news service, active lobbying of newspaper editors, and dozens of speakers, rallies, parades, as well as two hundred thousand pieces of literature delivered door to door and from street corners.[20]

What appeared to be missing from the campaign, however, was a robust synergy between direct democracy populists and the suffragists. In hopes of appealing to more mainstream voters, local suffragists distanced themselves from radical economic changes. The hands-off stance toward economic concerns was also reflected in the absence of a suffrage group comprised of trade unionists that could have advanced a targeted message to union members. Equi worked within the Progressive framework, not yet adopting a more radical stance, and served as a director of the College Equal Suffrage League (CESL), an import from the East Coast organized to train high school and college women to become effective advocates.[21]

Two out-of-state campaign consultants, Helen Hoy Greeley and Charlotte Anita Whitney, became stalwart friends and allies of Equi's in suffrage work and her political crises that lay ahead. Greeley, a Vassar graduate and an early woman attorney, obtained her law degree in 1903 and established a general law practice in New York before accepting an appointment to help revise the state charter. Once she concluded that "without the ballot, it was the old story of bricks without straw" for women, Greeley left her law practice to work on suffrage full time. She earned a reputation as a standout orator and a topnotch campaigner. Whitney had enjoyed a privileged childhood in Oakland, California, as the daughter of an attorney and a niece of a US Supreme Court Justice. She could have settled for an untroubled future, but after graduation from Wellesley College in 1899, she dreaded settling for a sheltered life and feared "being thought different" among her peers. She volunteered to do settlement work in New York and observed poverty firsthand. Then she studied social work and served as the first juvenile probation officer for Alameda County when she returned to California. Over time social work seemed to miss the mark for creating economic justice, and Whitney shifted her interests to woman suffrage. She led the Northern California chapter of the CESL, and, along with Greeley, helped win the 1911 suffrage vote in California.[22]

Greeley and Whitney recruited a large number of young women to the Oregon CESL, and they were especially effective helping the many suffrage groups collaborate and leverage their strengths. But no one could defuse the bickering and plotting that locked Oregon's Abigail Scott Duniway and her NAWSA opponents in contention. Anna Howard Shaw, NAWSA president, opened a back channel of support to Oregon with Esther Pohl Lovejoy and city market inspector Sarah Evans, keeping them apprised of opportunities to advance the cause and circumvent Duniway. When the discord appeared in the newspapers, Equi often figured in the stories as one of Duniway's lieutenants. In one instance Equi blocked a power play by Evans to undermine a local suffrage coordinating committee and replace it with a NAWSA-sponsored group that could then receive association funds.[23]

Equi fumed over the tactics by Shaw and her allies. In a six-page letter she castigated the NAWSA president for her "personal rancor and bias" against Duniway ever since the 1906 campaign. "It doesn't help your mental growth any, does it, dear woman?" she wrote. Equi recounted in detail how Evans,

Left: Abigail Scott Duniway led the Oregon woman suffrage effort through five campaigns and lived to witness victory with the sixth in 1912. Library of Congress, LC-DIG-npcc 3 3187. Right: Anna Howard Shaw, president of the National American Woman Suffrage Association, clashed with Oregon's suffrage leader. Library of Congress LC-F82-2574.

sometimes assisted by Lovejoy, stoked animosity among local women and between Duniway and Shaw. She charged that if the Oregon campaign were to lose once again, it would be due to "the bitterness engendered and fostered by you through your representative."[24]

Equi advised Shaw to resolve her longtime feud and "forget personalities, bury them deep." She knew this emotional territory, and she wrote, "You are still hot-blooded. I have hot blood in my veins, too, so (I) understand you, I think." But Equi set her limits. "Now, Anna Shaw, I love you, you understand that, but I am not afraid of the truth." She threatened to disclose to reporters what she considered traitorous acts to the cause of suffrage by Shaw's allies in Oregon. "They must keep hands off Mrs. D in the future," she warned, "Otherwise I will forget the CAUSE and remember only there is a woman sick, not only in body but in heart, a woman too old to be wearied and annoyed by heartless women who are filled with political greed." Equi appeared to take a familiar stance—defense of someone disrespected or treated unfairly—much like she had with Bessie Holcomb and Harriet Speckart. Equi and Duniway may not have developed a close, personal relationship, but each respected and appreciated the other.[25]

Equi's lengthy message, brimming with both advice and threats, reflects the intensity she brought to her intimate relations with other women. With

Shaw she shared a working-class background. Both had toiled as children in a textile mill, and both had struggled to obtain a medical license. Both were determined and passionate, and they loved other women. (Shaw maintained a thirty-year lesbian relationship with Lucy Anthony, niece of Susan B. Anthony). Although Equi challenged Shaw, she also expressed concern for her well-being and an understanding of her emotions. Shaw was perhaps too overwhelmed and fatigued with suffrage politics on every front to give much thought to Equi's letter, and there's little evidence that her antipathy for Duniway lessened as a result of Equi's intervention. Duniway was not the only independent, sometimes cantankerous state leader. Emma Smith DeVoe, a Washington State suffrage leader, had also rebuffed NAWSA from controlling her state's successful campaign in 1910. Kentucky's suffrage director Laura Clay had worked in the Oregon campaign as well, and she too advised the NAWSA board of directors to relent in their criticism. "We must exercise some courage in working with disagreeable women," she observed, "or we will be driven out of every state."[26]

The internal campaign politics of 1912 rattled Equi's certainty about suffrage. In the same letter to Shaw, in which she complained about tactics, she wrote of her misgivings:

> I have, since working in the campaign, changed my belief that women should vote—maybe they should, but politics is a dirty game, and whenever one gets in and wishes to hold their supremacy, they must do it at a cost of the highest moral sense; it is not conducive to the best in women.[27]

Equi managed her misgivings and kept her posts on the executive committees of the state suffrage association and the CESL. She also staged two media-savvy suffrage events—a parade by the Oregon Junior Booster Club, a twelve-member group with eleven boys and one girl, and an "all-suffrage wedding" in her downtown office. The *Oregonian* reported that Equi's suite was bedecked in suffrage yellow and white for the nuptials that were conducted by the president of the state suffrage association with Equi and another doctor serving as witnesses. The bride vowed to cherish rather than obey her future husband.[28]

While campaign organizers labored to keep their suffrage message on target, Equi became entangled in another dispute that distracted the public in a manner similar to the Speckart scandal before the 1906 campaign. Late in the evening of May 16, 1912, Equi and Bessie Gardiner, a thirty-four-year-old

University of Oregon medical student, were prevented from leaving the Medical Building where Equi kept her offices. They later told police officers that the elevator operators refused to transport them from the sixth floor to the street level by order of the building superintendent, George Prettyman. When they entered another physician's empty office to telephone the police, Prettyman confronted them and ordered them to leave. What happened next was either a firm but reasonable eviction or a knockdown assault that left Equi with dark and swollen marks on her body and in a state of "severe nervous shock," according to two doctor friends who later testified about her condition.[29]

In newspaper accounts, Prettyman claimed that Equi had previously refused to pay rent for her offices and had used "vile and intemperate language" to boast that she would remain without paying. On the night of the conflict, he said Equi and Gardiner had harassed him by throwing rotten eggs from the upper floor and repeatedly ringing for the elevator cars when they weren't needed. They were illegally occupying another doctor's office, according to Prettyman, and once he asked them to leave and then tried to escort them out of the building, Equi "put up a scrap."[30]

Equi charged that Prettyman attacked and assaulted her without provocation. She said he seized her by the neck, ripped her shirtwaist, threw her to the floor, held her immobile, and then beat her while calling her "vile and abusive names" and dragging her out of the office. She was so overwrought by the experience that instead of returning to the apartment she shared with Speckart in northwest Portland she stayed the night with a doctor friend in a downtown hotel.[31]

When police declared they had inadequate evidence to pursue the matter, Equi took her complaints to a grand jury that soon thereafter indicted Prettyman on assault and battery charges. Equi further retained attorney C. E. S. Wood to argue that Prettyman was hostile to her as a result of her medical care of a young woman whom he had infected with a venereal disease. In that dispute, she said, Prettyman struck her and threatened her with a pistol. The jury was not sufficiently persuaded, and Prettyman was acquitted after fifty minutes of deliberation.[32]

Whatever the dynamics of the brawl with Prettyman—how it began, how each side reacted—it had to have distracted the public from the suffrage question and dismayed the campaign leaders trying to stay on message. If there were complaints, none have been located. Also unknown is whether Harriet questioned Equi's budding involvement with Elizabeth Gardiner as that relationship continued and apparently deepened.

Long lines of voters turned out on a dreary, wet Election Day morning to cast their votes on a slew of propositions, including woman suffrage. After a nervous wait for election results, suffragists cheered the men of Oregon who finally approved women's right to vote with 52 percent in favor, a winning margin of just 4,161 votes. One newspaper touted, "Mrs. Duniway's Dream Comes True." The victory appeared to result from a mix of factors, primarily the influence of neighboring suffrage states, diminished opposition by liquor interests, greater support from labor unions, and enhanced fundraising with diverse marketing tactics. In western states overall, winning suffrage strategies appeared to have been influenced less by either a muted or a loud campaign than by significant fundraising and messages that were less threatening to perceptions of women's place in the world.[33]

Equi could celebrate the victory and be pleased with her own contributions and with the acclaim for Duniway as the Mother of Oregon Suffrage. On November 30, 1912, Governor Oswald West appeared with Duniway and asked her to sign Oregon's Equal Suffrage Proclamation that she had earlier transcribed. She was in her seventy-ninth year.[34]

Equi served as an impassioned, dedicated, and skilled leader in Oregon's suffrage campaigns, even if her loyal defense of Duniway distanced her from many of the national suffrage leaders. At the same time, the campaign experiences benefited her directly by exposing her to the local and national political landscape and introducing her to many of the most influential women of her day.[35]

The suffrage vote was critical for Oregon women in 1912, but the presidential contest that year became the "election that changed the country." The body politic roiled with the conflict between reformist fervor and business prerogatives. Labor strife, fear of immigrants, rampant industrialism, and a push for a radical restructuring of American life split the political parties and pitted reformists, radicals, and conservatives against each other.[36]

Eugene Debs, leader of the Socialist Party, proposed radical change by upending government and industry. He wanted to limit all three branches of government and guarantee collective ownership of corporations, banks, and real estate. He supported vastly improved labor conditions and explicitly endorsed full woman suffrage. Former president Teddy Roosevelt led the new Progressive Party and promised to regulate big business, establish a minimum wage, end child labor, and create a safety net of health insurance for the unemployed and elderly. The incumbent, William Howard Taft, dutifully remained at the top of the Republican Party ticket but with little interest in a second term. He warned that Socialists and Progressives were extremists and offered instead solid conservative leadership to keep the status quo. The Democratic candidate, Woodrow Wilson, urged moderate reform along with a promise to destroy business monopolies. He espoused social justice for the states to enact, not the federal government, and he voiced no support for African Americans or for women wanting a federal suffrage amendment.[37]

Wilson won the presidency with nearly 42 percent of the vote while Roosevelt took second place with 27 percent. Oregon sided with Wilson but gave Debs more than 10 percent of its vote, a significant show of yearning for fundamental change. Progressive women in the state, like Equi, had to wait another four years to vote in their first presidential election, but by then the onset of World War I in Europe commanded much of the nation's political attention.[38]

Portlanders might have hoped for a respite at the close of an intense political campaign year, but just three days after the 1912 election the arrest of a nineteen-year-old man triggered an explosive sex scandal in the city. Frightened during his questioning by the police, Benjamin Trout revealed the existence of a robust, sexually active homosexual underworld in the city. He described an extensive web of white, middle-class men who met in Portland's downtown district, especially Washington Street, one of the busiest commercial corridors, and in the males-only Lownsdale Park, and then arranged to have sex in nearby hotels, office buildings, or residences. A week after the young man spoke with the police, the *Portland News*, a working-class daily with a penchant for sensationalism, broke the story on its front page with a scare headline, "Rotten Scandal Reaches into the YMCA." The report described a raid conducted earlier in the day at the downtown YMCA that led to the arrest of twenty-five men for sexual activity, or, in the words of the *News*, "more than a score of 'men,' nice charitable, boy-loving men, were hauled before the juvenile court on charges of indecent and degenerate conduct." The disclosures rocked the city for days, and civic leaders grappled with a perceived threat to the city's youth, its institutions, and its closely tended reputation.[39]

With the scandal blown open by the *News*, Portland's mainstream dailies reported an increasing number of arrests—said to be more than fifty—that included well-known professionals, including two Marie Equi knew well. No right-to-privacy laws existed to shield consenting adults in their sexual conduct, and the men, whose names were revealed, could expect to be charged under the state's antisodomy law.[40]

Portlanders were accustomed to occasional newspaper reports of alleg-edly immoral activity among itinerant, foreign-born, working-class men—the denizens of the city's North End "vice district" —or to flamboyant, Old World celebrities like Oscar Wilde. But the 1912 same-sex scandal exploded pre-sumptions that homosexual practices were confined to those that society kept at a distance. Once the earnest and fastidious attorney Edward S. J. McAllister and the respectable physician Harry Start were implicated in the "vice clique scandal," as it became known, Portlanders and people throughout the Pacific Northwest were forced to acknowledge the presence of a white, middle-class, same-sex subculture in its midst.[41]

Edward Stonewall Jackson McAllister, age forty-five, was a promising, politically ambitious attorney who supported a raft of direct democracy initia-tives, including woman suffrage. He spoke frequently at suffrage events and was considered a major asset to the feminist campaign. But his rising star in Portland politics plummeted once he was charged with committing a "crime against nature" with a thirty-year-old man in his law office situated on Wash-ington Street. He was convicted and sentenced to one to five years in prison.[42]

Harry Start, a forty-three-year-old physician, resembled the scholarly, just-elected President Wilson. He had studied at the University of Oregon Medical School and had overlapped two years there with Equi. He graduated in 1905 and then studied further in Dublin, Ireland. He married, returned to Portland in 1910, and established his practice at the Medical Building, the same location as Equi's office. Start was also charged and convicted for having engaged in sex with a young man at his office. He eventually lost his medical license and left the country to work in the Philippines for several years before resettling in San Francisco.[43]

A review of trial testimony and later research by scholars revealed many fallacies advanced by the dailies, especially the *Portland News*. Al-though sexual trysts occurred in the YMCA building, it was just one of several favored spots for men seeking sex with men. The vice clique did not involve boys, although one was eighteen years of age and another was nineteen. And most of the accused men held midlevel positions—book-keepers, clerks, a florist, a salesman, co-owners of a restaurant—and did not represent Portland's elite. Yet the media frenzy and the anxious public reaction about the matter prompted further criminalization and punish-ment of men who engaged in same-sex affairs. In 1913 the state legislature amended Oregon's sodomy law to include "any act or practice of sexual perversity"—thus prohibiting oral sex as well as anal sex. It also tripled the maximum sentence for sodomy to fifteen years.[44]

Although the vice clique scandal did not involve women directly or implicate women in lesbian relationships, Equi and her circle were familiar with some of the men involved, and they had to deal with new public awareness of same-sex intimate relations in the city. They might consider their own interests distant from the activities of gay men, but they could not ignore that the fundamental issue involved same-sex attraction and its perceived threat to society. Equi was attuned to the different sexual and gender subcultures in Portland, given her personal and professional relationships. As a doctor she was comfortable, for example, with advising a transgender patient and presenting to the medical society her treatment of gonorrhea in the throat of a male patient. Yet the vice-clique affair had to have had a chilling effect on Equi and her circle, and it brought a thudding close to her period of relative calm and balance, one that she would not experience again.[45]

9
Soapbox to Jail Cell

Dr. Marie Equi, one of the brainiest women in the state . . . no woman in
Portland is closer to the women wage workers than Dr. Equi.
E. Hofer, president, Oregon State Editorial Association

For all its reputation as an engine of Progressive reform, Oregon also harbored radical sentiment among all classes during the early decades of the twentieth century. The city's sixty labor unions included five that were socialist and two that were aligned with the Industrial Workers of the World (IWW), a *One Big Union* founded in 1905 to place the means of production in the hands of all the workers together. Portland's mainstream activists sometimes protested the negative impacts of the industrialized economy, but radicals in the thick of frontline strife dismissed them as "parlor radicals" who operated from a comfortable remove. Critics may have lumped Marie Equi with this crowd in her early Progressive years, but the time came when she abandoned the parlor for the streets.[1]

Equi was no stranger to radical talk and protests. She kept company, for example, with C. E. S. Wood, the celebrated local attorney and poet, who espoused "absolute personal freedom" and nonviolent anarchism within a framework of "Philosophical Radicalism." In the years ahead, Wood defended Equi repeatedly in the courts for her political acts. Few who worked and lived in downtown Portland, as Equi did, would have missed the street riot that erupted during a December 1906 strike by trolley car workers. A few months later, the IWW first appeared on Portland streets three thousand strong to protest the trial of an IWW leader charged in the killing of a former Idaho governor. Wobblies, as IWW members were known, staged their first walkout in the Pacific Northwest the next month at lumber mills along Portland's waterfront. And in 1909 more than three thousand Portlanders—a mix of Socialists and union members—marched to protest labor conditions prevailing on the East Coast. Amid the organizing and protests, Equi initially resisted the pull of the far-left and kept her focus on Progressive reform.[2]

In the early morning drizzle of February 15, 1913, Equi waited outside the new south wing of the Multnomah County Courthouse in downtown Portland to be among the first women to register to vote. Dr. Mary Anna Cooke Thompson, age eighty-eight, Oregon's first woman physician, a longtime suffrage leader who also pushed for economic rights for women, held the honor of first in line. When it was Equi's turn, she declared herself a member of the Progressive Party, one of only nine women to do so that day. Two months later she stood witness as an eighty-four-year-old former slave, Mrs. Nanine Jones, with a scarf and shawl keeping her warm, registered for the first time. In a poignant gathering of her family, Jones sat at home on her front porch with her daughter, granddaughter, and two great-grandsons. A registration book lay open before them, and all three women signed their names and registered as Progressives. Equi stood behind them, solemn and dignified but with a slight smile.[3]

Equi joined the Progressive Party at her earliest opportunity, but fervor for the party had peaked with the 1912 election. Teddy Roosevelt had lost his bid for a return to the White House, and newly elected President Woodrow Wilson began pushing his own Progressive agenda. He backed the action by two-thirds of the states that started to regulate child labor more closely and to provide a degree of workers' compensation. Nine states limited work hours for women, and ten declared a minimum wage for them. The Democratic push for reforms diluted the need for a separate Progressive Party, some believed, and interest faded steadily over the next two years. Yet Equi served on the executive committee of Oregon's Progressive Party, working with the relatively few women members.[4]

In 1913 Portlanders endorsed yet another round of civic tinkering and created a new position—superintendent of a proposed woman's detention center—that piqued Equi's interest. The voters hoped to stop the revolving doors of vice control that simply processed women arrested for prostitution before shuffling them back to the streets after they paid a small fine. Under the new regimen, women would serve sentences of two years at the facility where they would develop job skills. Up to 175 women would be housed at the compound located outside the city, and the superintendent would receive an annual salary of $1,500.[5]

Equi's pursuit of the position suggests an eagerness to contribute to public health and social justice in an arena larger than her medical practice, and she encouraged her friends and allies to lobby the mayor-elect, H. Russell Albee, on her behalf. The Portland Card and Label League, a women's labor organization, wrote the mayor that Equi was "particularly fitted" to deal with unfortunate women in the city, and the Garment Workers Union noted her previous "moral uplift work." The president of the Oregon State Editorial Association recommended Equi as "one of the brainiest women in the state," and, he declared, "No woman in Portland is closer to the women wage workers." He added that Equi had been "one of the best reform workers during the past session of the legislature." Writing on NAWSA stationery, Charlotte Anita Whitney referred to Equi's "constructive ability" and her understanding of the plight of the unfortunate girls and women who get in trouble. The lobbying came to naught, however, as plans to build the facility and hire staff floundered for another five years.[6]

While Equi sought the city job, she also tried to place an important ballot measure before Oregon voters. She served as president of the Eight-Hour League of Portland, and in June 1913 she submitted a draft law to Oregon's secretary of state and then rallied support to place it on the upcoming ballot. She might have succeeded, but the state supreme court removed the measure due to laws for special elections.[7]

The eight-hour campaign on behalf of women was a classic Progressive Era concern—seeking protection for women as a separate class of workers rather than demanding justice and equity for both men and women across the board. Critics argued that a similar measure—the US Supreme Court's *Muller v. Oregon* ruling that upheld Oregon's ten-hour workday for women—established women as a vulnerable class requiring special government protection and ran counter to the long push for parity in the workplace. On this occasion, Equi opted for incremental change by first covering women and children. Oregonians, however, rejected the eight-hour initiative in November 1914 as well as a constitutional amendment for eight-hour workdays covering both men and women.[8]

Equi never allowed her more mainstream views to keep her from confrontation. In one incident reported in the dailies, she repeatedly challenged Dr. Clarence True Wilson, a prominent antisuffragist lecturer from Kansas who assailed feminists as mannish women and womanish men. He claimed such individuals were "hated far and wide." Two days later, a patrolman ordered Equi away from a downtown Portland street corner after an altercation with soldiers from the nearby US Army barracks. According to the *Oregon Daily Journal*, Equi had become "so radical in her remarks" during a socialist discourse that the officer told her to move to another corner. Not ready to stand down, Equi allegedly threatened to report the officer to the police chief, but no charges were filed. The account was the first published account to link her with radicalism.[9]

At first Equi was no different from most other Portlanders in late June 1913: all she knew about the strike at a fruit-processing cannery on the working-class eastside was what she read in the papers. Not until one of her patients who worked at the plant asked for medical care did she pay more attention. That night she made a house call in the area of East Eighth and Belmont streets and then stopped and watched the women picketing outside the Oregon Packing Company. Some of them she recognized as former patients. They called out to her to help them, and Equi mounted their tar barrel and urged the women still working to join the walkout. With that simple act, she altered the course of her life.[10]

The strikers told Equi they could tolerate no more. They had no control over their schedules as the managers adjusted shift hours to fit the fluctuating crop yields and deliveries. They struggled to arrange childcare, much less pay for it. Making matters worse, every day they endured filthy working conditions. Finally, on June 27, 1913, forty women refused to stem and sort cherries for five to eight cents an hour. The plant foreman dismissed a pay increase out of hand, and the walkout began. In the days ahead, more than two hundred women abandoned their stations in one of the Pacific Northwest's first strikes by women workers. They were unorganized, and, like most female laborers in Oregon, they had no union representation.[11]

Looking for allies and support, the strikers sought help from the local Socialist Party and, later, from labor unions. Tom Burns, a well-known Portland radical aligned with the Socialists and later the IWW, started a strike fund for them and helped organize a strike committee. Members of the IWW joined the dispute as well. The entry into the women's strike by the Socialists, Burns, and the Wobblies signaled the start of a more complicated and politically charged affair. Wobblies supported the strikers, but they also advanced their own agenda to increase their presence in the city. To do so they transformed the women's protest into Portland's first free-speech fight.[12]

Complaints about low wages and occupational hazards were precisely what Oregon's Industrial Welfare Commission was meant to address by a recent mandate of the voters. The women had reason to hope their voices might be heard. That spring the Oregon legislature had passed the nation's first compulsory minimum wage law for women. A delegation of cannery strikers pressed their case before the commission only to have the Catholic priest and chair of the group, Reverend Edwin O'Hara, urge them to retreat. He agreed to help as long as the women stopped picketing and "leave it to us." O'Hare's advice typified the Progressive desire for reform as well as control and the strategy to undermine radical proposals with more amenable compromises. The women rejected out-of-hand O'Hare's suggested ninety-day wait for a decision. By then, they shouted, they would lose the strike. The commission negotiated a one-dollar-a-day minimum wage and better working conditions, figuring an immediate improvement was better than protracted negotiations that might outrun the cannery season. But the women objected to not being consulted, and, besides, they wanted nothing less than a dollar and fifty cents per day.[13]

Next, the women on walkout lobbied Mayor Albee, but he offered little assistance. Instead, he insisted that no one resort to "indecent, vile or unreasonably abusive language," a particularly sore point for him. Within days, police made the first arrests with charges of disorderly conduct and abusive language against Mary Schwab of the Socialist Labor Party and her husband, Rudolph, a Wobbly organizer. Along with Tom Burns, the Schwabs emerged as the early leaders of the strike while Equi joined the picket lines. The next evening the IWW demonstrated on the streets of downtown Portland, bringing the conflict to the westside.[14]

Just as Mayor Albee struggled to establish his authority over the conflict, Oregon's Governor, Oswald West, intervened and persuaded the picketers to stop their protest until they met with him the next morning at city hall. Demonstrators, sympathizers, and the curious pressed into the council chamber Saturday morning. Tom Burns claimed the spotlight early on with a denunciation of the Industrial Welfare Commission's intervention. Governor West took offense and mounted the council table to shout a rebuttal. He had invested political capital into the success of the commission, and he would not tolerate having it maligned. Reverend O'Hara also complained. "I have preached that it is right to strike," he told Burns. O'Hara had done more than that. Along with social worker Caroline Gleason, he had crafted protective legislation ensuring minimum wages and better working conditions statewide and had taken the proposal to every town in Oregon.[15]

In this hothouse setting, Equi thrust herself into the center of attention. She stood on a chair and proclaimed her readiness to "shed her blood" on the picket line. She rolled up her sleeve to expose the large bruise from a policeman's club during an earlier street tussle. The newspapers latched onto Equi as the occasion's dramatic figure with her passionate, theatrical defense of the women. Thereafter she became the public face of the strike. She may have been grandstanding before the governor or she may have let her passion take control, but there is no indication she maneuvered to become the primary spokesperson. She was better known than Burns and the Schwabs, however, and she also carried the status of her profession. According to the *Portland News*, hundreds of people paid attention to the dispute once Equi mounted the soapbox. The *New York Times*, the *Washington Post*, and two San Francisco dailies followed suit and declared Equi the strike leader.[16]

Nothing much came from the governor's cramped, noisy five-hour conference. He advised the strikers to stay away from the plant and to wait ninety days for resolution. Mary Schwab and the picketers responded with a resounding "No." More than one hundred returned to the cannery and took up their pickets. Late that Friday afternoon, mounted officers charged the strikers, knocking several aside and injuring a few. That night Socialists and Wobblies reclaimed the downtown corner of Sixth and Washington.[17]

With street protests staged every night, the edgy tension and resentments between the deputies and the strikers festered. Three days after the meeting with the governor, the deputies arrested a string of strikers. First, Tom Burns was pulled from the soapbox. The highly critical dailies claimed he had predicted that the "red flag of anarchy" would soon fly over the courthouse. Then, Rudolph Schwab and eight others were picked off one by one from the box all on the charge of using profane language. One of the speakers dragged away was Agnes O'Connor, a thirty-year-old pregnant Native American. Equi witnessed the arrest and erupted in rage. "All the fighting Irish blood and the fighting Italian blood rose in my heart," she later told a reporter. Whatever blows Equi may have landed, the officers clubbed her with enough force to leave bruises. In full fury, Equi rallied the crowd to follow the police to the station—with O'Connor under arrest—and demand the release of all the strikers. Newspapers reported that Equi punched two officers in the face during a struggle at the jail and "opened her batteries of vituperation" on the sheriff and his deputies. The sheriff relented and released O'Connor but detained the others.[18]

Two nights later, Equi and other women strikers attempted a protest at Sixth and Washington, a downtown intersection the Mayor told strikers to avoid. Equi said later that she tried to discourage the women from protesting that night, but when they insisted, she joined them. The day had steamed at ninety-four degrees, and more than three thousand people crowded on the street and sidewalks to hear the women. Before Equi or anyone else could start, a massive show of force disrupted the gathering. A solid line of patrolmen

WOMEN ARRESTED FOR RIOTING ON STREET, PATROLMAN WHO WAS STABBED WITH HATPIN

Belle Goldish, Pauline Tooley, Marie Equi, and Mrs. Mary Schwab (left to right) were arrested for strike activity at a Portland cannery. *Oregon Daily Journal*, July 19, 1913.

cleared Sixth Street even while squads of officers some distance down the block pushed people back into the street. The situation worsened rapidly when police cavalry charged the street. Horses bucked and kicked, knocking people down. For thirty minutes police marched back and forth, clearing people away and clubbing dozens. Eighteen were arrested, including Equi, Mary Schwab, Agnes O'Connor, and two teenage girls. The county sheriff himself arrested Equi, who was holding a length of pipe used to assemble the speakers' platform. (The authorities described the pipe as a weapon.) She cursed him loudly and later recalled, "They threatened to split our heads open."[19]

On the way to the jail Equi stabbed a patrolman with a hatpin, according to one newspaper report. She had previously threatened to kill anyone who tried to keep her from speaking with a virus-dipped pin that would cause a "slow, lingering death." In her mind, it was a matter of free speech and not being told what she couldn't do. The officer cauterized his wound immediately and suffered no greater damage. Thereafter, the sensational hatpin assault—accurate or not—enhanced Equi's reputation, with even the *New York Times* describing the incident.[20]

The Portland police seldom dealt with a woman like Equi, who yelled, cursed, fought, kicked, threatened officers' lives, and refused to back down. Obstreperous women had certainly resisted arrest before, but few, if any, held Equi's professional status, standing in the community, and commitment to a cause. She faced criminal charges for disorderly conduct, inciting a riot, carrying concealed weapons, and assault with a dangerous weapon. Bail was set at $550, and the authorities threatened her with imprisonment or confinement in a mental institution. The *Oregonian* had already described her as "danger-ously insane," and the authorities assumed the right to subject her to a medical review to determine her sanity. Women considered unruly were routinely con-sidered quite "mad," as American suffragists later found when they undertook civil disobedience.[21]

Equi advanced her own explanation for why authorities tossed the in-sanity charge her way. "It was beyond the imagination of these people, who repeatedly attacked me, that a professional woman of established practice and reputation, of some money and high standing in the community could put these aside and get out and work for her unfortunate sisters and brothers—therefore I must be insane."[22]

Equi also charged that the police subjected her to rough, third-degree treatment at the jail. "What I underwent I cannot tell you. I am too much of a woman to want to go into the detail of it. . . . Three hours of torture, during which my womanhood revolted, and every now and then they asked if I would now go to California. Then they took me to a woman's cell and threw me in." The interrogation by officers and the curtailment of her free speech jolted Equi far more than she expected. At the police station she declared, "I started in this fight a Socialist but now I am an anarchist. I'm going to speak where and when I wish. No man will stop me." For her, a line had been crossed. Her rights as a citizen had been trampled, and her fierce independence had been threatened. She had lost faith in political reform, labor improvements, and the authority of the state.[23]

The next day Harriet Speckart tried to secure her companion's release with the help of a few friends. The police issued an ultimatum: keep Equi out of the state or expect her to be committed to an asylum. The group made plans for Equi to depart by midnight. Speckart purchased a rail ticket and drove Equi to Union Depot, but apparently no one had apprised Equi of the plan. When they finally did, she adamantly opposed the scheme. "It is principle with me—my duty," she told a reporter afterwards, "and don't ever believe that I will desert by taking a train to another state." To another, she said, "Honestly, now, did anyone imagine for a moment that I was a quitter? I'm here to see this thing through and I won't run." With that, Equi was returned to jail.[24]

The *Oregon Daily Journal* featured a front-page, three-photo spread the evening of her arrest with the three other women. In one photo, Equi assumed a stern, resolved stance, wearing a full suit like a coat of armor. A tough-looking Mary Schwab stood with her hands firmly on her hips. During a jail interview, Equi stated her case. "These girls want a living wage that is all. I want to help them and if I have to go to jail and stay there, it is all in the game." She denied stabbing the patrolmen and brushed aside her threat to use a deadly virus as something said in anger but never seriously considered. She also reflected on the consequences of her outbursts. "I lose my temper occasionally, and I do and say things which I wouldn't if I kept cool. But official brutality always did provoke me and when I'm mad—say, then is when they think I'm crazy."[25]

After three days in jail, Equi was released on bail. Charlotte Anita Whitney, her California suffragist ally, had intervened to free her early. Outside the jail, Equi's friends noticed bruises all over her body and complained to the police that she had been cuffed and mistreated. Equi admitted to being a "nervous wreck," and the psychological impact haunted her for years. Two months later her case was continued indefinitely and was never brought to trial. Equi believed the authorities dropped the matter to avoid her testimony about the rough handling she had received.[26]

The arrests and incarcerations of Equi and the other leaders broke the back of the strike. The Oregon Packing Company had already replaced the picketers with new hires, and the canning season was near its end. For the strikers, the walkout was a bust. Although the Industrial Welfare Commission obtained an increase in wages for the workers who remained on the job, the dollar-per-hour settlement was much less than the living wage the picketers wanted. The women never returned to work that season. The Socialists and Wobblies failed to empower the women, and the State Federation of Labor avoided trying to organize them for future labor action.[27]

The strike was not without impact, however. The women picketers grabbed the attention of Portlanders more accustomed to seeing men fight for better jobs. The repression of free speech prompted the American Federation of Labor to petition for a recall of Mayor Albee, and other community leaders threatened retaliation if free speech rights were not upheld. The federation's demands prevailed, and the mayor relented. The protest also exposed the Industrial Welfare Commission's limited, protective approach, and it broadened the rift between mainstream Progressives and Wobblies. Finally, Portlanders were introduced to the battle for free speech that would intensify as World War I drew near.[28]

Equi's strike involvement marked a watershed for her. It set her on a political trajectory from women's rights and other Progressive causes to the class struggle for economic equity and social justice. Her decision to join the picketers, mount the soapboxes, and risk jail and physical abuse demonstrated how much she differed from other Progressives who kept their distance from street protests. She had backed the strikers' full demands without urging a compromise, and she demonstrated a clear understanding and compassion for the plight of the picketers. The experience motivated, or forced, her to adopt a new political framework, Radical Socialism, and to leave much of Progressivism behind.

The quality of Equi's relationship with Speckart during this period of radicalization is mostly unknown, but the external political demands and Equi's relationship with Elizabeth Gardiner probably created strains for them both. In 1912, Equi and Speckart had relocated from the Nortonia Hotel to a quieter residence at the South Parkhurst Apartments, still on Portland's westside, but removed from the downtown hub. After the brawl at the Medical Building in 1912, Equi moved her offices again—this time to the nearby Central Building at Tenth and Alder Streets. In 1913, the city directory indicates that Elizabeth Gardiner resided at the same location.[29]

For many Americans, Wobblies had become a rowdy, dangerous threat to the country's economic and social order, and most newspapers stoked their fears. To its credit, the *Oregon Daily Journal* reprinted an impartial analysis of the IWW by Arno Dosch, a rising journalist from Oregon. Dosch described the Wobblies as more of a revolution than an organization. He quoted William "Big Bill" Haywood, an IWW founder, who explained, "We divide all the world into three parts: the capitalists, who are the employing class and make money from money, the skilled laborers, and the masses. The IWW represents the masses." Wobblies believed, he said, that once enough workers refused to endure their harsh working conditions, a general strike would paralyze capitalists' ventures and lead to control of industry by the masses. Dosch referred to a study for the US Steel Corporation that found employers could avoid the disruption of Wobbly action if they improved workers' conditions and provided a living wage. He concluded, "The IWW has an ability to organize discontent; where there is no serious discontent, it cannot operate." Few industrial titans accepted Dosch's prescription for peace between laborers and management, and the general public appeared to distrust all proponents of radical change.[30]

While the cannery strike troubled Portlanders during the summer of 1913, the nation slid into a recession. The downturn forced business activity into a 26 percent decline. Laid-off workers slept in doorways, huddled in breadlines, and begged food for their children. In Oregon and Washington the timber industry closed 40 percent of its mills and laid off a third of its labor force. Unemployment hovered at just over 4 percent, but nearly doubled the following year. In the autumn of 1913, several thousand jobless men migrated to Portland, hoping to fend off the cold and wet of the rainy season. They lined up outside the Salvation Army and the Men's Resort, but their numbers overwhelmed the services. The city hired several hundred men to work in Laurelhurst and Mount Tabor Parks and to round-out street corners, but the authorities screened applicants for "worthiness." They feared Portland might become a magnet for jobless men throughout the West, so they gave priority to local married men. All the rest were left to loiter on the streets and in the parks, frustrated and resentful at being shut out. In late December they adopted the Wobbly tactic of entering, or rushing, restaurants, ordering meals, and putting bills on the mayor's tab. In most cases, the police arrived and arrested the men or forced them outdoors.[31]

The mainstream press inflamed the discontent with the unemployed on the streets by stereotyping them as an "Idle Army" of freeloaders and trouble-makers. A Reed College study at the time found the majority of the men were just the opposite. Most were in their twenties and thirties and in the prime of their working lives. They had been out of work for several months and had spent their savings on living expenses and not on drink or debauchery, as often charged. Many of the jobless had belonged to a union, but only a small number were Wobblies.[32]

Equi strode into the unemployment crisis of 1913 determined to help right a wrong, and her efforts earned her another confrontation in the courts. She viewed unemployment as the result of the region's economic structure that treated workers as cogs in the industrial machine. The jobless did suffer from an overproduction of timber that drew vast numbers of men skilled at cutting lumber, but, with labor easy to obtain, employers felt no compunction to provide living wages or to offer jobs during the off-season. Equi assessed the situation and urged unemployed men and women to demand the jobs, food, lodging, and services they needed. On one occasion the men paraded through the streets of Portland to make their case, and this time the police did not intervene. "The sight of thousands of hungry, desperate men is not an inspiring one to the police," Equi told a reporter. As cold weather approached in the fall, Equi urged the city to open a public hall, the long-empty Gipsy Smith Tabernacle, in the North End as free lodging for the jobless.[33]

While many Portlanders spent the day before Christmas in 1913 prepar-ing for the holiday, Equi learned that unemployed men arrested for demand-ing food and lodging were being relegated to the rock pile. She rushed to the courthouse, where she found the judge mumbling the sentences. When she asked him three times to speak louder, he gave her a five-day fine for contempt of court. She tried to shame him with news that the old man he had sentenced the day before had died after only a few hours' busting rocks. For her impertinence, the judge increased her jail time. She refused to post the bail offered by her supporters.[34]

Equi spent a few hours in jail before the judge offered to release her if she apologized. She declined. The Christmas Eve standoff was resolved only when hundreds of men—"her army," the newspapers reported—packed the courtroom and hallways with a low, grumbling protest over the holding of the woman who had stood up for them. The judge relented and freed Equi. Although the dailies reported that Equi had apologized first, Helen Lawrence Walters, a Bohemian artist and socialist familiar with the incident, advised in her journal, "Don't believe it."[35]

Arresting jobless men for vagrancy effectively criminalized unemployment. In the Christmas Eve incident, none of the arrested men were released and the heavy sentences probably did not change, but the threat of the unemployed forced authorities to look beyond the rock piles. After the holidays, the city opened the Gipsy Tabernacle and provided shelter for nine hundred men. Another fifteen hundred were fed at the hall. The men managed the operation themselves in a smooth, efficient manner without trouble. The city forced the hundreds of others still without shelter to seek it out of town. Bands of the younger men started walking south on the highway and back roads in the cold, wet winter with damp clothes and empty stomachs, hoping small Willamette Valley towns would welcome them. They started out hopeful, singing Wobbly songs, and talking with people they met, but they found few jobs and, at best, overnight lodging before being forced on their way. At one point, they appealed to Equi by phone and asked her to intercede on their behalf. She advised them to end their march, but most continued before eventually returning to Portland or dispersing to other towns.[36]

The problem of joblessness continued to vex Oregon's leaders and advocates alike. In early February 1914, the State Federation of Labor gathered many of them together to define the issue and draft legislation. Equi joined Governor West, representatives from the Progressive Party, the State Grange, and the Unemployed League to debate strategies at the Central Library. Equi's involvement suggests that civic leaders respected, or tolerated, her involvement even after the uproar with the cannery strike. The meeting, however, came to a dismal end with a limp resolution to create a task force for further study.[37]

Ten days after the state meeting on joblessness, Equi attended the First National Conference on Unemployment in New York. As an official representative of Portland's Unemployed League, she joined six hundred delegates from across the country. Among the mayors, union leaders, and state labor commissioners, Equi held her own and delivered a blunt address unlike any other heard at the gathering. In her report of local conditions, she accused Portland authorities of dealing with thousands of jobless men by driving them out of town with "a wooden club." She blamed state Republicans for blocking relief bills proposed by Oregon's Democratic governor, and she castigated the newspapers for covering up the actual number of unemployed to avoid tarnishing Portland's boomtown reputation.[38]

In her talk Equi heralded the IWW as "the muckrakers of the world," unafraid to expose injustice when authorities were too timid to do so. She might have stopped there, but she did not. "I want to say right here that I am a radical Socialist," she said, and then added, "I think your hope will come from the West, because we will shorten the workday long before you will, and we will emancipate you." The delegates took her remarks seriously. Resolutions from the conference were practical and substantial, including unemployment insurance, vocational training, labor information bureaus, and improved labor statistics.[39]

Before leaving Portland for the conference, Equi had told the *Oregonian* she expected a busy trip of three to four months that would include postgraduate work at Massachusetts General Hospital with Richard Cabot, MD, the pioneer who established the nation's first in-hospital social services department. She also expected to boost the woman suffrage campaign in Massachusetts and push for child labor legislation in Pennsylvania. Little is known about those endeavors, but her family visit to New Bedford and her work with the unemployed in Boston were reported in local newspapers. The *New Bedford Standard* described Equi's role in Portland's cannery strike the year before. In the article, John Equi, Marie's father, advised that his daughter was "inclined to be overly enthusiastic about anything upon which she set her mind." Equi's enthusiasm for radical change seemed to beguile the newspaper's staff, and the editor devoted several columns to "the little fighting doctor" who staged a "one-woman fight . . . for the unemployed of Oregon and won."[40]

In an interview during this visit, Equi traced her journey from being an avowed Progressive to a radical socialist. She explained that as a professional worker, she was not eligible to join the IWW, but she admired Wobblies for being outspoken and willing to demand radical change and engage in confrontation. She said she had joined the Intercollegiate Socialist Society, a national group that recruited college students to the socialist cause. She favored a new economic order without bloodshed or revolution, she said, but she believed direct action, "in other words, militancy," was the only way to achieve better conditions for all. Paradoxically, she affirmed her support of President Wilson and the Democrats, more than any other political party, for their sound views and promise of real progress.[41]

Equi made her political passions clear. "How many wrecks do you see on every hand, men and women who have been broken on the industrial wheel of life?" she asked. "To my mind the liquor evil, the social evil, unemployment, and all the great social and economic problems that confront us are merely symptoms of the greater evil of capitalism." She thought the only way to avoid a bloody revolution was to undertake a complete change in the status quo. Foremost, she said, was the protection of free speech "which we certainly have not, no matter how much this is claimed."[42]

A few days later in a *Boston Globe* feature titled "Predicts Revolution Unless Aid Is Given to 5,000,000 Unemployed," Equi warned that men and women forced to the point of starvation by the current system had nothing to lose. "Very soon," she warned, "we shall be forced by them to take the consequences." She blamed the press for hiding the extent of the unemployed problem in the country. "I know my figures," she said. She ridiculed Portland's health officer for "frivoling over things like sex hygiene" in speeches to comfortable clubwomen. "It remained for a frayed, tattered, homeless man of the IWW to get on a soapbox and pound it into the minds of the people of Portland what terrible conditions existed in the canneries, though he knew he would go from soapbox to jail." When the reporter remarked that Equi was "noted" nationwide for her work for women and industrial conditions, Equi quipped, "Noted in the country, perhaps, but *notorious* in Oregon."[43]

During her Boston visit Equi spoke on the Common to a gathering of homeless men about the condition of Portland's unemployed. She shared the soapbox with Morrison Swift, a reformer, socialist, and writer committed to social justice who was known to have led every major protest by Boston's unemployed for the last twenty years. After her talk, twenty-five men marched to the elite Algonquin Club nearby to demand help with their plight. Police turned them away.[44]

Although Equi readily defended the unemployed and the underpaid, she was not reticent to seek lodging among the wealthy. In the *Globe* article, she deflected any criticism for her stay at the elegant Copley-Plaza Hotel a few blocks from the Common, explaining that just because she tried to get jobs and living wages for others didn't mean she should avoid comfort for herself. "None of them expect that and it's not necessary." More to the point, Equi underscored what activists on the front lines must do to survive:

> You must be one of two things, anyway, if you are going to take up the fight of the unemployed in this country. You must either have no money at all, so that nothing matters, or you must have enough to get you out of trouble when you are in it—and you are continually if you fight for the underdog. [45]

Returning to New York, Equi consulted with specialists about the nervous disorders she developed after the rough treatment from Portland police. She had a restful stay in Brooklyn with James and Agnes Warbasse, close family friends who were also longtime advocates for social justice. During her visit, the *New York World* profiled her work for the unemployed. On the day the feature appeared, the paper headlined the fierce battle the night before at Union Square when hundreds of Wobblies gathered to protest economic inequality in the country. Mounted police and four hundred officers on foot stormed the men with "unmerciful clubbing," according to the paper.[46]

Back in Oregon in the spring of 1914, Equi found conditions little improved for Portland's idle army. On April 1, Mayor Albee ordered an end to the three months of free lodging and meals for jobless men at the Gipsy Smith Tabernacle, and the displaced men returned to the streets with no job prospects. For the first time, slum conditions took hold in troubled neighborhoods like the North End, and that winter the city opened two boardinghouses for a thousand of the unemployed. Based on newspaper reports, Portlanders may have believed Equi led or joined every conflict involving Wobblies or the unemployed. But one story about her, in December 1914, highlighted a less-contentious move. She organized a committee of women to rent a forty-seven unit rooming house in the North End to provide lodging for jobless men. [47]

While Americans worried about political and labor strife, class conflict, and a still-struggling economy, the dark clouds of war hovered over Europeans. In June 1914, a nineteen-year-old Yugoslav nationalist killed Archduke Franz Ferdinand of Austria, triggering mutual declarations of war across the continent and the start of World War I. Stories of massive, startling casualties soon flooded newspapers in the United States. A million Russian soldiers died during a German offensive while French and German soldiers hunkered down in trenches at the Western Front, creating what would become an iconic horror of the war. For a time, there appeared to be an upside for Americans as factory orders for material of all sorts boosted the economy. But, overall, Americans were anxious about the pull of war, suspecting that joining the hostilities would forever change the country.[48]

10
The Company of Women

Here I met a stormy petrel of the Northwest, Dr. Marie Equi.
Elizabeth Gurley Flynn, radical labor activist

By spring 1915 Marie Equi achieved prominence in Portland matched by few other women. She was intelligent, forthright, good humored, and provocative, but her willingness to risk injury to herself and damage to her career for the rights of others set her apart. Her soapbox advocacy for strikers and the jobless elevated her as a woman of compassion and consequence among socialists, anarchists, and Wobblies nationwide. Yet her new commitment to radicalism upset the balance between her political and personal lives, and her relationship with Harriet Speckart suffered the most.

Speckart was not known to have engaged in the battles for a new social and economic order so important to Equi. She worried about her companion and was protective of her, but she was a private, reserved woman more accustomed to avoiding the limelight, her family's legal dispute notwithstanding. When Equi remained bruised and battered in jail during the cannery strike, Speckart intervened and agreed to the desperate demands of the authorities to deport Equi from the state in order to secure her release. The arrangement would have been a major disruption of her own life, but she proceeded with the plan nevertheless. She told reporters at the time, however, that she was baffled by Equi's street scuffling, her picketing with Wobblies, and her rousing homeless men to rush restaurants for free meals. After a year of Equi's radical pursuits and public exposure, Speckart had reason to question their future together.

Speckart's uneasiness peaked on March 18, 1915, when she married James F. Morgan, a forty-three-year-old mining engineer. Her reasons for getting married—and to Morgan in particular—remain a mystery. She already enjoyed financial security with her inheritance, and, if she objected to Equi's radicalism, Morgan was an odd choice. He was a seasoned Wobbly soapboxer himself, known for his cast-iron voice and fire-eating oratory. He had already led strikes and free speech fights on the West Coast, including a walkout near

Eugene, Oregon, and another in Salt Lake City that landed him in jail for sixty days. Only six weeks before marrying Speckart, Morgan joined a protest in Roseburg, Oregon.[1]

If Equi noticed Speckart's discontent, she did not temper her political work. The day before Speckart's nuptials, Equi led one hundred jobless men into Portland's courthouse to see how justice was delivered in the case of Mrs. Marcella Clark, a suffragist and friend of Equi's. Clark protested the divorce obtained by her husband, A. E. Clark, a former Progressive Party candidate for the US Senate from Oregon. The court was about to decide the basis of Clark's complaints and whether she was of sound mind. The *Oregonian* had weighed in earlier with a query, "Are all militant suffragists insane?" Equi sat quietly in the courtroom with "her boys," as she sometimes called the local Wobblies, while Clark was indeed found insane and placed in the care of a friend of her choosing.[2]

Speckart's union with Morgan ended abruptly after eleven days without the couple ever living together. On March 29, she sought a divorce on the grounds that Morgan had verbally abused her, threatened her with battery, and was afflicted with "a chronic and incurable sexual disease." She won the divorce and was awarded alimony of twenty dollars a month. Julia Ruuttila, a labor activist who was a girl at the time, remembered that Morgan appeared at her parents' home complaining bitterly that "a damn lesbian" had stolen his wife. But Morgan found no sympathy in the household. Equi's sexual orientation was well known in working-class and labor circles, and any misgivings over her personal life were far outweighed by appreciation for her generosity with free medical care. Ruuttila's father told her that anyone with any brains would avoid criticizing Doc.[3]

Speckart apparently wanted Equi's attention, but perhaps even more, she longed for a child. At the time, adoptions in Oregon often occurred informally before legal proceedings finalized the arrangements. A doctor sometimes acted as a go-between, matching women unable to care for a child and prospective parents seeking one. Equi facilitated the process frequently, according to one of her confidants, "She did an awful lot of placing children on her own without going through channels, but doctors did that then." Two weeks after Speckart's divorce, Equi adopted an infant girl with the assistance of a local judge.[4]

The child was born "Mary Everest" on March 15, 1915, at Portland's Multnomah Hospital to Edwin Elmer Everest, a laborer with no local residence, and Louise Vilandia Hanson, a waitress. Both were twenty-six years old. The attending physician who delivered the baby listed the birth as legitimate, but why the parents chose to place their child for adoption is unknown. Six weeks later, Equi completed the adoption procedures and registered a new name for the child: Mary Equi. The arrangement benefited all parties: the child was placed in a good home, Equi made her companion happy, and Speckart had a child to love and nurture. With her intervention, Equi achieved another distinction. She became a legally recognized unmarried mother known to be in a lesbian relationship.[5]

Equi and Speckart reached an understanding for childrearing that suited them both. Equi assumed responsibility as the legal parent and financial provider while Speckart promised to perform all hands-on childcare until Mary came of age. For a while the arrangement kept Equi and Speckart together, and Equi pursued her radical interests. As a child, Mary—who everyone called *Mary Junior*—referred to Equi as "Da" (for Doc, she later explained, since everyone called her that) and to Speckart as "Ma."[6]

By 1915 Equi had aligned herself with radical women activists who shared her belief in more fundamental political and economic change than what her Progressive colleagues endorsed. Her soapboxing during strikes and marching with the jobless enhanced her credentials in radical circles and introduced her to more experienced radicals, especially women. Prominent among them were Elizabeth Gurley Flynn, the IWW leader and organizer, and Emma Goldman, the anarchist reviled by much of America.

Few activists could claim as early an immersion in radical politics as Elizabeth Gurley Flynn. Her mother was a suffragist; her father, a Wobbly organizer. At the dinner table when she was a child in the early 1890s, her family discussed the work of Socialist leader Eugene Debs and the writings of Marx and Engels. The Flynns were poor, and times were hard for them in Manchester, New Hampshire, one of the dismal textile centers of the Northeast. The family later moved to New York and lived in "a cold-water, unheated, gas-lit flat" in the South Bronx, as she remembered it. Flynn was a high-spirited and headstrong girl, and she readily embraced the radical environment of her upbringing. At age sixteen, she delivered her first public talk—titled "What Socialism Will Do for Women"—before the Harlem Socialist Forum in January 1906, and the hearty response she received propelled her into a lifelong career of public speaking. The heady spirit of revolution and bohemianism coursed through New York's East Side denizens, and Flynn was readily drawn to the militant unionism of the IWW. She likened the radical organization to a "great comet across the horizon of the American labor movement." Flynn's appearance on the labor organizing circuit seemed equally bright to the mostly male IWW membership. She had dropped out of high school to become a full-time soapboxer, and in short order mesmerized her audiences with her passionate speech, flashing grey-blue eyes, and long black hair. Flynn brought passion and intensity to her talks, clenching her hands as she spoke and jabbing the air to make a point. Part of her immense appeal, even to more mainstream audiences, was her fresh and clearly "American" appearance that defied the stereotype of hardened immigrant radicals. The novelist Theodore Dreiser extolled Flynn as a "slender, serious girl" and described her in a magazine article as the "East Side Joan of Arc."[7]

At seventeen, Flynn joined Wobbly organizer and iron ore miner Jack Jones in the mining towns of the Mesabi Range in northeast Minnesota. In the subzero weather of January 1907, Flynn and Jones organized laborers at the great open-pit mines of the US Steel Corporation. Flushed with the thrill and adventure of radicalism, Flynn married Jones, became pregnant, and then lost the child in a miscarriage. But she did not slow down. She had become enthralled with travel, a wanderlust that held fast all her life. She joined IWW free speech fights—first in Missoula, Montana, and then, in the fall of 1909, in Spokane, Washington. Although she arrived in the Northwest fully pregnant again, Flynn was arrested and jailed on charges of conspiracy to incite a riot. Her account of the "orgy of police brutality" in Spokane was published and dispersed nationwide, gaining her further acclaim. But her impulsive marriage to Jones failed, and Flynn returned to her family in the Bronx where she gave birth to a son, Fred. In a move that typified her passions and priorities, she left her child with her mother and returned to the rails as a seasoned agitator.[8]

Through her associations with the anarchists and socialists of her late teens and early twenties, Flynn developed an eclectic but pragmatic philosophy that served her well. She believed that women had to achieve financial independence to function fully as human beings and citizens, but she recognized that too many women became trapped in low-wage, abusive jobs and felt forced to escape through marriage or, sometimes, prostitution. Flynn believed, as did Equi, that only radical economic change could free men and women, but Flynn launched herself as a radical agitator without a passage through liberal or Progressive work.[9]

By 1913 Equi's and Flynn's priorities were aligned. While Equi mounted soapboxes for cannery workers in Portland, Flynn helped organize the legendary Paterson, New Jersey, silk workers strike. Twenty-five thousand laborers from three hundred silk mills and dye houses had walked off the job to protest a steep hike in production quotas. Weavers and dyers picketed together in a collaboration that reflected the IWW's One Big Union with workers of different trades united to manage and govern workplaces. But the strike ultimately failed, the coalition of workers splintered, and several Wobbly organizers, including Flynn, were charged with inciting to riot. Her first trial ended in a hung jury, and New Jersey authorities held her indictment for more than two years hoping to keep her rabble-rousing out of the state.[10]

During the interim, Flynn embarked on a cross-country speaking tour. She visited Wobblies who already knew of her as the "Rebel Girl," the fearless young woman immortalized by IWW songwriter Joe Hill in a ballad of the same name. Flynn was passionate without being domineering or strident. She exhibited the clear-eyed enthusiasm of youth tempered with working-class values that inspired and gave hope to weary workers eager for change. In May 1915 Flynn stopped in San Francisco where she visited labor leader Tom Mooney and the suffragist and Socialist Charlotte Anita Whitney—Flynn described her as a "slender, beautiful" woman—who had befriended Equi. Flynn continued to Portland and later recalled first meeting Equi at Union Station: "Here I met a stormy petrel of the Northwest, Dr. Marie D. Equi, a successful woman doctor, who put me up at the swanky Hotel Multnomah. She entertained all the women speakers who passed through the City of Roses."

With their radical sentiments, working-class backgrounds, and strike experiences, the two women bonded readily. As girls, they had lived in northeastern textile cities with immigrant parents who struggled to feed their children. They learned of labor disputes at early ages, and they shared the fierce Irish resentment of oppression and determination to be free. But what especially connected Equi and Flynn was their intensity and steely commitment, their ease with working-class men and women, and their open-armed embrace of life. [11]

Fundamental differences separated the two as well, and these factors illustrate how two generations of women engaged the radicalism that swept the country during the late-nineteenth and early-twentieth centuries. Equi was eighteen years older than Flynn, and her childhood in the 1870s and 1880s coincided with the industrialization taking hold in northeastern cities. During her early years, Flynn, on the other hand, encountered a more thoroughly entrenched and formidable industrialism with its harsh effects readily apparent. In another contrast, Equi was forced to drop out of school and struggled to regain an academic toehold while Flynn abandoned her studies altogether and never looked back. For Equi, medicine became her base, her source of identity and security, but Flynn's natural abilities drew her to public speaking, labor organizing, and helping lead the organization that first inspired her. Flynn became much more of an organization woman who devoted her life to the IWW as long as it held together. But Equi's and Flynn's paths converged in the spring of 1915 when they met in Portland, and their relationship flourished into an alliance of mutual support.[12]

No woman in America was more notorious than Emma Goldman, and millions of people loathed and feared her. Newspapers, including the *Oregonian*, referred to her as "Queen of the Anarchists" and claimed she endangered America's democratic system. By 1915 Goldman had fought for radical causes for more than twenty years. She was punished with a year in prison for urging hungry, jobless people in New York to do anything necessary to get food and housing. With her reputation, Goldman traveled with a target on her back for authorities eager to stifle radical talk.[13]

Nearly every summer since 1906, Goldman had traveled to Portland and spoke of anarchism as a better way of life and governance, one without the harsh inequities of capitalism and industrialism. In 1908, she advised readers of the *Oregonian*, "Do not be alarmed, I have no dynamite in my pocket . . . education is the only bomb sanctioned by true anarchism, which stands for freedom in the truest and highest sense." Goldman presented a vision of people living and working collaboratively while sharing resources, yet, for most Americans, anarchism conjured chaos.[14]

Equi and Goldman might easily have met on several occasions given their radical interests, mutual acquaintances, and the frequency of Goldman's visits. The two women had much in common—they were close in age and both had worked in textile mills as girls and had taken nurse's training. Violent episodes had radicalized them—the cannery strike for Equi, the Haymarket Affair for Goldman—and both had done jail time for street protests. On a personal basis, each was passionate and quick tempered, intelligent, and sure of herself, although Goldman was more abrasive and flamboyant.[15]

Goldman treated women's health as both a personal and political issue fundamentally linked to social justice and personal liberation. During her August 1915 lecture in Portland, she spoke on "How and Why Small Families Are Best." The theme alone was controversial, but when Goldman addressed various means of contraception, city police arrested her and Ben Reitman, her companion and agent. Portland attorney C. E. S. Wood paid Goldman's $500 bail. At her trial, a Portland woman who had complained about Goldman's talk

Millions of Americans loathed and feared the anarchist Emma Goldman as a dangerous threat to moral authority and economic stability. Library of Congress LC-B2-4215-16

admitted she had done so at the request of Mayor Albee's office. Seven days later Circuit Court Judge William Gatens dismissed the charges due to insufficient evidence and remarked, "The trouble with our people today is there is too much prudery." He added, "We are shocked to hear things uttered that we are familiar with in our everyday life."[16]

During her stop in Portland the following year, Goldman decided she must add a discussion of abortion to one of her talks—titled "Free or Forced Motherhood"—and for doing so, she spent two weeks in jail. She believed that the plight of the working class and the ban on birth control information led to a dismaying number of abortions. Although Goldman boldly addressed abortion as contraception when few others would, she would not assume the risks of performing abortions. She was a trained nurse and had delivered babies and assisted with operations for mostly working-class patients. When women asked her to perform an abortion, however, she balked. Later she explained that she wanted to focus on the "entire social problem," not with one specific aspect. Besides, she wrote, "I would not jeopardize my freedom for that one part of the human struggle."[17]

Talking or writing about sex publicly wasn't for everyone in the early twentieth century, and Equi and Goldman approached such disclosures differently. Equi is not known to have ever discussed her own sexual preferences—or those of others—in public or in writing, but she lived openly with her partners in lesbian relationships and let those arrangements speak for themselves. Goldman, on the other hand, with a national audience and reputation, lectured about sex and free love. She did so in a matter-of-fact manner largely unprecedented in the United States. She believed that the state or other authority should not interfere with how men and women define their sexual lives. In that sense, she was much more of a *sex radical*, a woman thoroughly versed in the politics of sexuality and alternative relationships and willing to speak openly about them. Yet she did not acknowledge in her talks or writing her own intimate relationship with another woman, Almeda Sperry, a former prostitute who became a radical organizer after hearing one of Goldman's lectures on prostitution.[18]

The very next evening after her arrest for talking about birth control in Portland in 1915, Goldman addressed the topic "most tabooed in polite society, homosexuality." At the Turn Verein Hall, also known as Scandinavian Socialists Hall, at Fourth and Yamhill Streets, Goldman discussed "The Intermediate Sex, A Discussion of Homosexuality." She described the everyday realities for people who were variously called "inverts" or "intermediates" by sexologists. She asserted that scientific analysis, not moralizing, should shape an understanding of homosexual relations, and she opposed any regulation of sexual acts between consenting adults. Considering the high-profile, homosexual vice-clique scandal three years earlier, little was reported in the dailies about Goldman's talk, although the *Oregonian* published an advertisement for it. No arrest followed.[19]

With their radical positions and courage in presenting them, Flynn and Goldman secured a niche for radical ideas on the nation's front pages and in public discourse. However controversial their views, they acquainted local readers and audiences with the radical messages that Equi and others might then present. Equi also benefited from the camaraderie and support of these strong-willed women determined to work in political arenas largely defined by men. Yet Equi forged her own radical niche separate from Flynn's or Goldman's. Her devotion to medical care represented a defining difference between her life of radicalism and that of other leading women leftists. She remained grounded in medicine with a base in the Pacific Northwest, and she used her professional stature to further radical causes. But no accounts suggest that Equi aspired to lead a national organization, become nationally recognized, or undertake a national lecture tour.

Equi had concluded that woman suffrage promised only limited benefit to society if class disparities and economic injustice prevailed. Labor rights, free speech, and the unemployment problem loomed as far greater concerns for her, but in 1915 she was pulled into yet another suffrage conflict. She might have avoided the matter, but she felt her rights and prerogatives had been trampled.

Women's struggle to achieve full citizenship with the right to vote had languished for so many years with only occasional spikes of victory. Factionalism, frustration, and generational disputes among suffragists were inevitable. The most straightforward route to achieving full suffrage would have been for Congress to approve a federal amendment to the US Constitution granting women the vote and then forwarding it to the states for ratification. Suffragists had pursued this track since 1878, but the right-to-vote measure stalled in Congress repeatedly, leaving women to pursue laborious, often unsuccessful state campaigns. Once the number of suffrage states reached a critical mass, the veteran suffragists figured, Congress would be forced to act. But by 1914 only twelve states—all but two in the West—had enfranchised women, and neither Congress nor President Wilson was inclined to move on suffrage, especially with the distraction of the looming European War.[20]

Alice Paul, a bold, impassioned, and highly intelligent woman in her late twenties, decided to break through the logjam with different tactics. Seasoned by a stint working with militant British suffragettes, Paul and her associate, Lucy Jones, sought a bolder, more aggressive campaign for suffrage than what NAWSA, the long-established national suffrage organization, pursued. They launched a new organization, the Congressional Union, in 1914 with the sole intent to force Congress to act on a federal amendment. They scorned NAWSA's state-by-state strategy and abandoned the older group's nonpartisanship and cultivation of recalcitrant politicians. Anna Howard Shaw, NAWSA president, at first tried to work with and placate Paul and Jones. She hoped to cultivate younger suffragists, much like Susan B. Anthony had done with her, but she was unwilling to relinquish control to a militant faction that she feared would alienate suffrage supporters.[21]

Equi entered the fray when the Oregon chair of the Congressional Union, Mrs. Emma Carroll, excluded her from the roster of delegates selected to represent the state at the Union-sponsored National Convention of Women Voters, scheduled for mid-September in San Francisco during that city's world's fair. No explanation was given, but Carroll later expressed her disgust that the Congressional Union leaders appeared to prefer and need "one element of society *only*, namely the extreme radicals." Undeniably radical, Equi was nevertheless a Congressional Union member and a suffrage leader from a suffrage state. By all appearances, she deserved to be a delegate. Equi took offense and alerted the dailies of her intention to attend the convention and boarded a train to San Francisco. The next day Carroll refuted Equi's claim, and a personal and political tussle stumbled forward.[22]

Alice Paul convened the San Francisco meeting with a clever strategy in play. She had billed it as a gathering for all women voters, but she packed the halls with Congressional Union members to suggest a national consensus for the group's federal amendment strategy. On the first day of business, Equi was credentialed and took her seat, but Mrs. Carroll and her allies objected and apparently maneuvered a vote that unseated Equi.[23]

NAWSA members demanded an accounting of who could vote at the convention, and forced Paul to announce what might have been apparent all along: voting would be limited to Congressional Union members. When a vote on the federal amendment was later called, eligible women supported it wholeheartedly. Paul's strategy had prevailed with the "purr of the steamroller," according to the *San Francisco Chronicle*."[24]

The suffrage skirmishes hardly overshadowed San Francisco's extravagant Panama-Pacific International Exposition. The city trumpeted its resurgence since the 1906 calamity, and the vast fairgrounds spread its temporary opulence across the tracts of land where the Oregon doctors had set up emergency wards for earthquake victims. The women's conference closed with an evening gala and a sendoff for two envoys—one from Oregon, the other from California—on a cross-country road trip to the nation's capital. Upon arrival, they would present a three-mile-long petition signed by more than five hundred thousand women urging adoption of the federal amendment. Despite the show of unity, the Oregon delegation continued to bicker and feud. Alice Paul tried to make peace, but Carroll and another state leader resigned over the affair. Then Charlotte Anita Whitney, the chair of the California chapter of the Congressional Union, resigned her position to protest the "rank injustice" done to Equi. She also complained that the Congressional Union had become "an autocratic organization with its controls entirely in the hands of one woman." Paul decided to cut her losses. She dismissed Whitney's complaints and closed the Oregon office a few weeks later.[25]

Equi sued Carroll for $20,000 for slander and libel, accusing her of telling associates in Portland and San Francisco that she was "an immoral woman" who "conducts an illegal business." The charges in the suit were one of the few public references to Equi's lesbianism since the peak of the Speckart affair and the first to target Equi's abortion services. The case was dismissed when Equi neglected, or was unable, to provide details for her accusations, but she had taken a principled stand demanding a voice even for radical suffragists. As for her further engagement with suffrage, Equi had already become disillusioned with NAWSA, and now she had reason to distrust the Congressional Union as well.[26]

Elizabeth Gurley Flynn's upcoming trial in Paterson, New Jersey, drew Equi to the East Coast in late October 1915. On board a train from New York to Paterson, Equi did her best with other women friends to disguise Flynn as a society woman dressed in a mix of furs, hat, and a muff so she could slip by the ban on her return to the city. The local police, however, spotted her and kept her outside the assembly hall. Earlier that day Flynn was permitted to speak with President Wilson about the plight of the Wobbly prisoner Joe Hill—he was executed by firing squad a week later—but she was barred from addressing the women of Paterson. Instead, Equi and the others spoke to the restless audience.[27]

In the late afternoon of November 30, 1915, Equi awaited the jury's verdict in the Paterson courtroom with Flynn and Rose Pastor Stokes, the radical

Marie Equi (far left) supported Elizabeth Gurley Flynn in her trial for inciting a riot at the Paterson, New Jersey silk strike in October 1915. Library of Congress, LC-USZ62-96665.

socialist leader. She had earlier told the press that she traveled the long distance from Oregon "to see that the defendant got a fair deal." Flynn faced a jail sentence for allegedly urging strikers to get remaining workers out of the mills even if they had to "club them out, beat them out, or kick them out." The question before the jury was whether or not Flynn had uttered those words. The jurors entered and, in a solemn gesture, stood behind Flynn, Stokes, and Equi. The foreman intoned the verdict: Not guilty. Flynn flashed a smile, Stokes seized Flynn's hands and kissed her on each cheek, and Equi followed suit. Flynn told the press she was elated to be vindicated and then posed with Equi and others on the courthouse steps before departing for supper in New York.[28]

Equi later called on Flynn and her sister in their Bronx home, only to receive a jolt from an unexpected quarter. Elizabeth Gardiner, the medical student involved in the office brawl with Equi in 1912, had traveled to New York with Equi as her intimate companion. Little is known about their relationship, but the two women were involved enough for Gardiner to consider a future together. According to Flynn's later recollections, however, Gardiner delivered an ultimatum to Equi—either abandon her Wobbly protests and her involvement with Harriet Speckart's legal dispute or continue on alone without her. Equi would not comply, and Gardiner remained in the East alone to complete her medical studies. She lived the remainder of her life as a single, professional woman who later served with distinction as director of the Maternal and Childhood Health Division of the New York State Department of Health.[29]

11
"Prepare to Die, Workingman"

Marie Equi, MD, a rebellious soul—generous, kind, brave but so radical in her thinking that she was almost an outcast in Portland.
Margaret Sanger, birth control advocate

Across the country, 1916 was a troubling, contentious year fraught with foreboding and disruption. Americans felt uncertain and unsteady as the hostilities in Europe worsened and threatened the nation's tenuous neutrality. Strikes flared east to west with picketing shoe workers in Philadelphia, steel workers in Detroit, housemaids in Denver, and loggers in Washington. It was a presidential election year with war and peace, woman suffrage, and labor rights dominating the political campaigns. For Marie Equi, events tumbled forth in a jumble of complexity that thrust her into the public realm like never before.

In early June 1916, Mrs. Emmeline Pankhurst, England's foremost militant suffragette, stirred Portlanders with a glimpse of war on her country's home front. For years the American press had vilified the aggressive tactics of English suffragettes—the smashed windows, harassment of government officials, and hunger strikes in prison—leaving many Portlanders expecting to be appalled by Pankhurst. Instead, the petite and cultured fifty-seven-year-old woman surprised them with her gentle manner and pleasant voice. She spoke with persuasion not stridency, and she addressed Portlanders' beliefs about patriotism and their fears of what lay ahead.[1]

Pankhurst recounted the terror and destruction wrought on a defenseless Edinburgh, carpet-bombed by German zeppelins two months earlier. She described Londoners' edgy anticipation of more attacks, and she recounted the domestic unrest that flared during Easter Week that year when Irish republicans staged an uprising to wrest independence from England. In the midst of both panic and resolve, Pankhurst told Portlanders, she had shelved woman suffrage—her cause of twenty-five years—and joined the British war effort. Instead of clamoring for the vote, women marched fifty thousand strong in London and demanded the right to work in munitions factories, military hospitals, and every sort of civic endeavor. The women refused to accept that war service should be limited to men alone.[2]

Pankhurst lectured on behalf of the British government, and she zeroed in on her most important message. "Patriotism isn't enough," she declared. "Preparedness is necessary." Britain wanted the United States to join the Allies, but it judged "preparedness" a more palatable, initial step for Americans wary of the hostilities. The audience cheered Pankhurst and donated $1,000 to her fund for humanitarian relief in the Allied countries. For pacifists and suffragists like Equi, Pankhurst's story held great irony—a militant who had dropped her suffrage demands to support the war just as Equi retreated from suffrage to protest the war that the United States stepped closer to entering.[3]

Much of America accepted the message of preparedness as necessary self-defense even if they objected to a foreign military adventure. For a full two-and-a-half years, Americans resisted the pull of war and took comfort in their distance from the changing, dangerous world beyond the country's shores. At the same time, war boosters enthralled young men with visions of the glory that awaited them in the fields of France, far from their grinding factory jobs or farm work. Progressives feared that reform efforts at home would be scuttled by a government preoccupied with war and by a population consumed with nationalism. In this jumble of sentiments, a significant minority, including Equi, suspected "readiness" was a capitalist ploy that would inevitably lead to war with a grab for power and profits.

President Wilson had already distressed pacifists with a turnabout on military policy. Earlier he had kept the hostilities at a distance with his own fears of losing momentum for his reform agenda, but, as his reelection campaign neared, he abandoned the hands-off policy and adopted "reasonable preparedness." Progressives felt they had little choice but to "throw a monkey wrench into the machinery" and resist Wilson's initiatives. In 1915, several of the nation's foremost advocates of reform—including Jane Addams, the Chicago settlement organizer; Florence Kelley, the founder of the National Consumers League; and Rabbi Stephen Wise, an early Progressive—formed the American Union Against Militarism (AUAM) to lobby Congress, lecture, and organize local chapters. Members in Oakland, Seattle, and other cities staged peace demonstrations, and Equi joined the union as did her friends Charlotte Anita Whitney in California and Dr. James Warbasse of New York. In Portland, the AUAM claimed less of a presence but leaders in the East urged Equi to protest the government's plans.[4]

On June 3, 1916, Portland observed National Preparedness Day with the largest parade in the city's history. Fifteen thousand people marched along forty blocks downtown with their shoulders squared, heads held high, and spirits soaring. Hundreds carried banners with a one-word message—*Prepare*—while fifteen brass bands played martial airs and a dozen divisions marched in formation, grouped by profession and interest. A column of Civil War veterans hoisted flags behind a drum corps. A contingent of four hundred doctors and medical students, three hundred young men of the Athletic League, and five hundred suffragists—all stepped out for patriotism and readiness. It was a time of unity with the thrill of shared purpose and resolve.[5]

Equi was of a different mind, however. Earlier that day, she had motored around the city with an opposite message, daring for its difference. Then she steered her way into the parade route and approached the jubilant, patriotic crowd. She had mounted an American flag at the front of her automobile and strapped on the side a white banner that warned, "Prepare to Die, Workingman—J. P. Morgan & Co. Want Preparedness for Profit—Thou Shalt Not Kill." With brazen courage, she rolled into the march behind the Knights of Columbus and the local bar association, two contingents known for their preparedness fervor. Quick and fierce, the marchers attacked. According to Equi, the attorneys struck first, yanking the banner from her and striking her with it. "I was scratched and bruised, and my hand bled," she said. "They tore the banner to shreds and stomped on it." At one point, a mob of fifty angry men surrounded and taunted her, yelling, "That's what we do to your banner, now here's ours." The men thrust the American flag into her hands, daring her to rip it. Equi later admitted to tearing two strips from it, saying, "Your flag is no protection to me." She put up a fight until the police intervened and arrested her and two of the men. She vowed to file charges of disorderly conduct; the men accused her of desecrating the flag.[6]

Equi's protest inflamed many Portlanders, but she was committed to making a case for pacifism. On another occasion, she circumvented the police routine of pulling Wobblies from their soapboxes as soon as they started to speak. She borrowed a lineman's spurs and climbed high on a downtown telephone pole, out of reach of the officers below. From her perch she unleashed a banner—"Down with the Imperialist War"—and addressed the crowd that gathered. The police tried to enlist the fire department to get her down, but firemen were in no rush to harass the Doc who cared for their families. Only when she was ready did she climb down.[7]

With both protests, Equi upset a slew of expectations and norms for womanhood. The attorneys, marchers, and police officers reviled Equi's anti-war messages, but on another level her acts challenged the men's prowess and their traditional role of defending the nation. They had wrestled with a woman on the street, and they were taunted by a woman climbing beyond their reach. Women objected as well. Many had vowed to do their part by ensuring their homes promoted American values and patriotism. Others professed a duty to produce valiant sons ready to take up arms. From their prospective, Equi actively undermined the virtues of patriotic motherhood. If her message had been less confrontational and her behavior more ladylike, men and women might have accepted, or at least tolerated, her demonstration of prewar paci-fism. But she eschewed the norms to assert what patriotism meant to her.[8]

Equi was not alone with her dissent in Portland. At a public forum held the day after the big parade, a Reed College professor challenged Portlanders to reject noisy, emotional appeals and to seek reason instead. Rabbi Jonah B. Wise of Temple Beth Israel criticized plans for militarism as panic responses to conditions in Europe far different from those in America. C. E. S. Wood warned that repeated campaigns for preparedness fostered a militaristic spirit that posed a far greater danger than any foreign invasion. In the nation's capital, Oregon's US Senator Harry Lane, a progressive Democrat, complained that preparedness instigated an irrational "state of fear" that distracted Americans from dealing with the many pressing issues before the nation. Across the coun-try, the Women's Peace Party and the militant wing of the Socialist Party op-posed the military planning as well. Although Equi firmly supported the IWW, she disagreed with the radical group's hands-off approach to the preparedness debate. Wobbly leaders believed a dispute among capitalist nations held little importance to the class war they had undertaken. But stronger forces pre-vailed against the dissenters. Pressure groups like the high-powered National Security League, comprised of the nation's most powerful capitalists, and the American Public League, 250,000-members strong, rallied vigilant citizens to mobilize in their communities.[9]

Preparedness became a national watchword, and its spirit unified most Americans in the camaraderie of shared purpose. Throughout the summer of 1916, not only Portland but nearly every city and town outdid itself with a parade. In Chicago one million people rallied, waving flags and singing patriotic songs in an eleven-hour procession. New York City's outpouring drew two hundred bands and fifty drum corps. President Wilson led a march in the nation's capital, and, in Seattle, women garbed in white led a contingent of twenty thousand.[10]

Violence marred San Francisco's parade, and its impact shadowed labor and civil rights efforts for decades. On July 22, 1916, fifty-one thousand marchers assembled at the foot of Market Street around the Ferry Building. Thirty minutes into the parade, a bomb exploded with a force so great that it tore off legs and arms of bystanders, killing ten and injuring forty. No one knew who had placed the bomb, but the police arrested Tom Mooney, a radical Socialist and union leader, as well as Warren K. Billings, among others, who they suspected of promoting violence for political change. The proceedings against Mooney and Billings were scandalous from the start with obstructions to Mooney obtaining legal counsel for days. Evidence was specious; the witnesses, unreliable. Murder charges were drawn up by a jury selected by the district attorney, and a conviction followed. Only an international outcry kept Mooney from execution, and he and Billings were left to languish at San Quentin State Prison with life sentences. In the years ahead, Equi's own plight would often be likened to that of Mooney and Billings.[11]

Two weeks passed between the assault Equi suffered from Portland's marchers and her next confrontation with authorities. In the interim, she cared for patients at a new location, the Lafayette Building at Sixth and Washington Streets, at the intersection that served as the prime rallying spot for free speech fights. Dr. Alys Griff, Equi's good friend from medical school, kept her office down the hallway. Equi and Speckart passed their tenth anniversary together, in the company of Mary Jr., now a year old. Their bond had weakened over time, and the future threatened more tumult than the past.[12]

Nine days after Portland's Preparedness Parade, in the middle of June 1916, the *Oregonian* announced the imminent arrival of Margaret Sanger, the most persuasive advocate of birth control in the nation. A year earlier, local authorities had arrested Emma Goldman for daring to lecture on birth control, but during the interim Sanger had become a new sensation on the lecture circuit with her pleasing demeanor.[13]

After Goldman's 1915 visit, veteran Socialists and Wobblies organized the Portland Birth Control League, and it became the largest such group on the West Coast. Equi was an active member of the league, and she gave it greater visibility and credibility among radicals and poor and working-class women. The group drew sizeable crowds without incident to its monthly meetings held in the Central Library, and it staged rallies and lobbied to overturn laws that prohibited dissemination of contraception information and devices. In 1915, the league circulated a petition that reflected the sophistication of grassroots groups even before Sanger undertook her national tour. The document asserted a woman's right to determine the time and pacing for bearing children, that motherhood is "dignified and noble" only when it is planned and wanted, that "unwelcome or unfit children" should not be brought into the world, and that scientific knowledge cannot be judged obscene. As reasonable as these tenets seemed to advocates, they challenged the prohibitions of local government, courts, and churches. In early 1916, league members anticipated a surge of interest with Sanger's visit, and they helped organize her stop in the Rose City.[14]

Margaret Sanger launched her first national speaking tour on an emotional rebound following personal tragedy and a political triumph. Only six years earlier, in 1910, Sanger, her husband, and three children left their suburban New York home for a new life in bohemian Manhattan. While her husband worked as an architect, Sanger immersed herself in the turbulence of the city, first as a slum-visiting nurse and then as a Socialist Party organizer. The deplorable East Side slums exposed her to the harsh inequalities in America, and her party job left her feeling ineffective. What enlivened her and changed her life course was the passion and militancy of radicalism. She was especially drawn to the direct action tactics of the Wobblies, and she began writing articles in the radical press about women's concerns, including "What Every Girl Should Know." Her social and political circle widened to include Elizabeth Gurley Flynn, Emma Goldman, and William "Big Bill" Haywood, the IWW cofounder, and she joined several of the strikes they led.[15]

During a trip to Europe, Sanger became so enthralled with the widespread use of contraception in France that she embraced the cause as her life work. She endorsed the position of the American Left that withholding birth control information from the working classes left them struggling with overly large families and rendered them less able to fight exploitation. Like Emma Goldman, Sanger came to believe that birth control was especially important as a means to free women and empower them for positive sexual expression. After returning to the United States, she launched *The Woman Rebel*, a journal that asserted the rights of women to control pregnancy and express their sexuality. She challenged the federal prohibitions on disseminating birth control information, and the government obliged her with an indictment in August 1914 that threatened a forty-five-year prison sentence. At first she fled to England but then returned a year later even more passionate about the cause and ready to fight the indictment.[16]

Events rushed upon Sanger. As her trial date neared, her daughter, Peggy, became ill with pneumonia and then died in her arms. Early in 1916, she

Margaret Sanger was jailed in Portland, Oregon with Marie Equi in 1916 for advocating birth control. Library of Congress, LC-USZ62-29808.

suffered an emotional breakdown from the loss and her guilt for being away so long. Her doctor thought she was unable to stand trial, but she insisted. In the meantime, her allies publicized her case as persecution for exercising her free speech rights. They swayed public opinion to the extent that the authorities relented. In February 1916, all charges against Sanger were dropped. She was ebullient with the public recognition, and she undertook a vigorous schedule of lectures, filling assembly halls and plazas across the country.[17]

With the encouragement of Elizabeth Gurley Flynn and others, Sanger added the Pacific Northwest to her cross-country tour. She intended to flaunt local obscenity laws, claim her free-speech rights, and exploit any controversy to publicize the cause. She continued to distribute *The Woman Rebel* as well as copies of *Family Limitation*, a small, purse-sized booklet with details on practical, affordable methods for preventing pregnancy. In it she dispelled myths about sex and birth control, and she dared to extol the pleasures of intercourse. Everywhere Sanger stopped, women sought her advice before and after her talks, even appearing at her hotel room. Women confided their exhaustion and desperation over the prospect of repeat pregnancies, their struggles to hold families together, and their fears for their children. Sanger was moved by their fevered pleas, but their needs left her exhausted. In San Francisco, she collapsed and spent three days in bed before continuing to Portland.[18]

"My welcome in Portland was delightful," Sanger later wrote. On June 18 she was escorted to the grand, seven-storied Portland Hotel and then relaxed on the veranda, sipping loganberry juice over ice while talking with reporters. She appealed to Oregon's enfranchised women to repeal the puritanical laws that censored birth control information. "We wouldn't be so silly, puritanical, and narrow if we had a little more common sense," she said. Attorney C. E. S. Wood charmed Sanger with his personal welcome and sent flowers to her room. Equi also greeted Sanger on this, their first meeting. She impressed Sanger as one of the West's "robust, vital women."[19]

Portlanders found Sanger a compelling, attractive woman, trim and small with a kind face, a warm smile, and captivating green eyes. She appeared determined about her cause but she was more approachable than Emma Goldman. Equi could easily have believed that she had found a kindred spirit in Sanger, who she called "a little bunch of hellfire." They shared similar New England upbringings in immigrant, working-class, Catholic households. Sanger was also a middle child in a large family, and she had witnessed the debilitating effect of her mother's frequent pregnancies. She had hoped to be a doctor, but she dropped out of school to care for her ailing mother. Later she completed studies for nursing, and, like Equi, used her medical training to position herself for greater impact in political causes. Both Equi and Sanger were influenced by the radicalism of Emma Goldman and the labor organizing of Elizabeth Gurley Flynn, and they suffered the consequences of being strong, outspoken women who bucked the status quo. But like Goldman and Flynn, Sanger sought a national, even international, standing while Equi valued being a doctor in the Pacific Northwest.[20]

On the evening of June 19, at the Heilig Theater, Sanger addressed a full house. She knew from experience that a hush would settle upon the audience when she described the occasions when birth control was needed—the presence of transmissible disease, threats to the mother's health, parents who were adolescents or who already had "subnormal" children, and when family resources were too limited for another child. She advised young couples to delay parenthood for one or two years to adjust to marriage and to grow together.[21]

Toward the end of Sanger's talk, Portland police moved in and arrested three men for selling Sanger's pamphlets. Equi intervened and climbed atop a table to hand out pamphlets free to anyone who wanted them. Both the women followed the men to the police station where Sanger implored the captain to release them. She even offered to take their place. The captain refused, but he agreed to delay a trial until Sanger returned from lecture stops in Seattle and Spokane. Equi paid the seventy-five-dollar bail for the three men.[22]

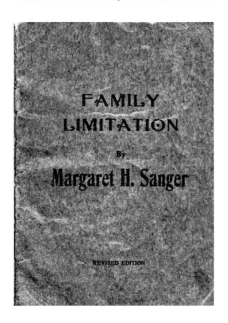

Marie Equi revised the birth control booklet *Family Limitation* in 1916 at Margaret Sanger's request. Booklet in author's collection. Photo: Michael Helquist.

While Sanger traveled, Equi revised *Family Limitation* as Sanger had requested to provide more of a medical perspective. To counter objections leading to the arrests, Equi toned down the text on sexual pleasure and dropped specific mention of abortion. She also targeted the pamphlet to working women and men, and especially union members. The inside cover castigated the "stupid persecution" by Portland authorities who arrested the three union men. West Coast labor leaders who promoted birth control were identified, and readers were encouraged to view contraception as a means to emancipate women and improve working conditions. With the prospect of the United States entering World War I, Equi also reminded women of their responsibility to limit the "human material for exploiters and militarists."[23]

In the meantime, Portland's city commissioners—all men—had rushed to call an emergency legislative session to criminalize distribution of any newly defined obscene material like Sanger's birth control booklet. Their act outraged Sanger's supporters who organized a protest meeting to coincide with her return. On June 29 Sanger appeared before a crowd packed into the Baker Theater in downtown Portland. Equi and others sold copies of the revised *Family Limitation* at the door. As soon as Sanger started to speak, the police arrested her along with Equi and two other women. The audience clamored in protest and more than one hundred women followed the arrestees to jail, calling out in solidarity and defiance, "We also have broken the law."[24] Portland had almost certainly never heard or seen such a march.

All four women refused bail, and they spent the night in the county jail. Sanger noted that the other female inmates, mostly young women, "scampered around talking over their troubles and complaints with Dr. Equi." She also later wrote, "Portland is the first city to interfere with my work since I left New York." Forty-eight Portlanders signed a petition to Mayor Albee to release the women. Anna L. Strong, a Seattle activist, wrote that wealthier women readily obtained birth control information from their physicians, but working women were barred from similar access.[25]

Over the next two days, Equi, Sanger, and the other women were tried separately from the men in proceedings that drew more than two hundred women to the Municipal Court trial. Several carried signs outside the courthouse reading "Poor Women Are Denied What the Rich Possess" and "Poverty and Large Families Go Hand in Hand." C. E. S. Wood argued the advocates' case and asserted that obscenity had not been proven and that no established criteria for defining obscenity existed, but the judge found all the defendants guilty for circulating a "lewd, obscene and indecent book." He claimed that birth control itself was not on trial, but he believed that the material could reach the "lascivious" minds of youth. He ordered fines of ten dollars, suspended, for the men and no fines for the women. Sanger bristled with indignation and declared the ruling a "cowardly decision." "It's practically the same old story," she said, "that knowledge, if it's hidden away on the musty bookshelves or in the narrow confines of the medical profession is moral; but as soon as it is distributed among the working people, the same book becomes obscene." Equi, according to the *Oregonian*, "vehemently protested" until the court warned her against contempt. Sanger completed her tour and found a surge of interest in birth control while Portland's local league found ways to distribute more copies of *Family Limitation*.[26]

Other physicians in Portland, no doubt, recognized the importance of birth control to women's health and independence, and many probably advised their patients how to prevent pregnancies. But none are known to have joined Equi and Sanger in defiance of a spurious municipal law or to have protested their incarceration. Three months after she visited Portland, Sanger opened the nation's first birth control clinic in the Brownsville district of Brooklyn. She had concluded that women were more likely to adopt birth control methods after speaking directly with doctors and nurses rather than by attending lectures. Clinics offered privacy for fittings of the best means of contraception—a vaginal diaphragm. Authorities continued to harass Sanger, but she helped establish a model operation that evolved into Planned

Parenthood clinics across the country. In Portland, ironically, two months after Equi's and Sanger's arrest over birth control, Emma Goldman lectured on the topic without incident. [27]

Following Sanger's departure, Equi sent her impassioned declarations of love and affection. She recounted the days and nights they spent together while awaiting the judge's verdict, and, in one letter, she wrote that Sanger's love for her had swept away the bitterness and pain she had experienced since being jailed during the cannery strike three years earlier. She described a "spiritual death" that had engulfed her during those difficult times, one that had burned out her "old rebellious attitude." In its wake Equi described feeling stronger but more remote as if her "higher senses had become inanimate." With Sanger's "beautiful love and friendship," Equi anticipated leaving behind the intolerance she had used as self-protection and thought she could forge "a new life out of the ashes of the old."[28]

Equi clearly reveled in the affection she had shared with Sanger. In one of her more intimate messages, she wrote, "Last night when you leaned over me—held me within the shelter of your arms—the very warmth and beauty of your nature became embodied within my heart and brain." She held back little, writing "My sweet girl I love you with an ecstasy, an understanding of spirit that you alone have imparted to me. . . . My arms are around you. I kiss your sweet mouth in absolute surrender." One letter from Sanger to Equi has been located in which she recalled, a few years later, their time together in 1916. She wrote, "Your picture is on my dresser always as I look into those blue, blue eyes, I remember our dinner, our ride, everything—*everything*."[29]

Sanger apparently did not continue to respond as passionately, and Equi shifted in her correspondence from fervent entreaties to more practical concerns. She applauded the idea of a birth control clinic as "the real thing," and she offered ideas for getting subscriptions to a new publication. But occasionally her feelings lingered, and she closed one letter with a plaintive note, "Am blue—lonesome for you—sometimes I wish I had never met you—*sense of loss*—mental detachment *love me, Peggy—do not wait too long before writing me.* I am a very sad—very lonely woman. I love you."[30]

Later that year, Sanger composed her thoughts in a note that she intended for Equi alone but never sent: "Marie Equi, MD, a rebellious soul—generous, kind, brave but so radical in her thinking that she was almost an outcast in Portland. Upon arrival she captures every well-known woman who comes to Portland. Her reputation is or was Lesbian but to me she was like a crushed falcon which had braved the storms and winds of terror and needed tenderness and love. She was living with a younger woman in Portland and had adopted a child—I liked Equi always."[31]

By mid-1916 Equi juggled her medical practice with what seemed full-time activism. In October of that year her antiwar sentiments clashed with the play of suffrage politics. During that year's presidential campaign, President Wilson faced off against Republican challenger Charles Evans Hughes. Wilson's backers touted his record—"He kept us out of war"—while Hughes charged the president with inadequately preparing the country for hostilities. At the same time, the candidates sought support from women who had won the vote, most of whom lived in western states. Wilson struggled to retain his constituency in the antisuffrage South, and he promised action on suffrage at a better, distant time. Hughes ultimately backed the federal suffrage amendment, hoping to boost his campaign in the West.

The choice for suffragists was far from black and white. Though NAWSA remained nonpartisan, it generally placed its faith in Wilson, trusting that years of lobbying his administration would ultimately deliver results. Critics disagreed. In June 1916, the Congressional Union transformed itself into the National Woman's Party (NWP), the first political party created by and for women. The NWP's one and only concern was the adoption of the Susan B. Anthony amendment to the federal constitution to ensure that the right to vote would not be denied any citizen on account of sex. The organization's leaders refused to back candidates of any political party that did not support the amendment. Alice Paul and her allies figured if women in the suffrage states voted against the Democrats, they could swing the outcome of the race and move suffrage through Congress. But for suffragists who were also pacifists like Equi, the peace candidate trumped the suffrage supporter.[32]

The conflict in Portland erupted in October 1916 with the arrival of the *Golden Special*—sleek Pullman cars bustling with East Coast suffragists—that had streaked across the country to rally women to vote for Hughes. When the emissaries gathered for a noontime rally in downtown Portland, Equi led other Wilson sympathizers in yells and catcalls loud enough to drown out the "Hughesettes," as they were called. She carried a banner painted with the words, "What Goose Laid the Golden Egg?" and charged that the easterners' train was financed by wealthy New York industrialists and their wives. That claim was mostly accurate. Besides the threat of war, Equi objected to eastern women from nonsuffrage states presuming to tell enfranchised women in the West how to vote. At another Hughes event, according to the Republican

Oregonian, Equi clashed with people waiting for the speeches to begin. She argued with a police officer, who then arrested her. Her friends paid her bail, and she returned to the streets for another protest.[33]

Equi was almost giddy in a letter to Margaret Sanger about the protests. "It sure has been a good Friday for me. . . . We sure did have a strenuous time— Put the Hughesites entirely out of business. . . . We had 5,000 people at Sixth and Alder. . . . Say it was the richest thing ever pulled off—and a complete surprise—even to the Democrats." Equi wrote that she "didn't believe in either Hughes or Wilson," but she believed the president was "the lesser of two evils."[34]

On Election Day, Oregon voters—including women for the first time in a presidential election—awarded the state's five electoral votes to Hughes. Equi and her allies had failed to swing the state to the peace candidate, and everyone awaited the news from California. A victory in the Electoral College hinged on California's tally in an extremely close race that extended late into the evening. Then, finally, the news arrived: Wilson carried the state by a mere four thousand votes. In the end, the president carried all the suffrage states except Oregon and Illinois. The power of the women's vote became apparent, and Democrats resolved to settle the suffrage issue before the 1918 midterm elections. Keeping the country out of the war was another matter.[35]

Three weeks after the Hughes protests, labor skirmishes in the timber town of Everett, Washington, flared into murderous attacks against Wobbly organizers. What became known as the "Everett Massacre" jolted Wobblies into yet another free-speech fight just as they planned to shift from street agitation to bringing workers into a more stable and permanent organization.[36]

Located thirty miles north of Seattle, Everett was a true company town developed in the 1890s by agents of John D. Rockefeller and the Weyerhauser Timber Company. In the spring of 1916, shingle weavers at one of the mills staged a walkout to protest a 20 percent pay cut. They were beaten for their action, and the local authorities obliged the mill owners by outlawing demonstrations downtown. The IWW tried to enter Everett to help the strikers, but the sheriff's department had already deputized men to keep Wobblies away. The deputies, often drunk and acting like thugs, attacked and blockaded the outsiders from the city. Their tactics were so brutal that more than two thousand Everett citizens protested at a street rally.[37]

Looking to bolster the picketers, 250 Wobblies boarded the passenger boat *Verona* in Seattle early in the morning of November 5 for the trip to

Everett. The sheriff and his fully armed posse waited for them at the Everett dock. Soon after the Wobblies made fast the bowline, a single shot rang out followed by volleys from each side, killing four Wobblies, two deputies, and wounding dozens. Another Wobbly died soon after the ship returned to Seattle, and most of the others were arrested for complicity in murder.[38]

Equi rushed to Seattle to provide medical care as soon as she heard of the trouble. "I have come of my own accord," she told a reporter, "and will speak in Everett shortly." She met Elizabeth Gurley Flynn upon her arrival, and together they comforted the Wobblies in jail and in the hospital. The men cheered her arrival, and several told her, "Good ole Doc. We *knew* you'd come to us." At the hospital Equi found one of the men, a twenty-two-year-old, suffering from a worsening bullet wound to his leg, and she demanded he be admitted to a private hospital for better care. She also determined that the last Wobbly to die would have recovered from his wound if he had received prompt surgical care. Her testimony to that effect was presented at the trial. Discouraged but determined after their visit, Equi and Flynn rallied support for the Everett defendants in talks throughout Western Washington and Oregon.[39]

Equi responded to the Everett crisis as a matter of course. It was what she did and how she understood her place in the world. She dropped everything to travel two hundred miles to stand with "her boys," to provide medical care, and to testify in their defense. She let it be understood that she was on-call for the men and women who risked their well-being and sometimes their lives for causes that meant everything to them. She simply did what she believed was necessary and what she felt was right.

Weeks later Equi described in a letter to Sanger that she would be part of a loggers' convention in the IWW headquarters in Portland. She intended to shed light on workers' demands for camp cleanliness, sanitary sleeping quarters, wages, and working hours. She wrote that she expected to "wake old Oregon up a bit." Soon thereafter, Equi served as the official IWW delegate from Oregon invited to help disperse the ashes of Wobbly songwriter Joe Hill. On the first anniversary of Hill's execution, six hundred small, sealed envelopes were distributed to Wobblies and their supporters. Printed on each packet were his likeness and an inscription that read "Joe Hill—murdered by the Capitalist Class, November 19th, 1915." One hundred fifty Wobblies gathered at his memorial in Chicago and recalled Hill's last song, an antiwar tune titled "Don't Take My Papa Away From Me." After the service, the delegates convened their tenth annual convention and adopted a resolution opposing war.[40]

12
"One of the Most Dangerous Anarchists"

Only traitors will now withhold their support from the President.
K. A. J. Mackenzie, MD, dean, University of Oregon Medical School

The specter of war infiltrated Americans' everyday lives in early 1917 with anticipation and foreboding. For many, the country's entry into the hostilities would entail an exercise of duty, a dose of adventure, and a show of national prowess. Others felt obliged to protest even more the march to war. Pacifists and antiwar radicals like Marie Equi assumed greater personal risks as outsiders resisting what was rapidly developing into a national purpose. Itching for action, the forces against dissent mobilized to stifle all objections, making citizenship itself a domestic battleground.

For a few of Equi's radical associates, the burden of protest became too great and the future too grim. Such was the case for Agnes Thecla Fair, a thirty-seven-year-old Wobbly agitator dubbed "the woman hobo" who had suffered brutal police treatment during the Spokane Free Speech fight in 1909. Fair was well regarded on the West Coast for her poetry, radical convictions, and willingness to sacrifice for the downtrodden. But one Friday afternoon in January 1917 she raised her arms and stepped in front of a speeding electric streetcar in southeast Portland and died instantly from the impact.[1]

Equi had once provided an abortion for Fair, and she knew her well. When Fair returned to Portland in late 1916, she suffered from nervous exhaustion and the early stages of tuberculosis. Equi was arranging convalescence for her in a Denver sanitarium, but Fair told friends that not being able to work among laborers in need made her life not worth living. Fair left instructions that she wanted her obituary to read, "She died from fighting for mankind." No more was needed, she had written, and added, "It's a good disease to die of." Equi organized Fair's funeral, and Wobblies filled the hall with Joe Hill songs.[2]

Equi understood the personal sacrifice that dogged union organizing and free speech fights. In an interview she gave years later, she commented: "Oh, it's very easy to attend a civic lunch, listen to a number of complimentary speeches from well-mannered and admiring people, while you wear your best clothes and play the part of a hero. But to go out and mount a soapbox and declare war against the organized forces of capitalism is quite a different matter. The task of veering public opinion was never an easy one." Equi knew the camaraderie and thrill of direct action could salve, but not heal, the wounds from family separations, rough living on the road, and, sometimes, harsh jail time. Her profession and income cushioned her from many of the hardships that other radical women endured on the front lines, but she accepted great personal risk and duress to confront injustice.[3]

Two years of war in Europe had devastated the combatant nations' economies, disrupted their social and political order, and sent millions to their deaths. The conflict had stalemated with the outcome largely dependent on munitions and supplies from the United States. In January 1917 Germany announced it would sink all vessels of any nationality or purpose that approached the waters off England and France. It was a calculated act intended to weaken and defeat the Allies before the United States could mobilize a credible retaliation. In America, the war seemed closer than ever before.

In early March 1917 Marie Equi witnessed the growing war fever when Oregonians rebuked one of their US Senators, Harry Lane, for his antiwar stance. Newspaper editors berated him for embarrassing the state and called him a traitor and a coward. Others urged a recall. Many of the Progressives who had once championed Lane as Portland's mayor now distanced themselves. Personal considerations and the demands of patriotism flared so intensely that even longtime colleagues like Dr. Esther Pohl Lovejoy, Portland's first woman health officer, withheld her public support. Lane refused to back down, even after German torpedoes sank three American ships.[4]

The United States might have steered clear of the European war, but by 1917 America's surging economy was tied to huge loans to Britain, and American leaders declared that democracy itself depended on an Allied victory. Many also understood the larger picture: the outcome of the war would likely determine the contours of a new world order with a realignment of nations and industrial power. On April 2, 1917, President Wilson asked Congress for a declaration of war against Germany, and most Americans previously reticent about preparedness shed their doubts with a full embrace of patriotic fervor. For decades many had expressed their citizenship by volunteering with civic clubs and uplift organizations, by promoting political reform, and by providing social services. With hostilities imminent, the government redefined citizenship to be first and foremost a vigilance to win the war and to secure for

America a new position as a world power. Public sentiment quickly embraced the war effort, and even Progressives dropped their earlier reticence with the belief that the war might strengthen national institutions, promote world peace, and lead to much-needed social reforms. Tolerance of antiwar beliefs largely evaporated across the nation and certainly in Portland. At the behest of local businessmen, Mayor H. Russell Albee—the same official who restricted free speech during the city's 1913 cannery strike—declared an immediate ban on any unpatriotic gathering. And Dr. K. A. J. Mackenzie, the medical school dean, spoke for many Americans when he told a Red Cross gathering in Portland, "Only traitors will now withhold their support from the President."[5]

Congress complied with Wilson's request, and the United States declared war on the Imperial Government of Germany on April 6, 1917. Oregon's Senator Lane was one of six senators who refused to concur, along with fifty members of the House of Representatives. Lane had been too ill to join the war debate, but he issued a statement, with sentiments similar to Equi's. "Commercialism is undoubtedly behind the war spirit," he wrote. Exhausted from the strain and vitriol over his vote, Lane sought medical treatment in San Francisco, but he died there of complications from a blood clot to the brain. At his memorial service in Portland's city hall, his recent detractors praised his honesty, courage, and dedicated service.[6]

Overnight the war came home, and activists were forced to accommodate the new reality. Margaret Sanger, who initially protested the war, undertook a strategic retreat and steered her birth control advocacy away from antiwar dissent. The suffrage group NAWSA took the advice of Emmeline Pankhurst, the British suffragist, and rallied to the war effort. Even before war was declared, NAWSA had distributed war service plans to each state chapter with detailed directions on Americanization classes, food drives, and fund raising. But pacifists among NAWSA members resented the shift toward militarism, and many either curtailed or dropped their support of the association. They felt NAWSA's position reflected a serious disconnect between the mostly middle-class suffrage movement and the more radical agenda of disaffected women. For its part, the National Woman's Party held tight to its suffrage-only policy and rebuffed calls to support the war.[7]

Equi found few allies among her medical colleagues in Portland. Most backed the war, and many of the male doctors whom she had known since the earthquake-relief mission enlisted. Women physicians sought to exercise their full citizenship by enlisting as well. They hoped war duty would improve their professional standing and demonstrate their clinical skills. Doctors Mae

Cardwell, Katherine Manion, and Mary MacLachlan reported for duty in the Medical Reserve Corps, but, like other female physicians, they were turned away unless they agreed to work as medical assistants. Only the American Red Cross offered women doctors service overseas, and several, like Portland's Esther Pohl Lovejoy, toiled in field hospitals.[8]

Members of Equi's family readily joined the war effort as well. One of her nephews, John Gay, the only child of her younger sister, Sophie, who had married and moved from New Bedford to southern California, enlisted on his own without waiting for a draft call-up. Gay was a popular seventeen-year-old sophomore at Pasadena High School when he joined the "Great Adventure" promised by war boosters.[9]

Equi's war dissent underscored her position as a political outcast, but she relied on radical allies and friends, including Hanna Sheehy-Skeffington, the Irish nationalist. Sheehy-Skeffington was renowned among Irish agitators for her own organizing for Irish independence. After British soldiers executed her husband, Francis, for opposing British rule, Sheehy-Skeffington acquired even more of a heroic status. Equi probably met her during the latter's lecture stop in Portland in May 1917. Portlanders received her well enough when she talked at Hibernia Hall, but once Sheehy-Skeffington assailed Great Britain—America's new wartime ally—for its repression of Irish nationalism, letters of protest appeared in the dailies. Equi bonded with Sheehy-Skeffington, who was five years younger, and nurtured a lifelong relationship with her. Equi also respected her own Irish heritage and the stories of her mother and grandmother about harsh British rule. On one occasion, she staged her own demonstration for Irish independence in Portland's Park Blocks. She stood next to a banner that read, "Ireland is the Only White Nation in Slavery—England Keeps Her in Chains."[10]

Equi marshaled courage and resilience to object to the war effort, but the Wilson administration soon upped the ante by exhorting Congress to enact the Espionage Act of 1917. The new law criminalized any speech or activity that might be construed as discouraging military service or as disrupting the nation's industries with demands for better working conditions. Offenses could lead to a prison sentence of twenty years. Congress readily obliged the president and passed the law. United States Attorney General Thomas Gregory delivered a chilling assessment of what labor activists and radicals could expect: "May God have mercy on them, for they need expect none from an outraged people and an avenging government." After his promises of keeping the peace, Wilson ushered in the most thorough assault on free speech in the nation's history.[11]

The first targets of the new, tough strictures were the nation's top anarchists, Emma Goldman and Alexander Berkman. What better demonstration of the government's intent to suppress enemy influences than by locking up the most reviled individuals in the country? For years Goldman's politics, free spirit, and unorthodox life had disturbed the public and politicians. Armed with wartime powers, the government seized its chance to be done with her and Berkman as well.

The two anarchists inflamed the fear that most troubled the Wilson administration—confronting the kind of pervasive draft riots that erupted during the Civil War. Fiercely opposed to the war, Goldman and Berkman founded the No Conscription League in May 1917 to advise conscientious objectors on how to resist the draft. Goldman later explained that she only dealt with men who had already decided to avoid registration, and therefore, she claimed under oath that she had not interfered with draft laws. Yet antidraft sentiment was high among immigrants, and No Conscription League rallies walked a fine line between encouraging resistance and empowering resisters. Federal agents were little interested in the nuances of dissent, and they arrested Goldman and Berkman for violating the Selective Service Act. Their conviction was a foregone conclusion as the government needed only to prove that they had a disruptive influence on conscription. Goldman and Berkman were convicted and sentenced to two years in prison and $10,000. They were deported as aliens and anarchists soon after their release from prison.[12]

Putting radicals behind bars represented only one phase of the government's strategy to manipulate public opinion. An expansive propaganda campaign instilled fear of the supposed dangers lurking in every community. A newly formed Committee on Public Information employed the most modern techniques of advertising. Posters, pamphlets, letters, newspaper features, films, and endorsements from prominent citizens were ubiquitous. Patrons seeking distraction from the war in the movie theaters found intermissions filled with patriotic talks by volunteers. The campaign fostered a sense of obligation among Americans—the ubiquitous "Uncle Sam Wants You" poster was an explicit reminder—but it also delved into a range of stereotypical images to stir hatred and fear. Prussians were portrayed as brutal, abusive invaders and women as victims or temptresses to soldiers.[13]

On another front, the Department of Justice exploited citizens' heightened sense of duty and exhorted them to report suspicious, possibly disloyal activity of their neighbors, colleagues, and acquaintances. The government helped create a coercive culture of vigilance and surveillance that infiltrated everyday relations and cast volunteer activities like patriotic marches, food drives, and fundraising as explicit tests of loyalty. One of the first reports about Marie Equi occurred less than a month after the declaration of war when a Multnomah County official informed William R. Bryon, Portland Chief for the Bureau of Investigation for the Department of Justice, of a conversation in which Equi told him, "If anybody was interned here, there would be serious trouble." Bryon did not act on the tip, but it alerted him to Equi as a possible threat to the nation.[14]

The potential for leftist and anarchist groups to disrupt the American war effort became apparent in June 1917 when the IWW shut down much of the lumber industry in the Pacific Northwest. Wobblies took advantage of workers' discontent and organized walkouts with demands for an eight-hour workday, safer operations, and more sanitary quarters. Equi had visited lumber camps and had widely complained of the wretched living conditions the men endured. She believed her challenges to the timber industry triggered intense antipathy toward her and enhanced the ensuing drive to silence her. The governors of Oregon, Washington, and Idaho coordinated a crushing retaliation with federal authorities, and they arrested hundreds of Wobblies. Then the government undercut the Wobblies further by installing a company union of its own making—the Loyal Legion of Loggers and Lumbermen—for what, in effect, became military service at the mills. The government basically reconfigured lumber operations into what it called the "Spruce Production Division" to fit its own needs for labor and output without giving workers any union rights. Ironically, the working conditions set by the government forced employers to adopt many of the strikers' longtime demands. Eventually one hundred thousand workers joined the Spruce Division after signing a no-strike clause and promising to support the war and oppose sedition. In a deft political and strategic move, the federal government suppressed the unions and organized the region's spruce production to total one million board feet every day.[15]

The suppression of dissent quickened, and on September 5, 1917, the Department of Justice mounted a nationwide raid that targeted Equi and hundreds of Wobblies, Socialists, pacifists, and labor agitators. They stripped her office of records, correspondence, and pamphlets in a search for evidence of treason. Equi did not resist, but she summoned attorney C. E. S. Wood to witness the raid. Few arrests occurred, but Attorney General Gregory announced that indictments would follow. Then, later that month, the government dropped the other shoe. A Chicago grand jury indicted 166 Wobblies, including leaders William

The Liberty Temple, erected on a busy downtown street, reflected the patriotic fervor of Portland, Oregon during World War I. Oregon Historical Society, bb005134.

"Big Bill" Haywood and Elizabeth Gurley Flynn, for violation of the Espionage Act. More mass arrests targeted activists in Sacramento, Wichita, Omaha, and Spokane. The broad sweep snared even smalltime offenders, including Oregon's first indictment under the Espionage Act, the postmaster of the tiny town of Tenmile, George W. France. He was sentenced to thirteen months in a federal penitentiary for circulating a pamphlet titled "War, What For?"[16]

The Wobbly arrests failed to intimidate Equi, and on Sunday afternoons she often mounted a soapbox in Portland's Park Blocks downtown and castigated the government's Liberty Loan operation. All citizens were expected to demonstrate their patriotism by purchasing bonds to help defray the enormous cost of the war. Anyone who failed to do so was reported to the authorities as a slacker. The operation incensed Equi. She objected to working-class people being intimidated into giving money for bonds they could not afford. "Why not ask Dupont Powder Works, who made sixteen millions, to divide 50 percent with the government?" she asked the crowds. Equi's daughter recalled accompanying her mother to the protests. Mary Jr.'s role was to carry her mother's valise and stand on the edge of the crowd. "If the police come," Equi told her, "You run." When Equi spoke before Wobblies in a hall, Mary Jr. wore a red dress and sat on a red chair on the platform. To her, it was an adventure, but she also remembered people yelling and spitting at them while they were walking downtown.[17]

In April 1918 Americans celebrated the first anniversary of the declaration of war with pageants and parades that attracted tens of thousands. The government launched its third Liberty Loan drive, and Portlanders erected a massive wood and plaster Liberty Temple in the middle of Sixth Avenue downtown as a show of the city's patriotism. Hundreds of Portlanders thrust wads of cash at clerks working at the temple, and in the first three days purchased nearly $12 million worth of bonds. Portland's achievements were repeated throughout the war—the city and the state regularly placed in the top ranks for fundraisers and appeals for all sorts of household materials. Equi could not have chosen a more prowar community to register her dissent.[18]

The US Congress, meanwhile, enacted an amendment to the Espionage Act that authorized vast new powers to curb and punish dissent. The new Sedition Act, signed by the president on May 16, 1918, prohibited anyone from speaking, writing, or publishing any "disloyal, profane, scurrilous, or abusive language" about the government, the armed services, the flag, liberty loans, the draft, or war industries. To dispel any uncertainty of the extent of its reach, the act outlawed anyone from saying or doing *anything* opposed to "the cause of the United States." [19]

Equi's reckoning came the following month when, on the evening of June 27, after a warm summer day, she delivered one of her regular rousing talks at the IWW hall. Her speech was not unusual and received no immediate notice in the dailies, but the US Army's Military Intelligence Division placed agents in the hall ready to find evidence against her. Afterward, they reported that Equi had uttered inflammatory and disloyal remarks. Two days later a grand jury indicted Equi with eight charges under the Sedition Act, including vowing allegiance to the red banner of industrial workers, accusing the ruling class of forcing laborers to fight against their brothers and relatives, and maligning the character of America's soldiers. The government also claimed she had urged the IWW to learn from Irish nationalists who sought their freedom while England struggled in the war.[20]

Federal officers apprehended Equi on Sunday, June 30, in the Lafayette Building where they found her in the offices of her friend Dr. Alys Griff drinking fine whiskey—at eight dollars a bottle. Deputy US Attorney Frank Berry, accompanied by Bureau of Investigation Agent William Bryon, arrested Equi and took her to the US Marshal's office without a fuss on her part. However, she later recounted that she "almost passed away" when informed of the $25,000 bail, an amount equivalent to several hundred thousand dollars today.

She negotiated a reduction to $10,000 and then set about collecting the full amount for bail from friends.[21]

While Equi was under arrest, federal agents appeared at the two-level Craftsman house that she and Harriet Speckart had rented the previous year in the eastside Mt. Tabor district. Armed with a search warrant, they demanded entry and Speckart stepped aside. The agents scoured the rooms and seized letters from IWW attorney George Vanderveer that they found taped behind a painting. Apparently, the documents were simple notes of appreciation for Equi's help with the defense of Wobblies. The operatives departed and left Speckart to explain to her three-year-old daughter what had just occurred.[22]

The charges against Equi were similar to a dozen others in Oregon and hundreds nationwide. On the same day Equi was arrested, federal agents targeted Eugene Debs, US congressman from Indiana and former presidential candidate for the Socialist Party. The government indicted him for his remarks about how dangerous it had become to exercise the right of free speech "in a country fighting to make the world safe for democracy." Debs was convicted of sedition and sentenced to ten years in a federal penitentiary. Federal officers also arrested Kate Richards O'Hare and Rose Pastor Stokes, the top two women leaders in the Socialist Party, on charges of discouraging enlistment and for false allegations about the government's motivations for going to war. Everywhere the message of the US government became, in the words of the attorney general, "Obey the law and keep your mouth shut!"[23]

Federal authorities crafted what seemed an excessive covert operation to secure Equi's conviction with at least eight agents from the Department of Justice's Bureau of Investigation and the US Army's Military Intelligence Division tracking her every move. Operators installed wiretaps in her rooms, shadowed her visitors and friends, and spied from rooms next to her medical practice and her hotel suite. The government deemed the surveillance necessary after receiving reports like one from the US attorney in Portland that Equi was "the very worst agitator we have in town." He held her to be "thoroughly disloyal and a woman of the Emma Goldman type." During Goldman's trial, prosecutors argued that her political views as well as her immoral personal life threatened fundamental American values. She became the reference for all the other disruptive, unconventional, and unbecoming women the government prosecuted under the wartime acts. Equi was not the only surveillance target in Portland, but the considerable resources assigned to her case reflected how much the government feared her influence.[24]

Irish nationalist and journalist Kathleen O'Brennan became Marie Equi's intimate companion. *San Francisco Chronicle*, February 17, 1922.

The arrival of another Irish nationalist in Portland in late July 1918 yielded an unexpected boost to federal agents overwhelmed by the number of suspects to monitor. They were able to spy on Equi and another agitator under the same roof. Kathleen O'Brennan, an independent single woman of twenty-eight years, had emigrated from Ireland to America in 1914 with hopes for adventure and work as a journalist. She undertook a national tour to speak on Irish culture and literature, and, in time, she drew on her family's troubled experience with Irish independence. Both her great-grandfather and her father had led rebellions against British rule, and, more recently, her brother-in-law, Eamonn Ceannt, was executed by the British for his role in the Easter Rising of 1916, an attempt to free Ireland in the middle of the war. British Intelligence had already placed O'Brennan under surveillance during her tour, and US agents assisted once she reached the West Coast.[25]

True to her reputation for welcoming important women to the city, Equi met O'Brennan within days of her arrival, and they soon became inseparable. With O'Brennan, Equi found an attractive, energetic, and politically engaged woman fourteen years her junior with whom she could share the rigors of labor and antiwar strife and receive the tenderness she had described to Margaret Sanger. In little time, she fell in love with a woman she called "my little rebel." Not surprisingly, her budding romance with Kitty, as everyone called O'Brennan, was serious enough to disrupt Equi's living arrangement with Harriet Speckart. After thirteen years of sharing their lives and a home together,

Equi and Speckart parted ways. Speckart could easily have tired of Equi's infatuations and affairs as well as the activities that brought federal agents to her door. She might also have sought relief from the bombast of the war years in Portland. With her daughter in tow, Speckart relocated to the Oregon Coast and took a home at Seaside. Equi rented rooms at the Oregon Hotel in downtown Portland. She remained in contact with Mary Jr. and Speckart, but the two onetime companions never lived together again."[26]

O'Brennan's intended adventure in America soured once she suspected she was being trailed in the Pacific Northwest. She registered at the venerable Portland Hotel upon her arrival, but soon suspected that British agents had taken rooms on either side of her own. Within days she discovered her belongings had been searched and that a dictaphone—a listening device—had been installed in her room. O'Brennan panicked and told her troubles to Equi, who responded in her usual restrained manner. She berated the military agents—who, she assured O'Brennan, were Americans, not British—threatened to shoot them through the wall, ripped out the dictaphone, and tossed it through the transom of the agents' room. Then she filed an anonymous complaint with the military authorities about the scandalous behavior of soldiers consorting with prostitutes in the hotel. Unsettled, O'Brennan left the hotel and moved into Equi's rooms.[27]

Equi may have seemed the perfect companion to O'Brennan. The older woman understood the Irish cause implicitly, she had dealt with federal authorities, and she had a reputation as a fearless advocate for working people. Besides, O'Brennan was a newcomer to Portland and its Irish community, and she found in Equi an entrée to politically engaged, impassioned individuals. Then there was the matter of infatuation and sex with another woman. O'Brennan's prior sexual experience and interests are not known, but Equi clearly gave her the chance for an intimate, sexual relationship with a woman of intelligence, good humor, and fierce convictions. The two lovers had little opportunity for peace and quiet, however. Equi was struggling to manage her attorneys and construct a defense to stay out of prison.

Federal authorities had already recruited an undercover agent, Margaret "Madge" Lowell Paul, to befriend O'Brennan and report on her activities. Paul, who the agents referred to as Informant 53, was known to support Irish independence, and the Bureau used that allegiance to endear her to O'Brennan. Paul was a confident, attractive, self-assured graduate of Radcliffe College, fluent in three languages, aware of current events, a good conversationalist, and a woman who mixed well in social circles. Her sympathetic, solicitous manner charmed Equi as well and prompted her to welcome the newcomer into her circle—just as federal agents had hoped. With one undercover agent they could build a case against Equi for espionage and another against O'Brennan for offenses meriting deportation.[28]

Paul followed a daily routine of telephone calls and personal visits with Equi and O'Brennan, often including lunch or dinner at one of Equi's favorite restaurants—Musso's, Bab's, and the Oyster Loaf—and ending with cocktails in Equi's office or hotel room. At some point, she slipped away to brief Agent Bryon and to submit a report that was shared with the US Attorney's office. As an informant trading in deception and manipulation, Paul's accounts of anything that might implicate Equi were suspect, but her observations of Equi's sometimes mundane, other times complicated personal and political dealings provide an otherwise unavailable glimpse of how she conducted her life while being hounded by the government.[29]

Equi spoke freely of her trial defense strategy, and Paul disclosed information moderately helpful for the government's purposes. The agent identified Equi's associate who helped solicit funds for her defense, and she described conflicts between Equi and her attorneys. She revealed that the American Federation of Labor had agreed to pay for the best attorney Equi could find, and she recounted that O'Brennan had successfully lobbied US Senator James Phelan of California to review Equi's case. Paul readily reported intimate details of Equi's and O'Brennan's private lives—the nights of poker and booze with friends, their endearments and spats, or an awkward encounter with Harriet Speckart in the hotel hallway.[30]

The intelligence units monitoring Equi and O'Brennan worked in conjunction with the US Attorney for Oregon, Bert Haney, who became the chief prosecutor in the case against Equi. Haney was an upright but small-minded man with little tolerance for political views or behaviors outside the mainstream. He was born and raised in the Willamette Valley town of Yamhill, and he earned his law degree from the University of Oregon, graduating the same year as Equi. Before taking the federal post, he served as a deputy district attorney and was considered an up-and-coming lawyer and prospective political candidate. Haney embraced the patriotism of the day, and, like other ambitious US attorneys, he treated the Espionage Act as a mandate for aggressive prosecutions and an opportunity to get noticed.[31]

To win the case against Equi, Haney needed proof that she had actually uttered the words attributed to her and that she *intended* to cause disloyalty and disruption of the war effort. But Haney pushed the federal agents even further.

He wanted them to interview all of Equi's contacts to unearth a predisposi-
tion toward disloyalty as evidenced by transgressions of any kind. During the
hypervigilance of wartime surveillance, the prospect of a visit by federal agents
struck fear into many Americans who wanted to avoid any association with
disloyalty. Yet, according to agents' reports, several of Equi's acquaintances
appeared all too ready to find fault with her. Dr. Belle Rinehart Ferguson, the
bemused object of Equi's infatuation in The Dalles in the 1890s, recalled how
she had tried to block Equi's graduation from medical school. She volunteered
that Equi would do anything, even use poison, to achieve her ends, and she
recounted an incident that occurred twenty-five years earlier in which Equi, in
anger, supposedly threatened to kill Bessie Holcomb. Another respondent, Dr.
Simon Josephi, the former medical school dean, recalled Equi's quick temper,
and he characterized her as a troublemaker. None of this amounted to real
evidence, but the investigations reflected how the government sought any
detail that might besmirch Equi's record before a jury.[32]

The investigations often veered off the mark. Attorney Haney tried to
link Equi to the 1913 Paterson silk strike, although she was battling the police
in the local cannery strike at the time. He pursued a twisted thread of suspicion
that one of Elizabeth Gurley Flynn's allies, the author Mary E. Austin, was the
same Mary Austin who had taught Equi high school history in New Bedford
many years earlier. Agents learned that the schoolteacher had lived above
suspicion and had died before the strike hit Paterson. Back on the West Coast,
agents delved into the Speckart affair, hoping to unearth unsavory details from
the detective agency hired by Speckart's uncle to investigate Equi. But former
operators recalled nothing damaging for all their efforts in 1906.[33]

Equi was neither the leader of a radical outfit nor the instigator of industrial sabotage. No one had suffered dire consequences from the purportedly
seditious words she spoke at the IWW hall. But her tenacity, her ability to
rouse people across class lines against injustice, and her refusal to be cowed
by the authorities particularly threatened US attorneys, federal agents, and the
men who wielded power in the Pacific Northwest. But there was more: Equi
seemed to stir an inordinate amount of loathing and fear.[34]

Agent Bryon, the Bureau chief, wrote his superiors in Washington, DC,
that Equi's menace grew daily, and his assessments expressed his own dislike
and disgust for everything about her. In a September 1918 report, Bryon detailed Equi's consorting with Kitty O'Brennan, and, he commented, "like all
of their kind they are perverts and degenerates." He described the account of
a woman guest at the Portland Hotel who overheard the carrying-on between

Equi and O'Brennan in the next room. The details, he explained, were "too lascivious" to be recorded. He likened Equi to a buzzard hovering over labor disputes expecting a feast, and he claimed that he was trailing "one of the most dangerous anarchists and plotters against constituted authority in the United States."[35]

No stranger to litigation, Equi nevertheless worried about how to proceed with her court appearance. Few attorneys were experienced with representing espionage defendants, and she vacillated on who to retain. She settled on E. E. Heckbert, the loyal, competent workhorse of an attorney who had represented Speckart in her family dispute, and James Fenton, whose calm but forceful manner she appreciated. Surprisingly Equi did not hire the more prominent and skilled C. E. S. Wood, who had already represented another Oregonian charged with sedition.[36]

A few days before her trial, Equi convinced IWW attorney George Vanderveer to lead her defense team. The two had crossed paths during the aftermath of the 1916 massacre in Everett, Washington, where he successfully defended one of the Wobblies charged with murder. Vanderveer was a good-looking man, solid and sturdy, who nevertheless appeared haggard and exhausted much of the time from his unrelenting work for IWW defendants. He took Equi's case on the heels of his devastating loss in the mass espionage trial of Wobblies in Chicago. But Equi and Vanderveer argued about everything from whether to insert IWW values in the defense to the advisability of recruiting character witnesses. (She initially wanted to avoid subjecting her friends to federal harassment.) Equi set out on one course of action, however, that Vanderveer could not dissuade her from. She tried to delay the start of her trial as long as possible. Like other radicals, she anticipated trumped-up charges, biased juries, and fraudulent court testimony. As a result, she adopted the wisdom of Elizabeth Gurley Flynn, who explained, "Time was our greatest asset." For radicals, Flynn believed, "A trial was tantamount to a lynching."[37]

Equi intended to feign illness to postpone the start of her trial, scheduled for November 6, 1918. She hoped a jury might be more sympathetic once the war had ended. At first she considered having her appendix removed and then requesting two weeks or more for recovery. Then she planned to ingest a noxious thyroid compound along with a morphine solution to induce fever and nausea. She settled on something less dire: rubbing an ointment in her nose that would trigger influenza-like symptoms. In normal times, her choice of faking the flu might have been inconsequential, but she figured her deception might merit empathy or even exploit fears of the influenza pandemic plaguing the nation.[38]

The first wave of the so-called Spanish influenza struck the East Coast and the Midwest in the spring of 1918. No one paid much attention to the peculiar flu that came on quickly and initially struck soldiers and sailors, and after a few weeks the number of cases dropped and the danger seemed to have passed. In the fall, however, a second, more virulent wave slammed the general population, especially young adults of all classes. The rapid onset of symptoms often meant a patient complained of fever, headache, and backache one day and then struggled to breathe the next before suffocating to death. Not until the onset of AIDS sixty-five years later would the nation exhibit so much panic and fear of a mysterious, deadly disease. Physicians struggled with an enormous demand for diagnosis and care although they had neither treatment nor vaccine to offer. During the course of the pandemic, nearly 30 percent of Americans became infected, and 675,000 died. Half of the fatalities among American soldiers in Europe were due to the epidemic. The psychological impact of this toll must have staggered the population.[39]

Portland's first Spanish flu case was believed to be a young soldier, diagnosed in early October 1918. The state's board of health quickly ordered all places of public gatherings closed: schools, theaters, churches, libraries, and assembly halls. No meetings were allowed, and people were advised to avoid crowded streetcars and wear gauze masks at all times. The number of cases soared so high that the public auditorium and several schools were converted into emergency hospitals. Portland registered 157 deaths the first week of November when Equi's trial was set to begin, but the federal court system disregarded the risks of transmission and announced plans to begin the fall session as scheduled. Equi put her ruse into effect and induced symptoms the night before her court appearance. That same evening she learned that an acquaintance of hers, a young Wobbly named Morgan, really was ill with the flu and had been taken to the emergency hospital.[40]

Equi's trial began on Wednesday, November 6, 1918, in Portland's federal courthouse at Sixth and Morrison Streets with Judge Robert S. Bean presiding. Bean was a dignified and distinguished judge who had previously served as Chief Justice of the Oregon Supreme Court before assuming a position as a US District Judge in Portland. As planned, Equi's attorney Heckbert informed Bean that she was ill with influenza and needed rest. Madge Paul had already informed US Attorney Haney of Equi's deception, and he requested that a court physician examine her and advise the court of her condition. The doctor determined Equi required, at most, forty-eight hours of rest. Bean ordered Equi to appear in court on Friday, November 8 or forfeit her $10,000 bail. During the same court proceedings, Haney revealed that he had received regular reports of Equi's activities and he knew of her ploy to delay her appearance. Equi was furious that her plan had been exposed. At first she blamed one of her attorneys, Heckbert, of double-crossing her; then she suspected Madge Paul but delayed a confrontation with her.[41]

A reflection of the intensity of the times came with a telephone call that evening from a nurse at the influenza ward who informed Equi that her friend Morgan was dying and begging to see her. When O'Brennan advised her to delay her visit, Equi exploded and yelled, "That dying boy is alone and wants me, and I'd go through hell to help one of my boys." She grabbed a bunch of red carnations from a vase, rushed to the patient's bedside, and stayed with him through the night until he died. She was distraught for days afterwards—angry with herself for not providing more care and furious with the government for keeping her from her patients.[42]

On November 7, George Vanderveer arrived in Portland, ready to serve as Equi's lead counsel the next day, but all plans were tossed aside once the dailies broke the news the war-weary public longed for: the war had ended. Portlanders erupted in deliriously happy, raucous celebrations. Longshoreman left the docks and marched downtown, whistling, shouting, and ignoring attempts by the police to maintain order. Office workers several stories above an impromptu street parade rained paper scraps on the revelers. Everyone ignored flu precautions and littered the streets with face masks. Oregon had sent thirty-five thousand men to fight, a full 14 percent of the state's adult population, and everyone wanted the dread scourge out of their lives.[43]

Equi took comfort in delaying her trial until after the war had ended, but several hours later all celebrations stopped when people on the streets, stunned and angry, learned there was no peace, not yet. The war continued. An overeager wire correspondent on the front lines in France had filed a premature report, and Germany had yet to surrender. The next morning, Equi's trial resumed.

13
Convicted for Conscience

I am firmly of the opinion that it would be a crime and
an outrage to send Dr. Equi to jail, even for a day.
Thomas Gough Ryan, deputy district attorney,
Multnomah County, Oregon

In the chill of Friday morning, November 8, 1918, with heavy frost on the ground, Portlanders returned to work, many of them tired and disgruntled from celebrating the false armistice the day before. Along the way they spotted bold-printed "Influenza" signs in windows to discourage visitors, and the more cautious among them donned their gauze masks again. The morning paper reported that a true end of the war was imminent as a German delegation awaited the terms of surrender. The day marked Marie Equi's first appearance to stand trial for wartime offenses, and she walked the short distance from her rooms at the Oregon Hotel to the historic US courthouse, a fine three-story, sandstone-clad edifice with a cupola. In the courtroom of Judge Robert Bean, she took a seat next to her attorneys, J. E. Fenton, E. E. Heckbert, and the recently arrived George Vanderveer, veteran counsel for the Industrial Workers of the World. Her nemesis, US District Attorney Bert Haney, sat ready to prosecute his most closely watched case yet, along with his deputy attorney, Barnett Goldstein. Prospective jurors, witnesses, and observers packed the room, curious to see if the indomitable Dr. Equi might possibly prevail.

Equi had informed friends that she doubted she would get a fair trial, and the jury selection did not encourage her. Men filled all twelve seats. (Although Oregon women had won the vote in 1912, they were still barred from jury service in state and federal courts.) All but three of the jurors were smalltown men—farmers, merchants, or proprietors. Yet they were chosen to sit in judgment of a professional woman from Portland who objected to a war that the majority of Oregonians earnestly supported.[1]

Much of Equi's first day in court slogged through procedural matters with Judge Bean over-ruling defense objections before adjourning for the weekend. During the few days off, the ravages of the Spanish flu demanded

Bert E. Haney, US Attorney, District of Oregon, prosecuted Marie Equi for her public opposition to the capitalist underpinning of World War I. Library of Congress LC-58-25138

Equi's attention. The daughter of her friends, Ina and John Hayes, fell ill and worsened rapidly. The girl pleaded to see her Doc, and her mother begged Equi to visit, which she did, leaving the girl's bedside only to have dinner with Vanderveer, O'Brennan, and undercover agent Madge Paul. Equi was sick of the trial, she told them, and she wanted to talk about cheerful affairs. Afterward, Equi returned to the girl and remained with her until she died the next day. Her passing unnerved Equi, who was already frustrated by frequent arguments with Vanderveer. That night she was infuriated to find yet another federal agent in the hallway outside her hotel room.[2]

On Sunday, November 10, at midnight the *Oregonian* announced the end of the war, this time for real. The news spread quickly, and hundreds of men and boys gathered and hollered once again on downtown streets. Meier and Frank's, Portland's large downtown department store, lit all its lights during the dark hours of the morning. Within hours crowds gathered all over the city in near pandemonium. The state declared the next day, November 11, a holiday, calling it Armistice Day, and the federal courts postponed all trials.[3]

When the trial resumed, prosecutors Haney and Goldstein set out to convince the jury that Equi's seditious intentions could be demonstrated by a history of defaming the country. They called as their first witnesses Sergeant Sutton C. Linville and James Brady, two operatives of the Military Intelligence Division who worked in the lumber mills. Both had been recruited to attend Equi's talk at the IWW hall, and they testified that she had urged the Wobblies to strike for freedom while their government masters were at war. On cross-examination the soldiers damaged their own testimony by admitting to difficulty staying awake during Equi's talk. Then they described comparing notes after the Wobbly meeting and agreeing what account to "stick with" under oath. A third witness testified that he had also attended the meeting and heard Equi describe the war as "nothing but . . . capital against labor, a rich man's war." He also claimed Equi swore her allegiance to the Wobblies' red flag.[4]

Haney then called city police officers to confirm offensive remarks Equi had allegedly uttered when a military funeral passed by an antiwar rally and again during the preparedness day parade. A detective recounted the flag-kissing incident at the parade and insisted Equi had told a Wobbly audience, "They wanted me to kiss that dirty little rag, that American rag, and I wouldn't do it. I wouldn't kiss any flag." Equi's attorney Vanderveer objected that these earlier incidents occurred before the Sedition Act made such talk illegal. Judge Bean over-ruled the objection, affirming that the defendant's "state of mind" was indeed relevant. The judge was asserting a critical interpretation of admissible information that later prevailed in other espionage cases despite legal challenges.[5]

Portland's mayor, George Baker, a six-foot-tall, irrepressible showman-turned-politician, testified that Equi's reputation as a law-abiding citizen was "very bad." Circuit Court Judge George Stapleton and the chief deputy US marshal, among others, concurred. George R. Funk, the head of Portland's Anti-Sedition League, a patriotic society known to intimidate and harass suspected dissenters, testified last. Such were the times in Portland that Funk, a wartime vigilante leader, also served as city auditor.[6]

Equi's attorneys faced an impossible challenge. They had to refute charges that they believed should never have been made based on a law that should never have been enacted. In his opening statement, Vanderveer presented Equi as the kind of citizen who made America strong. He spoke of her efforts to secure the eight-hour workday, better conditions in factories and forests, and housing and food for the unemployed. Through it all, he declared, she provided free medical care for the poor. He emphasized that Equi objected to government policies and to the role of big business in the war, but never to the government itself, its flag, or its soldiers and sailors.[7]

In normal times testimony by a popular former governor would represent a major coup for the defense, but Equi's most prominent character witness proved to be reluctant and equivocal. Oswald West, a one-term governor who had served at the peak of Oregon's Progressive Era, had known Equi for ten years and had tangled with her during the 1913 cannery strike. But when her attorney insisted that West state whether Equi was a peaceful, law-abiding, and loyal citizen, he hesitated and tried to reframe the question. Only when the judge demanded an answer did West respond that he had never known Equi's loyalty to be questioned prior to the indictment. Later there was much speculation that West had testified only because Equi possessed information that he wanted kept secret. In cross-examination Haney tried to maneuver the governor into admitting he had objected to Equi's behavior during the cannery strike. West allowed that she was "a little excited" at the time, but he added that several months prior to the trial he had agreed to help her with an application to serve in France. He never would have done so, he declared, if he had thought she was disloyal.[8]

The next witness, Dr. Charles Chapman, a former president of the University of Oregon and an editorial writer for the *Oregon Daily Journal*, was more forthcoming. Chapman had known Equi for twenty years, he said, and he had heard her talk fifty times in the past two years. "She is a good, loyal woman who devotes her life to good work," he asserted. He admitted she sometimes spoke disrespectfully of big corporations, but since the war began, he said, she had accepted the status quo like many others.[9]

The other defense witnesses assured the court they had never heard Equi make seditious remarks or resort to anything disloyal. Circuit Court Judge William Gatens, a respected Portlander who had known Equi since he helped Harriet Speckart with her family dispute, spoke highly of her. Two of Equi's medical colleagues—Viola Coe and Katherine Manion—testified to her good standing in the community. Even Deputy US Marshal Frank Berry, who had arrested Equi on the sedition charges, stood up for her, as did a Socialist Congressional candidate and the secretary of the Central Labor Council.[10]

Attorney Vanderveer then tried to undermine the prosecution witnesses. He called a Wobbly who denied that Equi ever called soldiers "skunks." She always referred to sailors and soldiers as "our boys," he testified. Erskine Wood, son of attorney C. E. S. Wood, remembered seeing one of the prosecution witnesses attack Equi during the preparedness parade. Vanderveer summoned a prosecution witness back to the stand and pressed him to admit that he had told a prostitute that the government may not have enough evidence but "we're going to get Dr. Equi one way or another." After he denied the statement, the woman in question testified he had lied. Given her occupation, little came of her accusation, except for harassment by the police. With the close of the trial's first full week, Vanderveer announced the defense would rest once Equi took the stand the following Monday.[11]

At two o'clock Monday afternoon, Equi strode into a packed courtroom, and no one, not even her attorneys, knew what she would say. She started with the basics: forty-five years of age, an Oregon resident for eighteen years, a member of the local medical society, and a fellow of the American Medical Association. She then credited her Italian father and Irish mother with her abhorrence of absolutism, monarchy, and oppression, and she reframed how others had described and vilified her. She declared her opposition to militarism and her support for labor rights as a responsible citizen concerned with injustice. She explained that she entered the Preparedness Parade with an anticapitalist banner because she felt people were being duped by corporate titans into supporting the war. A few men had tried to force her to kiss the American flag, she explained, and she refused to be bullied.[12]

Equi asserted her patriotism, disclosing that she had solicited help from the late Senator Harry Lane to arrange a Red Cross assignment for herself in France. She had also purchased $150 worth of War Stamps and a $50 Liberty bond, she said. But Equi castigated the banks that charged 8 percent on loans to hardpressed working people to purchase war bonds. And she objected that men were tarred and feathered for failure to buy bonds. The problem for her, she concluded, was not the government but the corporate profiteering that the government sanctioned.[13]

Attorney Haney's cross-examination triggered the stormiest exchanges of the trial. One of the dailies described the "battle of wits" with Equi as something seldom seen between a woman and a man in a courtroom. For several hours Haney brought to bear everything government agents had uncovered, and she batted them aside without a miss. When he pressed her on the Preparedness Parade, she countered that even President Wilson had opposed preparedness before he supported it. She asserted that she had always supported America and never Germany in the war. She denied calling the flag a "dirty rag," saying she had never heard anyone speak of the flag that way, not even Germans. But Equi acknowledged that she sometimes joined Wobblies to sing "The Red Flag" at their meetings. She was fired up and vented her months-long frustration over all the accusations lobbed her way even before the trial. She denied being an anarchist, asserted she had registered as a Progressive, and stated she had voted Democratic to keep America out of the war. She denied using objectionable language in public and asserted her right to free speech. Equi frustrated Haney to no end by answering his questions with several of her own. She refused to let him lead the examination, newspapers reported, and she expounded on issues important to her—industrialism, poverty, child labor laws, the draft, the Tom Mooney frame-up, and the right to strike.[14]

The strain of the afternoon drained Equi, and she was pushed too far when her own attorney queried whether she had ever referred to dead American soldiers as "dirty skunks and detestable scum." The *Oregonian* reported that Equi's eyes filled with tears, and her voice faltered. "I do not think I ought to be asked to deny such a charge," she said. The suggestion was too offensive. Vanderveer requested a brief intermission, and the day's session ended soon thereafter.[15]

That evening, undercover agent Madge Paul's cover was blown for certain. Vanderveer invited Paul to dinner and told her an informant of his own had exposed everything about her work for the Bureau. She dodged his accusation and countered that he was mistaken. Afterward, Equi never allowed Paul to think she was upset about the betrayal, and in a show of bravado, she told Paul several times that she had known about the ruse all along.[16]

On the last full day of the trial, Vanderveer observed that people like Equi had "always been misunderstood," and he asked the jury, in what may have seemed an odd turn, to try her as Jesus would. But assistant prosecutor Goldstein condemned Equi's morality, her life in Portland, and her work with the IWW. Haney saved his most caustic remarks for the closing statement. He dismissed the testimony of former Governor West with a snarky aside that he had more faith in Oregonians once they turned him out of office. He held nothing but contempt for Dr. Chapman, whom he dismissed as "another cheap intellectual." He referred to Equi and her *kind* as "Long–haired men and short-haired women." Haney's contempt tipped the government's hand, revealing the vitriol and homophobia that fueled the indictment. The prosecutor then pulled out more red-baiting. He warned, "The red flag is floating over Russia, Germany, and a great part of Europe. Unless you put this woman in jail, I tell you it will float over the world." He concluded by reciting *The Star Spangled Banner* up close, moving from one juror to another.[17]

Judge Bean instructed the jury to declare Not Guilty for three of the eight charges, due to lack of evidence. Then he explained that the alleged words and acts were only illegal during wartime, but it made no difference to their deliberations that the war had ended. Finally, he asked them to deliver a sealed verdict the next morning.[18]

On Thursday, November 21, Equi sat in the courtroom awaiting the decision that would shape the rest of her life. The twelve jurors filed into the courtroom, the foreman gave a sealed envelope to the judge, and he then announced the verdict—guilty on all remaining counts. For her one talk at the IWW hall, Equi faced a maximum sentence of one hundred years in prison and $50,000 in fines. "White as marble and with flashing eyes," Equi rose from her chair with complete silence in the courtroom, according to newspaper accounts. "I want to say a word," she announced. "For years I have been hounded in this town. During the cannery strike I was taken into the county jail, stripped, beaten, and spit upon." She objected to the charges against her and the excessive surveillance she had endured. When the judge finally prevailed and convinced her to stop, he ignored her comments and instructed her to refrain from public speeches until the final disposition of the case.[19]

"There is one more thing," Equi continued. "Barney Goldstein, who calls himself my friend, referred to me yesterday as an *unsexed woman*." She added, "When a Russian Jew comes to this country to sit in judgment of an American woman and makes such remarks as that about her, I think the court should require him to make public apology to me." Judge Bean declined, and Equi replied she would take care of it herself. Goldstein's remark reflected the slander that federal agents and court officers expressed regularly in their internal reports about Equi, but in the packed courtroom Goldstein flaunted official contempt for her and confirmed for the jury why she should be punished. For her part, Equi objected to the power exerted by a foreign-born man who enjoyed full citizenship when women still lacked the right to vote. But Goldstein's sexual slur may have also unleashed her resentment over the insults and accusations she had encountered for years about her lesbianism.[20]

In the hallway outside the courtroom, Equi held forth with her friends and attorneys as reporters gathered round. "What chance had a woman among those men head-hunters?" she asked. "It was a frame-up and everyone knows it. Four witnesses told the exact same story. If you know psychology, you know such a thing means a frame-up. They were out to get me because I have been pleading the cause of the poor and oppressed." Before Equi's attorneys could pull her away, she threatened any man or woman who questioned her loyalty or virtue. "I'll pull off the best little shooting you ever saw in this town," she promised, telling the reporters to publish her words.[21]

The full extent of what had befallen her registered by the time Equi addressed fourteen hundred supporters two weeks later. She mounted the stage to cries of "Dr. Equi, Dr. Equi," but she was unable to match their enthusiasm.

Marie Equi with her daughter Mary outside the federal courthouse in Portland, Oregon, 1920. Also present were her longtime companion Harriet Speckart (far left), her friend Ruth Barnett (right) and Barnett's husband. Oregon Historical Society, bb013177.

She criticized the prosecutors, but she spoke with little fire or passion. She claimed the lumber trust had targeted her for five years, and that they had finally succeeded. She concluded that she was now finished and that the authorities would put her away. She was grateful, she said, to have done her "little part" for the cause. Yet the occasion was a success: the crowd donated more than $200 to Equi's defense fund. Soon afterward, her attorneys filed a motion for a new trial, but they were denied and the court set her sentence hearing for the last day of the year. [22]

On Tuesday morning, December 31, 1918, Equi returned to the courthouse, holding the hand of her three-year-old daughter. Harriet Speckart, Ruth Barnett, and several other friends accompanied them, and they settled once again in Judge Bean's courtroom. With the session called to order, the judge asked Equi if she had any final words. She rose "white-faced, voice wavering," according to one report. She reiterated her innocence and disclosed that while her trial was underway, a nephew, a boy she said she had helped raise, was dying of injuries sustained on the front lines in France. "While I was being persecuted, not prosecuted, here," she said, "my boy gave his life there."[23]

Judge Bean suggested there were two classes of people in the country—those who supported the war effort and those who did not. "All the government asked was that those who did not would keep quiet and not embarrass the government in its conduct of the war." He said the evidence showed that Equi had not kept quiet, as if citizenship required silence. Equi's attorney Fenton requested leniency for his client, explaining that she tended to be impulsive and imprudent when agitated. Bean sentenced Equi to three years in federal prison and a fine of $500. He set her bail at $10,000.[24]

An explosive conflict awaited Equi outside the courtroom when she confronted federal agent Bryon face to face. His disgust for everything about Equi spilled out. He reportedly told her, "Well, I got you," and she replied, "I hope you're satisfied." One account said Equi called him a "dirty dog" several times. Bryon told her to get out of the way, and, according to Equi and newspaper reports, he grabbed her by the throat, struck her in the side, and shoved her to the floor. When Harriet tried to intervene, Bryon knocked her to the floor as well. Mary Jr. ran forward and yelled, "Leave my Da alone!" Bryon later gave his own version of the confrontation and said he may have brushed Equi aside and she fell backward. He noticed several Wobblies nearby and avoided a larger incident by ducking into the elevator and leaving the building. Equi and Speckart were left shaken and furious and held Mary Jr. close. The assault led to a barrage of criticism in newspapers with calls for Bryon's removal from the bureau.[25]

Before her federal imprisonment, Marie Equi sat for a series of studio photographs with her daughter Mary, 1920. Oregon Historical Society, bb013180.

14
Days of Reckoning

If ever an individual needed protection for free speech, free press, and free conscience, it is in time of war. People don't need constitutional guarantees at their picnics and prayer meetings.
Charles Erskine Scott Wood, attorney for Marie Equi

America was a transformed country after the wrenching experience of World War I and the ravages of the Spanish flu. The nation struggled to accommodate the returning soldiers and sailors seeking employment as well as the women and African Americans who wanted to keep their wartime jobs. Accustomed to government protections during the hostilities, industries resisted returning to greater competition and less-favored treatment. Women sought the long-delayed federal action on their right to vote, and Progressives and liberals lobbied for restoration of free speech and other civil liberties.

In Oregon, business activity in 1918 shattered previous records. The *Oregonian* proclaimed that every man who wanted a job could find one with unparalleled wages. Yet the region had also experienced one of the nation's most vigorous clampdowns on dissent, and the strife it caused hardly skipped a beat for the armistice. In addition, the federal and state governments inflamed a new postwar hysteria, stirring Americans' fears of radical immigrants and Bolshevik revolutionaries. A new Red Scare gripped the nation, and radicals like Marie Equi found little peace at war's end.[1]

Equi's conviction was one of hundreds delivered to radicals. In the mass trial of forty-six Wobblies in Sacramento, twenty received ten-year sentences, and all but three others were sentenced to terms of three to five years. The *Omaha Roundup* of sixty-four Wobblies was eventually dismissed, but not before the men had spent eighteen months in jail.[2]

Equi hoped the Ninth Circuit Court of Appeals in San Francisco would overturn her conviction, and she retained attorney James Fenton and, this time, C. E. S. Wood as her counsels. Wood, at age sixty-seven, had hoped to retire in San Francisco with his mistress, Oregon poet and suffragist Sara Bard Field, rather than tackling the US government's assault on free speech. But he found the wartime acts offensive to his personal and political beliefs, and he knew Equi well. In April 1919 he fired off a letter to the US attorney general, A. Mitchell Palmer, and objected to the government's use of the courts to silence Equi. He asserted that the charges against Equi accommodated "the privileged, wealthy classes of Portland and those who consider existing conditions sacred." President Woodrow Wilson had named Palmer, a Quaker-reared Progressive who never served in World War I, to the nation's top law enforcement post a month earlier. Palmer never responded to Wood's message, and Equi's attorney prepared for an appeal hearing in June.[3]

Equi's conviction failed to appease federal authorities in Oregon. As long as she remained free, they tried to silence her. Agent Bryon fumed in his reports to Washington about the public criticism of his courthouse clash with Equi, and he retaliated. An informant reported to him that on December 25, 1918, the local IWW had admitted Equi and Kitty O'Brennan—Number 439091 and Number 439090, respectively—as honorary members working on recruitment strategies. Bryon used the information first against O'Brennan to help deport her for working on behalf of Sinn Fein, the Irish revolutionary group. On January 14, federal authorities arrested O'Brennan at the Oregon Hotel. The *Oregonian* headlined the occasion with reference to her relationship with Equi: "Woman Who Shared Room with Dr. Marie Equi Taken Into Custody by Immigration Inspector."[4]

At O'Brennan's deportation hearing, government officials interrogated her about Sinn Fein and whether she favored the violent overthrow of British rule in Ireland. She denied raising money for the radical group but championed Irish freedom, no matter how it was achieved. After repeated questioning, she admitted to being an honorary IWW member. O'Brennan was released on her own recognizance, and a report of her hearing was submitted to officials in Washington, DC. Perhaps as a result of O'Brennan's connections with US senators, nothing further came of her case.[5]

Equi's own IWW membership—honorary or not—made her guilty of violating a new Oregon law meant to accomplish in the state what the Espionage and Sedition Acts had achieved nationally. Oregon and twenty-eight other states had enacted antianarchy laws—popularly known as criminal syndicalism acts— that prohibited utterances or publications that might trigger discontent or hostility toward the US government. In addition, any participation with the Socialist Party or the IWW violated the law. The US attorney general advised against prosecutions based on simple association with radical organizations, but local authorities, including state supreme courts, embarked on guilt-by-membership sweeps of suspect citizens. Fear of radicalism spiked across the nation, partly in reaction to the Great Steel Strike and the nation's first general strike in 1919. A walkout of 360,000 workers disabled the steel industry, and 60,000 local laborers shut down the city of Seattle for nearly a week.[6]

Portland police arrested Equi just before midnight on March 13, 1919, for violation of the state's criminal syndicalism act. She was charged with asking two men, a woman, and a girl to help her distribute Wobbly literature on downtown streets. After a night in jail, she was released for lack of evidence. Her detention reflected how authorities used the new law to exhaust radicals with arrests and jail time before reducing charges against them to misdemeanors.[7]

Equi left Portland for San Francisco two weeks later to take her case to the public under an arrangement with the Mooney Defense Fund. By aligning her circumstances with those of the internationally known prisoner of San Quentin, Equi gained a stature far greater than what she had achieved in Portland. She was thwarted from talking at Eagle's Hall in the city when the building owners learned the IWW sponsored her appearance, but she drew three hundred people at another location on Market Street and collected more than one hundred dollars.[8]

At an Oakland appearance, she challenged the audience to undertake nothing less than a widespread strike to free the thousands of political and class prisoners. "Political action is as dead as a Dodo—you can't do anything with it unless you have industrial organization first," she declared. She also spoke of class struggle. "You do not realize the class fear and the class hatred that is felt right now by the capitalist class. Talk about our class hatred. It is a puny affair next to their class hatred." Back in San Francisco, Equi reunited with Margaret Sanger, who was seeking solace in California after a bout of depression over the imprisonment of dissidents and the stalled efforts of the birth control movement.[9]

Equi's reckoning before the Ninth Circuit Court of Appeals came on June 4, 1919, in San Francisco's federal courthouse, the same location where Harriet Speckart's case had been heard years earlier. Equi appeared with her attorneys, Wood and Fenton. Kitty O'Brennan and six women supporters from the Bay Area, including Charlotte Anita Whitney, accompanied her. US Attorney Haney and Assistant Attorney Goldstein reappeared to defend their case before three judges led by William W. Morrow, a seventy-six-year-old Republican jurist with previous service in the Union Army and the US House of Representatives.[10]

Charles Erskine Scott Wood, prominent Portland
attorney and philosophical anarchist, defended
Marie Equi before the Ninth Circuit Court of
Appeals and submitted her appeal to the US Supreme
Court. Oregon Historical Society, bb018079.

Equi's attorneys reiterated that her activities prior to the Sedition Act should not have been admitted as evidence. They faulted Judge Bean for failing to protect her and claimed that she had become *tainted* before the jury as a result. In his remarks before the court, C. E. S. Wood presented a more profound argument. "If ever individuals need protection for free speech, free press, and free conscience, it is in time of war," he said. "People don't need constitutional guarantees at their picnics and prayer meetings." He argued that it mattered little if people found Equi disagreeable or if they found her speeches obnoxious. There was no treason, he said, in speaking one's mind.[11]

Wood knew that the circuit court judges were influenced by the Supreme Court's *Schenck v. United States* decision three months earlier. In that espionage case, Justice Oliver Wendell Holmes presented the situation of a man falsely shouting "FIRE" in a crowded theater as an example of limits to free speech. He established the *clear and present danger* test for utterances that Congress has a right to prevent. Wood countered that the fire-in-a-theater argument was irrelevant to a citizen criticizing her government since there was neither a threat nor damage to others. Instead, he countered, the US government, the press, and the moneyed classes had inflicted moral and political damage on the American public. One of Wood's biographers notes that his arguments were remarkable for assailing not only the political culture of the time but also the officers of the goverment, including the judges of the circuit court and the US Supreme Court.[12]

Attorneys Haney and Goldstein asserted that the war had required new demands of citizens. "We had to have men, we had to have money; and to get men and money, we had to have the proper spirit," Haney claimed. They reminded Judge Morrow of his previous finding that statements delivered prior to the war were clearly admissible. They claimed to confine their arguments to the record but then resorted to criticizing IWW and Socialist views and to deriding Equi for her "pose of martyrdom."[13]

The judges took the case under advisement, and Equi returned to Portland with O'Brennan. But she seemed unable to stop and rest for long. She traveled to Seattle and stood before fifteen hundred people to raise funds for those not fortunate to be released on bail. She made a point of identifying eight other women who faced terms of two to twenty years: Mollie Stimer, Flora Foreman, Louise Olivereau, Emma Goldman, Elizabeth Baer, Rose Pastor Stokes, Theodora Pollock, and Kate O'Hare. She understood how much these women, and many others, had upended gender norms of political power to protest the war and unjust labor conditions.[14]

Equi's life revolved around more than legal struggles and her expected imprisonment. Ruth Barnett, a younger abortion provider trained by Equi's friend Dr. Alys Griff, recalled long nights of partying. The three women worked in the Lafayette Building in three office suites and lived in the old Oregon Hotel, a few rooms apart.

"We worked hard and played hard," she later wrote. "After work we would whoop it up until all hours of the morning. . . . We'd go out to the roadhouses— *Twelve Mile* or the *Clackamas Tavern*. The doctor (Alys Griff) always had a big car, either a Winton or a Pierce Arrow. We had some great times. When you work hard, you appreciate the laughs, the big dinners, and the booze."[15]

Equi's drinking flew in the face of the Progressive Era's ban on alcohol sales and consumption in Oregon enacted in 1914. She had earlier regarded alcohol a threat to family life and individuals' well being, but, considering her looming imprisonment, she allowed herself some liberties.[16]

When Equi was fighting her conviction in San Francisco, senior staff at the Bureau of Investigation in Washingon D.C. questioned the merits of her case. A special assistant to the attorney general, Alfred Bettman, believed the charges were "the product of clamor rather more than truth." "I would certainly recommend dismissal of the prosecution," he advised if the circuit court reversed Equi's conviction. But three weeks later, on October 27, 1919, the Ninth Circuit Court affirmed the lower court's decision. They relied on precedents in other espionage cases and dismissed claims of First Amendment rights. Equi had partly expected the outcome, but she was staggered by the news nevertheless. "We're slaves," she told a gathering in downtown Portland four days later. "We may think we live in a free country, but we are in reality nothing but slaves."[17]

Only one legal option remained: a final appeal to the US Supreme Court. For this, Equi once again retained C. E. S. Wood with her own funds supplemented by $300 from Alexander Cook, the San Francisco merchant and husband of Bessie Holcomb, her longtime friend from New Bedford. She also recruited attorney Helen Hoy Greeley, an ally from Oregon's 1912 suffrage campaign, to lobby on her behalf in Washington, DC. They expected a decision from the nation's highest court at the start of the New Year.[18]

The clampdown on dissenters in America continued to surge, and radical suffragists were not spared the public's wrath. In Washington, DC, angry mobs attacked National Women's Party members who picketed the White House every day during the early months of 1919. They challenged President Wilson and Congress to ensure liberty for America's women as they had for European allies. The demonstrations led to arrests and beatings followed by hunger strikes and forced-feedings in prison. When the women were released, they toured the country by rail on a "Prison Special" to shame the government and further their cause. Congress finally submitted a federal suffrage amendment to the states in June 1919. More than a year later, on August 18, 1920, the amendment was ratified by two-thirds of the states and became enshrined as the Nineteenth Amendment to the US Constitution.[19]

A new free speech fight flared in the Pacific Northwest in November 1919 and drew Equi into its aftermath. A riot erupted between the American Legion and the IWW in Centralia, Washington, eighty-five miles south of Seattle. During the city's Armistice Day Parade, a platoon of American Legionnaires stormed the local Wobbly headquarters. Expecting an attack, Wobblies opened fire against the intruders, leaving three men dead and others wounded. One of the Wobbly shooters, Wesley Everest, a five-foot-seven-inch, thirty-three-year-old with dark red hair and blue eyes, ran from the scene and then reportedly shot and killed a Legionnaire who charged toward him. A mob captured Everest, beat him, and, according to eyewitnesses, rammed a spike through his cheek and broke his jaw before throwing him into jail. Later that night the men returned, pulled Everest from his cell, and hung him from a railroad trestle over the Chehalis River. Everest's death, and the trial of Wobblies charged in the battle, became yet another widely watched and much-condemned episode among labor radicals. George Vanderveer, Equi's recent attorney, mounted a defense, but most of the Wobbly defendants were convicted and sentenced from twenty-five to forty-five years in prison. Charges were never filed for the killing of Everest.[20]

Equi later told her daughter that she had visited the Wobblies in Centralia before the violence erupted and had tried to persuade Wesley Everest to leave the city while it was still safe. After Centralia, the Justice Department conducted another assault on radical organizations. Beginning November 7, 1919, in what became known as the Palmer Raids, named for the US attorney general, federal officers conducted mass arrests in thirty cities, including Portland, in an attempt to deport suspicious aliens and stifle antigovernment protests. The ongoing suppression of dissent demoralized radicals, and Equi wrote to Hanna Sheehy-Skeffington, her Irish nationalist friend in Dublin, that she was unable to give any talks because every assembly hall owner in Portland was threatened with arrest if a space was rented to her or to any other radical. Equi also felt badly, she wrote, about the attempt to deport Kitty O'Brennan. "Her arrest was brought about because she fought so hard for me . . . besmirching her took the spirit out of me somewhat." Equi continued to push for Irish independence, and she may have met Sinn Fein leader Eamon de Valera during his November 1919 visit to Portland. After de Valera's visit, Equi enlisted O'Brennan to lobby for her in Washington, DC, and to work with her attorney there. O'Brennan's trip east marked the end of the intense, intimate relationship that she and Equi had shared for eighteen months.[21]

As expected, the Supreme Court gave Equi no relief, and on January 26, 1920, the justices denied her request for review. Newspapers across the country carried the news, with the *San Francisco Chronicle* describing Equi as "the central figure in more episodes of turbulence in cities along the Pacific Coast for five years than any other woman." On a dreary day when more rain fell in Portland than at any time since 1903, Equi told the press, "Just what I expected. I am made to suffer for something I never said." She added, "I am no more guilty of the charges that take me to prison than is an unborn babe." She concluded that all she could do was await the start of her three-year prison sentence, but she actually kept fighting.[22]

Even before the Supreme Court decision, Equi initiated a new strategy with an appeal to President Wilson's secretary, Joseph Tumulty, to help her obtain presidential clemency. In a four-page letter remarkable for its straightforward portrayal of her situation, Equi declared her conviction resulted primarily due to the enmity of General Brice Disque, leader of the US Army's Spruce Division in Pacific Northwest forests. "I had dared to call attention to the failure of General Disque to do certain things to maintain an efficient morale among the workers and thus speed up production," she wrote. She claimed that Disque had told others he wanted to see her indicted and jailed. She also described how the two prime witnesses in her trial appeared incompetent to complete their task. She reiterated for him how they had agreed before the trial to "put words into her mouth" that would sound as damaging and disloyal as possible."[23]

Equi also detailed how the prosecution maligned her "private moral character." She charged that her same-sex preferences motivated federal agents and the US attorneys in Portland to mount their campaign against her. No other known lesbian convicted of federal offenses had presented such arguments to the nation's executive office. She wrote of the harassment inflicted on her—the wiretaps, the holes drilled through her doors, and the surveillance and intimidation of everyone with whom she came in contact. She closed with a complaint about Agent Bryon's physical assault on her, her companion, and her young daughter. She asked Tumulty simply for an examination of the testimony against her. She said she believed she deserved that much as an American citizen.[24]

Equi's friends and allies flooded the White House with letters and telegrams in support of clemency. Portland supporters sent a petition for a presidential pardon to Senator James Phelan of California who then conveyed it to the president. Thomas Gough Ryan, a former deputy district attorney of Multnomah County, wrote one of the most persuasive letters to the President. He declared his absolute opposition to the IWW and "all forms of radicalism" as well as his full support of the Espionage Act. Ryan was also an officer and active member of the Four Minute Men, the speakers' bureau that promoted voluntary registration during the war, and a host of other patriotic causes. He had known Equi for many years, he advised Wilson, and if she had made mistakes, they were "of the head rather than of the heart." He concluded, "I am firmly of the opinion that it would be a crime and an outrage to send Dr. Equi to jail, even for a day."[25]

Mary Frances Isom, Portland's librarian who had become embroiled in a patriotism dispute herself, added her plea for a presidential pardon, not just for Equi but for everyone caught up in what she described as "imprisonment for politics." An indication of Equi's influence beyond Oregon came with a letter from the wealthy and prominent Tammany Hall leader J. Sergeant Cram of New York. He wrote Attorney General Palmer that Equi had many influential friends in New York whom he would like to oblige. He dismissed her offense as "comparatively trivial" and advised, politician to politician, that "no public interest will be sacrificed by the exercise of clemency in her case."[26]

US Attorney Haney and Judge Bean, who had presided over Equi's case, attempted to counter the appeals from Equi's supporters. Haney declared to federal authorities that he "vehemently opposed clemency." The lobbying efforts, pro and con, captured the attention of the Department of Justice, and J. Edgar Hoover, the new head of what became known as the "Radical Division" of the Bureau of Investigation, requested a detailed memorandum about Equi's activities. Hoover would become FBI director in 1924 at age twenty-nine and maintain a fierce grip on the agency for forty-eight years until his death in 1972. He presented himself as a smart, cool operator, who modernized the agency even as he drove it into a morass of constitutional abuses and criminal acts. Historians have conjectured, and disagreed, whether Hoover maintained a longtime, closeted homosexual relationship with his deputy, Clyde Tolson, but there he was, nevertheless, requesting information about a lesbian who offended authorities by living her life openly.[27]

For several months in early 1920, Equi's attorney, Helen Hoy Greeley, labored in Washington, DC, over the application for a presidential pardon. The inordinate amount of effort required to complete the request led her to ask President Wilson for three separate sixty-day reprieves of the filing deadline. So much time transpired that even First Lady Edith Wilson expressed exasperation, writing to one of Equi's supporters in late August 1920 that "every opportunity is being given Dr. Equi to be heard fully," but "nothing can be done" until the application was submitted. When Greeley finally completed the one hundred–page document, Elizabeth Gurley Flynn—on behalf of the IWW Workers Defense Union—paid for its preparation.[28]

Several weeks later Equi was down to the final hours of her last reprieve from prison, and no one expected the president to grant a fourth delay. Attorney Greeley later revealed to Equi how close they had come to getting what they wanted. At the last moment before submitting a department recommendation, both the US pardon attorney and the assistant attorney general (who previously argued against Equi before the Supreme Court) had advised a full pardon. Attorney General Palmer himself shot down his subordinates' advice, according to Greeley. The night before Equi's last reprieve expired, Palmer wired Portland authorities that Wilson had commuted Equi's sentence from three years to one year and a day in a penitentiary to be determined.[29]

From the government's standpoint, a commutation reduced the length of punishment without any expression of forgiveness or fault by authorities.

But Equi proclaimed the move as a victory. "I'm going to prison smiling," she told the Portland dailies. "But I am not through. I shall keep on fighting until I die." She was keenly aware that her struggle was just one among many. "When they keep an old man like [socialist leader Eugene] Debs in prison—at 63 years of age—I have no complaint to make. There are better people in jail than I am."[30]

Equi was allowed a final night of freedom October 14, and she and her friends no doubt tapped her supply of bootleg liquor for the occasion. On Friday morning she appeared before Judge Bean to ask for extra time to get her affairs in order, but he turned away the request. She agreed to appear at the US marshal's office that afternoon. From there she would be escorted to jail to await her trip to prison.[31]

Two dozen friends accompanied Equi that afternoon. She carried a bouquet of red roses and walked beside five-year-old Mary Jr., who held Harriet Speckart's hand. Only that morning did Equi learn she would serve her time at San Quentin California State Prison in Marin County. (The federal penitentiary at McNeil's Island had been another option but it was not equipped for female inmates). The choice suited her, she said, much more than the women's reformatory in Rockville, Iowa. "I am too old to reform," she quipped. Her friends said goodbye at the jail. Her departure was widely covered in local and national media, including *La Tribuna Italiana*, Oregon's only Italian-language newspaper. To the *Oregon Daily Journal*, she spoke of her daughter: "I've had that little girl since she was three weeks old. She is as dear to me as if she were my own child." And she spoke of being humbled at "the wealth of friendship" extended to her that morning.[32]

Equi's transport to San Quentin was delayed several hours, but on Sunday, October 17, 1920, at 11:30 p.m. Southern Pacific No. 10 departed Union Station for points south. A US deputy marshal and a police matron who Equi knew well from her previous arrests accompanied her. Her sentence would not begin until she was received at San Quentin, and she wanted to get it started as soon as possible.[33]

15
The Palace of Sad Princesses

> *I have been in the women's sector there, and it is horrible. The women*
> *have no room for exercise and no work; they sit about and relate*
> *obscenities. I know the shame of the place that never wears off.*
> Charlotte Anita Whitney, California suffragist and radical

Marie Equi left behind the chaotic circumstances of her life as her prison-bound train rolled through Portland's eastside a few blocks from where she first mounted a soapbox. Earlier that night attorney George Vanderveer told an assembly of her supporters that he possessed evidence of a government frame-up and of perjury by government witnesses at her trial. But Equi had little time for the world of spies, lies, and rallies. She contemplated a life as a political prisoner at San Quentin.[1]

During the overnight trip south, Equi wrote the first of several letters to her daughter. She explained to Mary Jr. that her Da had to leave home to spend a long time in a Big House. "Someday you will come and see me," she wrote, "and put your little hand in mine, and the big door will open and you will lead me out to the beautiful, beautiful garden." She expressed her own wish for the future, "You will put your little arms around my neck, your sweet head against my breast, and joy and peace and happiness will be yours and mine." A month later the *Oregonian* published the letter along with a photograph of Mary Jr. on the beach at Seaside holding a large parasol with her dog at her feet.[2]

Equi's train stopped the next day in Richmond, a city north of Oakland, where she and her escorts boarded a ferry to San Quentin State Prison on the western shore of San Francisco Bay. During the half-hour crossing, the stark white prison buildings, standing isolated on a short stub of a peninsula, loomed ahead. Three large cellblocks formed a solid horseshoe-shaped front close to the shore. In the interior of the arc stood the desolate building that had housed female inmates since 1856. From the San Quentin dock, the US marshal transferred Equi to the custody of prison officials. She was registered as inmate number 34110 on October 19, 1920, marking the start of her term. She was fingerprinted, measured at five foot three inches, weighed

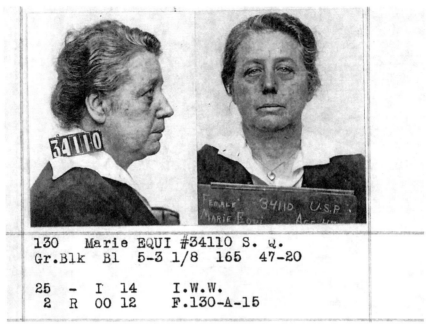

130   Marie EQUI #34110 S. Q.
Gr.Blk Bl   5-3 1/8 165   47-20

25 - I 14   I.W.W.
 2 R 00 12   F.130-A-15

Marie Equi at San Quentin State Prison on October 20, 1920, after her conviction under the Sedition Act. California State Archives, Sacramento, California.

at 165 pounds, photographed from the front and side. She was wearing her signature suit with broad lapels, a white blouse, and a necklace with a heart-shaped pendant.

Equi was known to be "finicky about her clothes" with a preference for lace shirtwaists and expensive suits, but she relinquished all her belongings in exchange for her prison trousseau—a fashion-bereft collection of blue-and-white striped suits, underclothes, shoes, stockings, bed linens, cotton flannel for sewing, and toiletries. For Sunday wear, she received a blue suit and a white waistcoat.[3]

The two-story women's jailhouse reminded Equi of a Spanish convent with high cement walls and floors. Others described the inner court as a mausoleum or a "lidless coffin." The forty-by-sixty-foot courtyard boasted only a fountain, a solitary tree, and an open-air sleeping room for tubercular women. Standing inside the courtyard, the high walls permitted views of only a patch of sky. Two stairways on either side of the court led to the inmates' cells upstairs, along three corridors, prosaically named Paradise Alley, Old Maid's Home, and Peaceful Alley.[4]

Equi was assigned to a room of her own, number 1 Paradise Alley, a tiny six-by-nine-foot cell behind a solid steel door with one window for light and air. She described in a letter to Kitty O'Brennan how much she had suffered during her initial weeks enclosed in such a small room. "I will never get used to hearing the locks snapped at night," she wrote. At 7 p.m. Equi and the other inmates returned to their rooms, dreading the moment when the trusty clicked the door padlocks shut. All lights were off by 9 p.m., and the women remained locked in their cells until the next morning.[5]

Equi shared the women's quarters with thirty-one other inmates. Many were married, a few divorced, a few widowed, and only one was single. The majority was white, but seven were African Americans and one was Native American. At forty-eight Equi was one of the oldest, although she reported the outrage of inmates at the arrival of a sixty-eight-year-old woman, "Grandma G," sentenced to serve five-to-ten years for assisting with an abortion. "When the dress is put on," Equi told a friend, "it is such a humiliating thing to do to a white-haired old lady." The women at San Quentin were imprisoned for charges in all three major crime categories—offenses against person, property, and public order. Several did time for homicides and larcenies, others for prostitution, and a few for botched abortions. Equi was the only *political,* as sedition offenders were called. Of all the women, Equi became closest to Kitty "KT" Wixson, a British woman of thirty-one, who later became her cellmate, and Rosina, a heartsick mother of seven.[6]

The days dragged for the women with few physical activities and no productive work. Female inmates clearly ranked second at San Quentin, even the large garden on the prison grounds was restricted to male prisoners only. For recreation the women played cards, listened to the Victrola, played the piano, and watched movies on Sunday evenings. Many crocheted for hours— endless hours, it seemed to Equi, who thought it served as a sedative. Some of the inmates played volleyball in the courtyard and attended Sunday religious services while a few took university extension courses. The matron ensured a few amenities, such as dining six to a table set with white tablecloths and with meals served on ceramic dishes not tin plates. On Monday nights she accompanied the women for walks on the prison grounds or, occasionally, on the hillside behind the prison where Equi loved to pick California poppies and lupines.[7]

Equi struggled with claustrophobia, even outside her own cell. She was unable to watch movies with the others due to the close, unventilated screening room. She suffered terrible headaches and "attacks with my circulation" that caused purple spots on her skin, so painful that she described them as "tortures of the damned." Even under the duress, she developed a good rapport with many of the women. Her own family background and her medical care for working-class patients helped her appreciate the women's experiences, and her abortion work reassured them she would not judge them. She also understood the psychological impact of their circumstances. "We are naked souls," she wrote to a friend, "and it takes infinite patience to keep us all comparatively in good humor." She observed that occasionally one of the women "blows off steam" and annoys everyone else, but she figured the acting out was only natural given the confinement and frustration from "the sex urge." The other women treasured Equi and referred to her as a "joy-bringer" for her kindness, her willingness to listen to them, and her wise advice.[8]

Unlike authorities at other state prisons and federal penitentiaries, the San Quentin warden placed no limits on the correspondence of the women inmates, and this simple measure vastly enriched their lives. For many, correspondence with the outside and periodic visitors rescued them from the depths of despair. Equi was particularly fortunate. During a four-month period for which records exist, she received letters from more than seventy friends, family, and acquaintances.[9]

Five months into Equi's sentence, the government's Bureau of Intelligence demanded copies of her correspondence from San Quentin authorities, with hope for disclosures about radical activities. Thereafter prison staff transcribed nearly three hundred letters, and sent three copies of each to the Bureau's San Francisco office. Two of these were forwarded to J. Edgar Hoover at the FBI headquarters in Washington, DC. As a result, Hoover's Radical Division preserved an account of Equi's experience as a political prisoner and a record of her relationships that would likely have been scattered and lost otherwise. Although Equi and many of her correspondents understood her mail was read and censored, the letters indicated minimal redaction. In any event, Equi revealed little about radical politics, the IWW, the Socialist Party, or other radicals that she had not already disclosed in her trial testimony and public speeches. Instead, she complained about government officials and business operators, who sent her to prison.[10]

With her family in New Bedford, Equi traded news about marriages, births, and high school graduations. She sent a photo of Mary Jr. to her sister and nieces, who apparently had only recently learned about the child. She was particularly close with her younger sister, Sophie, now living in Los Angeles, who continued to grieve the loss of her son in the war. Sophie had since adopted a young girl whom she named Marie, and both sisters shared news of their daughters. Equi also reminisced about their younger days: "It was a great crowd of kids—mother always enjoyed the fun." She recalled her last visit home and how much their father enjoyed the grandchildren while sitting on their sister Kate's broad porch. "He cooked me some dandy macaroni dinners," she added. "His fried pumpkin blossoms and young squash were a dish fit for an epicure."[11]

Harriet Speckart wrote Equi nearly every day, much more often than anyone else. In her messages she revealed a surprising depth of devotion and affection for Equi considering the disruption and distress she experienced in the last years of their living together. Her letters also reflect the layers of understanding the couple developed over the years. She explained that she "liked to talk" with Equi through her frequent letters, although, as happens with most daily correspondence, the content often relied on mundane details. She delighted in telling stories of Mary Jr., and every letter brimmed with their daughter's adventures, domestic duties, and her studies. In one letter she described Mary Jr.'s afternoon at a nearby swimming tank. "Just wait until you see our Mary swim, my Da, anyone for miles around will be able to tell by your joyful grin that you are a-belonging of Miss Mary's. She just throws herself on her little back and away she goes like a little flea. She is just bugs over it."[12]

Speckart appeared to thrive as a mother, and friends of hers and Equi's commented how happy she and Mary Jr. seemed at their Seaside home. She lived simply, filling her days with reading, mending her and Mary Jr.'s clothes, chopping firewood, cleaning house, and shopping. She accompanied Mary Jr. to the beach, to swimming lessons, and to visits with playmates. Her very steadiness with daily routines and her modest surroundings suggest how different her life had become from Equi's hectic, pre-prison days. She was not all-suffering, however, and on one occasion she rebuked Equi for her criticisms. "Please spare me, lady," she wrote, complaining that Equi's remarks had made her "fiercely cross." She also teased Equi, writing that Mary Jr. frequently came home after seeing friends and exclaimed, "Everybody loves me," just as Equi had often done. In the spring of 1921 she reminded Equi of the fifteenth anniversary of "our little friendship."[13]

The Speckart legal battle still troubled Harriet, and Equi sometimes advised her about how to deal with her "greedy brother," who Equi believed had treated Harriet poorly. But she also suggested that Harriet not worry about money, writing, "as long as I can make a living, you'll have part of it." Speckart's anxiety over money is curious, given the inheritance she received, but perhaps she simply wanted to keep to their agreement about Equi financing Mary Jr.'s upbringing. Equi continued to send her a stipend every month even while prison interrupted her own income. For all the earlier accusations that Equi had sought Harriet's money, Equi instead supported herself and their daughter.[14]

Equi created a magical world—a "Palace of Sadness"—to explain her imprisonment to her daughter. She described the inmates as "Enchanted Princesses" unable to leave the palace until a "Fairy Godmother" released them. She portrayed the warden as an "Old Ogre" for not letting her leave and the kindly matron as "Aunty Josephine." She described how she awaited the arrival of "Peter Seagull" with his mail delivery, weather permitting. "Old Peter Sea Gull didn't arrive at the Palace yesterday," she wrote in one letter. "I was up bright and early looking for him, but the wind was too much for him no doubt and kept blowing him farther out to sea." Equi placed herself in an unhappy realm but one in which she was surrounded by good and loving women. And she assured Mary Jr. that she would return as soon as she could ride the "Magic Carpet."[15]

When Equi and Aunt KT were assigned to a freshly painted room with new curtains, she brimmed with pride. She wrote that she kept Mary Jr.'s photo on the table: "I can see you all the time so you are right with me when I say "goodnight, all's well." When awakened in the morning, "I say, 'Good morning, Miss Mary, and how are you, old sweetie?'"[16]

On another occasion, Equi quipped, "Guess what happened to Da yesterday?" Then she recounted, "Why Da went to the dentist's office and had a big tooth pulled. O, my, but I made an awful face, I wasn't brave like Mary Jr. No siree! I just shook—almost shook my shoes off—(and) Aunty Josephine said, "Doc, don't kick the window out." Equi often seemed to use her letters to Mary Jr. to maintain her connection with Speckart, who she knew would read them out loud. She would sometimes close with an endearment, "Kiss Hatsy for me."[17]

For her friends, Equi stepped off the Magic Carpet. To Kitty O'Brennan she wrote:

> As I told you before, prisons are Houses of the Living Dead. We are real and unreal, we are living bodies, but, in reality, shadows. We laugh, we talk, we dance, we sing, but, always each and every one is

wrapped in sad, in seared thoughts. Only one's spirit can transcend prison walls and bars and, at times, even one's spirit is inert.

She explained to another friend that since her roommate was the trusty—a designated prisoner entrusted with certain responsibilities such as evening lockup—she was no longer locked up at night with "the rest of the prize poultry."

Yet, for all the difficulties, Equi's prison experience was far better than what other women endured in federal penitentiaries. The Socialist Party leader Kate Richards O'Hare, for example, struggled with forced labor—making overalls—nine hours a day with meals served cold and no respite from the summer heat of Jefferson City, Missouri.[18]

Equi's women friends especially helped her manage the isolation and deprivation she experienced. Anna Louise Strong of Seattle and Lena Morrow Lewis in San Francisco, both active in workers' rights and the Socialist Party, assured Equi she was beloved for her contributions to a more equitable society. Ruth Barnett, the Portland abortion provider, wrote, "I miss you so much, Marie, I do hope you can be back soon. . . . Please do take good care of yourself, old queen of the Bolsheviks." Margaret Sanger confided, "You have meant so much in my life. It is such a milestone to meet a real woman and you are a dozen of them packed into one." It was during Equi's imprisonment that Sanger expressed her fond memory of their earlier intimacies in Portland, writing, "Your picture is on my dresser always as I look into those blue, blue eyes, I remember our dinner, our ride, everything—*everything*."[19]

With her longtime suffragist friend Sara Bard Field, Equi was the one to offer support and comfort. She was much concerned about Field, whose seventeen-year-old son had died two years earlier in an automobile that crashed when Field was driving. In one letter Equi wrote, "Life has tolled heavily on you. You have gone through your Garden of Gethsemane and you wear your crown of thorns, my Sara. I have so deep an affection for you and want you to know it."[20]

In Charlotte Anita Whitney, the California suffragist-turned-radical, Equi had a kindred spirit. They knew each other's longtime friends and family. Whitney had graduated from Wellesley College in 1889 and would have known Bessie Holcomb, Equi's homestead companion. Mary Jr. wrote letters to her "Aunt Anita." "One friend like you makes life—even in Prison—a happiness," Equi wrote. She and Whitney had traveled similar political ground— from fighting for woman suffrage to opposing World War I, and getting ensnared by the wartime acts. They may also have become intimate during the course of their close relationship. Whitney never married, and no account has been unearthed of a romantic interest. Yet in her later years, she expressed surprise that her biographer had not inquired why she had never married. Whitney visited Equi in San Quentin every month, and each time she knew a cell on Paradise Alley might await her. Equi joked that her newly painted creamy-yellow room might soon be hers. "Think of the good time you can have in here," she wrote. "No phones ringing, no one asking for advice—your life is always so crowded."[21]

Whitney faced a fourteen-year sentence at San Quentin following her January 1920 conviction under California's Criminal Syndicalism Act, a statute like Oregon's. Whitney had been arrested in November 1919 for her participation at a Communist Labor Party meeting in Chicago earlier that year. Her charter membership in the party made her guilty under California's law. While awaiting the outcome of her appeal, Whitney moved from her East Bay home to a flat on San Francisco's Russian Hill. She called it her "nook" in the city, and she hoped that Equi would be her first guest.[22]

Strangers also wrote to Equi and expressed their admiration for her courage and her struggle for the sake of others. A woman from a small Minnesota farming town referred to an article about Equi she had read a year ago. She recognized that they both hoped for a day "when prison walls no longer enclose the thinkers and doers." She knew Equi was called a "Joy-bringer" and she closed with, "May this joy never grow dim." At times when imprisonment weighed on Equi the most, messages like this, she wrote to friends, helped her persevere.[23]

With one new acquaintance through her correspondence, Equi disclosed concerns about being *queer*. Mark Avramo was a twenty-five-year-old Russian immigrant who lived in New York and managed a factory in the Bronx. Several months after Equi's arrival at San Quentin, Avramo wrote and expressed sympathy for her cellmate, KT, whom Equi had described as a "big-bosomed" lifer six years into her sentence. But he felt a special empathy for Equi, "a feeling of friendship and common cause." Then he added, "What you say about yourself, your being queer, well—I must convince you that you are not. It is a fact that you have dared to do the un-established thing, and therefore the unapproved, that you are looked upon as queer. I believe there are those who cannot understand me that look upon me also as queer." He assured her, "You are perfectly sane, tho perhaps unusually out of the ordinary."[24]

Did Equi's naming her queerness reflect anxiety about her radical politics that separated her from the mainstream? Or did her comment reflect the sting of being called an "unsexed woman" at her trial? Perhaps she questioned her sexual preference for women. She might have also mentioned to Avramo her attraction to KT, a woman she found "highly intelligent (with) beautiful dark eyes." There is no way to know her meaning for sure. Prison circumstances generally fostered emotional and sexual relationships among female inmates, and sharing a cell with KT provided an opportunity for Equi to express her own sex urge. None of the inmates were likely to disclose sexual relations in letters to the outside, but there's little reason to believe the female inmates at San Quentin were different from those at other women's prisons. As for the term queer, it had entered usage among homosexuals by 1921 and appeared occasionally in mainstream newspapers as a reference to sexual outsiders or to any intimate behavior beyond the norm. But queer also remained a common reference for the unusual or peculiar. Apparently Equi did not revisit the matter of being queer in followup letters to Avramo, but her words revealed discomfort with being an outsider and feeling ostracized for it.[25]

For the women, visits from the outside boosted their well being and resilience, and Equi was especially fortunate with her frequent company. Her Italian and Irish cousins living in San Francisco visited her often, and she delighted in dashing off a letter to tell their news to her family in New Bedford. C. E. S. Wood and Sara Bard Field, now living together in California, called on Equi and relived their times together in Portland. Equi was especially pleased to see her former companions, Bessie Holcomb Cook and Mary Ellen Parker White, with whom she had stayed in contact since their years together. Bessie, then married for fourteen years, lived in a three-level, turreted mansion along the panhandle of Golden Gate Park with her husband and their three teenage children. Equi still referred to Parker as "Dr. Mary," and she was much-impressed with Mary Ellen's nine-year old son, Billy, who Equi thought was "extraordinarily brilliant." The boy would later become the famous mystery writer who published under the name Anthony Boucher. On another Saturday, Marie was thrilled when two of Eamon de Valera's children visited her. The Irish leader's nine-year-old daughter accompanied one of her younger brothers to San Quentin because, as Marie wrote to Mary Jr., "Marion's mother loves Da and knows that I love children." Three months later, in August 1921, de Valera became President of the Irish Republic.[26]

Marie Equi, inmate 34110, on Easter Sunday, 1921, at San Quentin State Prison. Oregon Historical
Society, bb013178.

For Easter greetings in 1921 Equi sent photographs to friends and family that showed a composed and serious woman. In one she posed behind the courtyard gate's bars appearing forlorn. In the other, a well-staged portrait, Equi stands in front of the gate, wearing her prison frock and a crocheted blouse. With one arm extended, she holds an Easter egg in her hand. In the other she has a plate of food. A calla lily is tucked in her belt.[27]

Equi reappeared in Portland's press in April 1921 when she refuted an offensive description of her prison stay by her cousin, Mrs. Marion Wall. Equi was incensed when Wall, who helped manage Equi's office in Portland during her absence, told a reporter, "The doctor is kept with Negresses, Indians, and the lowest dregs of womankind and that she could not help shrinking from it at times." Equi penned a fierce letter to her cousin, upbraiding her for having so little sympathy for the working classes. "You differ on many things from me. You go to Mass and believe in prayer, and I do not. You think an Irish woman a little bit better than an Indian woman." In a letter to the editor of the *Oregon Daily Journal,* Equi wrote, "This is no opinion of mine. I shrink from no fellow prisoners of mine, no matter what the color of her skin may be." She added that she had never recoiled from any woman no matter her circumstances that led to her conviction. She concluded, "Character alone counts with me."[28]

Equi's indignant reaction to the incident gave Portlanders a declaration of her fundamental values—colorblind and free of class bias—at a time when a global war had pitted nationalities and races against each other and racial discrimination and class tensions festered in the country.

Although Equi appeared stoic and even-tempered in her letters and photos and during visits with friends and family, she confided to a few that she forced herself to block thoughts of the injustice she endured. Otherwise, she explained, she would succumb to an attack of "brain fever." She concentrated instead on obtaining an early release from prison.[29]

Like all federal inmates, Equi was eligible for a reduced sentence based on good behavior, or "good time" as it is called. For her term of one year and a day, she could accrue six days for each month of good time, and, on that basis, she expected to be released on August 9, 1921. But she might have been released sooner if two other possibilities had not been blocked by her enemies: a presidential pardon or a general amnesty for all wartime political prisoners. Few observers expected Wilson to grant an individual pardon to Equi during his remaining months in office, but her friends and allies continued to urge such a move. Elizabeth Gurley Flynn, then the organizer for the IWW's Workers

Defense Union, dispatched a telegram to Equi vowing to push for her release, and Margaret Sanger wrote that she and many others were doing the same. After her defeat for an Oregon congressional seat in the 1920 election, Doctor Esther Pohl Lovejoy traveled to Washington, DC, to help with the petition for Equi's release. A delegation from the New York Women's Medical Association, led by pioneer physician Gertrude Kelly, met with Wilson's secretary, Joseph Tumulty, after sending the president a petition for Equi's release. He directed them to Attorney General Palmer in a fruitless mission since Palmer had already advised the president to deny Equi a pardon.[30]

As war fervor receded, the political climate appeared to favor a general amnesty for everyone convicted of seditious talk under the wartime acts. In late December 1920, hundreds of civic organizations lobbied Congress to support a general amnesty. Equi's attorney in the capital, Helen Hoy Greeley, argued before a Congressional committee that Attorney General Palmer had ignored the recommendation from Department of Justice staff to pardon Equi. She added that Equi had been punished and imprisoned at the behest of special interests in Oregon. Greeley was a respected and accomplished figure in Washington, and her testimony added credence to Equi's claim that lumber interests had fueled the political harassment that landed her in prison. She cited a New York official who had confirmed to her that Attorney General Palmer had obliged the Oregon parties opposed to Equi's release. Although the committee advised Greeley it would consider Equi's case, nothing came of it.[31]

Palmer also testified before the committee and disclosed that the government had handled 1,632 espionage cases as of January 15, 1921, a number that taxed the ability of federal agents and local courts. Palmer explained that even with a general amnesty, a case-by-case review of all affected individuals would be required and that such a process was already underway. The hearing and the testimony accomplished little with Wilson and Palmer rebuffing all entreaties for a general amnesty.[32]

Equi's final hope was a parole for good behavior. A parole would not reduce her term, but it would permit her to serve the remainder of her time outside the prison under supervision. She was eligible for such a release after serving one-third of her sentence, or four months, that would conclude in mid-February 1921.[33]

By all available accounts, Equi was an exemplary inmate. She was respectful of the warden and the matron, she did not stir discontent among the women, and the inmates appreciated her generosity. She often enlisted her friends to help finance a newly released woman's transition to the outside, and for Christmas 1920 she arranged to have gifts sent to all the women. She had earned her "good time," and she had every reason to expect a parole, but the February date passed without action. Apparently, her friends in Portland bungled her parole application. She erupted in frustration when she discovered that the wrong documents had been sent to the Department of Justice. "I was mad enough I can tell you," she wrote to a cousin. As the weeks dragged on, she complained to Charlotte Anita Whitney, "I must have been double-crossed somewhere. . . . I am here two months longer than I should be." She believed, accurately, that former US Attorney Bert Haney—then in private practice—was working to keep her behind bars. "He is a perjurer and a liar and a thief, for he attempted to steal my good name with his low lies, and he stole my Liberty. To me he is the lowest thing that crawls."[34]

The March 1921 inauguration of President Warren G. Harding stoked new hopes of an executive pardon or a parole. Equi's allies lobbied the new president, and, in mid-April, J. Edgar Hoover once again asked for a summary of her case. The three-page memorandum repeated the usual complaints about the allegedly most dangerous woman in the Pacific Northwest—her abortion practice, her rabble-rousing talks and protests, and her association with other radicals, including Elizabeth Gurley Flynn, Emma Goldman, and Charlotte Anita Whitney. Hoover's report concluded that Equi was a "menace to the good morals, happiness, and peace of the larger community." Perhaps most galling to him and other agents was that Equi "influences ignorant people to believe she has intimate relations with the highest government officials." He claimed a pardon would have "a disastrous effect" and would validate Equi's claims of persuasion with officials. Equi had already served time for her offense, and Hoover's recommendation suggested once again that the government's case against her had always been about more than sedition.[35]

Even after Equi's representatives filed a second set of papers with the Department of Justice, her parole went nowhere. By this time, one of Oregon's US senators, Charles McNary, stepped forward to get Equi's petition processed. He informed Equi's Portland attorney that she could expect a decision in a few days. Even the elderly Jonathan Bourne Jr., the former US Senator from Oregon who hailed from New Bedford, wrote Equi's attorney that her case made a very favorable impression, although he was not well enough to deal with the matter.[36]

Finally, on April 29 Equi appeared before San Quentin's warden and captain about her parole. The warden asked if in retrospect she thought she had spoken "indiscreetly or inopportunely" in Portland. The warden was kind to her, but the talk upset her greatly. She wrote a friend in Washington, DC, "It affects me, the injustice, the brutality of the prosecution, their smug lies, and I suffer inwardly, profoundly." She questioned whether to proceed with the parole. "That I have asked for pardon offends something deep within me, I have a sickening sense of loss." Nevertheless, the warden recommended a parole to the Department of Justice.[37]

During this time of increasing frustration, the espionage case of multi-millionaire Henry Albers erupted in Portland and may have damaged Equi's chances for an early release. Like Equi, Albers had been convicted in Judge Robert Bean's courtroom with US Attorney Haney serving as chief prosecutor. Once found guilty, Albers also took his case to the Ninth Circuit Court of Appeals. His attorneys, again like Equi's, objected to evidence presented at the trial for remarks Albers had made years before his alleged seditious statements. The circuit court refused to reverse the verdict. When Albers appealed to the US Supreme Court, however, he obtained a far different outcome from Equi's. The US solicitor general, representing the federal government before the Supreme Court, admitted that prior utterances should never have been admitted as evidence and that the Department of Justice had made an error. The judgments of the two lower courts were set aside, and Albers was free to get on with his life.[38]

The government's mistake and the release of Albers outraged public officials, civic organizations, and private citizens in Oregon who thought he was guilty and deserved punishment. The American Legion threatened to circulate a petition demanding a pardon for Equi if Albers was not retried. The Legionaires had little interest in Equi's freedom; they used her case to force the imprisonment of Albers. The protests escalated, and in late April 1921 the *Oregon Daily Journal* published front-page photos of Equi under the headline "She Wants To Get Out Too."[39]

Attorney Haney was shaken that his prosecution had been found incompetent. He told the *Oregonian* that if the confessed error applied to Albers, then it would affect every other similar case tried in his district. Exactly, according to Charlotte Anita Whitney who wrote to Equi, "Something surely popped in Portland when the news got out that Albers's case was revised while you were behind bars." Bud Warner, Equi's friend and former New York congressman, advised, "I don't think the fuss in Portland over Albers helped you at all in Washington." Although Equi might have been freed like Albers, the Department of Justice probably saw little value in poking another hornet's nest in the

Pacific Northwest by freeing one more convicted seditionist. The tumult over the Albers affair abated only when he suffered a paralyzing stroke that left him blind. His condition worsened and he died in late July 1921.[40]

When attorney C. E. S. Wood visited Equi in early May, he counseled her to accept a parole and complete her sentence outside prison. He believed her health had noticeably deteriorated, and he thought she should not stay in prison one more day than necessary. Equi admitted to a friend that she was "far from well" but confided that she did not want others to know her real condition. In fact, her long-dormant tuberculosis had begun troubling her with a flareup in her right lung. Yet she worried that accepting a pardon or parole was unprincipled. Several days after Wood's visit, she decided to take his advice.[41]

As it turned out, two days earlier the US Parole Board had recommended that Equi be granted a parole. But Attorney General Daugherty found a reason to block it. He explained to Equi's attorney that Albers had been pro-German and anti-Allies whereas Equi's offense was far greater for being anti-American, as if Albers's vow to commit all his wealth to defeat the US was less problematic than Equi's criticism of capitalists for their wartime profiteering.[42]

In most cases, parole applications did not proceed without the recommendation of the prosecuting US attorney and that of the federal judge at the trial. In Equi's case, both men objected to a parole and traveled to Washington, DC, to lobby against her. The attorney general could proceed without their assent, but he chose to hold Equi's application until it was no longer relevant.[43]

Once the chances for amnesty, pardon, and parole slipped away, all that remained for Equi was the more-or-less automatic "good time" credits. With her admirable behavior already established and a recommendation from the warden, federal authorities were hard-pressed to block this standard entitlement. As her August 9 release date neared, Equi wrote Whitney, "I am nearly out of purgatory, all except for my feet."[44]

In late June and much of July, Equi fell ill and struggled with lung troubles that left her weak from persistent night sweats and coughing. After she recovered, she complained of being in "a highly nervous state." She wrote Dr. Alys Griff in Portland that prison life had profoundly saddened her. "I do not moan over my own loss of personal liberty, but I have and do feel deeply for many of my fellow prisoners.[45]

Equi was anxious and uncertain about returning to the outside where she would be a woman who had done time, an exconvict in a much-changed world. But she yearned for freedom outdoors and time with her daughter. She also considered serving in Europe to assist with medical care, perhaps joining

Dr. Esther Pohl Lovejoy or her pacifist friend Anna Louise Strong. Other times bitterness took hold. She wrote in late July, "My life is not worth a tinker's damn in Portland. If I am going to be attacked again, I'll go to the pen for something, not for nothing." She no longer wanted to think of her conviction; instead, she wanted to deal with the "character assassinators" who had portrayed her as an "unmoral woman." She intended to pursue charges against Haney and others if she could obtain evidence. Or, she wrote, she might simply become a citizen of another country "where mob rule is not a popular pastime."[46]

On Tuesday, August 9, 1921, Equi collected her possessions, changed into the new clothes and hat provided by the state, and said goodbye to KT and the other women. She glanced at her tiny cell with the new curtains and then walked into the courtyard. The other inmates cheered her release, and she vowed not to forget them. She completed the required paperwork, took the five dollars cash allotted each discharged prisoner, and walked with guards through the gates. There one of her cousins waited to take her to the ferry and leave San Quentin behind.[47]

16
Nothing Is the Same

When the Armistice spread the black pall of silence over
fervid oratory and burning editorials, we felt a deep sense of
personal loss, something was missing from our lives.
Kate Richards O'Hare, socialist

An ideal refuge awaited Equi as she ferried across San Francisco Bay from San Quentin Prison. Charlotte Anita Whitney had taken a new apartment on Macondray Lane, a wooded, gardened walkway lined by a serpentine rock outcropping on one side and houses on the other, situated high above the bay on San Francisco's eclectic Russian Hill. From Whitney's one-bedroom home, Equi could see the Marin County headlands across the bay, although San Quentin, mercifully, did not mar the view. After months in close concrete quarters, she was just a few steps away from flowers, trees, and garden paths. No longer confined with strangers, she spent her days and nights with an intimate companion of her own choosing, and tried to make sense of her ordeal and what lay ahead.[1]

First, Equi needed to rest and recover from the health problems that flared in prison. Now on the outside, she also suffered from what prisoners called the "post-prison sweats"—flu-like symptoms with profuse perspiration that continued for several days, sometimes weeks. "I would wake up in the night with a choking feeling and a horrible sense that I was back in prison again," Equi told a reporter. Once she regained her footing, she visited her family and friends in the Bay Area, including C. E. S. Wood and Sara Bard Field, who were ensconced three blocks from Whitney's apartment. The longtime lovers were finally on their own—Wood had left his wife in Portland—and relished their perch on a hillside with a rambling garden. For months Equi had longed to talk with Field without the constraints of prison visits and to express how heartsore she was over the indignities she had suffered. She had written, "There is much cruelty in the modern prison system."[2]

Equi might have forsaken her activism, figuring she had done her part and had suffered too much as a result. Instead, she used the newsworthiness

Charlotte Anita Whitney, Equi's close
companion, was charged under California's
criminal syndicalism law. California
Records of the National Women's Party,
Library of Congress.

of her release to push for prison reform. She was convinced that California
authorities should transfer the women of San Quentin to another site as soon
as possible. The state had already authorized an "industrial farm" for women
inmates and had purchased a six-hundred-acre estate with a Victorian mansion
outside the Northern California town of Sonoma. But officials first wanted to
build a new hospital at the site. Equi felt keenly the empty days that plagued lif-
ers like her former cellmate KT, and she argued there was no time to lose. The
state's plans for a more woman-oriented institution—and Equi's advocacy for
the farm facility—reflected the thrust of prison reform for women since the
1870s. Advocates wanted to avoid the harsh architecture and design of men's
penitentiaries, preferring instead rural locations with cottages and a more domestic, nurturing environment. Yet many of the San Quentin prisoners who
Equi befriended did not fit the profile of young, first-time offenders who were
considered the best candidates for the new institutions.[3]

Free of the prison censors, Equi spoke more openly of the conditions
at San Quentin, but she calibrated her message for greatest effect. In a series
of Bay Area forums, she depicted the dire circumstances that prevailed in
prison—the cramped, claustrophobic cells, the inadequate toilet facilities,
and the mind-numbing inactivity—to prod audiences to demand changes.
But she also affirmed the humanity and dignity of women behind bars, and
she challenged stereotypes of the inmates as debased dregs of society. In an
Oakland Tribune interview, Equi extolled the liveliness of the inmates, tossing

jazz-era talk with a jaunty air. "San Quentin life is 'snap,'" she said. "The women ... roll 'em down, wear 'em high, and the sleek silk-clad ankle and high-heeled shoe are always in evidence at the parties." The women stepped to the latest dances—the Shimmy, the Bunny Hug, and the San Rafael Waddle. Equi also asserted that the "check passers, murderers, women of the street, forgers and narcotic addicts" were just like women on the outside.[4]

Like many prison reformers influenced by Progressive Era thinking, Equi believed in a wages-and-workplace approach to penal reform rather than assuming that a criminal woman offender needed to be locked away. She urged higher pay and better working conditions outside prison walls as an antidote to crime—a position consistent with her urging a radical restructuring of the nation's economic system. She understood that fundamental penal reform required an overhaul of America's criminal justice system, but she pushed for incremental change to benefit the inmates she knew.[5]

Equi's high-profile lobbying complemented the efforts of state reformers, and, five months after her lectures, the Sonoma facility admitted its first inmates. It flourished the first year, and the women spoke highly of their surroundings. But, tragically, fire destroyed the main building soon thereafter, and the legislature withheld funds for new construction. Reformers succeeded in getting a new three-story women's department built at San Quentin in 1927 to house more than one hundred prisoners. A new facility for women would not open until 1934, when the State Prison for Women at Tehachapi, located in an isolated mountain region of southern California, accepted its first inmates. Equi maintained contact with the women of San Quentin, and for several years after her release, she sent them gifts for Christmas.[6]

Equi remained in the Bay Area for six weeks and became more acclimated to the national mood. A great many Americans embraced President Harding's pledge for a new, happier era with "one spirit, one purpose, and only one flag, the American flag." They yearned for calm—for *normalcy*, in his words—after years of war, labor strife, and the flu pandemic, and political reform was shelved for the most part. For activists, it seemed that years of lobbying and protests for a more just and equitable system had achieved little lasting impact. The US Congress adopted a new fiscal policy that vastly favored upper-income brackets, leaving the people Equi cared about most—poor families, the working class, and the unemployed—shoved further aside. At the same time, the new US attorney general declared that the law of the land still prohibited dissent, and he appealed to the country's Americanism to justify the restrictions.[7]

On the evening of September 23, 1921, Equi departed San Francisco for Portland, ready with a message for the dailies. "I found myself that the entry into the prison was actually a relief from the persecution on the outside," she declared. Before she left Union Station for an overnight stay in town with her colleague, Dr. Alys Griff, Equi admitted to reporters that her health had declined in prison and that she needed rest. She hoped to complete a series of articles on prison conditions, she added, but she was uncertain whether she would remain in Portland or return to San Francisco. The next day she traveled to the Oregon coast to reunite with her daughter and Harriet Speck-art. Little else is known of their visit, but Equi and Speckart disagreed about their daughter's education. Equi favored sending Mary Jr. to a private school in northwest Portland, but Speckart insisted on keeping the child with her. Speckart prevailed, and Mary Jr. enrolled that fall at Jewell Preparatory near Seaside. They made no plans to live together as a family again.[8]

Back in Portland, Equi found little semblance of the radical groups she had left behind the year before. Prosecutions under the Espionage Act and the Criminal Syndicalism Act had decimated IWW ranks across the nation, and Wobbly leaders were hard-pressed to do more than mount legal defenses for indicted and convicted comrades. As early as November 1919, Portland Mayor George Baker declared that the IWW was not a threat in the city because they were not tolerated. He boasted that Wobbly meeting places had been taken from them and they had been driven from outdoor sites. The circumstances of the labor force had changed as well with fewer single and itinerant men seeking work than during the Wobblies' prewar heyday. Even when labor unrest festered and flared at the end of wartime production contracts—as it did with an unsuccessful 1922 strike by longshoremen and streetcar conductors—no clear and commanding Wobbly leadership channeled discontent into effective organizing and protests.[9]

The Socialist Party fared no better and suffered from rifts between mainstream members and its Left Wing Section. In Oregon, the party was isolated, disillusioned, and ineffective. More radical members split off and formed the Communist Labor Party in the summer of 1919. Communists rejected the idea of the IWW's One Big Union in favor of a worker's state with laborers claiming full control of production. In Oregon they recruited from the ranks of disillusioned Socialists and former Wobblies while maneuvering under the strictures of the state's revised criminal syndicalism law. (Oregon had strengthened the antiradical measure to be one of the most sweeping in the country.)[10]

The disarray and demoralization among Equi's former allies and the restructuring of radical interests made her reentry into radical politics difficult.

Kate Richards O'Hare, the Socialist leader imprisoned for sedition, described the despair she and other radicals experienced after the war. "When the Armistice spread the black pall of silence over fervid oratory and burning editorials," she wrote, "we felt a deep sense of personal loss, something was missing from our lives." Labor journalist and radical activist Mary Heaton Vorse bemoaned the dour Communists compared to the sparkling verve of the prewar left. "Where will you find today picturesque revolutionists like Jack Reed?" she asked. It seemed like her comrades had been "swept aside by the broom of time." Equi faced the state of radicalism through the prism of her own diminished energy. Her daughter commented years later that prison had broken her mother's spirits.[11]

The discouragement among radicals—and Progressives as well—was compounded with the rise of a protest organization that thrived in the United States. The Ku Klux Klan exploited Americans' anxiety over fundamental changes that seemed to tumble forth, including the direct democracy reforms in places like Oregon. Comprised largely of middle- and lower-class white Protestants, the KKK maligned the influence of those they despised: African Americans, Japanese, Catholics, Jews, and radicals. In Oregon the KKK reached its peak of influence in the early 1920s with an estimated twenty thousand members, and by end of the decade there were as many as fifty thousand. In 1922 the state organization helped elect twelve Republicans to the state legislature and nearly blocked the incumbent Republican governor from his party's nomination. The group managed to pass a compulsory school bill that required children, eight to sixteen years old, to attend public schools. The anti-Catholic measure was never implemented, and the US Supreme Court later ruled it unconstitutional. Another KKK-sponsored effort barred Japanese residents from owning property.[12]

Independent of her radical affiliations, Equi left prison with unfinished political business. She vowed to go after the "character assassinators" who had portrayed her as an amoral woman to Washington officials. She held former US Attorney Bert Haney most responsible, but she also set her sights on District Court Judge Robert Bean, federal agent W. R. Bryon, and Colonel Brice Disque, director of the US Army's Spruce Division in the region's forests. Even more than she knew, federal officials had maligned Equi's womanhood and her basic humanity. But with so little access to government documents or reports of internal conversations, she failed to uncover sufficient evidence of bias or of a frameup to use against them. The US Supreme Court's dismissal of the Albers case had embarrassed Haney and Bean, but neither suffered professionally. Haney, ironically, was later appointed to the US Court of Appeals for the Ninth District, and Bean remained on the federal bench until his death. Disque was criticized for mismanagement and hostility to workers' rights during the war, but he was promoted to the rank of brigadier general. Only the vindictive Bryon was knocked from his position leading the city's FBI office. He was forced to resign the month Equi returned to Portland—ostensibly to trim the bureau's budget, but mostly for his abrasive relations with colleagues and his role in the wartime sedition cases. Mayor Baker offered the former agent an investigative post with the city police force, but Bryon took a position as a special agent for Northern Pacific Railroad at Union Station.[13]

The prospects for Equi becoming a fulltime prison advocate were discouraging as well. Kate Richards O'Hare had already achieved national status as an authority on the subject in her own lecture tours. She had appeared in Portland in June of 1921, as did Louise Olivereau, the poet and anarchist from Seattle who had also been imprisoned for her antiwar protests. Another factor for Equi was her debilitated health after prison. The physical rigors of the lecture circuit would likely have been too much for her.[14]

Nor could Equi expect a state or local post, given her reputation and her prison record. At a time when women-oriented prisons had become more commonplace and the need for penal reform remained strong, there were few, if any, opportunities for Equi. She resorted to, or perhaps preferred all along, her medical practice, and she shared an office with her longtime friend Alys Griff. At San Quentin, Equi had pushed thoughts of her medical work from her mind to maintain her equilibrium, she wrote to a friend, but medicine remained her primary interest and her most ready means for a livelihood. But remaining in Portland could not have been easy for her. When she walked downtown, shopped at Meier & Frank's department store, or stopped at the Portland Hotel, she did so as a woman with a record, and she crossed paths with those who had helped send her to San Quentin. She found that many Portlanders, like other Americans after the war, turned away from anyone who reminded them of the troubles of the past.[15]

The Roaring Twenties became a mad dash from the suffering and strife of the previous decade. In movies, books, and magazines, Americans seemed to revel in prosperous times and everyone's life appeared on the upswing. The reality was far different with severe economic disparities. Six million families in the United States struggled with annual incomes below $1,000, while one-tenth of one percent of families enjoyed incomes equal to that of the six million. A few critics tried to pierce the illusion. In *Echoes of the Jazz Age*, F. Scott Fitzgerald wrote, "It was borrowed time anyway—the whole upper tenth of a nation living with the insouciance of a grand duc and casualness of chorus girls."[16]

Although the conservative interests of the moneyed classes prevailed during the successive Republican administrations of the 1920s, a resurgence of progressivism eventually appeared. In the early postwar period, civil libertarians as well as conservatives pushed back against the erosion of civil rights, and together they demanded limits to the wartime vigilantism. In the following years, New Progressives, as they were called, rejected the massive consumerism in the country. They developed alliances with rural reformers and factory workers that endured until the Democratic administrations of the 1930s ushered in strong labor legislation and economic reforms.[17]

Throughout the twenties, Equi kept to her medical practice although her reputation had suffered over the years. She spent a greater proportion of her time providing abortions, according to her daughter, but she had less reason to worry about prosecutions as public interest in abortion control and prosecution had waned. Sensational incidents still occurred, however, such as the case of Dr. Andre Ausplund who was well known to Equi. In 1921, Ausplund began serving time in the state penitentiary after exhausting court appeals of a manslaughter conviction for a botched abortion in 1915. Within two years he was paroled by the acting Oregon governor, and he reestablished his practice in Portland's Lafayette Building, the same location used by Equi. He became familiar enough in Equi's circles for her daughter to refer to him as Uncle Andre. In the years ahead when Equi closed her practice, Ausplund treated many of her abortion-seeking clients.[18]

Equi's patients experienced just as much difficulty obtaining birth control information and devices as when she spent a night in jail with Margaret Sanger in 1916. Portland officials remained adamantly opposed to contraception, and in July 1922 Mayor Baker rejected out of hand a proposed international birth control convention for the city. Portland had been selected as a convenient East-West site since the movement had embraced Asia-Pacific countries as well as the United States. "I don't know what's the matter with those people," Baker told the press, referring to the convention leaders. "Of all the cities in the world, Portland would be the least receptive to them and their doctrines."[19]

The birth control movement shifted during the 1920s with more professionalism and support from wealthy donors. Margaret Sanger, and the American Birth Control League she led, lobbied Congress to drop the restrictions that had hampered their work for so many years. In many ways the strategy succeeded, especially with a surge in acceptability during the hard times of the Great Depression. Condoms became more readily available, and the number of birth control clinics soared from fifty-five in 1930 to more than five hundred by 1938. Oregon became the first state, in 1935, to regulate the manufacture and sale of birth control devices and information, thus signaling the end of the Comstock Law. Two years later the American Medical Association finally dropped its opposition to birth control.[20]

Equi relied on her women friends to help her settle into postprison life, yet, for the first time in fifteen years, she lived alone and without a companion. She had carried a torch for Kitty O'Brennan ever since their parting the previous year, and she greatly anticipated O'Brennan's lecture stop in Portland in November 1921. From her new base in New York, O'Brennan worked as a top organizer for Irish independence. The previous year she had helped organize longshoremen in a refusal to unload British ships at the New York docks. On her tour O'Brennan was eager to talk about conditions in Ireland. Equi extended her usual robust welcome, but she was soon disappointed that O'Brennan spent little time with her.

Equi chided her in a letter after she departed, "Even if you do love a New Yorker, you might have been good to your prison bird a few days longer." She added, "Two nights away from me too in Portland. Takes real friendship to forget that hurt, after months of constant heart aches." O'Brennan returned to Ireland after her tour and in time set aside her political work. She devoted the rest of her life to literature and journalism.[21]

In February 1923, Hannah Sheehy-Skeffington stopped in Portland on her own national fundraising tour. After World War I, Sheehy-Skeffinton undertook prison reform and the release of political prisoners, and she sought donations for the families of the thirteen thousand Irish activists imprisoned by the British government. During a talk at the venerable Portland Hotel, Sheehy-Skeffington learned that her home in Dublin had been firebombed and destroyed. She took the incident in stride once she learned her young son, Owen, was safe.[22]

Parts of Equi's professional and personal life began to slip away as two close friends took their own lives. In October 1922, Janina Constance Klecan, a respected physician and pathologist in Portland, swallowed a vial of morphine to end her life. Equi had rushed to her friend's office after receiving a suicide note from her, and she had found Klecan lying on a couch unconscious. With two other doctors' help, Equi finally revived her, but Klecan died later in the hospital. Equi knew her friend suffered from depression and that she had experienced "soul torture" after C. E. S. Wood ended an affair with her. Wood had pursued a relationship with Klecan while also seeing Sara Bard Field.[23]

Two years later another tragedy took the life of Kathryn "Kitty" Beck Irvine, who had been a fervent correspondent to Equi during her months at San Quentin. Prior to Equi's trial, Irvine had led the local defense committee for the Wobblies charged with sedition. Irvine had also suffered from a breakup with C. E. S. Wood, her longtime employer and lover, who continued to see Field as his mistress. Seemingly doomed to troubled relationships, Irvine later married IWW attorney George Vanderveer, who wrestled with insolvency, alcoholism, and despair after the loss of Equi's case and that of the mass trial of Wobblies in Chicago. Once Irvine suspected her husband of seeing another woman, she started drinking excessively, and, in October 1924, she inhaled chloroform and suffocated herself. Equi grieved the loss of her friends, and she was appalled that Wood appeared to dote on his own emotional needs at the expense of the women he drew into his life. At one point she threatened to expose Wood's exploits, although it appears she did not do so.[24]

Between the deaths of her friends, Equi lost her father at age eighty-three in February 1924. Her sister Kate recalled in the local New Bedford paper that their father retained his reputation among neighborhood children as "Uncle Sam" for his full white beard and friendly manner. His survivors included four daughters, three sons, fifteen grandchildren, and five great-grandchildren. Equi wrote an obituary that appeared in the *Oregonian* and described her father as "a character in his home and a decidedly picturesque figure." Perhaps due to her failing health or the general weariness of her postprison life, Equi did not attend her father's burial services, held in the New Bedford church he had helped build.[25]

Six years after her release from prison, a series of events further disrupted Equi's personal and professional life and shaped her next decade. In December 1926, Elizabeth Gurley Flynn, the Rebel Girl of Wobbly fame, stopped in Portland to rally support for her causes. She spoke with the passion and commitment audiences anticipated, but below the surface she was emotionally battered and physically exhausted.

Throughout the war years, Flynn had led the Workers Defense Union and undertook nearly constant travel to raise money and organize protests for the release of political prisoners. She especially invested herself in the defense of two Italian anarchists, Nicola Sacco and Bartolomeo Vanzetti, accused of robbery and murder in Massachusetts, as well as her longtime lover, Carlo Tresca, arrested for disseminating birth control pamphlets. After Tresca was released, Flynn was staggered when he terminated their thirteen-year relationship. Soon thereafter she learned that Tresca had simultaneously romanced her sister, Bina, who gave birth to his child.[26]

Flynn dealt with the demands and losses in her life by assuming more obligations. She agreed to manage publicity for the Passaic, New Jersey, textile strike and then thrust herself into a massive relief effort to support the families of more than fifteen thousand strikers. She also undertook a demanding national tour to benefit Sacco and Vanzetti and the Passaic strikers.[27]

When Flynn reached Portland in December, she was already experiencing what she described as sharp pains in her spine, breathlessness, and a feeling that her heart was "as large as a football." She persisted with a half-dozen more stops in Oregon and Washington before she could do no more. She returned to Portland and sought medical care from Equi, who settled her in the two-level house in the Goose Hollow neighborhood she had purchased three years earlier.[28]

Equi arranged for Flynn to consult a heart specialist first. They were told her heart was normal, except for a few irregularities. The doctor advised complete bed rest and warned that Flynn risked an untreatable "heart lesion" if she did not end her excessive workload and stress. The diagnostician in Equi led her to seek another opinion, this time from a dental radiologist who identified an impacted molar that had triggered a streptococcal infection throughout her body. He pulled the tooth, but the extraction caused more rapid dissemination of the infection and a worsening of her condition. Penicillin and other antibacterial compounds had yet to be discovered, and Equi resorted to giving Flynn bootleg whiskey to ease her condition. Flynn's status worsened to the point that Equi summoned a "Bishop Brown," presumably a priest, to give a blessing. Flynn slipped into a periodic delirium that she later described as "bordering on madness." Mary Jr. remembered sitting with Flynn during her illness when the older woman "cried for the moon."[29]

In late February 1927, Equi wrote to Flynn's friends and colleagues and advised them that her condition did not permit a return to work. For Flynn to stop everything—lectures, organizing, meetings, and conferences—was a shock for the organizations depending on her, but they expressed immense gratitude for Equi's assistance. More than a month passed before Flynn left Equi's house for a ride in town. By early April, Equi sent another "Dear Friend" letter to report limited improvement. She also enlisted the help of another physician who had treated strep infections during World War I. He told Flynn that she needed complete rest and that she would not recover for at least five years. Equi could afford the best specialists in town, and their assessments reflected the limits of medical technology and therapeutics of the time.[30]

In the midst of the tumult of caring for Flynn, Equi assisted a woman doctor at the Oregon Coast, who was stricken with grief over the disappearance of her adopted six-year-old son. While being held in the Multnomah County jail for a minor offense, the frantic, overwrought woman undertook a hunger strike. Her story was reported in the dailies, and Equi sent the woman $160 to cover treatment in a sanitarium. The *Oregon Daily Journal* later remarked that Equi was the only Portlander who had helped the unfortunate doctor. The editor observed that "in many a humble home where Dr. Equi has ministered to the sick and from her own means bought and carried provisions to the hungry that name is blessed."[31]

Just as Equi had developed a daily routine for Flynn's care at home, she was shaken by news that Harriet Speckart had taken ill with symptoms of a cerebral hemorrhage. Equi arranged medical care for Harriet on the Oregon Coast and brought Mary Jr., now twelve years old, to live with her in Portland. Equi juggled crisis care for Speckart and nursing attention for Flynn in cities eighty miles apart—while also comforting a frightened daughter. Speckart's condition worsened rapidly, and she died at her home on May 26, 1927, at age forty-four. Her obituary in the *Morning Astorian,* an Oregon coast newspaper, identified her brother, Joseph, and her half-sister, Mrs. Emily Mailand, as Harriet's sole survivors. Equi handled all the arrangements, including a funeral service, cremation, and placement of remains at Lincoln Memorial Park in east Portland.[32]

Speckart's last six years are less well known than the ten months when she wrote almost daily to Equi in prison. She had lived a modest life in Seaside with simple pleasures. She had relinquished her family bonds in pursuit of justice, and she remained devoted through discord and disruption to her lesbian relationship. She shared twenty-one years with Equi in what she once called "our little friendship." No one else had been as intimately involved in Equi's life for so long a period.

At age fifty-five Equi assumed the role of sole parent with concerns and duties she never wanted and was ill equipped to perform. A few months after Mary Jr. arrived in Portland, Equi asked Charlotte Anita Whitney to take her daughter into her Oakland, California, home. The arrangement had to have been difficult for Mary Jr. so soon after Speckart's death. Yet Whitney's circumstances were perhaps the better alternative: she had remained single and her family's wealth provided for her own livelihood.

Whitney's life had become more settled with the threat of imprisonment lifted. In May 1927 the US Supreme Court upheld her conviction under the California criminal syndicalism law even while it restored free speech protections declared illegal under the Espionage and Sedition Acts. Ironically, Equi's wartime resistance would have been protected under the standards set in *Whitney v. California*. Whitney did not seek clemency from the governor of California. She worried she would receive special treatment due to her class, wealth, and prominence. Intense pressure from the Bay Area's civic, religious, and corporate leaders, however, persuaded the state's newly elected governor, Clement C. Young, to grant Whitney a full and unconditional pardon in June 1927.[33]

Elizabeth Gurley Flynn continued to improve through that summer under Equi's care, but she sorely missed her son, Buster, who she had frequently left behind to travel to one emergency after another. Equi intervened and paid for Buster to visit his mother and then for the two of them to vacation at Crater Lake National Park in southwest Oregon. Events continued to batter Flynn's emotional well being, however. In late August 1927, the anarchists Sacco and Vanzetti were executed, sparking violent protests worldwide. Flynn's seven years of defense work on their behalf had failed, and she sank into further despair and depression. Only after several more months did her health improve, allowing her to return to New York in November of that year. Evidently her strep infection, and not her heart, had been the primary cause of her difficulty, and the symptoms had lessened during her long period of rest.[34]

The year 1927 held one more upset for Equi. In December she developed pneumonia, after a years-long history of tuberculosis, pleurisy, and a back injury. In a sequence of events not entirely clear, Mary Jr. wired Elizabeth Gurley Flynn from Oakland and asked her to return to Oregon to care for her mother. Once again Flynn left her mother and son, after first relocating them in a new home in Brooklyn. After she assessed Equi's condition, Flynn urged Mary Jr. to return immediately to Portland with Whitney. And so, in the winter of 1927, Flynn and Whitney gathered with Equi to help each other recover from illnesses, legal defeats, and personal setbacks. They represented more than sixty years of political activism, two free-speech cases taken to the US Supreme Court, dozens of strikes and arrests, and jail and prison time. In the weeks ahead, Equi regained her health, and Whitney returned to Oakland to initiate a new, more radical phase of her life. Equi and Flynn, however, were about to take an extended leave from their activism, together in Portland. Flynn later wrote in her journal, "Should have stayed home and never gone back."[35]

17
Life with the Rebel Girl

I found in Oregon that one can have economic security,
leisure and rest, yet be frightfully unhappy.
Elizabeth Gurley Flynn, IWW radical

After her bout of pneumonia in late 1927, Marie Equi decided to keep her daughter nearby in Portland. She remained Doc for the child—the parent who spent her days at the office and made house calls into the night—but the household of Equi, Mary Jr., and Elizabeth Gurley Flynn was unsettled amid unfamiliar territory. Mary Jr. grieved the loss of a parent and her world of friends and familiar surroundings on the Oregon coast. In Portland she was expected to share her remaining parent with another woman, Flynn, who she hardly knew. Flynn by her own admission had never been the most attentive of mothers to her only child, and Equi held little interest in day-to-day childrearing. Yet there they were all together in a house in Portland—two of the best-known radicals in the Pacific Northwest with a girl seeking maternal attention.

Over time Mary Jr. became friends with Flynn, especially once the older woman paid attention to her and expressed interest in her schoolwork. They discussed literature and political history, and they made reading the assigned *Weekly Observer* one of their rituals. Mary Jr. later recalled how much she appreciated Flynn's kindness and understanding at the time, although she had wished Flynn would have defended her more often from her mother's reprimands.[1]

Mary Equi resumed her schooling in Portland, and in September 1929 she enrolled at Lincoln High School, the site of her mother's graduation ceremonies from medical school. In a yearbook photograph, she appears an attractive girl with her hair short in the style of the day. Mary—she had dropped Junior—excelled at mathematics, her favorite subject, and she liked swimming, hiking, and golf, but her real passion was aviation. Ever since ace flyers and aerial stuntmen Tex and Dick Rankin stormed the Seaside skies and landed their wartime biplanes, Mary had been enthralled with flying. She took her first flight at age eight with Tex Rankin and became his most frequent customer on the coast. In high

Mary Equi qualified for her first solo
flight and was touted "the youngest girl
flyer in the Pacific Northwest." Oregon
Historical Society, bb013182.

school she dreamed of flying solo, and she took lessons at the Rankin School of
Flying located on the Swan Island peninsula along the Willamette River. When
she was sixteen and a high school senior, Mary completed twelve hours of training and qualified for her first solo flight. She managed a sure takeoff, executed
three circles a thousand feet above the ground, and achieved a perfect landing.
The *Oregonian* touted her as the "youngest girl flyer in the Pacific Northwest"
and published a photo of her in a flight jacket and leggings, goggles, and cap.
Equi was mentioned in the article as her mother, but otherwise the account was
all about Mary. She had started to come into her own.[2]

Equi was a good provider, and she doted on her daughter, but she closely,
sometimes excessively, monitored Mary's activities. Margaret D., a family
friend, recalled that Equi tried to control her daughter's every outing, to the
point of determining which restaurant Mary and and her friend could go to
and what show they could see afterward. Margaret thought she understood
Equi's worry. "I think there was always a fear . . . because of the type of work she
did [abortion]," she said in an interview. "She had seen so many young lives
ruined by poor choices that she worried about her daughter."[3]

Mary graduated from high school in June 1932 and enrolled at Reed College, a liberal arts institution in Portland known for its emphasis on rigorous
development of intellectual skills and its support of leftist causes. Mary thrived

in the freedom Reed provided, and she became a popular student active in extracurricular activities. But Equi worried that students were permitted too much personal independence. She later wrote to her friend Hanna Sheehy-Skeffington that she wished she had sent Mary to study in Ireland instead to be among friends and family there.[4]

Equi's own freedom was restricted during these years by her caretaking responsibilities and her declining health, and she might easily have directed her frustration toward Mary. Yet she was also extremely proud of her daughter. A few years later in a letter to her longtime friend Dr. Belle Ferguson, she extolled Mary's "sheer force of intelligence and will" in restoring her Aunt Sophie's health during a trip to Pasadena, California. Equi wrote, "Am proud of our Mary as you would be and are."[5]

Elizabeth Gurley Flynn sank into lethargy and depression once she resettled in Portland, and she was unable to muster much motivation or initiative. She complained in a letter to Mary Heaton Vorse, the labor journalist and author, that she seemed to have "lost the knack" for doing much. Her thoughts of returning to New York faded. She offered a partial explanation, "It is so beautiful out here . . . I really don't care much when I go back." Flynn may have recovered from her earlier infection and heart trouble, but the disappointments in her professional and personal life left her with what appeared to be a loneliness of spirit, bereft of the affirmation and achievement enjoyed during her years of activism.[6]

Flynn's lengthy absence from work had forced her recent employer, the American Fund for Public Service, to hire someone else for her director position. She did not object, but she still felt the tug of activism. In March 1929 she ventured from Equi's house to speak at two labor meetings—one in Seattle to support Wobblies implicated in the Centralia conflict, the other in Portland at a rally to benefit Tom Mooney, who was still imprisoned at San Quentin. She reported in a letter to Mary Heaton Vorse that she felt little worse for wear other than some tiredness. Yet four months later she notified her comrades at International Labor Defense that she was still suffering the effects of her heart lesion, and she resigned her position with the group at a time when her expertise was sorely needed.[7]

Flynn stayed in Portland with Equi through all of 1928 and into the summer of 1929. It was a convenient arrangement for her; Equi provided lodging, meals, and medical care at no charge while Flynn was unemployed with no other means of financial support. Though Flynn coped with mental fatigue and depression, Equi seemed revitalized by the company of another woman. Mary recalled that her mother often became the "life of the party" around Flynn: "Sometimes she wrapped a towel around her head, grabbed a cane, and sang 'Johnny Comes Marching Home Again.'" [8]

Equi longed for a romance, however, and she looked to Hanna Sheehy-Skeffington as a prospect. In a saucy letter penned in February 1928, she described an outing to hear Portland police officers rehearse a popular song, "Please Come Out," for an upcoming event. She wrote how she settled herself before the men, sitting pretty and dignified with an ironic smile, given her rocky relationship with the officers. After a while everyone relaxed, and the police sang more songs for her, enjoying her company. Then, Equi shifted to an entreaty, "O Miss Hanna / Won't you please come out and take a walk." In a followup message, Equi asked if they might meet somewhere, anywhere, whatever the distance or expense. She wondered if her friend had earlier suggested a "white marriage" for the two of them. (The term referred to an unconsummated or companionate coupling.) She closed with an outright declaration of love. Sheehy-Skeffington's reply has been lost, and an intimate relationship never developed. [9]

Equi's yearning for a deeper, personal connection with a longtime friend suggests her romantic desires were not being met by Flynn. What her housemate offered was the company and comfort of a woman who understood her life experience, shared ten years of frontline activism, and commiserated over the state of postwar politics. Both women had lived the life of prominent radicals with all the sacrifices, strains on relationships, and the psychological buzz from being the center of attention. Each was alone without a lover, and their heady, political careers seemed over.

If Equi wrote love letters to Flynn when they were apart—as she had with Harriet Speckart, Kathleen O'Brennan, Margaret Sanger, and Hanna Sheehy-Skeffington—none have been located. (Many of Equi's papers were lost or destroyed after her death). Flynn's feelings for Equi, at least those evidenced in her journal and correspondence with others, suggest more of a respectful collaboration, a sense of obligation, and an appreciation for her care and assistance rather than a romantic or sexual attraction. But Flynn was mindful of her own stature, reputation, and legacy, and she may have chosen to keep secret her sentiments for a woman known to be a lesbian. (References to Flynn's lesbianism may also have been edited from her writings in a homophobic purge when they were archived by the Communist Party of the United States.) Given Equi's lesbianism and personal setbacks and Flynn's need for care and

Irish nationalist Hanna Sheehy-Skeffington (here with her son) toured the US to rally support for Irish independence and formed a close relationship with Marie Equi. Library of Congress, LOC LC-DIG-ggbain 23422.

comfort after her troubled relationships, they may very well have enjoyed a meaningful intimacy together that included sex. The only known suggestion of this was provided by Equi's daughter, Mary, who once remarked, as an adult, that she remembered her mother shared a bedroom for awhile with Flynn at their house. However, the longer the two women lived together, the more their relationship became entangled in dependency and frustration.[10]

By the summer of 1929 Flynn felt stronger and more robust, and she returned to her family in New York. She steadily improved and, in January 1930, she wrote to her friend Mary Heaton Vorse, "My mental troubles are pretty well eliminated." She was feeling well enough to express dismay to her friends in the city that the Communist Party she had joined earlier had become riven with factionalism. She confided that New York no longer satisfied her because it was too "nerve-wracking" and "too Jewish," a remark at odds with her stated values. Without employment and not wanting to be a financial burden to her family, Flynn's thoughts drifted to the secure life Equi offered in Portland.[11]

Oregonians might have heeded the warning signs of the coming disaster. Although the state's population increased steadily during the 1920s, markers of the local and regional economy declined—timber and wheat prices sank lower and residential construction in Portland dropped 50 percent. When the US stock market crashed on October 29, 1929, and lost a third of its value, the nation's economic infrastructure shattered from the shock. Devastation rippled across the country claiming the jobs, businesses, homes, and life savings of millions of Americans. Banks closed and trade plunged. Drops in crop prices plagued farming communities, and lumber losses eroded regional economies. The disruption reverberated worldwide with no nation strong enough to withstand the blows and stabilize its economy. President Herbert Hoover appeared unable to manage a remedy or provide a vision for recovery, and the public scorned him. In despair, hundreds of thousands of unemployed, homeless Americans resorted to living in shantytowns called "Hoovervilles"—vast tracts of public or unclaimed land crammed with shacks constructed of cardboard, scrap metal, and lumber. The denizens of Portland's Hoovervilles huddled under the Ross Island Bridge along the Willamette River, at Sullivan's Gulch in the southeast district, and at Guild's Lake, the former site of the 1905 world's fair.[12]

Unlike many Americans, Equi held onto her home and livelihood, but she also managed to invest in her future. A few months before the market crash, she purchased two hundred shares in a utilities conglomerate, and by the end of the year she added nearly five hundred more. Over the next two decades her portfolio swelled with stocks from foreign governments and in paper, oil, and nitrate concerns. She continued until her total estate reached a value of nearly $98,000, a sum comparable today to $850,000.[13]

Did Equi's investments in the stock market betray her belief that big business and corporate power obstructed economic and social justice? Apparently not to her way of thinking as she continued to both invest and support radical causes. Over the years she had honed a fierce determination to protect herself and ensure her independence, and her stock purchases fit that strategy. No social welfare safety nets existed, and Equi understood that no one else would take care of her financially. During the Depression, everyone focused on security—seeking it or holding on to what they could. Her portfolio—as well as purchasing a house—was her means of doing so.[14]

Equi also tried to ensure her daughter's future by battling with the Speckart family once again, this time over Harriet's estate. When Joe Speckart, Harriet's brother, initiated probate proceedings after his sister's death, he informed the court that she had died without a will and that he and Emily Mailand, his half-sister, were her only legal heirs. An administrator valued the estate at nearly $28,000, primarily in stocks and bonds. On the last day claims could be filed, Equi's attorney asserted that Mary Equi should receive all of Speckart's estate based on an oral agreement between Equi and Speckart about the child's upbringing. As part of that understanding, Speckart had agreed to leave all her estate to their daughter. Equi also contended that Speckart had received value in the form of "companionship, comfort and society" from the child since the time of her adoption.[15]

Equi's claim on her daughter's behalf had to have been one of the more unusual to come before the probate judge, George Tazwell of the circuit court: two unmarried and unrelated women sharing the upbringing of a child. Tazwell dismissed Equi's claim on Speckart's total estate, but he understood that the child had lived continually with Speckart since she was an infant. He sidestepped the question of Speckart's parental role and instead ruled that the girl's years of companionship to her mother held monetary value. He ordered an equal distribution of Speckart's net assets among her three heirs: her brother, half-sister, and her daughter. Each received $8,364, the equivalent of more than $100,000 today.[16]

Judge Tazwell had served on local courts since 1910, and he was acquainted with Equi. He would have known from newspaper reports that she had adopted a daughter and that she had lived with Speckart and the child. He was sympathetic to women's rights, having helped authorize the seating of the first all-female jury in Portland. Although his ruling in the probate case recognized only the nature and value of Mary's association with Speckart, it implicitly acknowledged Equi and Speckart's relationship by granting Equi standing in the case as the child's legal parent and by accepting as relevant their agreement for rearing the child. In effect, Tazwell's decision acknowledged the bond between two single adult women who chose an unorthodox arrangement for their alternative family in the early twentieth century.[17]

Equi would never again be fully immersed in the political issues of the day, but she did not disappear from the scene. In February 1929 she spoke at a meeting of twenty-five hundred supporters of Tom Mooney. (Elizabeth Gurley Flynn addressed the same meeting.) Mooney's attorneys were ready to present evidence that perjured testimony had led to his conviction for the Preparedness Day bombing in San Francisco, but Mooney received no reprieve from the courts. Although a public outcry demanded his release, he sent a statement to be read at the Portland meeting declaring that he would only accept a pardon that reflected no guilt on his part. Portland activist Tom Burns introduced Equi as someone who had also been framed and sent to prison, and she spoke of her prison experience and how she had seen Mooney at San Quentin.[18]

In April 1930 Equi suffered a heart attack that threatened to keep her bedridden indefinitely. Once again she turned to Elizabeth Gurley Flynn for help. Under the same arrangement as before, she offered lodging with all expenses paid if Flynn would rejoin her household. Flynn believed Equi had saved her life in 1927, and she wanted to reciprocate. With the additional impetus from the onset of the Depression and her own precarious finances, Flynn would have been hard-pressed not to agree.[19]

Equi struggled with heart problems for the remainder of the year and then suffered a relapse in July 1931 that forced her to bed again. She later wrote to Sheehy-Skeffington that doctors had not expected her to survive through the latter part of the year. Her dire condition prompted Charlotte Anita Whitney to rush from Oakland and stay with Equi for a month. With no prognosis for a full recovery, Equi retired from her medical practice in 1931 but kept her office open for several years under the management of Dr. Andre Ausplund, the well-known abortion provider who practiced in the same building. For twenty-eight years she had been Doc to hundreds of patients. Now she was forced to relinquish what had given her personal meaning and standing in the community. So accustomed to taking charge and directing others, she was now reduced to managing a household of three.[20]

Equi worried about her daughter's education and her prospects for a husband. She even tried matchmaking her daughter with Sheehy-Skeffington's son, Owen. "We'd get some sure enough grandchildren," she wrote. To help the process along, Equi proposed sending Mary to Ireland for the summer to see if the two were a good fit. She imagined all her future problems would be settled if they married. But Owen Sheehy-Skeffington had plans of his own: he married a French university graduate and became a lecturer at Trinity College in Dublin.[21]

While Mary Equi grew restless, Elizabeth Gurley Flynn sank further into discontent. She wrote to a friend, "I'm so lonely at times for my past activities, my old friends, and the places where life was so full—that I don't even try to think about them." She resented being sidelined by events, but she could not envision constructing a new life. In many ways her stay in Portland was too easy for her. Equi paid for everything; she even arranged for bootleg liquor to be dropped off at the house. Flynn wrote a friend, "The big cops come sneaking up with it for her. It's really amusing." Mary remembered that her mother and Flynn drank heavily at times, talked about life and politics, and sometimes argued all night—Equi in a low voice with Flynn shouting and screaming.[22]

Flynn never seemed to accept her circumstances or appreciate for long the respite in Portland. She spent her time reading the classics, Shakespeare,

Elizabeth Gurley Flynn, a
radical labor activist and
an eventual leader of the
Communist Party USA,
sought refuge in Marie
Equi's Portland, Oregon,
home during the Depression.
Library of Congress #b43883.

and science books, but she complained that she had become too stout and
had gained seventy pounds. She complained to her activist friend Agnes Inglis
that she "seemed to get marooned out there in Oregon caring for Dr. Equi and
her household." To her sister Kathy, she added, "I learned in Oregon one can
have economic security, leisure, rest, and yet be frightfully unhappy." Flynn
later confided in her journal that she had become "entangled in a situation
where when Dr. Equi became ill she expected me to remain with her "till she
died." Flynn's distress was understandable. She was forty-one years old, and
primarily sought the romantic company of men —even if her choices were
ill advised. She had thrilled to be in the thick of protests on the frontlines,
travelling from one labor dispute to another, and now she was sequestered
with Equi. Yet Flynn could have ended her arrangement, and Equi, if forced,
could have hired help from others.[23]

Portland activist Julia Ruuttila found the dynamic between Equi and
Flynn disturbing. "My first visit to the Doctor was followed by many others,
and each time I saw Flynn . . . she was acting as housekeeper to Equi." Ruuttila
recounted the drill. Equi summoned visitors, Flynn greeted callers and took
them upstairs to Equi who sat propped up in bed, wearing an ornate brocaded
gown. Equi then instructed Flynn to prepare coffee but never invited her to

join them. Ruuttila admired Flynn as an IWW hero, and she was embarrassed to see her treated like a servant. She concluded that Flynn felt "fettered" in Portland, but she believed that much of the distress was Flynn's own. "Gurley Flynn was one of those people who must have an organization around and behind her to function at full capacity," she later wrote. As she saw it, Flynn was embroiled in a struggle "to accept the fact that the organization which she had believed in and helped to lead in strikes and through frame-ups and struggles of the poor for twenty years had ceased to be a force in the continuing battle for economic and social justice."[24]

In the summer of 1933 Flynn visited her youngest sister, Bina, and her family in Miami, Arizona, for a month. She and her sister had since resolved the hurt and anger Flynn felt over Bina's affair with Carlo Tresca. In a photo taken at the time Flynn appeared tired and worn. Bina believed Equi was in love with Flynn and dominated her, and she pleaded with her sister to leave Portland. But Flynn felt badly about the harsh conditions Bina endured in Arizona, and she gave her sister the ticket to New York that she had hoped to use herself.[25]

Flynn's family was also worried that Equi's lesbianism would damage Flynn's reputation. Popular culture in the 1930s favored sinister depictions of lesbianism in novels and magazines with dire outcomes for women who strayed into forbidden sexual territory. In bohemian circles curiosity about same-sex love and experimentation with it prevailed, motivated partly by sexologists' talk of lesbianism. But mainstream Americans feared lesbian seduction. They worried especially about immoral practices rumored to take hold in women's schools and in the cities. People thought the severe financial straits of the Great Depression could force vulnerable women to grant sexual favors to wealthy predators for some financial relief. The prospect of two women engaged in a healthy sexual relationship and combining their resources to weather the economic storm never occurred or was repugnant to most Americans. Flynn's sister seemed to blame Equi for the domestic arrangement without acknowledging Equi's rescuing and providing for Flynn during dire times. Ironically, Equi faced the same charges of unhealthy influence that she encountered thirty years earlier when she began a romance with Harriet Speckart.[26]

Flynn's dissatisfaction matched the sour national mood that President Franklin D. Roosevelt, elected in 1932, referred to as the "grim problem of existence." In March 1933 more than twenty-four thousand jobless Portlanders registered with local employment bureaus, and forty thousand in the city were on relief.

Racial tensions compounded the economic woes, and at the start of that year Equi joined the outcry against an apparent frame-up of an African-American man convicted of killing a railway worker in Klamath Falls, Oregon. She wrote a letter condemning the imminent execution of the man, Theodore Jordan, and she consulted with the national representative of International Labor Defense for the case. Oregon's courts upheld Jordan's conviction, and his death was forestalled only after thousands of petitioners persuaded Oregon Governor Julius Meier to commute his sentence to life imprisonment.[27]

Equi directly benefited from one of the new president's initiatives. On December 24, 1933, Roosevelt granted a full pardon to her and fifteen hundred others convicted of wartime sedition. Twelve years after her release from prison, Equi regained her citizenship. Like hundreds of Wobblies, Socialists, and others swept up by the excesses of the wartime acts, Equi could once again vote, serve on a jury, and travel with a valid US passport. But she was not a Roosevelt fan, at least not in the early years of his presidency. In a 1934 letter, she objected to what she judged was his throttling of the press, and she criticized his "pacific talk" while getting the country ready for war, although World War II was five years off. She thought FDR dodged the real questions of war and peace with his banter, ready smile, and good cheer. He was "slippery as an eel" in her estimation and not a serious leader. She decried the "diplomacy, duplicity, deception" practiced by politicians in general. Her sentiments reflected a turning from FDR in some quarters, especially after his unsuccessful attempt in 1937 to "pack the court" with six new US Supreme Court Justices. As Europe edged closer to war in 1938, Equi wrote a letter to Sheehy-Skeffington, observing, "Better have a Hitler declaring himself openly than a Stalin with his underground machinations." She longed, she wrote, for the old IWW days when radicals were "all open and above board."[28]

Although the IWW limped through the Twenties with little clout, other forms of radical dissent flared in the Thirties, which saw twice as many strikes in industries nationwide. One of them led Equi to make an exception to her retirement when a tinderbox of trouble threatened West Coast ports. Longshoremen resented their eighty-five-cents-an-hour wages and their work shifts that extended from twelve to fifteen hours. Most of all the men on the docks objected to employers' control of hiring halls, an arrangement that effectively guaranteed a nonunion shop. When tensions erupted in a waterfront strike, Equi could not remain silent.[29]

In May 1934 longshoremen from Bellingham, Washington, to San Diego walked off their jobs. Portland members of the International Longshoremen's

Association (ILA) anticipated a long strike, and they cultivated support among farmers, grocers, and other unions. Within a week the other maritime unions joined the protest. In Portland alone seventy-five unions signed on to the action that became known as "The Big Strike." In short order the West Coast was closed to all maritime business, and the impact of the strike rippled through local economies with shortages in gasoline and oil supplies. Violence erupted in several coastal cities; open warfare on San Francisco streets killed three and left hundreds injured. Tension spiked in Portland when employers, with the support of local police, tried to force open the docks. Several skirmishes flared in early July and dozens of strikers were arrested.[30]

Equi left her house for the first time in two years to stand by the strikers on the docks. Many recognized her for the medical care she had provided their families or knew her by reputation. The next day on the same pier, picketers blocked strikebreakers who tried to force their entry into the terminal, and four strikers were wounded. On what became known as Portland's Bloody Wednesday, Equi left her home again and visited the local ILA headquarters. She told the association's publication, *The Hook*, that she "wanted to do something for the boys," and she donated $250—a considerable sum during the Depression—for the four wounded men. When a reporter asked her about her generosity, Equi quipped, "So a gift of $250 surprises you? Young man, money is a thing despised. I claim no honor or glory in giving this sum. If I had my name in the paper every time I gave away money, I'd look like a daily feature."[31]

Unbowed by the violence, the strikers held their ground even as the governor threatened to mobilize the National Guard. Two weeks later the longshoremen up and down the coast agreed to enter arbitration, and in the eventual bargain they obtained union recognition, higher hourly and overtime pay, a six-hour workday, and a greater voice in hiring halls.[32]

The Maritime Strike of 1934 marked Equi's last known public appearance for the cause of labor rights and social justice. However, in the following year, she wrote an article for the Seattle labor paper *Voice of Action* in which she asserted that behind the waterfront strike were "years of poverty and desperation, undernourishment of children." And she assured readers, "We shall win this struggle against the forces of wealth. We shall free our class from the oppression by organizing and unity." Elizabeth Gurley Flynn also wrote a piece for the paper and delivered a more ringing ultimatum: "There can be no peace, vindication of our martyred dead until there is no more a capitalist system."[33]

Although Equi's article reflected her steadfast identification with the workers' struggle, she did not support the far-left aims of the Communist Party.

She told Julia Ruuttila that she had once joined the party but later returned her membership card when the party's actions diverged from its goals. In the 1920s the Soviet Union held many in thrall over the possibility of revolution and socialism in action. These leftists listened to prominent Americans like Lincoln Steffens who wrote, "I have been over into the future and it works." But disillusionment with totalitarianism set in early for radicals like Emma Goldman, who criticized the Bolsheviks and abandoned her refuge in Russia. Yet, with the IWW sidelined and the Socialists in disarray, the Communist Party offered many radicals the only vehicle for their beliefs. In Portland, the Communists continued to be a force in the city and organized a chapter of the Young Communist League.[34]

Equi argued with Flynn over Communism, and their feelings would later disrupt their relationship. There's no account of whether Flynn disclosed to her that she had become a secret member of the Communist Labor Party in New York in 1926. She was drawn to communism because it closely aligned with the US-based radicalism that defined her first twenty years of activism.[35]

By 1936 Equi and Flynn had lived together for nine years. Mary Equi observed the interactions between her mother and Flynn more than anyone else, and she later described a "drawing power" between them, a kind of psychological dependence. She thought Flynn was a moth to Equi's lightbulb. The two women seemed to have developed an unwieldy interdependence that delivered just enough satisfaction to keep them together, but Flynn at least was terribly unhappy. In early 1936 Flynn's sister Bina and her husband drove to Portland from San Francisco where they were living and executed an intervention. Bina waited in a hotel while her husband drove to Equi's house and demanded that Flynn leave with him. Equi undoubtedly took offense at the intrusion, and she reportedly warned Flynn that she risked her health if she left. Flynn acquiesced to her brother-in-law's demands, or, perhaps, she jumped at the chance to make her exit. She traveled nonstop to San Francisco where she remained for three months before returning to New York.[36]

In her later years, Flynn offered several reasons for what she called her "Sojourn in the West," including how much she had cared about Mary Equi. In 1954, while serving a prison term for her Communist Party affiliation, Flynn reflected that she had become more "tolerant and sympathetic" of Equi. She understood better how Equi's time in San Quentin had affected her, she wrote, and she empathized with how much the prison conditions had assaulted Equi's dignity and personal privacy. The next year Flynn seemed more resolved about her experience. She allowed that Equi "was not the easiest person in the world to get along with," but that she admired Equi's "brilliant mind and progressive spirit."[37]

Equi complained of severe fatigue and of a "most trying period" when Flynn departed. She had little chance to absorb the change when, a few days later, Mary eloped to marry Tony Lukes, an older student at Reed College. Nothing about the occasion pleased Equi. Lukes was known at the college for his activism and travels to the Soviet Union. He also served as a district representative for the Young Communist League in Portland. Mary made an interesting choice, one that seemed particularly defiant of her mother's wishes. She had previously expressed little interest in politics, and she knew her mother was adamantly opposed to communism. Nevertheless, she married Lukes and the couple settled in southeast Portland. After nearly ten years of sharing her house with others, Equi at age sixty-three was living alone again.[38]

18
Queen of the Bolsheviks

*I see her as . . . a woman of passion and conviction
. . . a real friend of the have-nots of this world.*
Julia Ruuttila, longtime Oregon labor activist

A tonic for Marie Equi's bruised spirits after Mary's elopement and Elizabeth Gurley Flynn's departure appeared early in 1937 with the publication of an article that treated her antiwar protests with respect. Stewart Holbrook, a popular and prolific newspaperman, featured Equi in an eight-part series in the *Oregonian* on episodes of mass hysteria in the Pacific Northwest. Holbrook challenged Oregonians' beliefs that they were too solid of character to succumb to "public fevers." In the installment "Down with the Huns," he detailed the hyperpatriotism that engulfed the region in the World War I era. "The jails of every town and city in Oregon and Washington were soon full to bulging with Wobblies, young and old, native and foreign-born," he wrote. Holbrook described ordinary citizens, including Equi, whom the government harassed and defamed for exercising their right of free speech. Equi's enemies, in Holbrook's estimation, sent her to prison although they had "never accused her of anything much worse than honesty." Beneath a photo of her, the caption read, "Dr. Marie Equi was sentenced for saying what she thought of the big barbecue." Equi appreciated the even-handed tribute, and she thanked Holbrook in a note, "The line under the photo was very effective. You are writing trenchantly in your Sunday articles."[1]

The good press from Holbrook may have lessened Equi's indignation at having her reputation for radicalism overlooked on another occasion. When Portland's repressive Red Squad published a list of important radicals living in Portland, she was incensed to find her name missing. The Portland Police Bureau had long operated the Red Squad—a right-wing cadre dedicated to spying, harassing, and assaulting dissenters as well as liberal and radical organizations. But the group failed to designate Equi a major threat to American ideals. She dated her radical work to 1913, more than twenty years earlier, and she was one of two dozen Oregonians convicted under the Sedition Act.

Few Portlanders had been arrested as often as Equi for her principled stands, and she wanted due recognition. The slight made her "absolutely livid with annoyance," according to activist Julia Ruuttila. Equi telephoned the chief of police and threatened to sue the bureau unless the expose was revised with her name listed at the top as "Dr. Marie Equi, Queen of the Bolsheviks." The title harkened to the time after the Russian Revolution when revolutionists and all other radicals were lumped together in America as Bolsheviks. She probably also recalled the opening lines of the song her friend Ruth Barnett penned about her: "Mary was the Queen of the Bolsheviks / Everywhere she went her name was known." Nothing came of Equi's insistence for top billing, but the experience revealed how much her reputation meant to her.[2]

Even in her later years Equi attracted seasoned labor leaders and younger progressives and radicals. Ruuttila recalled accompanying a number of them to Equi's house in the evenings. Francis Murnane, president of the International Longshore and Warehouse Union, was a favorite. Once a Catholic seminarian, Murnane abandoned his thoughts of the priesthood after hearing a talk about the frameup of Tom Mooney. He considered becoming an attorney to defend those unjustly charged, but he undertook labor organizing instead. Others who trekked to see Equi were S. P. Stevens, fire union president, and John J. McNamara, charged with dynamiting the *Los Angeles Times* building during a bitter strike in 1910. Mary Equi recalled visits to her mother by Socialist and pacifist leader Norman Thomas and political activist and economist Scott Nearing.[3]

One of the new, younger leaders who sought Equi's advice and support was Monroe Sweetland, a labor man and community organizer in his mid-twenties. Sweetland led the influential Oregon Commonwealth Federation (OCF), a progressive association of trade unions, unemployment councils, farmers, and students. The OCF was the kind of bold, inclusive operation that appealed to Equi, and she welcomed Sweetland's visits. In 1937 she donated to the OCF campaign to oust Oregon's Democratic governor, Charles Martin, an antilabor, anticommunist extremist who had launched a police squad of "Red-hunters" two years earlier throughout the state.[4]

Visitors to Equi's house had to negotiate around a massive library desk and a heavily carved dining table with eight large chairs and a big buffet before finding a chair close to her bed where she sat poised for company. They often found her expansive and exuberant. According to Ruuttila, "She had a magnificent voice. Warm, deep, and eloquent. . . . She was fascinating to listen to—(but) you couldn't get a word in edgewise." Ruuttila knew by then that

Marie Equi ready to receive visitors at her house in the Goose Hollow neighborhood of Southwest Portland, Oregon, 1937. Oregon Historical Society, bb013174.

Equi took liberties with the facts for a good story, but she thought that made her more colorful. Besides, Ruuttila noted, "She was extremely honest in all ways that really mattered." But Equi's high spirits could be too much. "After two or three hours in her company," Ruuttila recalled, "I used to feel emotionally exhausted, and so did the men I went there with." Equi revealed to Hanna

Sheehy-Skeffington one of the reasons for her high spirits, "As in all lung cases consumed with fever, I sparkle into life after 4 p.m. until 2 a.m."[5]

In the latter part of her life Equi might have enjoyed her longtime bond with Charlotte Anita Whitney and she might have repaired her relationship with Elizabeth Gurley Flynn, but her strong dislike of communism distanced her from them. They both became leaders of the Communist Party USA. Whitney fell out of favor with Equi even further when it appeared that her onetime dear friend had taken advantage of an elderly sympathizer in order to inherit his estate. And she blamed her daughter's decision to wed a Communist on five years of "bad influence" from Whitney and Flynn that caused her "grief and slow death."[6]

No matter her Queen of the Bolsheviks claim, Equi was ever the political individualist. In 1939 she registered and presumably voted as a Republican rather than support FDR. As the troubles in Europe threatened to draw the United States into another world war, she apparently worried that the president would take the country to war as Wilson had done after she had voted for him.[7]

Equi strained to be positive about her daughter's marriage, but she wrote to Sheehy-Skeffington, "Life deals us blows through our children." She treated the couple kindly, but she remained "burned up with indigestion." She was displeased and unhappy about the situation, but she did not sink into vindictiveness or spite. Instead, she joked about Tony Lukes, "I call myself his out-law." She also helped the young couple by hiring a housekeeper for them.[8]

In time Equi's disgruntlement softened, especially with the arrival of grandchildren. Mary had returned to her studies and graduated from Reed College, and the family relocated to a house a few blocks from Equi's residence. Then, in the spring of 1938, Mary gave birth to her first child, Tony Jr. Six years later the Lukes celebrated the arrival of their second child, named Harriet Marie in honor of Mary's two parents. Equi became an attentive grandmother who provided childcare and offered advice about childrearing. On one occasion, she sent a note to Mary, describing how she sang hymns and recited nursery rhymes to help little Harriet sleep. When Mary and Tony enrolled their children in Portland grade schools and later at Lincoln High School, Equi assisted with tuition.[9]

Years later Arthur Champlin Spencer, a childhood friend of Tony Jr., remembered how much he was in awe of Equi. "She was not like any little old grandmother. She was regal . . . quite imposing," he said. "She sat bolt upright asking for her magazines and papers." He also recalled how much Equi was interested in history and that she had begun research on her family's genealogy.[10]

Equi employed nurses to visit or stay with her, but she had trouble keeping them, perhaps, as her daughter suggested, because she was too difficult to work for. Margaret D., the family friend, was an exception. Equi had delivered her as an infant, and she appreciated how much the older woman had encouraged her through nursing school. Margaret's job was to visit Equi at night, help her prepare for bed, and then stay overnight in one of the rooms upstairs. But the visiting and talking usually extended for hours, and Equi often kept Margaret awake until 4 a.m. On one occasion, Equi showed her several trunks and boxes filled with newspaper clippings, letters, San Quentin mementos, and the awards she had received for her earthquake relief work.[11]

As the 1940s began, Equi was in her late sixties, and several of her loved ones passed away. Her sister Sophie died in Los Angeles in 1942, followed two years later by Dr. Belle Ferguson, whom she first met in The Dalles during her homestead days. Equi followed the career of Hanna Sheehy-Skeffington, who taught school during World War II, and then, in 1943, stood unsuccessfully as a candidate for the lower house of the Irish parliament. She died three years later. In Equi's last known letter to her, she wrote, "I know now of no greater joy than in holding your hand and seeing you once again." She closed, "Au revoir and goodbye."[12]

Equi intermittently contacted other friends, and late one evening in 1943 she surprised Margaret Sanger with a telephone call. Sanger was discouraged that World War II distracted attention and funding from women's health care, and Equi commiserated. Sanger persevered to see the American Medical Association endorse the addition of contraception in regular medical services and in medical education. In 1952 she helped establish the organization that became the International Planned Parenthood Federation. But not until 1963—forty-seven years after Equi and Sanger spent a night in jail together— did a Planned Parenthood clinic open in Portland.[13]

Few accounts remain of Equi's final years of living alone, although Ruuttila described an occasion when Equi helped her. Ruuttila was fired from her newspaper position in 1948 for writing articles critical of Portland's treatment of the six thousand African-Americans made homeless when the Columbia River broke through a railway landfill and flooded the vast public housing community in north Portland called Vanport. Through a mutual friend, Equi learned that Ruuttila was unable to pay her gas bills and struggled to live without heat and hot water, and she sent payment to settle all of Ruuttila's accounts.[14]

In September 1950 Equi entered Good Samaritan Hospital in Portland after falling at home and fracturing her hip. She was seventy-eight years old, in frail condition, and she failed to improve. But she refused surgery and, therefore, never benefited from physical therapy. Ever the storyteller and charmer, she settled in with the hospital routine, entertained visitors, and became a favorite with the nurses. At one point, longshoremen remembered how she stood by them during the 1934 strike, and they sent a bouquet of thirteen red roses after hearing that she considered thirteen her lucky number. For the occasion, Julia Ruuttila wrote a poem for Equi that included the verse: "Fighter and friend to valiant end / Our champion to revere and defend."[15]

After more than a year at the hospital, Good Samaritan transferred Equi in February 1952 to a nursing home located outside Portland. Around midnight on July 13, 1952, she died of renal disease at eighty years of age. A rosary for her was said two evenings later in downtown Portland. The next morning a cortege left the funeral home and proceeded to St. Michael the Archangel, the Catholic church of the Italian community, on Fourth Street, a few blocks from many of her street protests. The service was conducted amid the simple wood and plaster walls of St. Michael's, a less grand space than the marble and granite of her family's church in New Bedford, but it served an immigrant community of working people important to her. Although Equi objected to many Catholic tenets, she believed it was important to die "in the church," she told a friend, because it offered "such wonderful hope."[16]

Ralph Friedman, a prolific Oregon writer and folklorist, observed that Equi would have been honored with a political funeral if she had not outlived so many who would have attended. One of Equi's friends suggested, "The problem with Doc is that she lived too long."[17]

Equi's entombment took place at Portland Memorial, a crematorium in southeast Portland. Today two vaults lay side by side and embedded in a brown-flecked marble wall. One is identified "Marie D. Equi, M.D. 1872–1952" and the other "Harriet F. Speckart 1883–1927." Presumably, Mary Equi Lukes arranged for her parents' remains to be placed together. After settling her mother's estate, selling her house, and divorcing, Mary remarried and relocated with her husband and children to northern California.[18]

Portland's newspapers eulogized Equi mostly for her combative spirit with nods to her medical work and her generosity to others. In the *Oregonian* she was "a firebrand in the causes of suffrage, labor, and peace." Another article titled "Generous Dissenter" described her as someone who added "yeast to the dough of the solid citizens." Equi's hometown paper, the *New Bedford Standard-Times,* recognized her, as a prominent social worker rather than a physician, as well as a suffragist, and a member of one of the first Italian-American families in the city. The *New York Times* and other newspapers carried an edited version of the New Bedford notice. [19]

After Equi's death, the Portland longshoremen's union adopted a resolution acknowledging her as an "outstanding fighter" who "braved personal dangers and hardships to preserve peace, freedom of speech, and the right of labor to organize." Former Oregon Governor Oswald West—the reluctant character witness at Equi's sedition trial—remarked upon hearing of her death, "She was a radical, but she had a heart as big as a watermelon." [20] Julia Ruuttila, a fiercely committed Oregon labor activist herself, perhaps described her best. Equi was, she said, "a woman of passion and conviction (and) a real friend of the have-nots of this world." She added, "I think she's the most interesting woman that ever lived in this state, certainly the most fascinating, colorful and flamboyant."[21]

Notes

PREFACE

1 "Six Slain, 44 Wounded in Battle between I.W.W. and Posse at Everett," *Oregonian,* November 6, 1916, 1; "State Troops Get Ready to go to Everett," *Oregonian,* November 6, 1916, 1; "Many Prominent Everett Citizens Wounded, One Killed by I.W.W.," *Oregonian,* November 6, 1916, 1.

2 Walker C. Smith, *The Everett Massacre,* www.gutenberg.org accessed December 2, 2012, 94; "IWW Go to Everett," *Oregonian,* December 4, 1916, 11; Charles Ashleigh, "Date Is Set For Trial," *Everett Defense News Letter,* January 27, 1917, content.lib.washington.edu, accessed December 2, 2012; "IWW Ask U.S. to Investigate," *Seattle Star,* November 10, 1916, 1; Elizabeth Gurley Flynn, *I Speak My Own Piece: Autobiography of "the Rebel Girl"* (New York: Masses & Mainstream, 1955), 220–24.

3 Report of Agent William Bryon, November 6 and September 9, 1918, Bryon to F.D. Simmons, September 9, 1918, DOJ Papers.

4 Karen J. Blair, "The State of Research on Pacific Northwest Women," *Frontiers: A Journal of Women Studies,* 22:3 (2001) 48-56; Kimberly Jensen, "A Bibliography of Regional Women's History," *Oregon Historical Quarterly,* 113:3, (Fall 2012), 505–14.

5 Chrystie Hill, "Queer History in Seattle, Part 1: to 1967," *HistoryLink.org, The Free Online Encyclopedia of Washington State History,* http://www.historylink.org/index.cfm?DisplayPage=output.cfm&file_id=4154 accessed January 15, 2015. Sarah Yesler (1822–1887) is noted for her intimate relationship with her friend Eliza Hurd. Yesler was married to Seattle pioneer and developer Henry Yesler; Susan Stryker and Jim Van Buskirk, *Gay by the Bay: A History of Queer Culture in the San Francisco Bay Area* (San Francisco: Chronicle Books, 1996, 9–27.

6 Mark R. Avramo to Marie Equi, March 31, 1921, United States Department of Justice. Mail and Files Division. "Department of Justice File on Dr. Marie Equi." Copies at Oregon Historical Society and at Lewis & Clark College Special Collections, both in Portland, Oregon, hereafter DOJ Papers.

7 Lucy I. Davis Collection on Oregon Women Medical School Graduates, Oregon Health & Science University Historical Collections and Archives, Portland.

8 The several interviews were conducted by Sandy Polishuk, Nancy Krieger, and Susan Dobrof and are cited throughout the Chapter Notes. All interviews are part of Oregon Historical Society Research Library Accession 28389, "Materials relating to research on Dr. Marie Equi," hereafter OHS ACC-28389-Equi. *Harriet F. Speckart v. Leopold F. Schmidt et. al.,* National Archives and Records Administration/San Bruno, Court Records, Record Group 21, Case 1908 US Court of Appeals, 9th Circuit, San Bruno, California; "Quarrel Among Speckart Heirs," *Sunday Oregonian,* May 27, 1906, 1.

9 DOJ Papers.

10 Newspaper articles are cited throughout the chapters. Publications most frequently cited are the *Oregonian, Oregon Daily Journal, Portland Evening Telegram, San Francisco Examiner, San Francisco Chronicle, The Dalles Times-Mountaineer, New Bedford Standard,* and the *New York Times.*

CHAPTER 1

1 "Jailed Three Times," *New Bedford Evening Standard*, March 7, 1914, 1; Katherine Commerford to Evelyn S. Hall, letter, *Application for Admission, Marie Aque*, Northfield Seminary, Sept. 6, 1889; "O.D. Taylor Chastised," *The Dalles Daily Chronicle,"* July 21, 1893, 3; "Start for Home on Saturday," *Oregon Daily Journal*, May 4, 1906, 4; Margaret Sanger to Marie Equi, 1916, MSP-SS as quoted in Margaret Sanger, Esther Katz, editor, *The Selected Papers of Margaret Sanger, Volume 1* (Champaign, Illinois: University of Illinois Press, 2007), 185; Elizabeth Gurley Flynn, *The Rebel Girl: An Autobiography, My First Life 1906–1926* (New York: International Publishers, 1973 edition), 197; Mark R. Avramo to Marie Equi, March 31, 1921, United States Department of Justice Files, National Archives, Civilian Records Unit (Archives II), Case File #9-19-1354-0 and Bureau Papers #9-19-1354, parts 1 and 2, hereinafter referred to as DOJ Papers.

2 Marie Equi to Sara Bard Field, May 29, 1921, Charles Erskine Scott Wood Collection, Huntington Library, WD 135 (53).

3 "Marine Intelligence," *New York Times*, May 23, 1853, 8; *Passenger Lists of Vessels Arriving at New York, 1820–1897*. Micro publication M237 Rolls # 95-580, National Archives and Records Administration, Washington, DC. Norman DaPrato, *Descendants of Michele Antonio Equi*, n.d. The author is indebted to Norman DaPrato for sharing his research of the Equi ancestry. The Equi cousins arrived in New York on May 21, 1853. The passenger roster lists Giovanni Equi's age as sixteen, not twelve, but his naturalization document lists his date of birth as January 15, 1841. *South Bristol Deeds,* Registry of Deeds, New Bedford, Massachusetts., v.35, 1857–1858, June 9, 1857. Dominic Equi purchased the lot from Joseph Grinnell, one of the most prominent business leaders in New Bedford for $363. J. H. Newton, "New Bedford Italian Colony Dates Back More than Half Century," *New Bedford Standard,* October 9, 1932, 4; Norman DaPrato to author, January 30, 2004.

4 Richard D. Brown and Jack Tager, *Massachusetts: A Concise History* (Amherst: University of Massachusetts Press, 2000).

5 J. H. Newton, "New Bedford Italian Colony Dates Back More than Half Century," *New Bedford Standard,* October 9, 1932, 4.

6 Paul A. Cyr, "New Bedford Foreign-Born Population, 1855–1915," *Portraits of a Port,* Kathryn Grover, ed., New Bedford Whaling Museum and *New Bedford Standard Times,* New Bedford, Massachusetts, 11; Dorothy and Thomas Hoobler, *The Irish American Family Album* (New York: Oxford University Press, 1995), 24.

7 Marie Equi to Sara Bard Field, May 29, 1921, DOJ Papers; Joseph Lukes to Nancy Krieger, letter, June 19, 1981, as cited in Nancy Krieger, "Queen of the Bolsheviks: The Hidden History of Dr. Marie Equi," *Radical America*, 17, no.5 (1983): 55–71. An Equi family story placed John Equi fighting with Garibaldi for Italian reunification, but Marie Equi's father would have been less than ten years old at the time of the early battles, and he was already living in America during the final victory. Sacramental Records, St. Lawrence, Martyr Catholic Church, New Bedford, Massachusetts (hereafter referred to as Sacramental Records). All the Equi family's early documents for marriages, births, baptisms, and funerals were located at the church.

8 Two of the adult children of John and Sarah believed their mother gave birth to ten children and that three died at birth or in early childhood. However, the Massachusetts Archives (vol. 223, page 134) and the Sacramental Records note the birth of another Aque child, Amelia, born July 25, 1870, the third child for John and Sarah. No documentation has been located to note her death, which likely occurred as an infant. For Marie Equi's birth, see Massachusetts Archives, Birth records, 1872, Volume 241, page 144, line 318. For Marie Equi's baptism, see Sacramental Records, April 17, 1872.

9 Thomas J. Schlereth, *Victorian America: Transformation in Everyday Life, 1876–1915* (New York: HarperPerennial, 1992), 274.

10 Sacramental Records; "Death Index," Massachusetts State Archives.

11 Mary Equi McCloskey with Sandy Polishuk, Interview, May 1, 1971, OHS ACC 28389-Equi. Note: For clarity, Equi's daughter is listed as Mary Equi McCloskey throughout the notes since that was her married name at the time of the interviews cited.

12 Leonard Bolles Ellis, *History of New Bedford and its Vicinity, 1602–1892* (Syracuse, New York: D. Mason & Co., 1892), 374. For analysis of New Bedford's decline and resurgence from one industry to another, see "From Old Dartmouth to Modern New Bedford," New Bedford Whaling Museum, www.whalingmuseum.org/kendall/oldnbindex.html, accessed November 2004; Thomas Austin McMullin, *Industrialization and Social Change in a Nineteenth Century Port City: A Study of New Bedford, Massachusetts, 1865–1900*, Thesis, University of Wisconsin, Madison, 1976, 14; Seymour Louis Wolfbein, *The Decline of a Cotton Textile City: A Study of New Bedford* (New York: Columbia University Press, 1944), 144. New Bedford also lost more than half its whaling fleet during the war, and watched as San Francisco and Honolulu became the new preferred ports for hunting bowhead whale in the Arctic. Local investors also failed to adopt new whaling techniques or to market whale oil as an ideal lubricant for the machinery of new technologies.

13 McMullin, *Industrialization*, 222; Herbert Gutman, "Work, Culture, and Society in Industrializing America, 1815–1919," *American Historical Review*, 78:3, June 1973, 531–88; Mary Equi McCloskey with Sandy Polishuk, Interview, May 1, 1971, OHS ACC 28389-Equi.

14 Ibid., *South Bristol County Deeds*, Registry of Deeds, New Bedford, Massachusetts, Vol. 76, 1873–1874, 105. The Equi family's address on James Street is variously indicated as *27, 60,* and *87* in city documents and directories. Bristol County Registry of Deeds, Southern District, New Bedford, Massachusetts, v. 35, 1857–1858, June 9, 1857. Richard D. Brown and Jack Tager, *Massachusetts: A Concise History* (Amherst: University of Massachusetts Press, 2000), 166; *South Bristol County Deeds*, Vol. 88, 1878, 446.

15 1880 Federal Census, New Bedford, Bristol County, Massachusetts, Roll 79_525, Film 1254525, 230C, Image 625; Mary Equi McCloskey with Sandy Polishuk, Interview, May 1, 1971, OHS ACC 28389-Equi.

16 Mary Equi McCloskey to Sandy Polishuk, March 31, 1971, OHS 28389-Equi; Lucy M. Wallbank,"50 Years Ago," *New Bedford Sunday Standard Times*, September 3, 1972, 2; *1881 City Document #6, Annual Report of the School Committee of the City of New Bedford together with the superintendent's report for the year 1880* (New Bedford: Mercury Publishing Co., City Printers, 1881); McMullin, *Industrialization, 127;* Katherine Commerfeld to Evelyn S. Hall, September 6, 1889, *Mary Aque Student Application, Recommendations*, Archives/Doblen Library, Northfield Mount Hermon School.

17 Mary E. Austin to Evelyn S. Hall, Northfield Seminary, September 6, 1889; Archives/Dolben Library, Northfield Mount Hermon School, Northfield, Massachusetts. Equi's school records from the New Bedford High School system could not be located upon inquiry, February 15, 2006; Federal Agent W.A. Winsor, Report, October 22 and December 4, 1918, DOJ Papers.

18 Massachusetts law required children, ages eight to fourteen, who worked in factories to attend school for twelve weeks every year. The statewide restriction was the first of its kind in the country, and it helped establish age fourteen as a demarcation for childhood protections. John J. Lalor, ed. *Cyclopaedia of Political Science, Political Economy, and the Political History of the United States by the Best American and European Writers* (New York: Maynard Merrill & Co., 1899), v. 2, Entry 50, Factory Laws, in paragraph II.50.6. Although Equi continued working at a textile mill in 1888, no certificate for her has been located among records at the New Bedford Free Public Library; South Bristol Deeds, Registry of Deeds, v. 119, 1886–1887, 515. The property was later designated 91 Tremont Street. Mary H. Blewett, *Constant Turmoil: The Politics of Industrial Life in Nineteenth-Century New England* (Amherst: University of Massachusetts Press, 2000), 49; Paul A. Cyr, Special Collections Librarian, New Bedford Free Public Library, Interview, October 27, 2004; Equi's two years of mill work is verified by Bessie Holcomb's letters to schools for Equi.

19   Kingston William Heath, *Patina of Place: The Cultural Weathering of a New England Industrial Landscape* (Knoxville: University of Tennessee Press, 2001), 75; Blewett, *Constant Turmoil*, 49; Paul A. Cyr, Interview, October 27, 2004.

20   Heath, *Patina of Place*, 161; Judith A. Boss and Joseph D. Thomas, *New Bedford: A Pictorial History* (Norfolk, Virginia: The Donning Company, 1983).

21   Birth Record, Commonwealth of Massachusetts, Office of the Secretary of State, Archives Division, B002595. For further information on the Holcomb family, see Zephanie W. Pease, *History of New Bedford, Vol. III* (New York: The Lewis Historical Publishing Company, New York, 1918), 537–38.

22   Wilma Slaight, Archivist, Wellesley College Archives, Margaret Clapp Library, Personal Correspondence with author, September 15, 2003; *Wellesley College Record, 1875–1900*, 160. Mabel Newcomer, *A Century of Higher Education for American Women* (New York: Harper & Brothers, 1959), 45–49; Alice Payne Hackett, *Wellesley: Part of the American Story* (New York: E.P. Dutton, 1949), 32–35.

23   Ned Kane, ed., "The History Project," *Improper Bostonians* (Boston: Beacon Press, 1998), 73; Lillian Faderman, *Odd Girls and Twilight Lovers: A History of Lesbian Life in Twentieth-Century America* (New York: Columbia University Press, 1991), 1–4, 11–36, 37–61.

24   Lisa Rubens, "The Patrician Radical, Charlotte Anita Whitney," *California History*, September, 1986, Vol. LXV, 158–71. Whitney also attended Wellesley College and undertook social work before shifting to Progressivism and Socialism.

25   Wilma Slaight, Wellesley College Archives, Personal Correspondence. September 15, 2003; Bessie B. Holcomb to Northfield Seminary, August 26, 1889, Archives/Dolben Library, Northfield Mount Hermon School, *Application for Admissions*, Northfield Seminary, September 6, 1889.

26   Bessie B. Holcomb to Northfield Seminary, August 26, 1889, Archives/Dolben Library, *Application for Admissions*, September 6, 1889.

27   Northfield Mount Herman School, www.nmhschool.org, accessed February 4, 2008.

28   Student File: Mary Aque, Archives/Dolben Library, Northfield Mount Hermon School; Equi gave her Bible from her Northfield Seminary days to her attorney and friend, C. E. Ambrose, of Portland, Oregon. Ambrose with Sandy Polishuk, Interview, May 5, 1972, OHS ACC 28389-Equi.

29   Marie Equi to Mary Vanni and Theresa Vanni, April 10, 1921, DOJ Files.

30   "Dr. Marie Equi Arrested," *New Bedford Standard,* July 20, 1913. Mary Equi McCloskey to Sandy Polishuk, March 31, 1971, OHS ACC 28389-Equi. The date of Equi's stay in Italy is unclear, but given her documented activities from 1882–1890, the period of 1890–1891 seems the most likely. Ira Glazier and William Filby, *Italians to America: Lists of Passengers Arriving at U.S. Ports, 1880–1899, v. 6, 280.* The surname Equi was common in northern Italy, and the Marie Equi who sailed on the ship *Werra* may have been a different person, but the age of the traveler by that name, the time period of travel, and the likely travel by steerage match the Marie Equi of New Bedford.

31   Wilma Slaight, Wellesley College Archives, Personal Correspondence, September 15, 2003.

CHAPTER 2

1   Douglas W. Allen, "Homesteading and Property Rights: Or, 'How the West Was Really Won,'" *Journal of Law and Economics*, 34:1 (April 1991), 1–23. Allen argues that the US government chose to "rush" homesteaders to certain western areas to establish a stronger American presence in lieu of losing vast tracts of land to Mexicans, Indians, British, Spanish, or Russians.

2   James M. Bergquist, "The Oregon Donation Act and the National Land Policy," *Oregon Historical Quarterly*, 58:1 (March 1957), 17–35. Lillian Schlissel, *Women's Diaries of the Westward Journey* (New York: Schocken Books, 1982), 156.

3   Lewis A. and Lewis L. McArthur, *Oregon Geographic Names, Sixth Edition* (Portland: Oregon Historical Society Press, 1992). Native Americans called the locality *Win-quatt,* a place

surrounded by cliffs. White settlers named the town *Dalles* and *Dalles City* but it was always referred to as *The Dalles*, a name officially recognized in 1966.

4   "Wiped Out by Fire," *The Dalles Times-Mountaineer,* September 3, 1891, 1.

5   *Homestead Application No. 4141,* Land Office at The Dalles, Oregon. National Archives and Records Administration, hereafter, NARA. Holcomb's claim was among 139 applications filed at The Dalles Land Office in the final quarter of 1891; "Homesteads in Oregon," Portland Chamber of Commerce (Portland Development Bureau: Portland, Oregon, n.d. but about 1918), 3–6.

6   "Chinookan Culture," *The Virtual Meier Site,* http://web.pdx.edu/~b5cs/virtualmeier/ society.html, accessed June 5, 2013; Francis Seufert, *Wheels of Fortune* (Portland: Oregon Historical Society Press, 1980), 6–7; "Editor's Notes," *The Dalles Times-Mountaineer,* January 10, 1892, 3.

7   *Homestead Proof, Testimony of Claimant.* December 22, 1896, Homestead Entry Application No. 4141. National Archives and Records Administration, hereafter NARA. At the conclusion of the five-year proving period, Holcomb listed the homestead improvements as the house, an eighteen by twenty-foot barn, outhouses, and fencing. Alice Day Pratt, *A Homesteader's Portfolio* (Corvallis: Oregon State University Press, 1993), xxxii.

8   Pratt, *A Homesteader's Portfolio,* xxxvi – xxxviii; Barbara Allen, *Homesteading the High Desert* (Salt Lake City: University of Utah Press, 1987), 79–80; "Trials of Homesteaders," *The Dalles Chronicle,* February 25, 1893, 3; William F. Willingham, "Family and Community on the Eastern Oregon Frontier," *Oregon Historical Quarterly,* 95:2 (Summer, 1994), 191–99. For discussion of the motivations of single women homesteaders, see Sherry L. Smith, "Single Women Homesteaders: The Perplexing Case of Elinore Pruitt Stewart," *Western Historical Quarterly,* 22:2, (May, 1991), 163–82.

9   "Items in Brief," *The Dalles Times–Mountaineer,* September 10, 1892, 1. Equi continued to use the "Aque" spelling of her surname for another nine years before she reverted to the original spelling.

10 Marie Equi to Constance M. Loftus, April 5, 1920. DOJ Papers.

11 The author's appreciation of an "East of the Cascades" character developed from several accounts including Dorothy Lawson McCall, *Ranch Under the Rimrock* (Portland: Binfords & Mort, 1968); Urling C. Coe, MD, *Frontier Doctor: Observations on Central Oregon and the Changing West* (Corvallis: Oregon State University Press, 1996 reprint), and several personal visits.

12 For a discussion of how women homesteaders experienced a new dynamic of sharing economic power and influenced perceptions of women's abilities and financial assertiveness, see Katherine Harris, *Long Vistas: Women and Families on Colorado Homesteads* (Niwot, Colorado: University Press of Colorado, 1993).

13 "The Facts," *The Dalles Times-Mountaineer,* July 24, 1893, 3; "O. D. Taylor Chastised," *The Dalles Weekly Chronicle,* July 28, 1893, 5; Susan A. Hallgarth, "Women Settlers on the Frontier: Unwed, Unreluctant, Unrepentant," *Women's Studies Quarterly,* 17: 3/4, Fall/ Winter, 1989, 25. For the experience of young female teachers in the West, see also Helen Guyton Rees, *Schoolmarms* (Portland: Binford & Mort, 1983).

14 *Catalog of the Wasco Independent Academy, 1890–1891,* held in archives at the Surgeons Quarters, Fort Dalles Museum, The Dalles, Oregon; "Where Is The Blame," *The Dalles Times-Mountaineer,* July 25, 1893, 3.

15 "Grand Dalles, The Magic City," *New York Times,* July 25, 1983, query.nytimes.com, accessed June 15, 2008; "North Dalles Story Detailed in 1904 History Book," The Klickitat Heritage, Klickitat County Historical Society, Goldendale, Washington, Summer, 1976. For further information on O. D. Taylor and his schemes, see the *Wasco County Historical Society Quarterly,* Winter, 2003.

16 "Grand Dalles," *The Dalles Times-Mountaineer,* September 21, 1891, 3.

17 E. Kimbark MacColl with Harry H. Stein, *Merchants, Money, & Power, The Portland Establishment, 1843–1913* (Portland: The Georgian Press, 1988), 306–10; "National Bank Failures," *Oregonian*, July 23, 1893, 1.

18 "The Facts," *The Dalles Times-Mountaineer*, July 22, 1893, 3 and "The Facts," *The Dalles Times-Mountaineer*, July 24, 1893, 3. The most extensive coverage of the horsewhipping and its aftermath was provided by *The Dalles Times-Mountaineer* with several articles, editorial notes, and letters to the editor in the July 21–27, 1893 issues.

19 "O. D. Taylor Chastised," *The Dalles Daily Chronicle*," July 21, 1893, 3.

20 Ibid.

21 Ibid.

22 "O. D. Taylor Horsewhipped," *The Dalles Times-Mountaineer*, July 21, 1893, 1.

23 "The Facts," *The Dalles Times-Mountaineer*, July 24, 1893, 3.

24 "Items in Brief," *The Dales Times-Mountaineer*, July 25, 1893, 3; "A Parson Cowhided," *Oregonian*, July 22, 1893, 6; "Flogged by a Woman," *San Francisco Examiner, July 22, 1893, 8;* "Grand Dalles, The Magic City," *New York Times*, July 25, 1893.

25 "Items in Brief," *The Dalles Times-Mountaineer*, July 21, 1893, 3; "Editorial," *The Dalles Weekly Chronicle*," July 28, 1893.

26 For a full account of the Mitchell case, see F. L. Slim, "Alice Mitchell and the Murder of Freda Ward," in Jonathan Katz, ed., *Gay American History, Lesbians and Gay Men in the U.S.A.* (New York: Avon Books, 1976), 82–90 and Lisa Duggan, *Sapphic Slashers* (Durham, North Carolina: Duke University Press, 2000) 9–11, 114; *Cincinnati Lancet-Clinic*, Vol. 28, No. 5 (January 30, 1892), 154; "Another Medical Man Testifies," *Oregonian*, July 26, 1892, 2.

27 "O. D. Taylor in Portland," *The Dalles Times-Mountaineer*, July 29, 1893, 3; "O. D. Taylor's Arrest," *The Dalles Times-Mountaineer*, August 24, 1895; "Rev. O. D. Taylor's Case," *The Dalles Time-Mountaineer*, December 19, 1896. "Williams, George Henry," Biographical Directory of the United States Congress, bioguide.congress.gov/scripts/biodisplay.pl?index=WOOO498. George H. Williams served as US senator from Oregon (1865–1871), US attorney general (1872–1875), and withdrew his name due to a scandal after President Ulysses S. Grant nominated him as chief justice of the US Supreme Court. Williams later served as mayor of Portland, Oregon, 1902–1905).

28 "Items in Brief," *The Dalles Times-Mountaineer*, July 29, 1893, 3. The Dalles High School today is located on the original site of the Wasco Independent Academy.

29 K. A. Davis, "Dr. Belle Cooper (Rinehart) Ferguson (7.1)," *Lewis and Elizabeth Rinehart and Descendants: A Family History*," n.d., privately published, copy at The Dalles Wasco County Library; Fred Lockley, "Impressions and Observations of the Journal Man," *Oregon Daily Journal*, February 23, 1936, February 26, 1936, March 1, 1936. Report of Agent Keller, Interview with Belle Cooper Rinehart, September 11, 1918, DOJ Papers. The Department of Justice at the time of this interview was seeking incriminating evidence against Equi prior to her espionage trial, and federal agents were notorious for filing inaccurate and biased reports. But an infatuation for Equi at age twenty-one appears plausible, and it seems unlikely that the agent would have fabricated the details of Rinehart's recollections. Marie Equi to Dr. Belle Ferguson (Rinehart), April 6, 1936, OHS ACC 28389–Equi.

30 "A Study of Women Graduates of UO Medical School and Willamette University," The Lucy Davis Phillips Collection, Oregon Health & Science University, Historical Collections & Archives, 2004-030.

31 Fred Lockley, "Impressions and Observations of the *Journal* Man," *Oregon Daily Journal*, March 1, 1936, 8. See also articles in February 23, 26, and March 1, 1936 issues.

32 *The Dalles Times-Mountaineer*, August 1, 1896, 3.

33 Certificate 2652, Application No. 4141, February 11, 1897, NARA. At the time of Holcomb's "proving up" declaration on December 22, 1896, she estimated the value of the property improvements (house, barn, outbuildings, and fencing) at $275.

34 MacColl and Stein, *Merchants, Money, & Power*, 335–337; "News Item," *The Dalles Times-Mountaineer*, March 16, 1897.

CHAPTER 3

1 Frank R. Mills and Ev Mills, *Shasta Route* (North Highlands, California: History West, Pacific Chapter Railway & Locomotive Historical Society, 1981), 7–123 with a photo of Southern Pacific's *Solano*, "one of the largest train ferries in the world," 120, and a photo of Oakland Mole, 123.

2 B. E. Lloyd, *Lights and Shades in San Francisco* (Berkeley: Berkeley Hills Books, 1999), 17–32.

3 Campbell Gibson, *Population of the 100 Largest Cities and other Urban Places in the United States: 1790 to 1990* (Washington, DC: Population Division, US Bureau of the Census, June 1998) www.census.gov/population/www/documentation/twps0027.html, accessed January 10, 2008.

4 Photo, Donohoe Building, Historical Photograph Collection, San Francisco Public Library, AAC-4754; Block 191, Sanborn Map, sfgeneaology.com, accessed July 10, 2008.

5 *Crocker Langley San Francisco Directory, 1898* (San Francisco: H.S. Crocker Co., 1898). "Miss Marie Equi" worked as a cashier at Miss T. Taylor, residence 16 Donohoe. Edan Wilton Hughes, *Artists in California, 1786–1940* (San Francisco: Hughes Publishing Co., 1989), 262; "New Names in Art that Show Promise," *San Francisco Call*, November 26, 1905, 19.

6 Joseph Equi owned lot #531 on the periphery of the Sonoma town square; the lot was later described as being two full blocks on Fifth Street East between Denmark and Prussia Streets. *Sonoma Historical Map and Directory, 1877.* Joseph Equi's produce store and home was located at 1514 Dupont (now Grant Street) between Union and Filbert. *Crocker Langley San Francisco Directory, 1876* (San Francisco: H. S. Crocker Co, 1876); "Flogged By A Woman," *San Francisco Examiner*, July 22, 1893, 8.

7 US Bureau of the Census, *Historical Statistics of the United States, Colonial Times to 1970*, Part I, Series D 11–25, 128; Theodore Caplow, Louis Hicks, and Ben J. Wattenberg, *The First Measured Century: An Illustrated Guide to Trends in America, 1900–2000* (Washington, DC: AEI Press, 2000), 44–45 as quoted in Donald M. Fisk, "American Labor in the 20th Century," Bureau of Labor Statistics, US Department of Labor, http://www.bls.gov/opub/cwc/cm20030124ar02p1.htm#7, accessed June 20, 2013; County Deed Records, Grantee, Mary D. Equi, (indirect); microfilm reel Y-401, 402, Wasco County Courthouse, The Dalles, Oregon.

8 Susan Stryker and Jim Van Buskirk, *Gay by the Bay: A History of Queer Culture in the San Francisco Bay Area* (San Francisco: Chronicle Books, 1996), 8–19.

9 "American Barbarism," *San Francisco Daily Chronicle*, March 30, 1882, www.sfmuseum.org/hist5/wilde.html, accessed June 27, 2013; Roy Morris Jr., "Wilde About California," *Los Angeles Times*, May 5, 2013, http://articles.latimes.com/2013/may/05/opinion/la-oe-morris-oscar-wilde-in-california-20130505, accessed June 27, 2013; Peter Boag, *Same-Sex Affairs, Constructing and Controlling Homosexuality in the Pacific Northwest* (Berkeley: University of California Press, 2003), 125–35.

10 *College of Physicians and Surgeons of San Francisco Medical Department, Sixth Annual Announcement, 1901 and 1902.* College announcements for the years prior to 1901 are unavailable; however, the P&S curriculum was competitive with the other schools in San Francisco. The author appreciates the assistance of Dorothy Dechant, PhD, Museum Curator of the Institute of Dental History and Craniofacial Study at the University of the Pacific School of Dentistry. In 1904 the University of California Medical Department added two years of college preparatory work as an entry requirement, leading to a huge drop in enrollment. Nancy Rockafellar, PhD, "A History of UCSF 1868–1959," http://history.library.ucsf.edu/curriculum_reform.html, accessed June 8, 2008.

11 Paul Starr, *The Social Transformation of American Medicine* (New York: Basic Books, 1982), 79–116.

12 Regina Markell Morantz-Sanchez, *Sympathy & Science: Women Physicians in American Medicine* (New York: Oxford University Press, 1985), 232–65; Mary Roth Walsh, "*Doctors*

Wanted: No Women Need Apply": Sexual Barriers in the Medical Profession, 1835–1975 (New Haven: Yale University Press, 1977), 184–85.

13 Erik K. Curtis, *A Century of Smiles, 1896–1996: One Hundred Years at the College of Physicians and Surgeons* (San Francisco: University of the Pacific School of Dentistry, 1995), 23; D. A. Hodghead, MD, "The College: A Brief History," *CHIPS, Volume V,* San Francisco, College of Physicians and Surgeons, 1904; Mary Equi McCloskey with Sandy Polishuk, Interview, March 12, 1980, OHS ACC 28389–Equi.

14 The college was located on Fourteenth Street between Mission and Valencia Streets. Mary Ellen Parker was the daughter of William and Anne Jane Parker. Mary Ellen had one sibling, her younger brother Patrick, who became a district attorney and superior court judge of Mono County, California. *Sixth Annual Announcement, 1901–1902, Medical Department, College of Physicians and Surgeons of San Francisco,* 10–27.

15 "The Imperial Future of San Francisco," *San Francisco Chronicle,* December 31, 1899, special feature, 1, 3. See also: Gray Brechin, *Imperial San Francisco: Urban Power, Earthly Ruin* (Berkeley: University of California Press, 1999).

16 Howard Zinn, *A People's History of the United States, 1492–Present* (New York: HarperCollins, 2003), 315; "The Imperial Future of San Francisco," *San Francisco Chronicle,* December 31, 1899, special feature, 1, 3.

17 1900 Federal Census. San Francisco, California; Roll: *T623 104*; Page: *9B and 10A*; Enumeration District: *166.*

18 "A History of UCSF," The Regents of the University of California 2013, http://history.library.ucsf.edu/, accessed June 28, 2013.

19 *University of California Directory of Graduates, 1905* (Berkeley: University of California, 1905). The California State Constitution prohibited barring admission to any of the collegiate departments of the State University on account of sex. Rockafellar, "A History of the UCSF School of Medicine"; Helen MacKnight Doyle, *Doctor Nellie: The Autobiography of Dr. Helen MacKnight Doyle* (Genny Smith Books, 1983), 237–40, 254–55.

20 For more on the plague in San Francisco, see Marilyn Chase, *The Barbary Plague: The Black Death in Victorian San Francisco* (New York: Random House, 2003).

21 *Crocker Langley San Francisco Director,* (San Francisco: H.S. Crocker Co., for the years 1900 and 1905). Wagner Leather Co. was located at 306–308 Clay Street.

22 Alice Wexler, *Emma Goldman* (Pantheon Books: New York, 1984), 31–38.

CHAPTER 4

1 E. Kimbark MacColl with Harry Stein, *Merchants, Money, & Power: The Portland Establishment, 1843–1913* (Portland, Oregon: The Georgian Press, 1988), 335–37; Carl Abbott, *Portland in Three Centuries: The Place and the People* (Corvallis: Oregon State University Press, 2011), 31, 50–55, 62–63, 70; "Another Tribute to Portland's Centennial," *Oregonian,* September 10, 1901, 1. Abbott, *Portland: Planning, Politics, and Growth,* 11, 56.

2 Willamette University and the University of Oregon Medical Department, now the Oregon Health & Science University, continue operation today, although the medical departments of the two institutions merged in 1913 under the state university system. For a history of medical education in the state, see Thelma Wilson, "A Century of Medical Education in Oregon," *Northwest Medicine,* 1967, Portland, Oregon. *Sixteenth Annual Announcement of the Medical Department of the University of Oregon, Session 1902–1903* (Portland: Anderson Printing and Duniway Company, 1902). Variations in Equi's surname continued to appear in several public records—e.g., the 1900 Census lists her as Mary "Aqua"—but she reverted to the original "Equi" once she moved west. *Fifteenth Annual Announcement of the Medical Department of the University of Oregon, 1901–1902* (Portland: Anderson Printing and Lithograph Co., 1901).

3 Alexander Flexner, *Medical Education in the United States and Canada: A Report to the Carnegie Foundation for the Advancement of Teaching* (New York: The Carnegie Foundation for the Advancement of Teaching, 1910), 291–92.

4 Mary B. Purvine, *Mary B. Purvine, Pioneer Doctor* (Santa Barbara, California: Johnck and Seeger, 1958); Esther C. P. Lovejoy, "My Medical School, 1890–1894," *Oregon Historical Quarterly* 75:1 (March, 1974) 7–35. Mary Equi McCloskey with Sandy Polishuk, Interview, May 1, 1971, OHS ACC 28389–Equi.

5 Mary Equi McCloskey with Sandy Polishuk, Interview, May 1, 1971, OHS ACC 28389–Equi; photograph of Equi and Parker, Courtesy, The Lilly Library, Indiana University, Bloomington; Indiana. Mary Equi McCloskey to Sandy Polishuk, March 31, 1971, Interview, OHS ACC 28389–Equi; Mrs. Annie Parker to Mary Ellen Parker, letter, March 17, 1903, White Mss., Manuscripts Department, Lilly Library, Indiana University. Equi and Parker rented an apartment near the medical school campus at 703 Northrup Street. *Harriett F. Speckart v. Leopold F. Schmidt, Henrietta Speckart, the Olympia Brewing Company, and the Bellingham Bay Brewing Company*, National Archives and Records Administration, San Bruno, California, Records Group 21, Ninth Circuit Court of Appeals, Case #1908, 1670–72, hereafter, referred to as *Speckart v. Schmidt*.

6 Report of Agent Keller, September 11, 1918, DOJ papers. The sole source of information about Rinehart's intercession with the university dean is a report filed by an agent of the federal Bureau of Investigation. Reports filed by federal agents involved in investigations of political radicals of the time were often inaccurate and biased toward the government's case. It's not surprising that Dr. Rinehart or Dr. Josephi would speak to a federal agent or that Rinehart might recall an incident many years earlier that disturbed her. On March 28, 1903, the university faculty verified that Equi had complied with the rules of the school and recommended that the board of regents grant her a degree of doctor of medicine. "Faculty Minutes," Oregon Health & Science University, Historical Collections & Archives, ACC 1999-Box 1, vol. 1. See footnote 3 and also: Oregon Health Sciences University, *1887–1987: 100 Years: Reflections of Yesterday*, (Portland: Oregon Health Sciences University, 1987).

7 "A Fool? Take That," *Oregonian*, March 14, 1903, 14. Title IX of the Education Amendments of 1972 states: "No person in the United States shall, on the basis of sex, be excluded from participation in, be denied the benefits of, or be subjected to discrimination under any education program or activity receiving federal financial assistance."

8 "Nine New Doctors," *Oregonian*, April 1, 1903, 9; "Good Advice to Young Physicians," *Oregonian*, April 12, 1903, 34. Portland High School was located at Southwest Fourteenth and Morrison Streets until it was renamed Lincoln High School and moved to its current South Parks Blocks location. Today the building is Lincoln Hall, a part of Portland State University.

9 *Statistics of Women at Work, Based on Unpublished Information Derived from the Schedules of the Twelfth Census: 1900.* US Government Printing Office, Washington, DC, 1907, Table XXIII, 34; "Members of the Graduating Class of the Medical Department of the University of Oregon," *Oregonian*, April 2, 1903, 10. Olof Larsell, *The Doctor in Oregon: A Medical History* (Portland: Binfords & Mort, Oregon Historical Society, Oregon, 1947), 491–93; Oregon Board of Medical Examiners, telephone interview, May 27, 2003. Equi's license number was 00717, issued on April 9, 1903. *General Register of the Offices and Alumni of the University of Oregon, 1873–1904,"* University of Oregon, March 1904.

10 Starr, *The Social Transformation*, 123–34.

11 Starr, *The Social Transformation*, on homeopathy, 93–110; *Speckart v. Schmidt*. According to Equi's testimony in the Speckart case, she undertook advanced study in San Francisco from April through September or October of 1903. Information on Dr. Parker's internship in San Francisco has not been located. Edi Mottershead, "Florence Nightingale Ward, MD: Medical Sectarian or Medical Scientist?" Thesis, Mills College, California 2004, 4–15, 37.

12 Starr, *The Social Transformation*, 93–112; Kimberly Jensen, *Oregon's Doctor to the World: Esther Pohl Lovejoy & A Life in Activism* (Seattle: University of Washington Press, 2012), 51–52.

13 Sophie B. Kobicke, a San Francisco native, served as adjunct to the school's chair of gynecology and abdominal surgery. William Harvey King, MD, LLD, *History of Homeopathy and Its*

Institutions in America, (New York: The Lewis Publishing Co., 1905), 238, 396. *Speckart v. Schmidt,* 1667-69.

14 *Polk's Directory for Baker City, LaGrande, and Pendleton,* 1903. For a full description of Pendleton, Oregon, to 1975, see Gordon McNab, *A Century of News and People in the East Oregonian, 1875–1975* (Pendleton: East Oregonian Publishing Co., 1975).

15 Ibid. For additional information on the practice of medicine in Pendleton, see C. J. Rademacher, *History of Medicine in Central Oregon* (Bend, Oregon, publisher unknown, 1971).

16 *Physicians and Surgeons Register Book I,* page 143, Umatilla County Courthouse, Pendleton, Oregon. The author greatly appreciates the assistance of Virginia Roberts of the Umatilla County Historical Society with information about medical practitioners in Pendleton in the early 1900s. *Official Register and Directory of Physicians and Surgeons in the States of California, Oregon, and Washington, 1904.* Medical Society of the State of California, Sixteenth Edition, 1904; "Lady Physician," *East Oregonian,* October 20, 1903, 5; Notice, *East Oregonian,* November 21, 1903, 11.

17 Urling C. Coe, MD. *Frontier Doctor: Observations on Central Oregon and the Changing West* (Corvallis: Oregon State University Press, 1996), 43-59; Fred deWolfe, "Early-Day Woman Doctor Made Mark with 'Radical' Reforms," *Oregon Daily Journal,* November 25, 1971, 4; *Oregon Biographies–Dr. Marie Equi,* Oregon History Project, Oregon Historical Society.

18 Rademacher, *History of Medicine in Central Oregon; Speckart v. Schmidt.* Author's correspondence with Sally Schwartz, archivist, Old Military and Civil Records, National Archives and Records Administration, Washington, DC, July 2, 2004; "Lady Physicians," *East Oregonian,* October 20, 1903, 5. An editorial published July 26, 1893, in *The Dalles Times-Mountaineer* refuted statements made by the *Pendleton Tribune* related to the horsewhipping incident.

19 *Speckart v. Schmidt.*

20 Equi and Parker set up their practices in room 513. Morantz-Sanchez, *Sympathy & Science,* 92, 133. Morantz-Sanchez reflects upon the "wide spectrum of emotional options" that women physicians pursued while developing their practices and that many found "various degrees of emotional commitment" among other women. Equi's and Parker's address was 440 Jefferson which today would be on the 1200 block of Jefferson in downtown Portland. A common practice among renters at the time was to relocate frequently, and Equi and Parker resided at 514 Jefferson (on today's 1500 block of SW Jefferson) in 1905. Equi would live at more than half a dozen additional sites in Portland in the years ahead.

21 Berta Van Hoosen, *Petticoat Surgeon* (Chicago: Pellegrini & Cudahy, 1947) as quoted in Cathy Luchetti, *Medicine Women: The Story of Early-American Women Doctors* (New York: Crown Publishers, 1998), 213–14.

22 Larsell, *The Doctor in Oregon,* 570.

23 "Nervousness in Children," *Oregonian,* February 17, 1905, 14; "Nervousness in Children," *Medical Sentinel,* March 1905, 732.

24 George M. Robins, MD, *History of the Multnomah County Medical Society, 1884–1954* (Portland, Oregon: Multnomah County Medical Society, 1993), p. 18–19. My appreciation to George Painter for providing a copy of this document. Fifty-two women had graduated from the two Oregon medical schools before the society admitted any as members. In 1903 the eleven women elected were Drs. Gertrude French, Kittie P. Gray, Esther Pohl, Ethel Gray, Edna D. Timms, Elsie Patton, Sarah Whiteside, Jessie Mr. McGavin, Eugenia G. Little, Amelia Ziegler, and Sarah Marquam Hill. Mae H. Cardwell, MD, "The Medical Club of Portland—Historical," *Medical Sentinel* 13:7 (July 1905). Other members of the Medical Club included, in 1906, E. E. Van Alstyne, Gertrude French, Ethel Gray, Sarah Marquam Hill, Eugenia Little, Katherine Manion, Jessie McGavin, Elsie Patton, Esther Pohl, Edna D. Timms, and Sarah Whiteside. See Morantz-Sanchez, *Sympathy & Science,* 181–83 for an analysis of the importance of women's medical societies.

25 Abbott, *Portland,* 50–51, 79. Oregon pioneered different approaches to obtain a state version of direct election of US senators, including instructing state legislators to select the electorate's choice to serve in the posts. The Seventeenth Amendment to the US

Constitution authorized the direct election of senators in 1913. Robert D. Johnston describes the roots of the Oregon System from 1884 until the early twentieth century in *The Radical Middle Class: Populist Democracy and the Question of Capitalism in Progressive Era Portland, Oregon* (Princeton: Princeton University Press, 2003), 121–26, 156–59.

26 Johnston, *The Radical Middle Class*, 123–26. Johnston profiles the contributions of William S. U'Ren, "direct democracy's mechanic," 127–37.

27 Jensen, *Oregon's Doctor to the World*, 91–95, 75–97. For more on social feminism and civic housekeeping, see Annette K. Baxter, Preface in *The Clubwoman As Feminist: True Womanhood Redefined, 1868–1914* in Karen J. Blair (New York: Holmes and Meier, 1980), xi–xii; Blair, *Clubwoman*, 118; Sandra Haarsager, *Organized Womanhood: Cultural Politics in the Pacific Northwest, 1840–1920* (Norman: University of Oklahoma Press, 1997), 188–89.

28 Ruth Barnes Moynihan, *Rebel for Rights: Abigail Scott Duniway*, (New Haven: Yale University Press, 1983), 82. Moynihan concluded that "there was at the core of her personality, nourished by the hardships of her childhood and marriage, a profound insecurity." Abigail Scott Duniway, *Path Breaking: An Autobiographical History of the Equal Suffrage Movement in Pacific Coast States* (New York: Schocken Books, 1971), reprinted from James, Kerns & Abbott edition, 1914, photo caption, 268.

29 Moynihan, *Rebel for Rights*, 84–196.

30 Moynihan, *Rebel for Rights*, 1–11, 26–84. Duniway's first novel was later revised with a new title in 1905, *From the West to the West*; Rebecca J. Mead, *How The Vote Was Won: Woman Suffrage in the Western United States, 1868–1914* (New York: New York University Press, 2004), 97–118.

31 Duniway, *Path Breaking*, 40–41, 84–211. Duniway founded the Oregon State Equal Suffrage Association with two other women in November of 1870. Duniway, *Path Breaking*, 40–41, 84–211.

32 G. Thomas Edwards, *Sowing Good Seeds: The Northwest Suffrage Campaigns of Susan B. Anthony* (Portland: Oregon Historical Society, 1990), 164–66, 178–81, 292–96.

33 Robert Rydell, "Visions of Empire: International Expositions in Portland and Seattle, 1905–1909, *Pacific Historical Review*, 52:1 (February, 1983), 37–65.

34 Carl Abbott, *The Great Extravaganza: Portland and the Lewis and Clark Exposition* (Portland: Oregon Historical Society, 1981, revised edition, 1996), 24, 44. The Forestry building measured 105 feet by 209 feet with pillars of natural tree trunks at the entry. Inside, columns of more trees supported the ceiling and balcony and created a massive exhibition space, a cathedral of natural wonders.

35 "Medical Societies—Portland Medical Society," *Medical Sentinel*, January 1905, vol. 13, #1 www.books.google.com, page 674.

36 Deborah M. Olsen, "Fair Connections: Women's Separatism and the Lewis and Clark Exposition of 1905," *Oregon Historical Quarterly*, 109:2, (Summer, 2008), 174–203. Olsen discusses feminists' attempts to present women's concerns at the nation's expositions and their desire to highlight women's contributions to the planning of such major civic occasions. Their attempts represented a move from "female separatism" with its focus on primarily women's affairs. Olsen also argues that in addition to commanding attention for the NAWSA convention, women organizers directed public attention to the unveiling of a statue of Sacajawea, the Shoshone woman who was widely touted as a guide for explorers Lewis and Clark and was presented as an example of women's contributions to society.

37 Ida Husted Harper, ed., *History of Woman Suffrage*, Vol. 5 (New York: National American Woman Suffrage Association, 1922), 117–50; Edwards, *Sowing Good Seeds*, 210–15.

38 "Portland Leads Pure Food Fight," *Oregonian*, Aug. 14, 1905, 7; Mayor Harry Lane to Frances E. Gotshall, Recording Secretary, Oregon Equal Suffrage Association, August 11, 1905. PARC, A2000-003, 0256-01, H-Women Organization 1905; "Mayor Lane Has Others On List," *Oregonian*, August 12, 1905, 8; "Mayor Deposes Board of Health," *Oregonian*, August 8, 1905, 1; "Lane Calls Health Board Careless," *Oregonian*, August 10, 1905, 16.

39 Minnie (Montieth) Van Dran's family founded Albany, Oregon, in 1847. "Mrs. Van Dran Died of Poison," *Oregonian*, August 14, 1905, 1, 14; "Marshall Makes Full Confession," *Oregonian*, August 24, 1905, 16. Also, May 8 and 11, 2008, correspondence with Ellen West Lilja, playwright, of "Don't Drink the Ginger Ale!" a production based on the Van Dran poisoning.

CHAPTER 5

Material in this chapter was previously presented in different forms: in the lectures "KAJ Mackenzie, Marie Equi, and the Oregon Doctor Train: Portland's response to the 1906 San Francisco Earthquake," delivered on May 12, 2006, at the Oregon Health & Science University, and "Lesbian to the Rescue," delivered on April 11, 2006, at the Eureka Valley/ Harvey Milk Memorial branch of the San Francisco Public Library; and in "Portland to the Rescue: The Rose City's Response to the 1906 San Francisco Earthquake and Fire," in *Oregon Historical Quarterly* 108, no. 3 (Fall 2007): 384–409. Reprinted by permission of the publisher.

1   *Speckart v. Schmidt*. The Hill was located at Lucretia Place, Washington Street. The five-story building remains at the site today at 2235 SW Burnside.

2   *Speckart v. Schmidt*, 1671.

3   Adolph Speckart was Henrietta Speckart's second husband. Her first, Laurenz Heinrich Ludwig Disch, died shortly after the birth of their daughter, Emmy Disch, in 1866. The author thanks Karen Able for her generosity in sharing Speckart family history and collaborating on research into the Speckart family legal cases.

4   *Speckart v. Schmidt*, 8–9.

5   Ibid. 1673–4, 12. "Suffrage Delegates," *Sunday Oregonian*, January 28, 1906, 14. Equi was elected to represent Oregon at the Baltimore convention; another account stated that she was elected as an alternate delegate. Deed Records, Grantee (indirect), Mary D. Equi, microfilm rolls 401–402 and Grantor (direct) Mary D. Equi to Bessie B. Cook, microfilm roll 38–278, County Clerk Office, Wasco County Courthouse, The Dalles, Oregon. Holcomb granted Equi one-half interest in the Oregon homestead property on March 29, 1898, for one dollar; Equi returned her one-half share to Holcomb on September 23, 1904, for ten dollars; both transactions occurred in San Francisco. Wasco County Deed Records, Alex Cook et al. to Ross and Alice Ornduff, microfilm roll 102–435. Bessie's children sold the property October 15, 1945, for $500. *Speckart v. Schmidt*, 1674, 12.

6   Susan B. Anthony to Mrs. Barnes, January 31, 1906, NAWSA Suffrage Scrapbook, 1897–1911; Edwards, *Sowing Good Seeds*, 259–60; "Miss Susan B. Anthony Died This Morning," *New York Times*, March 13, 1906, 1.

7   Jensen, *Oregon's Doctor to the World*, 100–04; "Suffrage Parlor Meeting," *Oregonian*, April 18, 1906, 5; Edwards, *Sowing Good Seeds*, 294–95.

8   "Lynching Mob Scored by Folk," *Oregonian*, April 18, 1906, 1; "Help for the Sufferers," *Oregonian*, April 18, 1906, 2; "On Wire at Time of Quake," *Oregonian*, April 19, 1906, 18.

9   "Portlanders in San Francisco," *Oregonian*, April 19, 1906, 12.

10 Gladys Hansen and Emmet Condon, *Denial of Disaster: The Untold Story and Photographs of the San Francisco Earthquake and Fire of 1906* (San Francisco: Cameron, 1989), 47.

11 For Portland's relief efforts, see Michael Helquist, "Portland to the Rescue, The Rose City's Response to the 1906 San Francisco Earthquake and Fire," *Oregon Historical Quarterly*, 108:3 (Fall, 2007). For women's civic activism, see Sandra Haarsager, *Organized Womanhood: Cultural Politics in the Pacific Northwest, 1840-1920* (Norman: University of Oklahoma Press, 1997), 188–89; Portland Woman's Club, Records, 1895, MSS 1084, Oregon Historical Society Research Library, Portland.

12 "Corps of Nurses and Doctors," *Oregon Daily Journal*, April 19, 1906, 6.

13 "To Avert Pestilence," *Oregonian*, June 18, 1903, 5. Mackenzie also directed a medical mission to a small town in Eastern Oregon devastated by a flash flood. "Corps of Nurses and Doctors," *Oregon Daily Journal*, April 19, 1906, 6; "Forty on Errand of Mercy," *Oregon Daily Journal*, April 20, 1906, 12.

14 "Flashlight Photograph of Portland Nurses Taken Before They Left On Last Night's Train,"
    Oregonian, April 20, 1906, 1; "Relief Train Is on the Way," *Oregonian,* April 20, 1906, 12;
    "Hospital Relief Train Dispatched," *Portland Evening Telegram,* April 20, 1906, 17.

15 "Will Need Aid for Months Yet," *Oregonian,* May 9, 1906, 10. A combined issue of the three
    San Francisco dailies, with its first page reprinted in the *Oregonian,* reported on April 19 that
    martial law was declared.

16 The Oakland Mole was also known as the Oakland Long Wharf. For maps and photos, see
    http://cprr.org/Museum/Maps/Long_Wharf_Oakland.html.

17 "Dr. Mackenzie on Relief Work," *Portland Evening Telegram,* May 8, 1906, 2. The Harbor
    View district is now known as the Marina District. Arno Dosch, "City's Health Is Good,"
    Oregonian, April 26, 1906, 1. Oregon National Guard physicians also traveled on the doctor
    train; they were ordered to convert a local school, Wilmerding School of Mechanical Arts
    at Sixteenth and Utah Streets, as an emergency hospital. "Oregon Hospital Corps finishes
    relief work in Bay City," *Oregon Daily Journal,* May 10, 1906, 4.

18 Helquist, "Portland to the Rescue," 394; Henry H. Rutherford, "Experiences of an Army
    Medical Officer During the San Francisco Earthquake," *Military Surgeon* 79 (1936): 208–10;
    Gaines M. Foster, "The Demands of Humanity: Army Medical Disaster Relief," Center of
    Military History, US Army, Washington, DC, 1983, 62. The US Army General Hospital
    was later designated *Letterman General Hospital,* and in World War II it became the largest
    army hospital in the US. The hospital closed in 1992, and today several of the buildings,
    including Building No. 1016 where Equi worked, have been converted for use by nonprofit
    organizations.

19 "Twenty-three Babies Born in Oregon Ward," *Oregon Daily Journal,* May 4, 1906, 1; "Dr.
    Marie Equi Praises the Work of Portland Nurses in San Francisco," *Portland Evening
    Telegram,* May 9, 1906, 10.

20 "Dr. Marie D. Equi Seizes a Motor Car," *Oregon Daily Journal,* May 1, 1906, 8.

21 "Doctors and Nurses Help," *Sunday Oregonian,* April 29, 1906, 1. For more on Laughlin's
    relationship with Sperry, see "Dr. Mary A. Sperry Leaves Estate to Woman Companion,"
    San Francisco Chronicle, May 22, 1919, 10; "Mother Fights Mary Sperry's Will in Courts,"
    San Francisco Chronicle, May 8, 1920, 1. For more on Laughlin, see Ruth Sargent, *Gail
    Laughlin, ERA's Advocate* (Portland, Maine: House of Falmouth Publishers, 1979).

22 "Insult Makes Doctors Angry," *Portland Evening Telegram,* May 7, 1906, 1; "Oregon Doctors
    Offered Insult," *Oregonian,* May 7, 1906, 1; "Dr. Mackenzie on Relief Work," *Portland Evening
    Telegram,* May 8, 1906, 2.

23 "Insult Makes Doctors Angry," *Portland Evening Telegram,* May 7, 1906, 1; "Resolution Was
    Born In Frenzy," *Portland Evening Telegram,* May 10, 1906, 7.

24 George C. Pardee, Governor of California, to George E. Chamberlain, Governor of Oregon,
    April 19, 1906, George Pardee Papers; Online Archive of California, Bancroft Library,
    BANC MSS C-B 400; "Doctors and Nurses Not Needed," *San Francisco Call,* May 5, 1906, 1.

25 "Express Deep Gratitude of California for Aid of Oregon," *Oregonian,* May 12, 1906, 4;
    "Words of Praise for Oregonians," *Oregonian,* May 13, 1906, 24; "Disease Appears in City,"
    Oregonian, May 6, 1906, 4; "Work of Oregon Nurses Good," *Sunday Oregon Journal,* May
    6, 1906; "Splendid Work of Organizers," *San Francisco Chronicle,* May 4, 1906, 11; "Start
    for Home on Saturday," *Oregon Daily Journal,* May 4, 1906, 9. My appreciation to Heather
    Lukes for confirming that a medal awarded for Equi's relief services had been among her
    possessions.

26 Several of the "Oregon Doctor Train" physicians developed successful careers. Mackenzie
    became dean of the University of Oregon Medical School (UOMS) in 1912. Ralph C.
    Matson became one of the nation's most prominent specialists in tuberculosis. Joseph
    McCusker became assistant professor of obstetrics at UOMS, served as Portland health
    officer in 1914, and as president of the Oregon State Medical Society in 1921. M. B.
    Marcellus taught anatomy at UOMS and helped secure municipal legislation in 1915
    to authorize school health inspection. Joseph Bilderback was Portland's first practicing

private pediatrician. He helped found Doernbecher Memorial Hospital (now Doernbecher Children's Hospital) in Portland and became dean of the UOMS Pediatrics Department.

27 Edi Mottershead, *Florence Nightingale Ward, M.D., Medical Sectarian or Medical Scientist*, dissertation, Mills College, CA, May 9, 2004. Cook's business was located on Clay Street in the city's old produce district, now the site of the Embarcadero Center.

28 "Food Needed by 400,000 People," *Oregonian*, April 20, 1906, 1; "Popular Fund for Stricken," *Oregonian*, April 20, 1906, 12; "More than $100,000 in Cash Already Raised in Portland," *Oregon Daily Journal*, April 20, 1906, 1; "Willing Hands are at Work," *Oregonian*, April 22, 1906, 14; Helquist, "Portland to the Rescue," 389–91, 395-98, 401. "Food and Rooms for Refugees," *Oregonian*, April 23, 1906, 16; "Portland Nobly Answers Call from Stricken San Francisco," *Oregon Daily Journal*, April 20, 1906, 1. Portland's total contribution to the San Francisco sufferers, $250,000, is today equivalent to more than $5 million.

29 "Dr. Marie D. Equi Praises the Work of Portland Nurses in San Francisco," *Portland Evening Telegram*, May 9, 1906, 10; "Woman Doctor Goes to Aid of Suffering," *Oregon Daily Journal*, April 28, 1906, 2.

CHAPTER 6

1 Equi testified in a court hearing that she never saw Speckart as a patient and only diagnosed anemia during her visit in San Diego. *Speckart v. Schmidt.*

2 "Quarrel Among Speckart Heirs," *Sunday Oregonian*, May 27, 1906, 1.

3 See Gloria E. Myers, *A Municipal Mother:Portland's Lola Baldwin, America's First Policewoman* (Corvallis: Oregon State University Press, 1995) for a discussion of measures taken to protect young women in Portland during the Progressive Era.

4 Everett D. Graff, *Resolutions and Memorials of the Territory of Montana, Passed by the First Legislative Assembly*, Newberry Library. books.google.com accessed October 20, 2013. The age of majority for males was set at twenty-one years at the time of this act, 1864. "Quarrel Among Speckart Heirs," *Sunday Oregonian*, May 27, 1906, 1.

5 Schmidt also owned the Centennial Brewing Company of Butte, Montana, and the Salem Brewing Company of Salem, Oregon.

6 "Quarrel Among Speckart Heirs," *Sunday Oregonian*, May 27, 1906, 1.

7 Ibid.

8 "Family Troubles Aired in Portland," *Seattle Post-Intelligencer*, May 27, 1906, 1; "Girl Wished to Give $1200 To Dr. Equi," *Daily Olympian*, May 29, 1906, 1; "Heiress Victim of Hypnotist," *San Francisco Call*, May 28, 1906, 1.

9 "Olympia Girl Tells Strange Tale of Intrigue and Conspiracy," *Oregon Daily Journal*, May 28, 1906, 1; "Dr. Marie Equi Denies Charges, Her Relation with Miss Speckart Only that of Friend," *Portland Evening Telegram*, May 28, 1906, 1.

10 Ibid. "Dr. Marie Equi Denies Charges," *Portland Evening Telegram*, May 28, 1906, 1.

11 Ibid.

12 Ibid.

13 "Heiress Victim of Hypnotist," *San Francisco Call*, May 28, 1906, 1.

14 Agent A. R. Dutton, Seattle, to Headquarters, Bureau of Investigation, Washington, DC, September 17, 1918, DOJ Papers.

15 Lillian Faderman, *To Believe in Women: What Lesbians Have Done for America—A History* (Houghton Mifflin Co.: Boston, 1999), 15–39. Faderman also profiles Reverend Anna Howard Shaw (40-60) and Carrie Chapman Catt (61–78). Faderman describes how Shaw hid from the public her preferred choice "to play masculine" and instead adopted "feminine charm" for the good of the cause.

16 Faderman, *To Believe in Women*, 30–39, 40-60, 61–78.

17 Abigail Scott Duniway, *Path Breaking: An Autobiographical History of the Equal Suffrage Movement in Pacific Coast States* (New York: Schocken Books, 1971), 156-58.

18 "Will Fight Equal Suffrage," *Oregonian,* January 23, 1906, 10. The two most prominent groups were the Anti-Suffrage League and the Oregon State Association Opposed to the Extension of Suffrage to Women. Manuela Thurmer, "'Better Citizens Without the Ballot': American Anti-suffrage Women and Their Rationale During the Progressive Era," in Marjorie Spruill Wheeler, ed., *One Woman, One Vote: Rediscovering the Woman Suffrage Movement* (Troutdale, Oregon: NewSage Press, 1995), 203–20. For a discussion of class issues in suffrage campaigns, see Ellen Carol Dubois, "Working Women, Class Relations, and Suffrage Militance: Harriet Stanton Blatch and the New York Woman Suffrage Movement, 1894–1909," *The Journal of American History,* 74:1, June 1987, 34–58.

19 Edwards, *Sowing Good Seeds,* 271–72; Rebecca Mead, *How the Vote Was Won: Woman Suffrage in the Western United States, 1868–1914* (New York: New York University Press, 2004), 142–43.

20 Mead, *How the Vote Was Won,* 103–04; G. Edwards, *Sowing Good Seeds,* 265–69; Paul E. Fuller, *Laura Clay and the Woman's Rights Movement* (Lexington: University of Kentucky Press, 1975), 97–104; Sara Hunter Graham, *Woman Suffrage and the New Democracy* (New Haven: Yale University Press, 1996), 67–68. Robert D. Johnston, *The Radical Middle Class, Populist Democracy and the Question of Capitalism in Progressive Era Portland, Oregon* (Princeton: Princeton University Press, 2003), 147–52. Johnston argues that Portland's *direct democrats* failed to develop an effective collaboration with suffragists through the 1906 and into the 1912 suffrage campaigns.

21 Harriet F. Speckart to Aunt Katie, February 26, 1906, *Speckart v. Schmidt.*

22 Edwards, *Sowing Good Seeds,* 285–87.

23 Johnston, *The Radical Middle Class,* 147–52; Jensen, "Neither Head nor Tail to the Campaign," 350–83; Beverly Beeton, "How the West Was Won for Woman Suffrage," in Marjorie Spruill Wheeler, ed., *One Woman, One Vote,* 99–115; 289–303.

24 Aque, Sarah A. (Mullins), Massachusetts Death Index, v. 72, 481, no. 227; "Died," *Morning Mercury,* February 14, 1907, 8.

25 Ibid.

26 Paul A. Cyr, "The Rise of Textiles" in *Portraits of a Port: New Bedford, New Bedford Standard Times* and the New Bedford Whaling Museum, 2002, 1, 11.

27 *Death Certificate, Aque, Sarah A. Mullins,* Massachusetts Archives; Aque, Sarah A. (Mullins), Massachusetts Death Index, v. 72, p.481, no. 227; Obituary, *Republican Standard,* New Bedford, Massachusetts, February 21, 1907, 12. Catherine Mullen, Marie Equi's maternal grandmother, was also buried in this cemetery; she died January 11, 1891, at age 85.

28 "Portland's Rose Parade a Triumph," *Oregonian,* June 22, 1907, 1; "Successful Rose Fiesta Week Ends," *Sunday Oregonian* June 23, 1907, 8. Fifty dollars in 1907 is equivalent to more than $1,200 today.

CHAPTER 7

Material in this chapter was previously published in a different form by Michael Helquist in, "'Criminal Operations,' The First Fifty Years of Abortion Trials in Portland, Oregon," *Oregon Historical Quarterly,* 116:1 (Spring 2015): 6–39. Reprinted by permission of the author and publisher.

1 Equi started her practice in Portland in 1905. In a 1915 libel suit against Emma Carroll, Equi claimed that Carroll had maligned her with rumors of her conducting an illegal business. This is the first-known reference to Equi's abortion practice. *Marie Equi v. Emma B. Carroll,* Oregon State Circuit Court case #63125. See Chapter 10, 211–14.

2 James C. Mohr, *Abortion in America: The Origins and Evolution of National Policy, 1800–1900* (New York: Oxford University Press, 1978), 147; Linda Gordon, *The Moral Property of Women: A History of Birth Control Politics in America* (Urbana: University of Illinois Press, 2007), 24–34; Leslie J. Reagan, *When Abortion Was A Crime: Women, Medicine, and Law in the United States, 1867–1973* (Berkeley: University of California Press, 1997),8–18, 80–112.

3   Mohr, *Abortion in America*, vii, 229–30; Gordon, *The Moral Property of Women*, 24–34;
    Reagan, *When Abortion Was a Crime*, 8–18, 80–112.
4   Janet Farrell Brodie, *Contraception and Abortion in Nineteenth-Century America* (Ithaca:
    Cornell University Press, 1994), 253-58; Mohr, *Abortion in* America, 3; *The Moral Property*,
    26; Reagan, *When Abortion Was A Crime*, 8–11, 83–85, 109–110.
5   *Journal of Proceedings of the House of the Legislative Assembly, 1864* (Portland, 1864) and
    Journal of Proceedings of the Senate of the Legislative Assembly of Oregon, 1864 (Portland, 1864).
    The new law read:
    "If any person shall administer to any woman pregnant with a child any medicine, drug
    or substance whatever, or shall use or employ any instrument or other means, with intent
    thereby to destroy such a child, unless the same shall be necessary to preserve the life of
    such mother, such person shall, in the case of the death of such child or mother be thereby
    produced, be deemed guilty of manslaughter."
6   Reagan, *When Abortion Was A Crime*, 61–70, 3, 40–70. Reagan indicates that turn-of-the-
    century physicians mostly debated when a woman's physical condition required an abortion,
    such as excessive vomiting or when the mother had tuberculosis. Willing doctors could use
    these concerns to justify abortions to women who they understood wanted to end their
    pregnancies.
7   Oregon Statutes, chapter 3, section 13 (1854); *Journal of the Council of the Legislative
    Assembly of the Territory of Oregon . . . Begun and Held at Salem, Fifth of December, 1853* (Salem,
    1854), as cited in Mohr, *Abortion in America*, 138, and footnote 4, 293, 119–46, 200–26.
8   Barnett, *They Weep*, 30–31. Alys Bixby Griff kept offices in the Lafayette Building in down-
    town Portland. Myers, *Municipal Mother*, 75–90, fn. 23, 199. Police officer Lola Baldwin
    listed the following abortionists who practiced in Portland: Courtney, Von Falkenstein,
    Atwood, McCormick, Pierce, Walker, Armstrong, Candiani, McKay, Watts, Mallory, King,
    and Ausplund; Reagan, *When Abortion Was A Crime*, 46–61. C.N. Sutter, MD, "A Plea for the
    Protection of the Unborn," *Northwest Medicine*, July 1908, 305–10.
9   Reagan, *When Abortion Was A Crime*, 9–10, 26; Myers, *Municipal Mother*, 83. "Disgrace
    Drives Girl to Poison," *Oregonian*, April 6, 1908, 5. One suicide case linked to an unwanted
    pregnancy was reported in April 1908 and involved a twenty-one-year-old single woman
    in Portland who killed herself with rat poison when her friends learned of her unwanted
    pregnancy.
10 "True Bill Found," *Oregonian*, November 7, 1873, 3; "Set for Thursday," *Oregonian*,
    November 11, 1873, 3.
11 Advertisement, "The Eclectic Dispensary," *Oregonian*, October 25, 1873, 4.
12 "Tried for Manslaughter," *Oregonian*, November 14, 1873, 3; "Found Guilty," *Oregonian*,
    November 17, 1873, 4.
13 Michael Helquist, "'Criminal Operations,' The First Fifty Years of Abortion Trials in
    Portland, Oregon," *Oregon Historical Quarterly* 116:1 (Spring 2015): 14–17 for table of
    abortion trials, 6–39 for the overall difficulties with abortion prosecutions. In the 1889
    case, Hattie Reed survived the abortion. A jury first found the practitioner, Dr. William E.
    Morand, guilty, but, when the judge allowed a second trial, Reed withdrew her charges.
14 "Dr. Atwood Is Arrested," *Oregonian*, April 8, 1907, 14. "Accused of Criminal Operation,"
    Oregonian, February 24, 1906, 11; "Dr. Semler Goes Free," *Oregonian*, March 15, 1906, 11.
    The Atwood case was not the first abortion trial in Portland in the twentieth century, but
    it was the first that led to a community-wide campaign against the practice. In February
    1906 Dr. Paul J. A. Semler was tried on abortion charges involving a fifteen-year-old girl in
    Portland. He was acquitted when the woman involved changed her account of what had
    occurred.
15 Federal Census, Year: 1900, Census Place: Eugene, Lane, Oregon; Roll: T623_1349;
    Page: 15A, Enumeration District: 34; "Will Drive Out Criminal Doctors," *Portland Evening
    Telegram*, May 16, 1907, 12. "Dr. Atwood Is Arrested," *Oregonian*, April 8, 1907, 14. Myers, *A
    Municipal Mother*, 8–24.

16 "Dr. Atwood Is On Trial," *Oregonian*, May 15, 1907, 2; "Slow Progress Is Made," *Oregonian*, May 18, 1907, 11; "Jury Cannot Agree," *Oregonian*, May 19, 1907, 11. The District Attorney explained that W. B. Holdiman had pleaded guilty to a statutory crime against Hattie Fee, but he was not immediately sentenced, pending his possible testimony in court against Dr. Atwood. "Jury Cannot Agree," *Oregonian*, May 19, 1907, 11; "New Trial for Atwood," *Oregonian*, May 21, 1907, 10. "Case Against Atwood Dismissed," *Oregonian*, June 11, 1907, 9.

17 "Will Drive Out Criminal Doctors," *Portland Evening Telegram*, May 16, 1907, 12; "The Oregon Situation," *Northwest Medicine*, January 1906, 30–31 and "Dr. McCormack and the Profession of Oregon," June, 1906; "Misleading, Mischievous, False Say Doctors in Reply," *Oregon Daily Journal*, March 7, 1906, 14. Rickie Solinger in *Pregnancy and Power, A Short History of Reproductive Politics in America* (New York: New York University Press, 2005), 79–83, notes that the right to privacy in medical matters was closely linked to economic status with the middle class obtaining services "free from state or community interference."

18 Rickie Solinger, *The Abortionist*, page x. Solinger observed that "when an activity is simultaneously illegal, culturally taboo, and perceived as one of life's necessities for women, the opportunities abound for exploiting women while enhancing the power of men."

19 Kimberly Jensen, *Oregon's Doctor to the World:Esther Pohl Lovejoy and a Life in Activism* (Seattle: University of Washington Press, 2012), 75–91. "Death Certificate Conceals Crime," *Sunday Oregonian*, February 2, 1908, 10. The X-Radium Institute was located at Third and Alder Streets. "Turning Light on Rowland Scandal," *Oregonian*, February 4, 1908, 11; "Death Certificate Conceals Crime," *Oregonian*, February 2, 1908, 10; "Coroner Finley Explains," *Sunday Oregonian*, February 9, 1908, Sec. 3, 10.

20 "Constable Closes Institute," *Oregonian*, February 6, 1908, 7; "Death Certificate Conceals Crime," Oregonian, February 2, 1908, 10; "Heymans Is Still In Hiding," *Oregonian*, February 6, 1908, 7.

21 "Crusade Is Opened," *Oregonian*, February 17, 1908, 5.

22 "Criminal Doctors to be Prosecuted," *Sunday Oregonian*, February 23, 1908, 12.

23 Reagan, *When Abortion Was A Crime*, 21–22, 67–68. Reagan argues that when the *private sphere* of abortion discussions went public, coupled with women's ongoing demands, the legal and political climate for abortion changed.

24 Helquist, "Criminal Operations," 6–39; the twenty-seven abortion trials, 14–17, the estimated number of abortions, 12. Barnett, *They Weep on My Doorstep* (Beaverton, Oregon: Halo Publishers, 1969), 8–15, 20–29, 36. Barnett named five full-time abortion providers: Drs. Albert Littlefield, George Watts, Edward Stewart, Maude K. Van Alstyne, and Alys Bixby Griff. The estimate of the number of annual abortions is based on an extrapolation of Barnett's observations, suggesting that one provider might perform four to five abortions each workday for a total of 1,000 to 1,250 each year. The work of five providers could total 5,000 to 6,250 abortions annually. Other physicians and the city's many unlicensed practitioners may have performed another 1,000 abortions, boosting the annual total to 6,000 or more. Joffe, "Portraits of Three 'Physicians of Conscience,'" 46–67.

25 Helquist, "Criminal Operations," 6–39. Historian Sandy Polishuk researched Multnomah County court records and found no account of Equi's involvement in an abortion trial in Portland. Equi practiced medicine from 1903 until 1930 when she retired due to health problems. For a discussion of Equi's birth control advocacy, see Chapter 11.

26 Myers, *A Municipal Mother*, 83; fn. 23, 199. Baldwin tracked fourteen men known for their abortion practices; six of them had faced prosecution. Barnett, *They Weep on My Doorstep* 11–25. Five physicians were identified by Ruth Barnett, a naturopath who learned the abortion trade from one of them. *Fifteenth Annual Announcement of the Medical Department of the University of Oregon, 1901–1902* (Portland, Oregon: Anderson Printing & Litho Co., 1901), 27; *Sixteenth Annual Announcement of the Medical Department of the University of Oregon, 1902–1903*, 29.

27 Barnett, *They Weep*, 11–25. Solinger, *The Abortionist*, 7.

28 Jessie Laird Brodie, MD, interview with Susan Dobrof (date uncertain, 1981–1982), Oregon Historical Society Research Library, Accession 28389, "Materials relating to

research on Dr. Marie Equi" (hereinafter OHS ACC 28389–Equi); Mary Equi McCloskey with Sandy Polishuk, Interview, March 20, 1980, OHS ACC 28389–Equi.

29 Lew Levy with Sandy Polishuk, Interview, April 5, 1976, OHS ACC 28389–Equi. Levy was an Oregon member of the Industrial Workers of the World.

30 Sandy Polishuk, *Sticking to the Union: An Oral History of the Life and Times of Julia Ruuttila* (New York: Palgrave MacMillan, 2003), 92–93. Julia Ruuttila with Sandy Polishuk and Nancy Krieger, Interview, Portland, Oregon, June 6, 1981, OHS ACC 28389–Equi. Ruuttila also revealed that she once sought an abortion from Equi but that by then she had closed her practice. Equi instead referred Ruuttila to a trusted colleague.

31 Margaret D. with Sandy Polishuk and Susan Dobrof, Interview, February 2, 1982, OHS ACC 28389–Equi. "Margaret D." requested that her identity not be disclosed.

32 Jessie Laird Brodie, MD, nterview with Susan Dobrof (date uncertain, 1981–1982), OHS ACC 28389-Equi. In the early 1900s in Portland, women physicians had few, if any, privileges at the city's hospitals, and Equi would be unlikely to accept requests for late-term abortions given the greater complexity and risks from the procedure. She probably performed abortions only at her office. Sadie Ann Adams, "We Were Privileged in Oregon"" Jessie Laird Brodie and Reproductive Politics, Locally and Transnationally, 1915–1975," Masters Thesis, Portland State University, 2012, 7.

33 Carol Joffe, *Doctors of Conscience: The Struggle to Provide Abortion Before and After Roe v. Wade* (Boston: Beacon Press, 1995), Preface vii–xiii. Joffe describes "physicians of conscience" as those who were medically competent and active in mainstream medicine, who provided abortion services for their patients' benefit rather than from a desire for remuneration, and those who did not exploit their patients.

34 Salvarsan remained the most effective syphilis treatment until the 1940s when penicillin replaced it as the medication of choice. Starr, *Social Transformation of American Medicine*, 134–135; *History of the Multnomah County Medical Society, 1884–1954, 1993, 28*; Ray Matson, MD, "The Principles of ChemoTherapy, and the Relation of the Wasserman Reaction to Syphilis," *Northwest Medicine*, Vol. 3, No. 4, April 1911, 101–03; Portland City and County Medical Society, meeting of January 13, 1911. Report in *Northwest Medicine*, Vol. 3, No. 3, March 1911, 86.

35 "Baby Home Draws Physicians' Fire," *Oregonian*, March 16, 1911, 4.

36 "Home Is Criticized," *Oregonian*, March 20, 1911, 9. Drs. Florence S. Manion, E.J. Labbe, and George R. Storey also filed statements of concern about the Baby Home with the newspaper after Equi's charges were publicized. "Baby Home Criticized," *Oregonian*, September 8, 1910, 4; "Baby Home Exonerated," *Oregonian*, March 18, 1911, 14.

37 "Police Are Castigated," *Oregonian*, September 3, 1912, 9; "Not Portland Police," *Oregonian*, September 4, 1912, 10; Peter Boag, *Re-Dressing America's Frontier Past* (Berkeley: University of California Press, 2011), 23–31.

38 "Woman Known to Friends as Man," *Oregonian*, December 12, 1906, 1; Peter Boag, "Go West Young Man, Go East Young Woman: Searching for the Trans in Western Gender History," *Western Historical Quarterly*, 36:4, (winter, 2005), 479–80, 485–87; "Nan Pickerell Wants a Job as a Longshoreman," *Portland News*, June 12, 1912.

CHAPTER 8

1 Harriet Speckart testimony, *Speckart v. Schmidt*, 1685. The Elton Court was located at 415 Yamhill in 1906; today that location is at the corner of Eleventh and Yamhill, across the street from the Multnomah County Central Library.

2 "Inland Folk Hear Call of Ocean," *Oregonian*, July 4, 1909, 4; "Brilliant Close to Horse Show," *Oregonian*, October 18, 1908, 3.

3 Defendant's Exhibit No. 187—Letter, Dated February 26, 1906— "Hattie" to "Aunt Katie," *Speckart v. Schmidt*, 25; Margaret Sanger to Marie Equi, 1916, MSP-SS as quoted in Sanger, *The Selected Papers of Margaret Sanger, Volume 1,185*. Margaret Sanger, Gail Laughlin, Charlotte Anita Whitney, and others were either known to have intimate relations with

women or respected those who did. Lillian Faderman, *Odd Girls and Twilight Lovers* (New York: Columbia University Press, 1991), 303–08.

4   Advertisement for Medical Building in Portland, *Sunday Oregonian*, May 13, 1908, 9. Equi's office was in suites 324 and 325. The other women doctors with offices in the same building were Gertrude French, Edna Timms, and Amelia Ziegler. "Medical Building, Alphabetical Directory," *Oregonian*, May 6, 1908, 13. The building was later known as the Park Building.

5   Mary Roth Walsh, *Doctors Wanted: No Women Need Apply: Sexual Barriers in the Medical Profession, 1835–1975* (New Haven: Yale University Press, 1977), 185–86. Walsh notes that 1900 saw 7,387 women in medical practice or 5.6 percent of the total with a jump to the peak in 1910 of 9,015 or 6 percent. By 1920 the numbers dropped and represented 5 percent of all doctors.

6   Mary Ellen Parker's mother was also in poor health and that may have prompted her return to Bridgeport. 1920 US Federal Census, Bridgeport, Mono, California; Roll T625_121, Page 1B, Enumeration District 60, Image 1094. C. Crawford to author, November 28, 2005, Physician Record Search for Parker (White), Mary Ellen, National Geneological Society. Although Parker retained her Oregon State Medical Association membership for a few years, there is no record of her obtaining a medical license in California. Jeffrey Marks, *Anthony Boucheron: A Biobibliography* (Jefferson, North Carolina: McFarland, 2008), 9–15.

7   Discrepancies exist about when Equi and Speckart relocated to the Nortonia Hotel. "Nortonia Hotel Opening," *Sunday Oregonian*, March 15, 1908, Sec. 3, p. 7. The building today is the Mark Spencer Hotel. Harriet Speckart to Miss Louise H. Maitland, (postcard), April 16, 1909. The author thanks Karen Able for sharing this item.

8   "Mr. Dolph Gets Verdict," *Oregonian*, June 30, 1918, 6. The second attorney hired by Harriet Speckart later testified that he had secured from her mother and uncle a settlement in the inheritance case, one that would have equaled $100,000 in cash and stocks. Speckart refused the deal and fired the attorney.

9   *State Ex Rel. Speckart v. Superior Court*, Case #7048, Decided Dec. 20, 1907, 141; *Washington Reports*, Vol. 48, *Cases Determined in the Supreme Court of Washington, Dec. 8, 1907–March 17, 1908*, Bancroft-Whitney Co., Seattle, 1908. Leopold Schmidt had claimed the Speckart estate was subject to community property law in Montana, which would grant half the estate to Mrs. Speckart with the remainder split three ways among her, her daughter, and her son. But Montana did not have a community property law, and the Washington State Supreme Court set aside Schmidt's claim.

10 *State Ex Rel. Speckart v. Superior Court*, Case #7048. The Supreme Court ordered that Harriet Speckart was entitled to receive $96.75 in court costs; but Leopold Schmidt, her uncle, tried to avoid paying the court fees and was nearly successful until her attorneys discovered the ploy and challenged it.

11 *Speckart v. Schmidt*, Case No. 1358, US Circuit Court, Western District of Washington, Western Division, January 29, 1910. On September 28, 1907 Speckart first filed in the US circuit court in Washington State and demanded an accounting of the estate and payment of her share. That case, #1316, was dismissed. Five months later she tried again in the same court, and that bill proceeded as case #1358, in the western district of Washington court. Note: The US circuit court later merged with the district court.

12 *Speckart v. Schmidt*, October 2, 1911.

13 *Speckart v. Schmidt*; 1909 Fed. 499, 111 Circuit Court of Appeals, 331. "Speckart Case in a Big Tangle," *Oregonian*, October 1, 1909, 16; "Heckbert Told to Return Coin," *Oregonian*, October 12, 1909, 6. The appellate court returned the case to the US district court for settlement. For uncertain reasons, eleven years passed before a decision was delivered. Other newspaper accounts referred to $119,000 that Speckart received and $135,000 that she was offered but refused. A definitive accounting is elusive after an extensive review of legal documents and newspaper reports. Dollar conversion estimate based on Consumer Price Index statistics from the *Historical Statistics of the United States* (USGPO, 1975) and the annual *Statistical Abstracts of the United States* as cited http://www.westegg.com/inflation.

14 "Lots Sell for $26,000," *Oregonian*, March 30, 1911, 9 and "Lot Shows Rapid Advance," April 2, 1911, 9; *Appeal from Circuit Court Multnomah County; Robert Tucker, Judge; Action by Chester V. Dolph against Harriet F. Speckart, The Pacific Reporter,* Vol. 186, St. Paul, Minnesota: West Publishing Co., 1920, 32–36. "Heiress Sued for Fee," *Oregonian*, September 26, 1909, 11. Speckart hired six different attorneys during the course of her dispute and often paid them only under court order, *Oregonian*, Oct. 2, 1909, 4. The court established the value of the stocks Speckart received from her mother in 1909 at $43,432 in addition to the $57,000 in cash.

15 *Speckart v. Schmidt,* "Decree," February 24, 1922.

16 "Documents," *Superior Court of the State of Washington, County of Thurston.* In her Last Will and Testament, Mrs. Speckart directed that her daughter Harriet Speckart receive ten dollars, that her daughter by her previous marriage, Emmy Marie Mailand, receive ten dollars in addition to the thirty thousand shares of real estate stock previously awarded, and that her son, Joseph Speckart, receive all the remainder of her holdings.

17 Faderman, *To Believe in Women,* 266–68. Faderman discusses how the very traits needed to be a successful attorney—assertiveness and confrontation—were considered unwomanly and inappropriate.

18 Campaign advertisement of Dr. Sam C. Slocum for county coroner, *Oregonian*, April 14, 1912, 14; "Suffrage Leaders' Session Stormy," *Oregonian*, March 9, 1912; "Editor Testifies for Dr. Marie Equi," *Oregonian*, November 15, 1918, 1.

19 "Ballot Goal for Women," *Oregonian*, Jan. 25, 1908, 12; "Never Give Up the Ship," *Oregonian,* June 4, 1908, 5; "Will Try New Plan, Suffragettes to Ask Ballot for Women Taxpayer," *Oregonian*, August 30, 1908, 10; "Home Rule Leads, Majority Small," *Oregonian*, November 7, 1910, 1. Paul E. Fuller, *Laura Clay and the Woman's Right Movement* (Lexington: University of Kentucky Press, 1992), 101. Kentucky suffragist Laura Clay, one of the few eastern funders of Duniway's suffrage organization, withheld her support in light of this campaign tactic. She thought it would deny the vote to working women who most needed it. The property-owning proposal failed in New York as well. Ellen Carol Dubois, "Working Women, Class Relations, and Suffrage Militance: Harriet Stanton Blatch and the New York Woman Suffrage Movement, 1894–1909," *The Journal of American History,* 74:1, June 1987, 34–58.

20 Ruth Barnes Moynihan, *Rebel for Rights: Abigail Scott Duniway* (New Haven: Yale University Press, 1983), 214–16; "Suffrage Branch Gets Aid in East," *Oregonian*, March 13, 1912, 15; Jensen, "'Neither Head Nor Tail,'"384–409;

21 Rebecca J. Mead, *How the Vote Was Won: Woman Suffrage in the Western United States, 1868–1914* (New York: New York University Press, 2006), 97–118, 119–149. Kimberly Jensen, "Neither Head Nor Tail to the Campaign," *Oregon Historical Quarterly,* Fall 2007, v. 108, no. 3, 362, 372. Jensen notes that the Central Labor Council and the Oregon State Federation of Labor endorsed the 1912 suffrage campaign, but of the twenty-three suffrage organizations, none identified as trade unionist groups. Robert D. Johnston, *The Radical Middle Class: Populist Democracy and the Question of Capitalism in Progressive Era Portland, Oregon* (Princeton: Princeton University Press, 2003), 147-52. Although east Portland, the city's bastion of middle-class direct democrats, favored suffrage, Johnston argues that the final prosuffrage tally could have been greater if populists had made suffrage a higher prior-ity and suffragists had targeted them with appeals to economic justice. Ellen Carol Dubois, "Working Women, Class Relations, and Suffrage Militance: Harriet Stanton Blatch and the New York Woman's Suffrage Movement, 1894–1909," *The Journal of American History,* 74:1, June 1987, 34–58. Dubois describes how Blatch urged recognition of working women and trade union women in New York suffrage campaigns with positive results.

22 "College League Forms," *Oregonian*, February 21, 1912, 6. Ida Husted Harper et al., *History of Woman Suffrage* Vol. VI, 33; "Pioneers in the Law: The First 150 Women: Helen Hoy Greeley, 1926," State Bar of Wisconsin, www.wisbar.org accessed April 22, 2008; "California Woman Leads Equal Suffrage Cohorts of Oregon," *Oregonian*, August 6, 1912, 11; "College Suffragists Elect," *Oregonian*, May 8, 1912, 11.

23 "Suffragists Outline Campaign Plan," *Oregon Daily Journal*, March 6, 1912, 7; "Suffrage Leaders Session Stormy," *Oregonian*, March 9, 1912, 4; Ida Husted Harper, *The History of Woman Suffrage*, Vol. V, 544–49; "Early Death Fate of Suffrage Body," *Oregonian*, March 17, 1912, 12.

24 "Dr. Equi to Anna Howard Shaw," *Abigail Scott Duniway Scrapbook, Vol. 11*, 1912, Oregon Historical Society Research Library, 1.

25 Ibid.

26 Moynihan, *Rebel for Rights*, 214; Fuller, *Laura Clay*, 100.

27 "Dr. Equi to Anna Howard Shaw," *Abigail Scott Duniway Scrapbook, Vol. 11*, 1912, Oregon Historical Society Research Library, 1.

28 "Chinese Women Dine with White," *Oregonian*, April 12, 1912, 16; "Women Pay Honor," *Oregonian*, April 16, 1912, 20; "Mrs. LaFollette to Speak," *Oregonian*, April 16, 1912, 11; "Woman of World Prominence Here," *Oregonian*, September 29, 1912, 16. Equi appeared in the photo accompanying this article (second from far right in second row). "Boys Like Suffrage," *Oregonian*, April 24, 1912, 15; also "Boys Work for Equal Suffrage," *Oregonian*, April 16, 1912, 11. "Suffrage Bride Taken," *Oregonian*, April 11, 1912, 9. The author thanks Kimberly Jensen for sharing the article on the boys' suffrage club.

29 Equi's offices were in rooms 422 and 423. *Polk's Portland 1912, City Directory*, 585; *Polk's Medical Register and Directory of North America* (Detroit: R.L. Polk & Co., 1912), 1410–22; "Gun Play Figured, Declares Dr. Equi," *Oregonian*, Nov. 9, 1912, 4. Dr. Alan Welch Smith and Dr. Mary MacLachlan—the doctor who filed charges with Equi against Portland's Baby Home in 1911—testified that they found black marks and contusions on Equi's arms, neck, back, and legs and that she was in a state of nervous shock.

30 "Dr. Equi Is Accused," *Oregonian*, August 10, 1912, 8; "Dr. Equi Hurled Eggs Assert Two Witnesses, *Portland Evening Telegram*, June 9, 1912, 2; *Equi D. Equi v. Pacific Trust Co.*, Judgment No. 52584, June 12, 1913, Complaint, 4; "Gun Play Figured, Declares Dr. Equi," *Oregonian*, November 9, 1912, 4.

31 Equi and Speckart lived at the South Parkhurst Apartments, at Twentieth Street North; today the address is 1204 NW Twentieth at the corner of Northrup. Equi spent the night with her friend Dr. Mary MacLachlan at the Cornelius Hotel.

32 "Prettyman Indicted on Dr. Equi's Charges," *Portland Evening Telegram*, May 25, 1912, 7; "Dr. Equi Asks Jury to Investigate Case," *Oregon Daily Journal*, May 1, 1012, 10; "Equi Case Goes to Trial," *Oregonian*, May 25, 1912, 14; *State v. Prettyman*, Multnomah County Circuit Court, case # 50340; "Gun Play Figured, Declares Dr. Equi," *Oregonian*, November 9, 1912, 4; "Dr. Equi Loses in Suit, *"Oregonian*, Nov. 10, 1912, 15; "Find Prettyman Not Guilty, Out 50 Minutes," *Oregon Daily Journal*, Nov. 10, 1912, 4. George Prettyman remained superintendent of the Medical Building after his acquittal, but he continued to face scrapes with the law.

33 Jensen, "Neither Head nor Tail," 372–74; Carrie Chapman Catt and Nettie Rogers Shuler, *Woman Suffrage and Politics: The Inner Story of the Suffrage Movement* (Seattle: University of Washington Press, 1969 Reprint), 130; Holly T. McCammon and Karen C. Campbell, "Winning the Vote in the West: The Political Successes of the Women's Suffrage Movements, 1866–1919," *Gender and Society*, 15:1, February 2001, 55–82. McCammon and Campbell argue that "expediency" messages that emphasized women's maternal and nurturing effect on the body politic were more persuasive to western voters than assertions of women's rights that challenged the social order.

34 "Mrs. Duniway's Dream Comes True," *The Spectator*, November 16, 1912, 6; Oregon Blue Book, http://bluebook.state.or.us/state/elections/elections06b.htm accessed March 21, 2012.

35 Moynihan, *Rebel for Rights*, 214–16; Mead, *How the Vote Was Won*, 118; Abigail Scott Duniway, *Path Breaking: An Autobiographical History of the Equal Suffrage Movement in Pacific Coast States* (New York: Schocken Books, 1971), 268. Duniway includes photographs of dozens of "Equal Suffragists" in her volume, including national and Oregon leaders and

extending back to the early days of suffragists from the nineteenth century. Equi is profiled on page 268.

36 James Chace, *1912: Wilson, Roosevelt, Taft, and Debs—The Election That Changed the Country* (New York: Simon & Schuster, 2004), 163–67.

37 Ibid, 169–87, 213–215.

38 Ibid, 238–40.

39 "Rotten Scandal Reaches into the YMCA," *Portland News*, November 15, 1912, 1; Peter Boag, *Same-Sex Affairs: Constructing and Controlling Homosexuality in the Pacific Northwest* (Berkeley: University of California Press, 2003), 1–11, 89–124.

40 "Six Indictments in Vice Inquiry," *Portland Evening Telegram*, November 30, 1912, 1; "One Attempts Suicide; Eleven Under Arrest," *Oregon Daily Journal*, November 17, 1912, 1; "Clubs Take Action," *Oregonian*, November 20, 1912, 1; "The Mothers Are with the News in this Fight . . . Read and See," *Portland News*, November 25, 1912, 3.

41 The *Oregon Daily Journal* first coined "vice clique" to describe the 1912 same-sex scandal in a November 17, 1912, report. For more on the Portland sex scandal, see George Painter, *The Vice Clique: Portland's Great Sex Scandal* (Portland: Espresso Book Machine, 2013). The author appreciates the information and assistance of George Painter with research of this event. "Clique" was often used at the time to describe a tightly knit group, often as a pejorative reference.

42 *Seventeenth Annual Announcement of the Medical Department of the University of Oregon, Session 1903–1904*; Boag, *Same-Sex Affairs,* 168–179.

43 Boag, *Same-Sex Affairs,* 139–141; 217–18. The Oregon Supreme Court eventually overturned the convictions of McAllister and Start based on the lower court's decision to allow testimony about their previous homosexual activity as evidence of their likelihood to commit the offenses for which they were charged. Basically, the lower court ruled that a history of alleged homosexual acts predisposed defendants to breaking the law and were thus admissible in court. Freed by the higher court's decision but still deeply shamed, McAllister left Portland to live in Southern Oregon, his professional and political life ruined. Harry Start sought refuge from the persecution in the United States by accepting an invitation from nationalist leader Dr. Sun-Yat Sen to practice medicine in China, but ultimately he worked as an urologist in the Philippines for the next three decades.

44 The *Portland News* named eleven men in its third *Extra!* edition about the vice scandal. One was a nineteen-year-old drugstore clerk. Delvin Peterson, age eighteen, occupation unknown, was not included in the newspaper list, but his name was placed on the Multnomah County Register as an offender. Painter, *The Vice Clique*, 49; Boag, *Same Sex Affairs,* 193–200.

45 Equi presented her findings and treatment to the Multnomah County Medical Society during the group's January 18, 1911 meeting, as reported in *Northwest Medicine*, February, 1911. My thanks to George Painter for providing this information. The medical society held meetings twice a month in the Medical Building where Equi maintained her practice.

CHAPTER 9

1 Editorial, *Eugene Register Guard*, October 29, 1919, 3. The editor referred to C. E. S. Wood, sometime attorney for Marie Equi, a "high-brow parlor anarchist." Robert D. Johnston, *The Radical Middle Class: Populist Democracy and the Question of Capitalism in Progressive Era Portland, Oregon* (Princeton: Princeton University Press, 2003), 101–02. Johnston discusses three solidly Progressive Portlanders who embraced radical agendas and defended radical positions: small businessman and labor leader Will Daly (99–114), architect of much of Oregon's direct democracy reforms William S. U'Ren (127–37), and Portland's mayor and later US Senator Harry Lane (307–47). "In the Field of Labor," *Oregonian*, February 24, 1907, 41.

2 Robert Hamburger, *Two Rooms: The Life of Charles Erskine Scott Wood* (Lincoln: University of Nebraska Press, 1998), 126–29, 143–46; Carlos A. Schwantes, "Free Love and Free Speech on the Pacific Northwest Frontier," *Oregon Historical Quarterly*, 82:3, (Fall, 1981),

271–93; "In the Field of Labor," *Oregonian*, February 24, 1907, 41; "Success of Tie-up Is Due to Crowds," *Oregonian*, December 16, 1906, 2; "Editorial Reports," *Oregonian*, March 6, 1907, 8.

3 Registration Cards, Division of Registration, 1912–1913, Film File No.19; Multnomah County Records Administration; Warren Marion Blankenship, "Progressives and the Progressive Party in Oregon, 1906–1916," Thesis, PhD, University of Oregon, August 1966.; "Ex-Slave to Vote," *Oregonian*, April 20, 1913, 10.

4 "Bull Moose Meet, Multnomah County Progressive Club Launched," *Oregonian*, October 15, 1913, 15; *New Bedford Evening Standard*, March 17, 1914, 3. Note: Due to inability to obtain microfilm copies of the *New Bedford Standard* and the *Boston Globe*, the author has been unable to confirm titles and page numbers for a few articles.

5 E. Kimbark MacColl, *The Shaping of a City: Business and Politics in Portland, Oregon, 1885–1915* (Portland: The Georgian Press, 1976), 435–46.

6 "Detention Homes Are Recommended," *Oregonian*, July 20, 1913, 14; Portland Archives & Records Center, hereafter referred to as PARC, 12000-003, 0201-01, Applications, various positions, 17-07 20/1; MacColl, *The Shaping of a City*, 460–61.

7 "Supreme Court Rules 8 Hour Law Off Ballot," *Medford Mail Tribune*, July 29, 1913, 1; *Daily Capital Journal*, July 3, 1913, 1. *Marie Equi and Mrs. J. B. Oaman v. Ben W. Olcott* asked the court to require the state to place the eight-hour bill proposed by a ballot intiative on the special election ballot slated for November 1913. The state supreme court declined to do so.

8 Nancy Woloch, *Muller v. Oregon, A Brief History with Documents* (Boston: Bedford/St. Martin's, 1996), 21–40, 144-50; Elaine Zahnd, "Protective Legislation and Women's Work: Oregon's Ten-Hour Law and the *Muller v. Oregon* Case, 1900–1913," PhD. Diss.: University of Oregon, 1982. Special thanks to Janice Dilg for directing me to this work. For a discussion of historians' evolving and conflicting views about the meaning and impact of the Muller decision, see Johnston, *The Radical Middle Class.*

9 "Anti-Vote Talk Stirs," *Oregonian*, August 8, 1912, 2; "Dr. Equi Ordered Off Corner with Her Talk," *Oregon Daily Journal*, August 10, 1912, 8.

10 "Woman Socialist's Hard Experience on Pacific Coast," *New York World*, April 5, 1914, sec. m, 4.

11 "Work Is Hampered," *Oregonian*, June 30, 1913, 7. For more on the 1913 cannery strike, see Greg Hall, "The Fruits of Her Labor: Women, Children, and Progressive Era Reformers in the Pacific Northwest Canning Industry," *Oregon Historical Quarterly* 109:2 (Summer 2008), 226–51 and Adam Hodges, "The Industrial Workers of the World and the Oregon Packing Company Strike of July 1913," (MA thesis, Portland State University, 1996). For information on the role of the Consumer's League of Oregon in the cannery strike, see Janice Dilg, "'For Working Women in Oregon' Caroline Gleason/Sister Miriam Theresa and Oregon's Minimum Wage Law," *Oregon Historical Quarterly*, 110:1, (Spring, 2009), 96–129.

12 "Strikers' Views Told," *Oregonian*, July 3, 1913, 18; *Portland News*, July 8, 1913, 1.

13 Dilg, "For Working Women in Oregon," 98–99, describes the minimum wage law adopted in 1913. E. Kimbark MacColl, *Merchants, Money, and Power* (Portland: Georgian Press, 1988), 443-44; PARC, 0200/0201-01: Mayor (Archival)—Albee, Harry Russell—Subject Files, 17-07-25/1; Johnston, *The Radical Middle Class*, 24–26;"Minimum Wage Scale Reached," *Oregon Daily Journal*, July 1, 1913; "They Weren't Told About It," *Portland News*, July 5, 1913, 1.

14 PARC, 0200/0201-01: Mayor (Archival)—Albee, Harry Russell—Subject Files, 17-07-25/1; "Strikers Views Told," *Oregonian*, July 3, 1913, 18; "Strike Trouble Comes to Head," *Oregon Daily Journal*, July 9, 1913, 2; "Patience of Mayor With Agitators Now at Breaking Point," *Oregon Daily Journal*, July10, 1913, 1; "Disturbers Force Cannery to Close," *Oregonian*, July 11, 1913, 12. Rudolph Schwab's life had been defined by radical action ever since his father, Michael Schwab, was convicted for a role in the violent Haymarket Affair of 1886. "Schwab Jury Is Unable to Agree," *Oregonian*, July 16, 1913, 12.

15 "Governor West Takes Hand in Strike at Packing Plant," *Oregon Daily Journal,* July 11, 1913, 1; "Father O'Hara Talks," *Oregonian,* July 12, 1913, 11; "Strike Trouble Comes to Head," *Oregon Daily Journal,* July 12, 1913, 1; Dilg, "For Working Women," 96–129.

16 "Strike Agitator Arouses Ire of Governor West," *Oregon Daily Journal,* July 12, 1913, 1; "1000 Join in Riots," *Sunday Oregonian,* July 13, 1913, 2; "Women Agitators Put in Bastille," *San Francisco Chronicle,* July 18, 1913, 2; "Poisoned Pin Her Weapon," *New York Times,* July 20, 1913, 3; "IWW Women Taken to Jail for Disorder," *San Francisco Call,* July 18, 1913, 2.

17 "Strike Agitator Arouses Ire of Governor West," *Oregon Daily Journal,* July 12, 1913; "Officers Ride into Belligerent Crowd at Packing Plant," *Oregon Daily Journal,* July 13, 1913, 1.

18 "1000 Join In Riot At Packing Plant," *Oregonian,* July 13, 1913, 1; "Cannery Strikers Are Charged by Police," *Oregon Daily Journal,* July 13, 1913, 1; "IWW Calls For A General Strike," *Oregon Daily Journal,* July 13, 1913, 4; "IWW Deny Demonstration," *Oregonian,* July 17, 1913, 12; "Dr. Equi 'Biffs' Deputies," *Oregonian,* July 16, 1913, 3; "Start War to Finish On IWW," *Oregon Daily Journal,* July 16, 1913, 1; "Woman Socialist's Hard Experience on Pacific Coast," *New York World,* April 5, 1914, 2.

19 "Officials Decide to Continue IWW Campaign," *Oregon Daily Journal,* July 19, 1913, 1, 5. Photo of women arrested, including Equi and Officer "stabbed" with hatpin. *Portland News,* July 18, 1913, 1; Cannery Strike Arrest Records, v. 1913, 178, lines 861–78, PARC; "Mayor Refuses to Lift Ban on Street Speaking," *Oregon Daily Journal,* July 17, 1913, 1.

20 "Poisoned Pin Her Weapon," *New York Times,* July 20, 1913, 3.

21 "Officers, Defied, Charge Agitators," *Oregonian,* July 18, 1913, 1, 5; "Five Are Arrested in Running Fight," *Oregonian,* July 19, 1913, 1. See Jean H. Baker, *Sisters: The Lives of America's Suffragists,* (New York: Hill & Wang, Farrar, Strauss & Giroux, 2005) for occasions when the perceived misbehavior of unruly women was often described as evidence of madness.

22 "Predicts Revolution Unless Aid Is Given to 5,000,000 Unemployed," *The Boston Globe,* March 25, 1914.

23 "Woman Socialist's Hard Experience on Pacific Coast," *New York World,* April 5, 1914, 2; "Lingering Death Is Promised to Any Who Stops Her Speaking," *Oregon Daily Journal,* July 17, 1913, 1.

24 "Police Arrest IWW as Vagrants," *Oregon Daily Journal,* July 18, 1913, 1; "Officers, Defied, Charge Agitators," *Oregonian,* July 18, 1913, 1, 5; "Five Are Arrested in Running Fight," *Oregonian,* July 19, 1913, 1, 4; "Dr. Equi Declines All Prison Food Though Not On Hunger Strike," *Oregon Daily Journal,* July 19, 1913, 1, 5. The *Oregonian* reported that Equi was taken to the depot twice and each time refused to board the train. "Dr. Equi Will Not Leave," *Oregonian,* July 19, 1913, 8.

25 "Five Are Arrested in Running Fight," *Oregonian,* July 19, 1913, 1.

26 "Agitators Are Let Go," *Oregonian,* July 22, 1913, 9; "Personal Mention," *Oregonian,* April 11, 1914, 8.

27 Testimony of E. J. Stark, Oregon State Federation of Labor, "Industrial Relations, Final Report and Testimony, US Commission on Industrial Relations, Vol. V, 1916 (hearings held in mid-1914), http://books.google.com/, accessed October 12, 2013. The author thanks Janice Dilg for sharing this information and the document.

28 The Industrial Welfare Commission determined that a single woman in Portland needed twenty dollars a month for room and board alone. The IWC recommended a weekly wage of $8.64. *Oregon Daily Journal,* July 30, 1913, 1. In early August 1913, the commission enacted the first instance of compulsory minimum wage legislation in the country with one dollar a day stipulated for all women and girls. Dennis E. Hoffman and Vincent J. Webb, "Police Response to Labor Radicalism in Portland and Seattle, 1913–1919," *Oregon Historical Quarterly,* 87:4, (Winter, 1986), 341–66. For an analysis of source of friction between Progressives and the IWW, see Adam J. Hodges, *The Industrial Workers of the World,* 1996. "Agitators Would Restrain Mayor," *Sunday Oregonian,* July 27, 1913, 5.

29 The South Parkhurst Apartments were located at South 260 Twentieth N; the current
    address is 1204 NW Twentieth Northrup Street and the building is known today as The
    Belvedere. Equi and Speckart remained at these apartments from 1912 until 1914–1915
    and perhaps later. Equi's office location in 1913 and 1914 was in suite 403 of the Central
    Building at SW Tenth and Alder.

30 Arno Dosch, "What the I.WW. Is," *Oregon Sunday Journal*, August 3, 1913, 6. The article was
    first published in *World's Work* for August 1913. Arno Dosch, a member of the prominent
    Henry Dosch family of Portland, became a highly respected war correspondent during
    World War I.

31 "600 Family Men Go To Work This Week," *Oregonian*, December 22, 1913, 18; "Mob
    Demands Food," *Oregonian*, December 22, 1913, 10.

32 Arthur Evans Wood, *A Study of the Unemployed in Portland, Oregon*, Social Services Bulletin
    No. 3, 1914; Reed College, Portland, Oregon, December 1914, http://books.google.com,
    accessed September 15, 2012.

33 Adam J. Hodges, "The Industrial Workers of the World and the Oregon Packing Company
    Strike of July 1913," Thesis, Portland State University, 1996, 10–11; "Predicts Revolution
    Unless Aid Is Given to 5,000,000 Unemployed," *Boston Globe*, March 25, 1914. The Gipsy
    Smith Tabernacle stood at the northeast corner of SW Twelfth and Morrison Streets. The
    building was name for a British evangelist.

34 "Deputy Sheriffs Summoned When Dr. Equi Leads 100 'Unemployed' into Court,"
    Oregonian, March 18, 1915, 14; "Predicts Revolution Unless Aid Is Given to 5,000,000
    Unemployed," *Boston Globe*, March 25, 1914.

35 Michael Munk, "The Diaries of Helen Lawrence Walters," *Oregon Historical Quarterly*, 106:4
    (Winter, 2005), 606–07.

36 Hoffman and Webb, "Police Response to Labor Radicalism, 341–66. Groups of the
    unemployed stopped in Oregon City, Woodburn, Salem, Tangent, Shedd, Independence,
    Albany, Harrisburg, and Eugene. "Idle Army Is On March," *Oregonian*, January 9, 1914, 5;
    "Idle Army Turned Down in Woodburn," *Oregonian*, January 11, 1914, 10; "Idle Army's
    Agent Travels on Trains," *Oregonian*, January 15, 1914, 5.

37 "Panacea for Idle Army Hard to Find," *Oregonian*, February 19, 1914, 4.

38 Delegate Goes to New York," *Oregonian*, February, 22, 1914, 12; "Jailed Three Times,"
    New Bedford Standard , March 17, 1914, 3; "Proceedings," *First National Conference on
    Unemployment*, American Labor Legislation Review, American Association for Labor
    Legislation, New York: #2, publ. 25, http://www.ebooksread.com, accessed September 2,
    2012; "Discuss the Unemployed," *New York Times*, February 28, 1914, 5.

39 "Proceedings,*" First National Conference on Unemployment*.

40 "Delegate Goes to New York," *Oregonian*, February 22, 1914, 12; "Dr. Marie Equi Arrested,"
    New Bedford Standard Times, July 20, 1913; "Jailed Three Times," *New Bedford Standard* ,
    March 7, 1914, 1.

41 "Jailed Three Times," *New Bedford Standard*, March 7, 1914, 1.

42 "Predicts Revolution Unless Aid Is Given to 5,000,000 Unemployed, *Boston Globe*, March
    25, 1914.

43 Ibid.

44 Ibid. "Dr. Equi Speaks," *New Bedford Evening Standard*, March 23, 1914, 3.

45 *Ibid.*

46 "Woman Socialist's Hard Experience on Pacific Coast," *New York World*, April 5, 1914, sec.
    m, 4; "Police Clubs, Fists and Horses Rout I.W.W. Rioters in Fierce Battle at Union Square,"
    New York World, April 5, 1914, 1.

47 "Police Clubs, Fists and Horses Rout IWW Rioters in Fierce Battle at Union Square,"
    New York World, April 5, 1914, 2; Dmitri Palmateer, "Charity and the 'Tramp': Itinerancy,
    Unemployment, and Municipal Government from Coxey to the Unemployed League,"
    Oregon Historical Quarterly, 107:2 (Summer, 2006): 242–49; "Home for Idle Rented,"

Oregonian, December 18, 1914, 9. The rooming house was located at Second Street and Everett.

48 E. Kimbark MacColl, *The Shaping of a City*, 461–62; Carl Abbott, *Portland: Planning, Politics, and Growth in a Twentieth-Century City*, (Lincoln: University of Nebraska Press, 1983) 74–75.

CHAPTER 10

1 Marriage Certificate, Oregon State Vital Records; Oregon Birth Certificate, # 379; "Changes of Names and Adoptions," Oregon Laws, 987, Oregon State Archives. My thanks to Karen Able for sharing this document. Robert L. Tyler, *Rebels of the Woods: The IWW in the Pacific Northwest* (Eugene: University of Oregon Press, 1967), 59; William M. Adler, *The Man Who Never Died: The Life, Times and Legacy of Joe Hill, American Labor Icon* (New York: Bloomsbury, USA, 2011), 36–39.

2 "Five Physicians to Pass on Mrs. Clark," *Oregonian*, March 13, 1915, 12; "Mrs. Clark Found Insane by Doctors," *Oregonian*, March 17, 1915, 13; "Deputy Sheriffs Summoned When Dr. Equi Leads 100 'Unemployed' into Court," *Oregonian*, March 18, 1915, 14.

3 Divorce #4213, May 29, 1915, Judgment # 61143, Multnomah County, Oregon; Julia Ruuttila with Sandy Polishuk and Nancy Krieger, Interview, June 6, 1981, OHS ACC 28389—Equi; Mary Equi McCloskey with Sandy Polishuk, Interview, March 12, 1980, OHS ACC 28389—Equi; Franklin Rosemont, *Joe Hill: The IWW and The Making of a Revolutionary Workingclass Counterculture* (Chicago: Charles H. Kerr Publishing Company, 2003), 273–97.

4 Margaret D. to Sandy Polishuk, Interview, February 2, 1982, OHS ACC 28389—Equi. Margaret D. was a nurse who cared for Equi in her later years. She requested of the author that her surname not be used.

5 Oregon Birth Certificate, # 379; Marriage certificate, Oregon State Vital Records. *Oregon Adoptions and Name Changes, 1876–1918*, General Laws, 987, 1915. In later years, several individuals suggested that the IWW martyr Wesley Everest was Mary Equi's father. These were inaccurate understandings or false representations.

6 Petition of Marie D. Equi, Probate No. 28, 462, Harriet F. Speckart, Deceased, Multnomah County Circuit Court. Mary Equi McCloskey with Sandy Polishuk, Interview, May 1, 1971, OHS ACC 28389—Equi. Equi's daughter confirmed in an interview that her nickname for Equi, "Da," referred to "Doc" and not for "Dad" or something similar. Mary Equi McCloskey with Sandy Polishuk, Interview, May 1, 1971, OHS ACC 28389—Equi.

7 Elizabeth Gurley Flynn, *The Rebel Girl: An Autobiography, My First Life (1906–1926)* (New York: International Publishers, revised edition, 1973), 9–11, 23–40, 53–55, 61–70; Helen C. Camp, *Iron in her Soul, Elizabeth Gurley Flynn and the American Left* (Pullman: Washington State University Press, 1995), 1–16. "Elizabeth Gurley Flynn: Statement at the Smith Act Trial," delivered April 24, 1952, http://americanrhetoric.com/speeches/elizabethgurley-flynn.htm , accessed October 31, 2012.

8 Flynn, *The Rebel Girl*, 83–88, 95–115; Camp, *Iron in Her Soul*, 18–25.

9 Camp, *Iron in Her Soul*, 1–16, 47–55. Flynn worked as an organizer in several strikes before the 1913 Paterson silk dispute, notably among railway workers in Philadelphia and the textile workers of Lawrence, Lowell, and New Bedford, Massachusetts.

10 Flynn, *The Rebel Girl*, 127–46. Elizabeth Gurley Flynn, *The Truth about the Paterson Strike*," in Joyce L. Kornbluth, *Rebel Voices: An IWW Anthology*, (Chicago: Charles H. Kerr Publishing Company, 1988).

11 Flynn, *The Rebel Girl*, 191–98, 182–84; Camp, *Iron in Her Soul*, 57–59. In San Francisco, Flynn spoke at the IWW hall at 3345 Seventeenth Street and at Carpenters Hall on Valencia Street. "Woman Labor Leader to Speak," *Oregonian*, May 20, 1915, 13; "Miss Flynn Speaks on Labor," *Oregonian*, May 22, 1915, 16; Flynn's choice of "stormy petrel" reflected either an association with radical causes in the late 1890s and early 1900s or its seafaring reference to birds that presaged a storm.

12 Flynn, *The Rebel Girl*, 201–02, 217–68. Flynn noted that as early as 1915, ten years after its founding, the IWW struggled with how to hold its transient, fluctuating membership.

She wrote of "a growing demand by then to get out of the purely agitational state and build constructive and permanent organizations." Although the Wobblies "abandoned the soapbox," labor flareups in Everett and Centralia, Washington and, later, the defense of indicted and imprisoned Wobblies overwhelmed the organization.

13 "1000 Anarchists Parade in Gotham," *Oregonian*, March 22, 1914, 4.

14 Terence Kissack, *Free Comrades: Anarchism and Homosexuality in the United States, 1895–1917* (Oakland, California: AK Press, 2008), 133–49; "Says Anarchism Means Freedom," *Oregonian*, May 24, 1908, section 4, 10; "Chaos Promoter to Speak Here," *Oregon Daily Journal*, May 21, 1907, 14.

15 Equi was familiar with Goldman's attorney in Portland, and she had every reason to attend Goldman's talks especially when she pursued more radical causes herself. Goldman did not mention Equi in her journals or other writings. Frank Harris, *Contemporary Portraits* (New York: Brentano's, 1923), 224, as quoted in Pal Avrich, Karen Avrich, *Sasha and Emma: The Anarchist Odyssey of Alexander Berkman and Emma Goldman* (Cambridge, Massachusetts: Harvard University Press, 2012), 23.

16 "Emma Goldman Is Put Under Arrest," *Oregonian*, August 7, 1915, 12; "Miss Goldman Free," *Oregonian*, August 14, 1915, 9. When C. E. S. Wood paid bail for Goldman, he left Reitman in jail.

17 Emma Goldman, *Living My Life* (New York: A. A. Knopf, 1931), 186, 313; "Emma Goldman to Speak," *Oregonian*, August 16, 1916, 12.

18 Katz, *Free Comrades*, 3–6, 127–28, 141-43; Nicholson, *Emma Goldman* 170–77. Sperry's letters to Goldman and the latter's response, as quoted in Lillian Faderman, *Odd Girls and Twilight Lovers*, 33–34.

19 Emma Goldman, "The Unjust Treatment of Homosexuals (1900–1923)", www.angelfire.com/ok/Flack/emma.html accessed October 15, 2012; Correspondence 1915, J-Anarchists, 10/53, 17-07, 10/1, PARC. Kissack, *Free Comrades*, 141–46. "Emma Goldman," *Oregonian*, advertisement, August 6, 1915, 7.

20 States granting woman suffrage by the end of 1914 were Wyoming, Colorado, Idaho, Utah, Washington, California, Oregon, Arizona, Nevada, Montana, Kansas, and Illinois.

21 Sara Hunter Graham, *Woman Suffrage and the New Democracy* (New Haven: Yale University Press, 1996), 81–98; Rebecca Mead, *How the Vote Was Won: Woman Suffrage in the Western United States, 1868–1914* (New York: New York University Press, 2004), 151–74. For a full account of the Congressional Union and, later, the National Woman's Party, see Christine A. Lunardini, *From Equal Suffrage to Equal Rights: Alice Paul and the National Woman's Party, 1910–1928* (San Jose: toExcel Press, 2000). For the trade unionist suffrage initiatives, see Ellen Carol Dubois, "Working Women, Class Relations, and Suffrage Militance: Harriet Stanton Blatch and the New York Woman Suffrage Movement, 1894–1909," *The Journal of American History*, 74:1, June 1987, 34–58. Dubois argues that suffrage militancy relied not solely on the British suffragette experience but had "indigenous roots" in the United States.

22 "Suffrage Workers Meet Today," *Oregonian*, September 13, 1915, 14; "Personal Mention," Oregonian, September 14, 1915, 11; "Suffrage Officers for State Chosen," *Oregonian*, September 9, 1915, 5.

23 Mrs. Emma Carroll to Virginia Arnold (Congressional Union officer), correspondence, September 29, 1915, National Woman's Party Papers: The Suffrage Years, 1913–1920, Library of Congress. "Women Voters in an Uproar," *San Francisco Examiner*, September 16, 1915, 6; "Suffragist Camp Upset and At War," *San Francisco Examiner*, September 26, 1915, 1; "Suffrage Union Spikes Enemy Guns," *Oregonian*, September 16, 1915, 4.

24 Jensen, *Oregon's Doctor*, 119; "Radical Suffragists Win Fight, Anthony Amendment Indorsed," *San Francisco Examiner*, September 17, 1915, 4; "Women Ask S. B. Anthony Amendment Or Nothing," *San Francisco Chronicle*, September 17, 1915, 1; "Dr. Equi Is Aided by Miss Whitney," *San Francisco Chronicle*, September 25, 1915. Note: Apparently Equi voted during the convention proceedings but was unseated as an Oregon delegate. Different accounts contribute to the lack of clarity.

25 Dr. Equi Is Upheld," *Oregonian*, September 24, 1915, 4; "Suffrage Plea, 3 Miles Long, Off Tonight," *The San Francisco Call and Post*, September 16, 1915, 7.; Charlotte Anita Whitney to Mrs. William (Elizabeth) Kent, September 26, 1915, National Woman's Party Papers, Library of Congress; "Women's Union Closes," *Oregonian*, October 5, 1915, 8. Sara Bard Field represented Oregon and Frances Joliffe represented California for the journey east, although illness kept Joliffe from completing the trip.

26 "Women In Turmoil," *Oregonian*, September 21, 1915, 11; "Personal Mention," *Oregonian*, September 13, 1915; "Dr. Equi Not Named Delegate," *Oregonian*, September 16, 1915, 9; "Dr. Equi Sues Suffragist," *Oregonian*, October 9, 1915, 4; Marie Equi vs. Emma B. Carroll, Oregon State Circuit Court case #63125.

27 Flynn, *Rebel Girl*, 172; "Miss Flynn, in Disguise, Invades Paterson in Vain," *New York Tribune*, November 12, 1915, 1; Camp, *Iron in Her Soul*. 62–63; Adler, *The Man Who Never Died*, 329–33; "Hillstrom Is Shot Denying His Guilt," *New York Times*, November 20, 1915, http://query.nytimes.com, accessed November 7, 2012.

28 "Gurley Flynn Free; To Keep Talking," *New York Times*, December 1, 1915, 1; "Miss Flynn's Trial Is Test of Police Power," *The Sun*, November 30, 1915, 14; "Noted Women Aid Miss Flynn in Paterson Court Fight," *Kingston Daily Freeman*, Kingston, New York, December 2, 1915, 1.

29 Correspondence, Rosalyn Baxandall to Sandy Polishuk, April 23, 1972 with notes on Elizabeth Gurley Flynn's letter of July 14, 1956, to her sister while at the Alderson, West Virginia, penitentiary, OHS ACC 28389—Equi. Gardiner received her medical degree at Women's Medical College of Pennsylvania. "Obituary," *New York Times*, July 9, 1956, 23.

CHAPTER 11

1 "Militant Is Coming," *Sunday Oregonian*, June 4, 1916, 10; "Mrs. Emmeline Pankhurst," *Sunday Oregonian*, June 4, 1916, 7.

2 "Mrs. Pankhurst Is For Preparedness," *Oregonian*, June 7, 1916, 20.

3 Ibid

4 David M. Kennedy, *Over Here*, 32–34; "Wilson Ahead of His Party," *Oregonian*, May 10, 1916, 10; "Strong Opposition to Training Voiced," *Oregonian*, January 14, 1917, 2; "'War Parade Opposed," *Oregonian*, May 29, 1916, 7; Alan Dawley, *Changing the World: American Progressives in War and Revolution* (Princeton: Princeton University Press, 2003), 107–40, 116–20; Al Richmond, *Native Daughter: The Story of Anita Whitney* (San Francisco: Anita Whitney Seventy-Fifth Anniversary Committee, 1942), 69–70.

5 "Preparedness Is Cry of Thousands," *Sunday Oregonian*, June 4, 1916, 1. A similar march in Chicago that day attracted 130,000 and lasted nearly twelve hours. "Tide of Humanity Surges for Hours," *Sunday Oregonian*, June 4, 1916.

6 "Dr. Marie Equi Nearly Causes Riot in Preparedness Parade," *Oregon Daily Journal*, June 4, 1916, 6; "Mob Brushes Woman Desecrating Flag," *Oregonian*, June 4, 1916, 1. Interview with Palmer L. Fales, attorney, by Bureau of Investigation Agent E. H. Keller, September 11, 1918 or thereabout, DOJ Papers.

7 Johnston, *The Radical Middle Class*, 41–45. Interview with Julia Ruuttila by Sandy Polishuk and Nancy Krieger, June 6, 1981. This incident was also recounted in an interview with Portland activist Lew Levy by Sandy Polishuk, April 5, 1976, OHS ACC 28389—Equi. Gurley, *Rebel Girl*, 198–200.

8 Kathleen Kennedy, *Disloyal Mothers and Scurrilous Citizens: Women and Subversion during World War I* (Bloomington: Indiana University Press, 1999), 1–17, 91–107. Kennedy and other historians argue that the government identified and promoted women's obligations during wartime through propaganda into a construct reflected in the term "patriotic motherhood." Women seen to reject these norms were often prosecuted ostensibly for their offenses under the wartime espionage and sedition acts but often their greater transgressions appeared to be their disorderly, unbecoming, and unwomanly conduct. Susan Ziegler describes how the government helped shape popular culture to transform meanings of

"manhood" and "motherhood" into service of wartime goals. Susan Ziegler, "She Didn't Raise Her Boy to Be a Slacker: Motherhood, Conscription, and the Culture of the First World War," *Feminist Studies*, 22:1, (Spring, 1996), 6–39.

9 "Anti-Defense Men Talk," *Oregonian*, June 5, 1916, 11; Kennedy, *Over Here*, 30–32; Dawley, *Changing the World*, 120–23; Capazzola, *Uncle Sam Wants You*, 119–23.

10 "New York Ready for Big Parade," *New York Times*, May 13, 1916; "Peace Parade Billed, Too," *Oregonian*, June 21, 1916, 13.

11 Page Smith, *America Enters the World: A People's History of the Progressive Era and World War I* (New York: McGraw-Hill Book Company, 1985), 501–03. The Mooney and Billings case figured prominently in the prewar labor strife and continued as an international controversy with critics objecting to fraudulent trial proceedings and unjust imprisonment.

12 Equi's office is listed in the 1917 Portland, Oregon, City Directory at the Lafayette Building. Her office was located on the same floor as that of Dr. Andre Ausplund, an abortionist charged in 1915 for a "criminal operation" in which a patient died. He was later imprisoned for the offense. See Chapter 10, note 15.

13 "Sanger Talk Set," *Oregonian*, June 12, 1916, 12.

14 Margaret Sanger, *The Selected Papers of Margaret Sanger, Volume 1: The Woman Rebel, 1900–1928*, Esther Katz, Cathy Moran, and Peter Engelman (eds.) (Urbana: University of Illinois Press, 2003), 184, 136; "League for Birth Control Founded," *Oregonian*, January 26, 1916, 1; "Some Consequences of Birth Control," *Oregonian*, May 17, 1916, 13; Linda Gordon, *The Moral Property of Women: A History of Birth Control Politics in America* (Urbana: University of Illinois Press, 2007), 152–53; Julia Ruutilla with Sandy Polishuk and Nancy Krieger, Interview, June 6, 1981, OHS ACC 28389-Equi; Sandy Polishuk, *Sticking to the Union: An Oral History of the Life and Times of Julia Ruutilla*, (New York: Palgrave Macmillan, 2003), 25.

15 Ellen Chesler, *Woman of Valor: Margaret Sanger and the Birth Control Movement in America* (New York: Anchor Books, 1992), 56–73, 74–88.

16 Gordon, *The Moral Property of Women*, 3–4, 138–50; Chesler, *Woman of Valor*, 89–104.

17 Chesler, *Woman of Valor*, 128–49; Margaret Sanger, *Margaret Sanger: An Autobiography* (New York: Dover Publications, 1971), 192–209; Chesler, *Woman of Valor*, 126–27. While Sanger took exile in England, her husband, William Sanger, was arrested for distributing copies of *Family Limitation*, the birth control pamphlet Margaret Sanger had drafted before her quick departure. His trial, conviction, and thirty-day prison sentence gained considerable public sympathy that worked in his wife's favor as her trial approached.

18 Sanger, *Margaret Sanger*, 199–203. In straightforward, explicit language, the pamphlet advised women about using a vaginal douche with household and prescriptive formulas, the effective use of a condom and a diaphragm (called a "pessary" at the time), sponges, and suppositories. Sanger had drafted *Family Limitation* before she fled the US for Europe in August 1914. Her radical friends and the IWW distributed hundreds of thousands of copies of the pamphlet during her absence. Margaret Sanger, *Motherhood in Bondage*, (Columbus: Ohio State University Press, 2000); Margaret Sanger Papers Project, "Motherhood in Bondage: The Ultimate Horror Story," https://sangerpapers.wordpress.com/tag/motherhood-in-bondage/.

19 Sanger, *An Autobiography*, 204–06; "Mrs. Sanger Is Here," *Oregonian*, June 17, 1916, 15.

20 Chesler, *Woman of Valor*, 142; Gordon, *The Moral Authority of Women*, 158.

21 Sanger, *An Autobiography*, 204–06.

22 Ibid., Michael Munk, "The Diaries of Helen Lawrence Walters," *Oregon Historical Quarterly*, 106: 4, (Winter 2005), 607; "Book Sale Stopped," *Oregonian*, June 24, 1916, 18; "Virtue Not Made by Ordinance," June 28, 1916, 10; "Portland Moral or Ridiculous," *Oregonian*, June 21, 1916, 10; Receipt, #4603, City of Portland, Dept. of Public Safety, Municipal Court, copy located in the Huntington Library, Charles Erskine Scott Wood Collection, Box WD 135, folder 47. My thanks to Dona Munker for providing references from the C. E. S. Wood Papers.

23 Sanger, Margaret H., *Family Limitation*, Revised Edition, n.d. but likely 1916. Personal collection of the author. Sanger retains use of "working class" in the text although she gradually

shifted to "working women" and less class analysis in later revisions. Joan M. Jensen, "The Evolution of Margaret Sanger's 'Family Limitation' Pamphlet, 1914–1920," *Signs*, Vol. 6, No. 3, (Spring 1981), 548–67. The president of the Portland Birth Control League wrote to Mayor Albee that references to the "pleasurableness" of intercourse were deleted from the booklet distributed at the second rally on June 29 specifically to address the city's objections. H. C. Uthoff to Mayor H.R. Albee, July 18, 1916, Portland Archives and Records Center, 0201-01, A2000-003, Birth Control Correspondence, 13/39, 17-07-34/1.

24 "Book Sale Stopped," *Oregonian*, June 24, 1916, 18; "Sanger Birth Control Protest Meeting," Advertisement, *Oregonian*, June 29, 1916, 11; Margaret Sanger, *Margaret Sanger: An Autobiography* (New York: Dover Publications, 1971), 206.

25 Sanger, *Margaret Sanger*, 206; "Mrs. Sanger, Arrested, Wants Woman Jury," The Free Press, filed July 2, 1916 from Portland, Oregon, no city of publication noted. Also, Anna L. Strong to Mayor Albee, July 5, 1916, and petition, July 1, 1916. All three in Portland Archives and Records Center, 0201-10, A2000-003, Birth Control—Margaret Sanger, 13/39 and 13/40, 17-07-34/1.

26 Sanger, *Margaret Sanger*, 206; Margaret Sanger, "A 'Birth Control' Lecture Tour," August 9, 1916, Margaret Sanger Papers Project, www.nyu.edu/projects/sanger, accessed November 27, 2012. "Mrs. Sanger, Arrested, Wants Woman Jury," *The Free Press*, filed July 2, 1916, from Portland, Oregon, no city or publication noted. Also, Anna L. Strong to Mayor Albee, July 5, 1916. Both in PARC, 0201-10, A2000-003, Birth Control—Margaret Sanger, 13/39 and 13/40, 17-07-34/1. "Two Birth Control Trials in Court," *Oregonian*, July 1, 1916, 16; "Sanger Cases Are Now Up to Court," *Sunday Oregonian*, July 2, 1916, 15; "City of Portland vs. Carl Rave, C. L. Jenkins, and Ralph Chervin" and "City of Portland vs. Margaret Sanger, Mrs. F. A. Greatwood, Miss Maude Bournet and Dr. Marie D. Equi," 0201-01, A2000-001, Birth Control—legal decision, PARC; "Mrs. Sanger Book Declared Obscene," *Oregonian*, July 8, 1916, 16.

27 Chesler, *Woman of Valor*, 146–52; "For Birth Control Clinic," *New York Times*, September 12, 1916, 11; Gordon, *The Moral Authority of Women*, 156; "Emma Goldman to Speak," *Oregonian*, August 1, 1916, 12.

28 Marie Equi to Margaret Sanger, Saturday, October 20, 1916, Margaret Sanger Papers, Sophia Smith Collection, Smith College, hereinafter MSP-SS included in Margaret Sanger, *The Selected Papers of Margaret Sanger, Volume 1: The Woman Rebel, 1900–1928*, Esther Katz, Cathy Moran, Peter Engelman (eds.), (Urbana: University of Illinois Press, 2003), 184.

29 Marie Equi to Margaret Sanger, October 2, 1916; Margaret Sanger to Marie Equi, April 9, 1921, San Quentin Prison Correspondence, DOJ Papers.

30 Marie Equi to Margaret Sanger, November 2, 1916, MSP-SS.

31 Margaret Sanger to Marie Equi, 1916, MSP-SS as quoted in Sanger, *The Selected Papers of Margaret Sanger, Volume 1,185*.

32 Rebecca J. Mead, *How the Vote Was Won: Woman Suffrage in the Western United States, 1868–1914*, (New York: New York University Press, 2004), 166–68; Christine A. Lunardini, *From Equal Suffrage to Equal Rights: Alice Paul and the National Woman's Party, 1910–1928*, (San Jose: toExcel Press, 2000), 50–70; Kimberly Jensen, *Oregon's Doctor to the World: Esther Pohl Lovejoy and A Life in Activism* (Seattle: University of Washington Press, 2012), 114–120; "Women to Work Only for Votes," *Oregonian*, June 6, 1916, 1. The NWP's anti-Democrat campaigns in 1916 outraged NAWSA as congressional supporters were affected, and some were defeated, as a result.

33 "Woman's Party Vote Unpledged," *Oregonian*, October 14, 1916, 1. Lunardini, *From Equal Suffrage to Equal Rights*, 88–93. The Progressive Party backed Republican Hughes; the Socialist and Prohibitionist Parties also supported the federal suffrage amendment but their candidates were not major contenders. Candidate Hughes backed the federal amendment on August 1, 1916, following the Republican convention. Lunardini, *From Equal Suffrage to Equal Rights*, 88–93; "Wilson Forces Try to Stop Speakers," *Oregonian*, October 15, 1916, 13.

34 Marie Equi to Margaret Sanger, October 2, 1916, Box 80, Reel 51–52, Margaret Sanger Papers, Manuscript Division, Library of Congress, Washington, DC.

35 Warren Marion Blankenship, "Progressives and the Progressive Party in Oregon, 1906–1916," Thesis, University of Oregon, August 1966, 361–66; Lunardini, *From Equal Suffrage to Equal Rights*, 101–03. The Republicans and Progressives had vigorously recruited Oregon women volunteers into the campaign and had employed the communication and outreach strategies that helped win suffrage in 1912.

36 Flynn, *Rebel Girl*, 201–03.

37 Philip S. Foner, *Fellow Workers and Friends, I.W.W. Free-Speech Fights as Told by Participants* (Westport, Connecticut: Greenwood Press, 1981), 183–89; Robert L. Tyler, *Rebels of the Woods: The I.W.W. in the Pacific Northwest* (Eugene: University of Oregon Press, 1967), 62–84.

38 Tyler, *Rebels of the Woods*, 62–84.

39 Walker C. Smith, *The Everett Massacre*, www.gutenberg.org accessed December 2, 2012, 94; "IWW Go to Everett," *Oregonian*, December 4, 1916, 11; Charles Ashleigh, "Date Is Set For Trial," *Everett Defense News Letter No.,* January 27, 1917, content.lib.washington.edu accessed December 2, 2012; "IWW Ask U.S. to Investigate," *Seattle Star*, November 10, 1916, 1; Flynn, *The Rebel Girl*, 220–24.

40 Equi to Sanger, November 2, 1916, MSP-SS; Inez Rhodes to Nancy Krieger, April 17, 1981, as referenced in Nancy Krieger, "Queen of the Bolsheviks: The Hidden History of Dr. Marie Equi," *Radical America*, 1983, vol. 17 (5), 58, fn. 18. Inez Rhodes was an active IWW member in Seattle who spread Hill's ashes with Equi. Franklin Rosemont, *Joe Hill: The IWW and the Making of a Revolutionary Workingclass Counterculture* (Chicago: Charles H. Kerr Publishing, 2003) 143–55, 134; "Joe Hill's Ashes Divided," *New York Times,* November 20, 1916, 22; William M. Adler, *The Man Who Never Died*, 340.

CHAPTER 12

1 "Agnes Thekla Fair Is Dead," *The Blast*, Vol. 2, No. 1, January 15, 1917, 6; Rosemont, *Joe Hill*, 299–304; Julia Ruuttila with Sandy Polishuk and Nancy Krieger, Interview, June 6, 1981, OHS ACC 28389—Equi. Camp, *Iron in Her Soul*, 17.

2 "I.W.W. Hold Rites," *Oregonian*, January 15, 1917, 8; "Agnes Fair At Rest; Red Flowers Bedeck Casket; IWW Sings," *Oregon Daily Journal*, January 15, 1917, 5.

3 "How to Struggle," *New Bedford Standard,* date uncertain, 1927.

4 "Lane Repudiated by Entire State," *Oregonian*, March 6, 1917, 1, 6; "Harry Lane Held Coward, Traitor," *Oregonian*, March 6, 1917, 5; "Lane County Deeply Stirred," *Oregonian*, March 6, 1917, 5; Johnston, *The Radical Middle Class*, 41–43; Jensen, *Oregon's Doctor to the World*, 122–23; Kennedy, *Over Here*, 74.

5 Dawley, *Changing the World*, 143–44; *Oregonian* reports on April 4, 1917: "Spies Honeycomb National Capitol," 1; "Gag on Enemies Wanted," 1; "Disloyal Cannot Parade," 1; "Today at Majestic Theater," 9; "Drill Taxes Club Gym," 9; "Monster Rally Is Held by Red Cross," 9. Christopher Capozzola, *Uncle Sam Wants You: World War I and the Making of the Modern American Citizen*, (Oxford: Oxford University Press, 2088), 3–20, introduction. Capozzola argues that Americans accepted and promoted "coercive voluntarism" before the war and were thus more likely to accept requirements for military conscription and war bond contributions during the war.

6 "Senate Adopts War Resolution," *Oregonian*, April 5, 1017, 1; "Senator Lane, Ill, Ordered to Rest," *Oregonian*, April 8, 1917; Johnston, *The Radical Middle Class*, 41–45; "High Officials to Pay Lane Tribute," *Oregonian*, May 28, 1917, 6.

7 Ellen Chesler, *Woman of Valor: Margaret Sanger and the Birth Control Movement in America* (New York: Anchor Books/Doubleday, 1993), 160–63; Sara Hunter Graham, *Woman Suffrage and the New Democracy* (New Haven: Yale University Press, 1996), 99–105, 128–46. Graham cites Leslie Fishbein, *Rebels in Bohemia: The Radicals of The Masses, 1911–1917* and Margaret C. Jones, *Heretics and Hellraisers: Women Contributors to the Masses, 1911–1917*. Graham acknowledges NAWSA's growth as an effective organization that nevertheless demoted spontaneity and democratic decision making, disengaged from militant demands

to seek greater economic equality, and marginalized immigrants, trade unionists, leftists, and ethnic minorities.

8 Olaf Larsell, *The Doctor in Oregon: A Medical History,* (Hillsboro, Oregon: Binfords & Mort, 1947) 614–18. Dr. K. A. J. Mackenzie established a base hospital unit through the Red Cross; Drs. M. B. Marcellus, R. H. Ellis, and Ray Matson were also in military service.; Kimberly Jensen, *Mobilizing Minerva: American Women in the First World War* (Chicago: University of Illinois Press, 2008) 77–87, 88–90; Lettie Gavin, *American Women in World War I: They Also Served* (Niwot, Colorado: University Press of Colorado, 1997) 157–74; Ellen S. More, "'A Certain Restless Ambition'": Women Physicians and World War I," *American Quarterly,* 41:4, (December 1989), 636–660; Jensen, *Oregon's Doctor,* 122–44.

9 Kennedy, *Over Here,* 184–85; "Yank Willingness to Rush Into Battle Shortens War," *Oregonian,* January 5, 1919, 6.

10 "Ireland Will Be Theme," *Oregonian,* May 19, 1917, 4; "British Militarism and Its Relation to Democracy," advertisement, *Oregonian,* June 8, 1917, 11; "Result of Attacks on Britain," (letter), May 24, 1917, 11; "Mrs. Skeffington's Protest Is Inopportune Says Rancher," *Oregonian,* June 13, 1917, 10. Photo of Equi with Irish Republic sign provided by the National Library of Ireland, MS 41, 511/1.

11 Geoffrey R. Stone, *Perilous Times: Free Speech in Wartime, From the Sedition Act of 1798 to the War on Terrorism* (New York: W.W. Norton & Co., 2004) 146–53.

12 Kennedy, *Disloyal Mothers,* 39–53; "Convict Berkman and Miss Goldman, Both Off To Prison," *New York Times,* July 10, 1917, query.nytimes.com accessed January 1, 2013.

13 Dawley, *Changing the World,* 148–150; Capozzola, *Uncle Sam Wants You,* 3–8.

14 Capazzola, *Uncle Sam Wants You,* 117– 43; Report of Agent William Bryon, May 25, 1917, DOJ Papers.

15 Tyler, *Rebels of the Woods,* 85–102; "Logging Work Is Hard Hit by IWW," *Oregonian,* August 3, 1917, 14; "National 8 Hour Day Bill Drafted," *Oregonian,* August 14, 1917, 4; "Propaganda Spread in City," *Oregonian,* July 31, 1917, 6; "Yakima Jail Is Crowded," and "19 Are Jailed at Moscow," both in *Oregonian,* July 17, 1917, 4; Kennedy, *Over Here,* 262–66; Robert Justin Goldstein, *Political Repression in Modern America: From 1870 to 1976* (University of Illinois: Champaign, Illinois, 2001), 115–16. "The U.S. Army Spruce Production Division Mill," Fort Vancouver National Historic Reserve, National Park Service, 2008.

16 "IWW Subject to Nation-wide Raid," *Oregonian,* September 6, 1917, 1; "Federal Raid Made on IWW Quarters," *Oregonian,* September 6, 1917, 4; Report of Agent Bryon, September 9, 1918, DOJ Papers. Raids on IWW offices also took place in Seattle, Los Angeles, Missoula, Salt Lake City, Fresno, Great Falls, Everett, Butte, Denver, and Miami, Arizona. "Blow at I.W.W.," *New York Times,* September 29, 1917, 1; "50 More Arrests in IWW Roundup," *New York Times,* September 30, 1917, nytimesquery.com, accessed January 6, 2013.

17 Testimony of Dan Kellaher, Judgment Roll #8099, FRC 20349x; Report of Agent Elton Watkins, October 23, 1917, DOJ Papers; Wayne E. Wiegand, "Oregon's Public Libraries during the First World War," *Oregon Historical Quarterly,* 90:1(Summer 1989): 45–55; US Attorney Reames to US Attorney General Davis, October 24, 1917, and Davis to Reames, October 25, 1917, DOJ Papers; Mary Equi McCloskey with Sandy Polishuk, Interview, May 1, 1971, OHS ACC 28389—Equi.

18 "Oregon Is First to Boost Loan Over," *Oregonian,* April 13, 1918, 1.

19 Stone, *Perilous Times,* 184–91; Gregory, as quoted in Kennedy, *Over Here,* 80–81. Note: Even former president Teddy Roosevelt objected to the Espionage Act amendments and threatened to test its provisions if passed. Stone, *Perilous Times,* 180; Hiram Johnson to C. K. McClatchey, April 11, 1918, as quoted in Kennedy, *Over Here.* For a full discussion of the Espionage and Sedition Acts during World War I, see Stone, *Perilous Times,* 136–233. The Sedition Act was repealed by Congress on December 13, 1920.

20 Judgment Roll, #8099, *United States v. Marie Equi,* Registrar No. 7968, Indictment, June 29, 1918.; US Attorney Bert Haney to US Attorney General, November 22, 1918, DOJ Papers.

21 Judgment Roll 8099, *United States v. Marie Equi,* Registrar No. 7068, Indictment, 29 June 1918; Report of Agent Byron, April 27, 1920, *United States v. Dr. Marie Equi,* DOJ Papers; "Dr. Equi

Obtains Bondsmen," *Oregonian,* July 1, 1918, 16; Report of Informant 53, August 30, 1918, DOJ Papers. (The relative value in 2015 of $10,000 ranges from $157,000 to more than two million dollars, depending on the calculation used, www.measuringworth.com) Katherine "Kitty" Beck was an intimate of C. E. S. Wood before she married Lloyd Irvine, MD, one of the doctors who had tried to rescue Equi from jail during the cannery strike of 1913.

22 Report of Agent Ralph Jones, July 1, 1918, DOJ Papers. Equi and Speckart lived at what is today 2214 SE Fifty-Second Avenue in the Mount Tabor district.

23 Stone. *Perilous Times,* 196–98; "Eugene Debs Arrested by Marshall," *San Francisco Examiner,* July 1, 1918, 1; "Find Debs Guilty of Disloyal Acts," *New York Times,* September 13, 1918. Stephen Martin Kohn, *American Political Prisoners: Prosecutions Under the Espionage and Sedition Acts* (Westport, Connecticut: Praeger Publishers, 1994), 97, 99. Equi's case and that of millionaire Henry Albers were the two most prominent espionage convictions in Oregon. Flora Foreman was the only other Oregon woman imprisoned for sedition. *War Time Prosecutions and Mob Violence from April 1, 1917 to March 1, 1919,* National Civil Liberties Bureau: New York, 1919, libcudl.colorado.edu accessed January 12, 2013; "Socialist Is Held," *Oregonian,* November 6, 1917, 7; "Albers Indicted By Federal Jury Upon Six Counts," *Oregon Daily Journal,* November 2, 1918.

24 Kennedy, *Disorderly Conduct,* 18–38 (O'Hare), 39–53 (Goldman), 54–68 (Stokes), 69–71 (Sadler), 71–79 (Olivereau), 90–92 (Strong), and 97–100 (Equi); Clarence Reames, US Attorney, as noted in E. Kimbark MacColl, *The Growth of A City: Power and Politics in Portland, Oregon, 1915 to 1950* (Portland, Oregon: Georgian Press, 1979), 145; Report of Agent William Bryon, June 28, 1917, National Archives Record Group 165, US MID, Surveillance of Radicals in the US, Washington, DC; William H. Thomas Jr., *Unsafe for Democracy: World War I and the U.S. Justice Department's Covert Campaign to Suppress Dissent* (Madison, Wisconsin: University of Wisconsin Press, 2008), 32–33, 60–62. The Portland bureau placed a female undercover agent, #50, among local women believed to be sympathetic to Germany. The Portland bureau chief also complained that it was impossible to meet all the demands of surveillance.

25 *New York Passenger Lists, 1820–1957, ancestry.com,* accessed January 14, 2013; "That Reminds Me," *Capuchin Annual,* 1936, 243; Letter of introduction, Marie Sweeney to Hon. John W. Willis, October 8, 1915, National Library of Ireland collection, MS 41,509 (1); "Miss O'Brennan Is Here for Short Stay," *San Francisco Chronicle,* October 23, 1916, 6; Agent E. W. Bryon Jr., May 31, 1918, Great Falls, Montana, File 209551, Roll 619, Microfilm 1085, National Archives, Washington, D.C.; A. Bruce Bielaski to Marlborough Churchill, June 12, 1918, Personal File 11436, MID, RG 165.

26 Report of Informant 53, September 14 and 21, 1918, DOJ Papers. Equi regularly purchased groceries and had them delivered to Harriet and Mary Jr. at their home on the Oregon coast.

27 Reports of Informant 53, August 28, 1918, and September 4, 1918, DOJ Papers.

28 Report of Agent William Bryon to A. Bruce Bielaski, December 14, 1918, DOJ Papers.

29 Report of Agent William Bryon, September 3, 1918, DOJ Papers. Equi apparently referred to the restaurant Progress as Musso's since she knew the proprietor Joseph Musso well. He and a partner founded the business in 1910 in Portland and later relocated it to Los Angeles where it continues today as *Musso & Frank Grill.*

30 Report of Informant 53, September 26, 1918, DOJ Papers. Equi apparently secured the union's support only after she enlisted the help of one of her brothers, an American Federation of Labor member in Washington, DC.

31 Montague Colmer and C. E. S. Wood. *History of the Bench and Bar in Oregon* (Portland, Oregon: Historical Publishing Company, 1910), 147; *Four Minute Men News,* December 24, 1918, and other documents, Thomas Gough Ryan Papers, MSS 1599, Oregon Historical Society Research Library. Oregon's *Four Minute Men* chapter also included Mayor Baker, former Governor Oswald West, Will Daly, and attorneys C. E. S. Wood, E. E. Heckbert, and Thomas Mannix.

32 Capozzola, *Uncle Sam Wants You,* 3–11; Report of Agent Elton Watkins, November 14, 1918; report of Agent E. H. Keller, n.d., DOJ Papers.

33 Reports of Agent Thomas B. Smith, October 25, 1918; Agent W. A. Winsor, October 24, 1918, Agent S. C. Schlein, October 24, 1918; Agent W. H. Bryon, September 9, 1918; Agent B. F. McCurdy of Spokane, September 15, 1918, and Agent A. R. Dutton of Seattle, September 16 1918, DOJ Papers. The report from the Thiele Detective Agency was most likely destroyed per company policy to purge files every six years. Agent A. R. Dutton report, September 17, 1918, DOJ Papers.

34 William H. Thomas Jr., *Unsafe for Democracy: World War One and the U.S. Justice Department's Covert Campaign to Suppress Dissent* (Madison: University of Wisconsin Press, 2008), 60–62.

35 Ibid. Report of Agent William Bryon, November 6 and September 9, 1918, Bryon to F. D. Simmons, September 9, 1918, DOJ Papers.

36 Report of Informant 53, November 1, 1918, DOJ Papers; "Ramp Convicted on Sedition Charges," *Oregonian*, February 2, 1918, 1. Floyd Ramp, a young farmer and Socialist from Roseburg, Oregon, was convicted for warning young army recruits they would be defending John D. Rockefeller's money.

37 Lowell S. Potts and Ralph Bushnell Hawley, *Counsel for the Damned: A Biography of George Francis Vanderveer* (Philadelphia: J. B. Lippincott Co., 1953), 236–39. Flynn, *The Rebel Girl*, 235–38. Flynn, Carlo Tresca, and a few others successfully severed their cases from the mass trial of Wobblies with the plan to tie up their cases in legal knots until the war ended. Their cases never went to trial.

38 Report of Informant 53, September 25, October 13, October 30 and November 5, 1918, DOJ Papers. "Dr. Equi Ill; Trial Is Put Over to Friday," *Oregon Daily Journal*, November 7, 1918, 3.

39 For more on the influenza pandemic, see Crosby, Alfred W. *America's Forgotten Pandemic: The Influenza of 1918*. 2nd ed. New York: Cambridge University Press, 2003.

40 "Portland Closed, Mayor Gets Order," *Oregonian*, October 11, 1918, 1; "Influenza Spreading in City and in State," *Oregonian*, October 18, 1918, 8; Ivan M. Wooley, "The 1918 'Spanish Influenza' Pandemic in Oregon," *Oregon Historical Quarterly* 64 (September, 1963): 246–58; "Soldier En Route to Training Camp May Be Influenza Victim," *Oregon Daily Journal*, October 4, 1918, 4; "Influenza Encyclopedia: The American Influenza Epidemic of 1918–1919, Portland, Oregon," University of Michigan Center for the History of Medicine and Publishing, University of Michigan, quod.lib.umich.edu accessed on January 21, 2013; Report of Informant 53, October 30, 1918, DOJ Papers.

41 Report of Informant 53, November 12, 1918, DOJ Papers. Portland's federal courthouse at the time of Equi's trial is known today as the Pioneer Courthouse.

42 Ibid. November 6, 7, 1918.

43 "Nation Victim of Heartless Hoax," *Oregonian*, November 8, 1918, 1; "Armistice Is Signed, World War Is Over," *Oregonian*, November 11, 1918, 1; "Looking Back," *Oregon Daily Journal*, November 18, 1918, 10.

CHAPTER 13

1 http://kimberlyjensenblog.blogspot.com/2011/08/oregon-attorney-generals-decision.html, accessed February 4, 2013. Jensen notes that Oregon's attorney general ruled that the 1912 adoption of woman suffrage in Oregon did not qualify women to serve on juries in the state; Charles Henry Carey, *History of Oregon* (Chicago: Pioneer Historical Publishing Co., 1922) 908. Oregon voters approved jury service for women on June 7, 1921; "Lumber Trust Wins," *The Defense Bulletin of Seattle District*, No. 39, December 1, 1918, 5.

2 Report of Agent Madge Paul for November 8, 9, and 10, 1918, DOJ Papers.

3 "Armistice Is Signed, World War Is Over," *Oregonian*, November 11, 1918, 1; "Looking Back," *Oregon Daily Journal*, November 18, 1918, 10; Report of Agent Madge Paul for November 11, 1918, DOJ Papers; "Armistice is Signed, World War Is Over," *Oregonian*, November 11, 1918, 1; "Biggest Day in History Breaks," *Oregonian*, November 12, 1918, 1.

4 *A Bill of Exception*, February 27, 1919, Judgment Roll #8099, US District Court Oregon, Seattle Federal Archives and Records Center, Record Group 21. Writers from several Socialist and anarchist publications around the country attended Equi's trial as well.

5 Testimony of Russell E. Butler and Dan Kellaher, *A Bill of Exception*, February 27, 1919.

6 "Dr. Equi In Tears On Stand," *Oregon Daily Journal*, November 19, 1918, 1; "Dr. Equi Is Accused of Boosting I.W.W.," *Oregonian*, November 14, 1918, 8.

7 "Dr. Equi In Tears On Stand," *Oregon Daily Journal*, November 19, 1918, 1.

8 When Equi directed O'Brennan to ask Governor West to testify on her behalf, she indicated she had information that would compel him to speak, according to the report of Agent Bryon for April 26, 1920, DOJ Papers. Bryon's summary report on Equi was based on information obtained from Informant 53. Report of Agent A. E. McMahon for November 13, 1918, DOJ Papers. A government agent asked the French consul in Portland and the director of the department of nursing for the American Red Cross whether Equi had ever applied for volunteer placement. Each reported having no knowledge or record of such an application.

9 "Editor Testifies for Dr. Marie Equi," *Oregonian*, November 15, 1918, 1.

10 "Dr. Equi To Take Witness Stand On Own Behalf," *Oregon Daily Journal*, November 16, 1918, 2.

11 "Dr. Equi To Take Witness Stand On Own Behalf," *Oregon Daily Journal*, November 16, 1918, 2; "Ex-Governor West Recalled To Stand," *Oregonian*, November 16, 1918, 7; "Editor Testifies for Dr. Marie Equi," *Oregonian*, November 15, 1918, 1.

12 "Dr. Equi In Tears on Stand," *Oregon Daily Journal*, November 19, 1918, 1; "Wilson Her Model Dr. Equi Asserts," *Oregonian*, November 19, 1918, 1.

13 "Dr. Equi In Tears on Stand," *Oregon Daily Journal*, November 19, 1918, 1.

14 Ibid, "Wilson Her Model Dr. Equi Asserts," *Oregonian*, November 19, 1918, 1.

15 "Dr. Equi In Tears on Stand," *Oregon Daily Journal*, November 19, 1918, 1.

16 Report of Agent Madge Paul for November 18, 19, and 20, 1918. Equi gave Paul a book of poetry by C. E. S Wood in an odd gesture of friendship to someone who had betrayed her. The Bureau later arranged a safe house in Portland for Paul and then escorted her to her ranch in Trout Lake, Washington.

17 "Equi Case Will Reach Jury Today," *Oregon Daily Journal*, November 20, 1918, 1; "Jury to Decide Fate of Dr. Marie Equi," *Oregonian*, November 21, 1918, 12; Flynn, *The Rebel Girl*, 252.

18 *Instructions, R.S. Bean, D.J.*, Judgment Roll #8099, FRC 20349x, US District Court Oregon, Seattle Federal Archives and Records Center, Record Group 21.

19 "Dr. Equi Is Guilty of Disloyalty," *Oregon Daily Journal*, November 21, 1918, 1; "Jury Finds Dr. Equi Guilty of Treason," *Oregonian*, November 22, 1918, 12.

20 "Dr. Equi Is Guilty of Disloyalty," *Oregon Daily Journal*, November 21, 1918, 1. Equi's "Russian Jew" reference is curious and problematic, given her own heritage as a child of immigrants and her association with Emma Goldman, born to Jewish parents, and with many other Jews in her political and social circles.

21 Ibid.; "Jury Finds Dr. Equi Guilty of Treason," *Oregonian*, November 22, 1918, 12.

22 Reports of Agents M. J. Doyle and W. M. Hudson for December 5, 1918, (with announcement flyer) DOJ Papers; "Equi Appeal Asked," *Oregonian*, December 22, 1918, 7; *I.W.W. Summary for Week Ending November 14, 1918*, Intelligence Office, US Army, December 14, 1918, DOJ Papers.

23 "Dr. Equi Gets 3 Years and Fine of $500," *Oregon Daily Journal*, December 31, 1918, 1.

24 "Dr. Equi Sentenced To 3 Years In Prison," *Oregonian*, January 1, 1919, 14; "Prison for Woman Under Espionage Act," *San Francisco Chronicle*, January 1, 1919, 5. Judge Bean quote from Carolyn M. Buan, ed., *The First Duty: A History of the US District Court for Oregon*, (Portland: US District Court of Oregon Historical Society, 1992), 156–57; Stephen P. Kohn, *American Political Prisoners, Prosecutions Under the Espionage and Sedition Acts*, (Westport, Connecticut: Praeger Publishers, 1994), 83–114. See Kathleen Kennedy, *Disloyal Mothers and Scurrilous Citizens, Women and Subversion during World War I* (Bloomington: Indiana University Press, 1999) for profiles of several women tried under the wartime acts.

25 Report of Agent Bryon, April 3, 1919, DOJ Papers. For several months thereafter, Agent Bryon took to defaming Equi, referring to her as "the above named creature" in one report to headquarters; Mary Equi McCloskey with Sandy Polishuk, Interview, May 1, 1971, OHS ACC 28389—Equi; "Dr. Equi Gets 3 Years and Fine of $500," *Oregon Daily Journal*, December 31, 1918, 1.

CHAPTER 14

1 "Great Record Is Established in 1918," *Oregonian*, January 1, 1919, 1.

2 Kohn, *American Political Prisoners*, 17–18.

3 Flynn, *The Rebel Girl*, 90; C. E. S. Wood letter to Palmer, April 28, 1919, as cited in Hamburger, *Two Rooms*, 268–71. The appeal process was underway in early 1919; on February 27 a district judge granted the filing of a *writ of error*, followed by a *Bill of Exceptions*, and receipt by the court of a $10,000 bond from Equi, Katherine Irvine (a friend who worked in the office of C. E. S. Wood), Alys Griff, and P. H. Dunn. The plaintiffs were charged to appear before the Ninth Circuit Court within ninety days.

4 "Labor condemns William R. Bryon," *Oregonian*, January 9, 1919, 1; Report of Agent Bryon for September 3, 1919, DOJ Papers; "Woman Denies Treason Charge," *San Francisco Chronicle*, February 14, 1919, 2; "Miss O'Brennan Arrested," *Oregonian*, January 16, 1919, 12. Reports suggested several IWW members objected to admitting Equi and O'Brennan since they were not wage earners.

5 "IWW Affiliation Denied," *Oregonian*, January 22, 1919, 10. Adam J. Hodges, "At War Over the Espionage Act in Portland," *Oregon Historical Quarterly*, 108:3, (Fall 2007), 474–86. In their own realms, O'Brennan and Agent Bryon argued vastly different versions of the IWW and free speech conflicts in Portland.

6 Kohn, *American Political Prisoners*, 20–21.

7 "Dr. Equi Is Re-Arrested," *Oregonian*, March 14, 1919, 11; "Dr. Marie Equi Released," *Oregonian*, March 15, 1919, 9; Adam J. Hodges, "Thinking Globally, Acting Locally: The Portland Soviet and the Emergence of American Communism, 1918–1920," *The Pacific Northwest Quarterly*, 98:3 (Summer, 2007), 115–29. "H. M. Wicks Quits as Leader of Radicals," *Oregonian*, March 1, 1919, 9. Two weeks earlier H. M. Wicks, the leader of the Council of Workmen, Soldiers, and Sailors of Portland and Vicinity (a leftist group of Wobblies, Socialists, and WWI veterans modeled after a Bolshevik soviet) had resigned his post to protest the more radical sentiment of members; he especially identified his disgust with a talk given by Equi.

8 Report of Agent Bryon for March 30, April 1, May 6, and May 11, 1919; "Equi's Talk Banned," *Oregonian*, May 12, 1919, 4; Equi was to speak at Eagles Hall located at 568 Golden Gate Avenue; instead she spoke at 1254 Market Street.

9 The Oakland appearance was reported in the *Oakland World News*. Charlotte Anita Whitney to Attorney General Palmer, telegram, May 30, 1919, DOJ Papers; Ellen Chesler, *Woman of Valor: Margaret Sanger and the Birth Control Movement in America*, (New York: Doubleday, 2007), 172–73.

10 "Dr. Equi with Wilson, Says Her Attorney," *Oakland Tribune*, June 7, 1919, 3; bioguide. congress.gov for William W. Morrow, accessed February 17, 2013.

11 "Brief for Plaintiff in Error," *Equi v. United States*, US Circuit Court of Appeals for the Ninth Circuit, No. 3328; Hamburger, *Two Rooms*, 271–75.

12 "Rhuberg Verdict Upheld," *Oregonian*, February 27, 1919, 12; *Schenck v. United States*, 249 U.S. 47; C. E. S. Wood, *Free Speech and the Constitution in the War* (privately printed by Wood in 1920), as quoted in Hamburger, *Two Rooms*, 271–75; "Sedition Laws Invalid, C. E. S. Wood Asserts," *Oregonian*, June 7, 1919, 1. For further discussion of *Schenck v. United States*, Stone, *Perilous Times*, 192–95.

13 "Brief of Defendant in Error," *Marie Equi v. United States*, US Circuit Court of Appeals for the Ninth Circuit, No. 3328.

14 Equi spoke in Seattle at the ILA Hall for the meeting sponsored by the Soldiers and Sailors organization. Content.lib.washington.edu accessed February 19, 2013.

15 Ruth Barnett, *They Weep On My Doorstep* (Beaverton, Oregon: Halo Publishers, 1969), 16–19.

16 Dale Soden, "The Women's Christian Temperance Union in the Pacific Northwest: The Battle for Cultural Control," *Pacific Northwest Quarterly* 94, no. 4 (Fall 2003), 197–207. Soden emphasizes that the WCTU sought to enact a broad range of social reforms that would reshape the West's saloon culture dominated by male interests into community life free of social evils, especially for women and children.

17 Alfred Bettman to Mr. Porter, May 12, 1919, DOJ Papers. Bettman also noted that the "whole community seems to have divided sharply and with extreme opinions one way or the other," a characteristic he found typical of the Pacific Northwest. "Dr. Equi Jail Term Sentence Upheld," *Oregonian*, October 28, 1919, 2; "'We're Slaves,' Says Convicted Dr. Equi," *Oregonian*, November 1, 1919, 9.

18 Equi to C. E. S. Wood, letter, March 3, 1920, Huntington Library Collection, WD 135 (47). The author appreciates the assistance of Dona Munker in identifying this document. State Bar of Wisconsin, "Pioneers in the Law: The First 150 Women," www.wisbar. og/AM/Template.cfm?Section=History_of_the_Profession&TEMPLATE=/CFM/ ContentDisplay.cfm&CONTENTID=21490 (accessed May 26, 2006). From 1918 to 1920, Greeley obtained rank for army nurses in her role as counsel of the National Committee to Secure Rank for Army Nurses. *Marie Equi v. United States of America*, No. 666, October Term, 1919, File No. 27,421. In his brief for review by the US Supreme Court, Wood noted that the Ninth Circuit Court's admission of acts prior to the wartime laws differed from rulings by the Seventh and Eighth Circuit Courts.

19 "Prison Special," noted in Flynn, *The Rebel Girl*, 278.

20 Tom Copeland, "Wesley Everest, IWW Martyr," *The Pacific Northwest Quarterly*, Vol. 77, No. 4 (October, 1986) 122–29; "Radical Lynched by Centralia Mob," and "Centralia Reds Fire on Parade," *Oregonian*, November 12, 1919, 1; "20 Radicals Taken in 6 Portland Raids," *Oregonian*, January 3, 1920, 1.

21 Mary Equi McCloskey with Sandy Polishuk, Interview, May 1, 1971, OHS ACC 28389—Equi; "Vanderveer Found Guilty Second Time," *Oregonian*, May 2, 1920, 8; Wm. D. Haywood, General Defense Committee, to Kathleen O'Brennan, August 16, 1920, DOJ Papers; Adam J. Hodges, "At War Over the Espionage Act in Portland," *Oregon Historical Quarterly*, 108:3, (Fall, 2007), 474–86; Marie Equi to Hannah Sheehy-Skeffington, May 11, 1920, National Library of Ireland, Hannah Sheehy-Skeffington Papers, MS 22.691 (ii); "Soldiers Take Down Flag of De Valera," *Oregonian*, November 15, 1919, 4.

22 "Petition for Writ of Certiorari," *Marie Equi, Petitioner v. United States,* Supreme Court of the United States, No. 666, October Term, 1919; Record Group 267, US Supreme Court, Case File 27421, Folder 1, tabbed, Box 6509, 17E06/03/03; "Dr. Equi Loses Fight Against Term in Prison," *San Francisco Chronicle*, January 27, 1920, 3; "Equi Appeal Denied By Supreme Court, *Oregonian*, January 27, 1920, 3; "Upholds 3 Espionage Convictions," *New York Times*, January 26, 1920.

23 Equi to Tumulty, San Quentin State Prison, 29: Inmate Case Files 1890–1958, Folder F3750:1–800, Commitment number 34110, 1920, California State Archives, Sacramento, California.

24 Ibid.

25 "Friends Ask Wilson to Pardon Dr. Equi," *Oregonian,* February 10, 1920, 4. Clark was the former wife of prominent Oregon politician and attorney A. E. Clark. Thomas Gough Ryan, Attorney, to President Wilson, December 26, 1919, Thomas Gough Ryan Papers, MSS 1599, file 16, Oregon Historical Society Research Library.

26 Isom to Tumulty, February 6, 1920, DOJ Papers; Wayne Wiegand, "Oregon's Public Libraries During the First World War," *Oregon Historical Quarterly*, 90:1 (Spring, 1989), 39–63; Sargeant Cram to Attorney General Palmer, March 13, 1920, DOJ Papers.

27 Report of Agent Bryon for April 2, 1920, 11, DOJ Papers; J. Edgar Hoover to Mr. Grimes, April 20, 1920, DOJ Papers; Report of Agent Bryon for April 26, 1920; J. Edgar Hoover to Mr. Ruch, April 27, 1921, DOJ Papers. J. Edgar Hoover to Mr. Grimes, April 20, 1920, DOJ Papers; Report of Agent Bryon for April 26, 1920; J. Edgar Hoover to Mr. Ruch, April 27, 1921, DOJ Papers. Athan G. Theoharis and John Stuart Cox, *The Boss: J. Edgar Hoover and the Great American Inquisition* (Philadelphia: Temple University Press, 1988), 108; Rhodi Jeffreys-Jones, *Cloak and Dollar: A History of American Secret Intelligence* (New Haven: Yale University Press, 2003), 93; Warren Johansson and Percy William, *Outing: Shattering the Silence* (Binghamton, NY: The Haworth Press, 1994), 85–88.

28 Helen Hoy Greeley to Elizabeth Gurley Flynn, letter, July 9 and July 24, 1920, uncertain source; records provided to author by the Office of Pardon Attorney, US Department of Justice. Reprieves to Equi were granted on April 17, June 12, and August 13, 1920; Correspondence, the White House (a representative for Mrs. Wilson) to Mrs. Ina B. Hayes. August 30, 1920, National Library of Ireland, .MS 41, 511/2; William Haywood to Kathleen M. O'Brennan, August 16, 1920. National Library of Ireland, MS, 41, 511/2. Kathleen O'Brennan requested financial assistance from the General Defense Committee of the IWW, but William Haywood sent his regrets, stating the committee was already overwhelmed with helping one thousand men awaiting trial.

29 Helen Hoy Greeley to Marie Equi, April 21, 1921, DOJ Papers. Copy of Commutation document provided by the Office of the Pardon Attorney, US Department of Justice, Washington, DC, to the author; "Dr. Equi Term Cut by Wilson," *Oregonian*, October 14, 1920, 1.

30 "Sentence of Dr. Equi Cut to One Year," *Oregon Daily Journal*, October 14, 1920, 1; "Dr. Equi Surrenders to Begin Sentence," *Oregonian,* October 16, 1920, 6; "Dr. Equi Smilingly Starts for Prison," *Oregonian*, October 18, 1920, 1.

31 "Dr. Equi Is Asked to Appear Today," *Oregonian*, October 15, 1920, 22.

32 "Dr. Equi To Be Taken to San Quentin," *Oregon Daily Journal*, October 15, 1920, 1; "Dr. Marie Equi Escorted To Her Cell" (photo caption), *Oregon Daily Journal*, October 16, 1920, 1; "Dr. Equi Surrenders To Begin Sentence," *Oregonian,* October 16, 1921, 6; "Dr. Equi Leaves for Penitentiary," *La Tribuna Italiana*, October 22, 1920, 2; "Jail Door Clicks on Dr. Marie Equi," *Oregon Daily Journal*, October 16, 1920, 1. The author thanks Kimberly Jensen for sharing a copy of the article in *La Tribuna Italiana*.

33 "Dr. Equi Smilingly Starts for Prison," *Oregonian*, October 18, 1920, 3.

CHAPTER 15

1 "Equi Conviction Rapped," *Oregonian*, October 18, 1920, 5.

2 "Dr. Equi Sighs For Girl," *Oregonian*, November 21, 1920, 20.

3 Nancy Ann Nichols, *San Quentin Inside the Walls* (San Quentin, California: San Quentin Museum Press, 1991), 22–24; *Register and Descriptive List of Convicts Under Sentence of Imprisonment in the State Prison of California*, Registration, MF: 1–9 (15) roll 6, California State Archives, Sacramento; *Topical Mug Books Ca. 1916–1943*, Inventory of Department of Justice Criminal ID and Investigation Records, Crime Category: Miscellaneous, Folder 3672:54:IWW; Mary Equi McCloskey with Sandy Polishuk, Interview, May 1, 1971, OHS ACC 28389—Equi.

4 "San Quentin More Like Cloister Than Prison, Is Impression of Dr. Equi," *Portland Evening Telegram*, August 31, 1921, 1; George C. Henderson, "The Caged Woman," *Oakland Tribune*, Sunday feature section, April 17, 1921; Estelle B. Freedman, *Their Sisters' Keepers, Women's Prison Reform in America, 1830–1930* (Ann Arbor: University of Michigan Press, 1981), 9–15.

5 Marie Equi to Kathleen O'Brennan, January 10, 1921, *Papers of Kathleen O'Brennan*, MS 41, 509/1 1911–1919, National Library of Ireland; Marie Equi to Sara Bard Field, December 27, 1920, C. E. S. Wood Collection, The Huntington Library Collection, WD 135 (51). The author thanks Dona Munker for identifying this document.

6   1920 US Census, California, Marin, San Quentin township, Enumeration District 88, State
     Prison; Marie Equi to Kathleen O'Brennan, January 10, 1921, *Papers of Kathleen O'Brennan*,
     MS 41, 509/1 1911–1919, National Library of Ireland.

7   George C. Henderson, "The Caged Woman," *Oakland Tribune*, Feature Section, April 17,
     1921.

8   Henderson, "The Caged Woman." *The Sunday Oregonian* published an excerpted version of
     this article. "Dr. Equi 'Joy-Bringer,'" *Oregonian*, February 20, 1921, 14.

9   Equi's prison letters are included in the DOJ Papers.

10 Bureau Chief to Special Agent E. M. Blanford, San Francisco office, March 22, 1921 and
     Blanford to Bureau Chief, Headquarters, April 5, 1921, DOJ Papers. The department's
     collection of Equi's letters spans the period from March 21 to July 26, 1921. J. E. Hoover to
     Mr. Ruch, April 27, 1921, DOJ Papers.

11 Teresa Valli to Marie Equi, n.d., probably in spring 1921; Mary Vanni to Marie Equi, March
     21, 1921; Marie Equi to Constance M. Loftus, April 5, 1921; Mrs. Vincent (Kate) Vanni to
     Marie Equi, April 20, 1921; Marie Equi to Mrs. J.C. Gay, April 7, 1921, May 3, 1921; Mrs.
     J.C. Gay to Marie Equi, March 30, 1921, May 20, 1921, June 20, 1921, all in DOJ Papers.

12 Harriet Speckart to Marie Equi, May 21, 1921, DOJ Papers.

13 Marie Equi to Harriet Speckart, May 10, 1921, DOJ Papers; Harriet Speckart to Marie Equi,
     April 1, 1921, April 3, 1921, May 18, 1921, and May 21, 1921, DOJ Papers.

14 Marie Equi to Harriet Speckart, May 22, 1921, DOJ Papers.

15 Marie Equi to Mary Jr. Equi, April 4, 1921, April 6, 1921, April 9, 1921, April 21, 1921,
     May 1, 1921, and May 22, 1921, DOJ Papers. Kate Richards O'Hare referred to prisons as
     "Cities of Sorrow" in her account of doing time, *In Time*, (New York: A.A. Knopf, 1923),
     Dedication.

16 Marie Equi to Mary Equi Jr., April 21, 1921 (mistakenly transcribed as "1920"), Marie Equi
     to Mary Equi Jr., April 9, 1921, DOJ Papers.

17 Marie Equi to Mary Equi Jr., April 9, 1921, DOJ Papers.

18 Marie Equi to Mrs. George Warner/Kitty O'Brennan, April 24, 1921; Marie Equi to Mr.
     Whitaker, April 1, 1921, DOJ Papers.

19 Ruth Barnett to Marie Equi, March 28, 1921; Margaret Sanger to Marie Equi, June 12,
     1921; Margaret Sanger to Marie Equi, April 9, 1921, DOJ Papers.

20 Marie Equi to Sara Bard Field, May 29, 1921, C. E. S. Wood Collection, Huntington Library
     Collection, WD 135 (53).

21 Marie Equi to Charlotte Anita Whitney, April 13, 1921, DOJ Papers; Lisa Rubens, "The
     Patrician Radical, Charlotte Anita Whitney," *California History*, Vol. LXV, No. 3 (September
     1986), 161.

22 Al Richmond, *Native Daughter: The Story of Anita Whitney* (San Francisco: Anita Whitney
     Seventy-Fifth Anniversary Committee, 1942), 90–140; Carol E. Jensen, "Silencing Critics:
     Guilt by Association in the 1920s," in *Historic U.S. Court Cases: An Encyclopedia,* John
     W. Johnson, editor (New York: Routledge, 2001), 850–53; Lisa Rubens, "The Patrician
     Radical, Charlotte Anita Whitney," *California History*, Vol. 65, No. 3 (September 1986),
     158–71; Al Richmond, *Native Daughter,* 90–140; Charlotte Anita Whitney to Marie Equi,
     May 6 and May 22, 1921, DOJ Papers.

23 Irene Benton to Marie Equi, March 27, 1921, DOJ Papers.

24 Mark R. Avramo to Marie Equi, March 31 and April 8, 1921; Equi to Avramo, May 20,
     1921; all DOJ Papers.

25 Marie Equi to Sophie Gay, April 7, 1921, DOJ Papers; *Los Angeles Times*, November 19,
     1914, 10, in which the Ninety-six Club was composed of "queer" people and that "at these
     'drags,' the 'queer' people have a good time." Also, a 1914 reference in the *Journal of History
     of Sexuality*, 1995, 5, 593, with "Fourteen young men were invited . . . with the premise that
     they would have the opportunity of meeting some of the prominent 'queers.'" Thanks to
     George Painter for sharing his research on the terminology.

26 Marie Equi to Charlotte Anita Whitney, May 8, 1921. DOJ Papers. Bessie Holcomb Cook
    lived with her family at 301 Lyon Street in San Francisco. Her children were Alexander,
    Clare, and Elizabeth. The building today is a San Francisco Historic Landmark, known as
    the "Clunie Mansion," after the first owner. The homestead property was sold on October
    15, 1945, to Ross and Alice Ornduff for $500. Deed Records, Wasco County Courthouse,
    The Dalles, Oregon, A. Cook (grantor) to R. and A. Ornduff. As an adult, William Allen
    White, "Billy," became a mystery writer and a science fiction editor for the *San Francisco
    Chronicle*, and he founded the *Magazine of Fantasy & Science Fiction*. After his death in 1968,
    the annual Bouchercon convention of mystery writers was established in his honor. Phyllis
    White and Lawrence White, *Boucher: A Family Portrait* (Berkeley: Berkeley Historical
    Society, 1985). Marie Equi to Mary Equi Jr., May 15, 1921, DOJ Papers.

27 Marie Equi to KT, April 2, 1921, DOJ Papers.

28 Marie Equi to Mrs. Marion F. Wall, May 2, 1921, DOJ Papers; Marie Equi, Letter to the
    Editor, *Oregon Daily Journal*, April 28, 1921, 2.

29 Marie Equi to Mrs. Marion "Molly" Wall, May 1, 1921, DOJ Papers.

30 Press Release, Workers Defense Union, Room 405, 7 East Fifteenth Street, New York.
    The text of Flynn's telegram to Equi was included in the document. Workers Defense
    Union, Press Release, no date but refers to Equi beginning her sentence today—she did
    so on October 19, 1920. Margaret Sanger to Marie Equi, April 9, 1921, DOJ Papers; "Irish
    Flag Adorns Desk of Tumulty," *Washington Times*, November 18, 1920, 2. The previous
    December Dr. Kelly was arrested while marching against the imprisonment of antiwar
    dissenters.

31 Testimony of Helen Hoy Greeley, *Amnesty and Pardon for Political Prisoners*, US Senate,
    Subcommittee of the Committee on the Judiciary, Washington, DC, 41–44. Greeley said
    that a Department of Justice representative inadvertently told her that a pardon for Equi had
    been recommended by the department's pardon staff but that the US attorney general had
    decided not to follow the advice. The full text of the committee hearings are available online
    at http://archive.org/details/amnestyandpardo00stergoog, accessed March 15, 2013.

32 http://archive.org/details/amnestyandpardo00stergoog, accessed March 15, 2013. Of the
    total cases, 581 resulted in convictions, 736 had been otherwise disposed, and 315 remained
    pending. Attorney General Palmer also testified that as of January 15, 1921, a total of 17,900
    cases under the wartime acts had been handled by the department. Nearly 16,000 of these
    were for alleged offenses under the Selective Service Act.

33 Newly elected presidents were inaugurated on March 20 in the year following their election
    until the ratification of the Twentieth Amendment to the US Constitution in 1933.
    Thereafter, Inauguration Day was set for January 20. Also note: The parole of any federal
    inmate, whether incarcerated in a federal or state prison, must be approved by the US
    attorney general. *AGSRP*, 1939, US Department of Justice.

34 "Freedom Coming for Marie Equi," *Oregon Daily Journal*, May 29, 1921, 2; Ruth Barnett,
    They Weep On My Doorstep, 18. The parole request required notarized signatures from
    individuals supporting the application and proof of Equi's former employment. Marie Equi
    to Marion Wall, April 1, 1921, and Marie Equi to Charlotte Anita Whitney, April 7, 1921,
    DOJ Papers.

35 J. Edgar Hoover to Mr. Ruch, April 27, 1921, and J. Edgar Hoover to Mr. Smith, April 29,
    1921, DOJ Papers; W. Grimes to J. Edgar Hoover, April 1921, DOJ Papers.

36 "Billy" to Marie Equi, April 11, 1921, and James E. Fenton to Marie Equi, April 26, 1921,
    DOJ Papers.

37 Marie Equi to Marcella Clark, April 29, 1921, and Jonathan Bourne Jr. to James E. Fenton,
    April 20, 1921, DOJ Papers.

38 "Henry J. Albers Faces Court on Espionage Charge," *San Francisco Chronicle*, January 25,
    1919, 3; "The Albers Case," *Sunday Oregon Journal*, May 8, 1921, 4; "Who Would Try
    Second Albers Case?" *Oregon Daily Journal*, May 8, 1921, 1.

39 "Protests Pile Up Over Albers Case," *Oregonian*, May 6, 1921; "Legion Men Demand
    Retrial of Albers," *Oregonian*, April 29, 1921, 11; Portland Federation of Churches to H. M.

Daugherty," May 20, 1921, DOJ Papers; "She Wants To Get Out Too," *Oregon Daily Journal*, April 28, 1921, 1.

40 "Not Ended, Says Humphreys," *Oregonian*, April 28, 1921, 1; Charlotte Anita Whitney to Marie Equi, May 4, 1921, DOJ Papers; Marie Equi to Charlotte Anita Whitney, May 8, 1921, DOJ Papers; Bud Warner to Marie Equi, June 23, 1921, DOJ Papers; "Paralysis Fatal to J. Henry Albers," *New York Times*, July 29, 1921. Attorney Haney resigned his post in 1920. His successor, Lester Humphreys, declared his intention to re-try Albers until the latter's worsening condition made such an action untenable.

41 Marie Equi to Charlotte Anita Whitney, May 8, 1921; Marie Equi to Mrs. A. E. Clark, April 8, 1921, DOJ Papers; Marie Equi to Hannah Sheehy-Skeffington, March 24, 1938, National Library of Ireland, Hannah Sheehy-Skeffington Papers, MS 41, 177 (16).

42 Marie Equi to Mrs. A.E. Clark, June 13, 1921, DOJ Papers.

43 Marie Equi to Charlotte Anita Whitney, May 8, 1921; Marie Equi to C. E. S. Wood, May 9, 1921, DOJ Papers; Chief, Bureau of Investigation, to Agent Bryon, June 17, 1921; Marie Equi to Marcella Clark, June 13, 1921, DOJ Papers; "Prisoner on Parole, Case No. 5371," Federal Bureau of Prisons. A month after Equi was released from prison, the attorney general returned the papers to his staff who noted on an attached memorandum, "No action as term had expired."

44 *Attorney General's Survey of Release Practices (AGSRP), Volumes 1 and 4*, 1939, US Department of Justice. Good-time credits were liberalized and graduated to increase with the length of sentence in 1902 with five days allowed for sentences of up to one year and six days for a sentence of one to three years. Email communication, Archives of Office of Public Affairs of the Federal Bureau of Prisons with the author, February 18, 2004. Equi earned a six-day reduction for every month of her sentence, thus her twelve-month sentence accrued seventy-two days of good time. Marie Equi to Charlotte Anita Whitney, May 8, 1921, DOJ Papers.

45 Marie Equi to Mrs. A. E. Clark, June 13, 1921, DOJ Papers; Marie Equi to Alys Griff, June 24, 1921, DOJ Papers.

46 Marie Equi to Mrs. A.E. Clark, July 17, 1921, DOJ Papers; Marie Equi to Mrs. Marion "Molly" Wall, July 26, 1921, DOJ Papers.

47 *Congressional Series Set*, US Government Printing Office, January 1922, 125 www.books. google.com, accessed June 14, 2012.

CHAPTER 16

1 "Woman Pacifist Cheered As She Leaves Prison," *San Francisco Call*, August 31, 1921, 3. Whitney rented an apartment at what was then 58 Macondray Lane from June through August 1921. The address was later changed and is number 60 today. She later purchased the building at 74 Macondray Lane and lived there for many years. Macondray Lane served as the inspiration for the fictional Barbary Lane in Armistead Maupin's *Tales of the City* in a *San Francisco Chronicle* serial in the 1980s and later in several novels, a television series, and a stage musical.

2 "San Quentin Life Is 'Snap,'" *Oakland Tribune*, August 29, 1921, 1. Hamburger, *Two Rooms*, 287–92. Wood purchased the house at 1020 Broadway in 1919; it is still standing. Marie Equi to Sara Bard Field, April 3, 1921, C. E. S. Wood Collection, Huntington Library, WE 135 (52).

3 Estelle B. Freedman, *Their Sisters' Keepers: Women's Prison Reform in America, 1830–1930* (Ann Arbor: University of Michigan Press, 1981), 67–106. Freedman describes how these first women-centered prisons failed to meet expectations due to the difficulty in recruiting suitable staff, the influence of administrators who were less liberal in their prison philosophy, and the relatively small numbers of prime candidates for the prisons.

4 "San Quentin Life Is 'Snap,'" *Oakland Tribune*, August 29, 1921, 1. The article was accompanied by a photo of Equi smiling. The report was also published in the *Portland Evening Telegram*, August 31, 1921, 1. "Rouge Aplenty Used in Jail," *New Bedford Evening Standard* , September 12, 1921.

5   Equi wrote to several friends and allies about prison reform, including to her cousin Marion
    Wall, April 1, 1921; Rev. Robert Whitaker, April 1, 1921; activist Lena Morrow Lewis, April
    8, 1921; radical Anna Louise Strong, May 9, 1921, and her friend Mrs. Sheldon Coons, May
    9, 1921, all in DOJ Papers.

6   Freedman, *Their Sister's Keepers,* 121–2. The California legislature approved farm facilities
    for women prisoners in 1919 (California Penal Code, 4100–4137). Cyndi Banks, *Women in
    Prison: A Reference Handbook* (ABC-CLIO, 2003), Google eBook, 24-27, books.google.com,
    accessed October 30, 2013; "Report Work on State Industrial Farm for Women, *Berkeley
    Daily Gazette,* January 4, 1923, 4; "Women Prisoners Become Home-Makers on State
    "Ranch,'" *San Francisco News,* September 11, 1934; "Dr. Equi Donates Turkeys to Women at
    San Quentin," *Oregon Daily Journal,* December 25, 1930, 1.

7   "Law Violators Given Warning by Daugherty," *Oakland Tribune,* August 31, 1921; Albert
    F. Gunns, *Civil Liberties in Crisis: The Pacific Northwest 1917–1940* (New York: Garland
    Publishers, 1983), 63.

8   "Prison Found Refuge After 'Persecution,'" *Portland Evening Telegram,* September 24, 1921,
    1; "Dr. Marie Equi in City," *Oregonian,* September 24, 1921, 8; Marie Equi to Mrs. Sheldon
    Coons, May 9, 1921, DOJ Papers; Transcript, Mary Equi, from Jewell Preparatory in
    Seaside, Oregon, to Lincoln High School in Portland, 1929, information provided by the
    alumni director of Lincoln High School, January 13, 2004.

9   "No Danger Here—Baker," *Oregonian, November 13, 1919,* 7; Robert L. Tyler, *Rebels of the
    Woods: The IWW in the Pacific Northwest* (Eugene, Oregon: University of Oregon Books,
    1967), 185–217. For an examination of the decline of the Socialists and Wobblies and for-
    mation of the Community Labor Party in Portland, see Adam Hodges, "Thinking Globally,
    Acting Locally: The Portland Soviet and the Emergence of American Communism,
    1918–1920," *Pacific Northwest Quarterly,* Vol. 98, No. 3 (Summer, 2007), 115–129.

10 Gary Murrell, "Hunting Reds in Oregon 1935–1939," *Oregon Historical Quarterly,* 100:4,
    (Winter 1999), 375; Alan Dawley, *Changing the World: American Progressives in War and
    Revolution* (Princeton: Princeton University Press, 2003), 323–27.

11 "Convictions Will Stand," *Oregonian,* March 22, 1921, 1; Tyler, *Rebels of the Woods,* 185–217;
    Jeff Johnson, "The Heyday of Oregon's Socialists," *Sunday Oregonian, Northwest Magazine,*
    15–18. For an examination of the decline of the Socialists and Wobblies and formation of
    the Community Labor Party in Portland, see Adam Hodges, "Thinking Globally, Acting
    Locally: The Portland Soviet and the Emergence of American Communism, 1918–1920,"
    Pacific Northwest Quarterly, Vol. 98, No. 3 (Summer, 2007), 115–29; Kate Richards O'Hare,
    The Kate O'Hare Booklet: Americanism and Bolshevism (St. Louis: F. P. O'Hare, 1919), 5,
    http://pds.lib.harvard.edu/pds/view/3013742, accessed June 14, 2010; Mary Heaton
    Vorse, *Daily Notes,* 1926, Box 79, Wayne State University as cited in Dee Garrison, *Mary
    Heaton Vorse: The Life of an American Insurgent* (Philadelphia: Temple University Press,
    1989), 196. Dawley, *Changing the World,* 8. For the anti-Red campaign in Oregon, see Gary
    Murrell, "Hunting Reds," 374–401.

12 "Oregon Is Invaded by Ku Klux Klan," *Oregonian,* July 21, 1921, 14; Abbot, *Portland,*
    100–102; Johnston, *The Radical Middle Class,* 243–47; David A. Horowitz, "Social Morality
    and Personal Revitalization: Oregon's Ku Klux Klan in the 1920s," *Oregon Historical
    Quarterly,* 90:4 (Winter, 1989), 365–84.

13 "History of the Federal Judiciary," Federal Judicial Center, www.fjc.gov accessed April 6,
    2013; "Robert S. Bean," www.oregon.gov accessed April 8, 1921; "Answer Is Declined by
    General Disque," *Oregonian,* December 26, 1918, 12; "W. R. Bryon Asked To Resign From
    Secret Service by W. J. Burns," *Portland Evening Telegram,* August 31, 1921; "Mr. Bryon
    Gets Position," *Oregonian,* October 14, 1921, 11. The bureau chief to Attorney General
    Daugherty, November 3, 1917, DOJ Papers. The chief noted that Bryon had considerable
    difficulty with agents and other division superintendents. Also, US Attorney Clay Allen in
    Portland asserted in a lengthy memo that Bryon has "never been of any great value to this
    office . . . ." No date, DOJ Papers.

14 Freedman, *Their Sisters' Keepers*, 143–151; "Kate O'Hare in Portland," *Oregonian*, June 27, 1921, 5; "Ex-Convict Is Speaker," *Oregonian*, May 5, 1920, 4; Sally M. Miller, *From Prairie to Prison: The Life of Social Activist Kate Richards O'Hare* (Columbia: University of Columbia Press, 1993), 226–28; "Cedars Now Open," *Oregonian*, August 11, 1918, 13. Kate Richards O'Hare took a position as an assistant administrator in the California Corrections System in 1938 with a focus on San Quentin prison.

15 Equi's contemporary, Margaret D., often visited her at the office she shared with Dr. Griff. Margaret D. with Sandy Polishuk and Susan Dobrof, Interview, February 2, 1982, OHS ACC 28389—Equi.

16 Economic statistics from a Brookings Institution study as noted in Howard Zinn, *A People's History of the United States*, (New York: Perennial Classics, 2001), 382–83.

17 Capazzola, *Uncle Sam Wants You*, 140–43; Dawley, *Changing the World*, 313–30.

18 Mary Equi McCloskey with Sandy Polishuk, Interviews, May 1, 1971 and March 12, 1980, OHS ACC 28389—Equi; "Love of Humanity Dominates Radicalism of Dr. Marie Equi," *New Bedford Standard Times*, June 1, 1924, 8; Jessie Laird Brodie, MD, Interview with Susan Dobrof (date uncertain, 1981–1982), OHS ACC 28389—Equi; Michael Helquist, "'Criminal Operations,' The First Fifty Years of Abortion Trials in Portland, Oregon," *Oregon Historical* Quarterly, 116:1 (Spring 2015): 6–39; "Doctor's Fate in Doubt," *Oregonian*, June 30, 1920, 12; "Dr. Ausplund in Prison," *Oregonian*, March 24, 1921, 14; "Medic May Lose License," *Oregonian*, June 4, 1930, 22; *Portland City Directory*, 1930, (Portland: R. L. Polk, no month but usually published in September); C. E. Ambrose, attorney, with Sandy Polishuk, Interview, May 5, 1972, OHS ACC 28389—Equi. Ambrose confirmed that Dr. Andre Ausplund acquired Equi's office and patients after her retirement in 1930.

19 "Portland to Get New Convention," *Oregonian*, July 30, 1922, 13; "Birth Control Sect Barred in Portland," *Oregonian*, July 30, 1922, 13. The previous conferences had been convened in European cities, and Portland would have had the honor of hosting the first outside Europe and in the United States. Instead, New York hosted the event.

20 Reagan, *When Abortion Was A Crime*, 36, 132–34. Reagan notes that dire economic conditions in the 1930s contributed to a surge in the number of abortions performed in the county as many women were unable to afford a child and as physicians tried to maintain their incomes by providing abortions. Sadie Ann Adams, "We Were Privileged in Oregon," 7.

21 "Resent MacSweeney's Fate," *New York Times*, September 9, 1920; "Miss O'Brennan to Speak," *Oregonian*, November 16, 1921, 9; US Dept. of Justice: British Espionage in the United States, February 15, 1921, MID Document 9914 A-178 at http://www.marxists. org/history/usa/government/dept-justice/1921/0215-doj-britespionage.pdf, page 5. Marie Equi to Kathleen O'Brennan, December 22, 1921, Eamonn and Aine Ceannt, and Kathleen and Lily O'Brennan Papers, 1874–1952, Collection, Ms. 41, 509 (2), National Library of Ireland; "Papers of Eamonn and Aine Ceannt, and of Kathleen and Lily O'Brennan," MSS 13,069-13,070; 41,478-41,522, pages 6, 46–53.

22 "Mrs. Skeffington Talks on Ireland," *Oregonian*, February 24, 1923, 1; "Mrs. Skeffington A Judge," *New York Times*, August 27, 1920, 3; Leah Levenson and Jerry H. Natterstad, *Hanna Sheehy-Skeffington, Irish Feminist* (Syracuse: Syracuse University Press, 1986), 132–34.

23 "Suicide Committed by Woman Physician," *Oregonian*, October 10, 1922, 1; Hamburger, *Two Rooms*, 215–16, 218, 232–233, 276, 294.

24 Hamburger, *Two Rooms*, 301–2, 327; "Beck, Kathryn, "Kitty" (?-1924) http://editorsnotes. org/topic/beck-kathryn-O'Brennan-1924/#article, accessed April 15, 2013; Christine Stansell, "Talking About Sex: Early Twentieth-Century Radicals and Moral Confessions," 283–308, in Karen Halttunen and Lewis Perry, *Moral Problems in American Life: New Perspectives on Cultural History* (Ithaca: Cornell University Press, 1998).

25 "City's Oldest Italian Dies," *New Bedford Standard Times*, February 13, 1924, 1; "Dr. Marie Equi's Father Dies," February 14, 1924, 11. The New Bedford Death Registry lists "mitral insufficiency and arteriosclerosis" as "disease or cause of death." "Love of Humanity Dominates Radicalism of Dr. Marie Equi," *New Bedford Sunday Standard*, June 1, 1924. The article includes several inaccuracies and reprints an article in *Industrial Solidarity*.

Sacramental Records, Death Records, St. Lawrence, Martyr Catholic Church, New Bedford, Massachusetts.

26 Camp, *Iron in Her Soul*, 111–21; Baxandall, *Words on Fire*, 20–30, 30–33, 141–46. Flynn's account of the Sacco-Vanzetti defense campaign and trial appears in Flynn, *The Rebel Girl*, 297–332.

27 Camp, *Iron in Her Soul*, 114–15, 118–20. The "Garland Fund" was the popular name for the American Fund for Public Services, an organization financed with $1 million by Charles Garland, a young man who used his inheritance from his father, a Wall Street broker, for leftist causes. The Passaic woolen mill workers strike became known as the first successful Communist-led labor action in the United States. Elizabeth Gurley Flynn to Mary Heaton Vorse, December 23, 1926, Mary Heaton Vorse Papers, ACC LP000190, Wayne State University.

28 Camp, *Iron in Her Soul*, 125–26; Multnomah County Property Tax Records. Portland's addresses and street names were renumbered and renamed in 1931; interview by author with current owner of the property, August, 21, 2003. The property is located today on the 1400 block of SW Hall Street.

29 Camp, *Iron in Her Soul*, 111–23, 126–37; Baxandall, *Words on Fire*, 126–31. Comment on Flynn's state of health by Mary Heaton Vorse, as quoted in Baxandall, *Words on Fire*, 30. Ralph C. Walker, MD to Marie Equi, January 11, 1927, and Walter T. Brachvogel to Marie Equi, February 4, 1927, both in *Sojourn in the West*, microfilm, Elizabeth Gurley Flynn Papers, Tamiment Library. Camp, *Iron in Her Soul*, 125–27; Mary Equi McCloskey with Sandy Polishuk, Interview, March 12, 1980, OHS ACC 28389—Equi.

30 Baxandall, *Words on Fire*, 23–30; Marie Equi to "Dear Friend," January 11, 1927, *Sojourn in the West* microfilm, Elizabeth Gurley Flynn Papers, Tamiment Library; Marie Equi to "Dear Friend," April 5, 1927; Camp, *Iron in Her Soul*, 125–27.

31 "Woman Continues on Hunger Strike," *Oregon Daily Journal*, March 4, 1927, 6; "One Good Samaritan," *Oregon Daily Journal*, March 13, 1927, 6.

32 "Obituary," *Morning Astorian*, May 28, 1927, 4; Certificate of Death, Oregon State Department of Health, State Registered #92, May 31, 1927.

33 Woodrow C. Whitten, "Criminal Syndicalism and the Law in California, 1919–1927," from *Transactions of the American Philosophical Society*, New Ser., Vol. 59, No. 2 (1969), 3–73. The US Supreme Court at first decided, in May 1927, to dismiss the Whitney appeal due to lack of jurisdiction, but in October 1927 the court reconsidered the case. For analysis of the Supreme Court's evolution of thinking about free speech cases in general, and in *Whitney v. California* specifically, see Stone, *Perilous Times*, 523–25. "Won't Ask Pardon, Cell Is Certainty for Miss Whitney," *New York World*, October 22, 1925, 1, as reported in Al Richmond, *Native Daughter*, 126–34.

34 Camp, *Iron in Her Soul*, 126–27; Flynn, *Rebel Girl*, 297–332.

35 Elizabeth Gurley Flynn journal excerpt noted in Dorothy Gallagher, *All the Right Enemies: The Life and Murder of Carlo Tresca* (Rutgers University Press: New Brunswick, New Jersey, 1988), 118.

CHAPTER 17

1 Mary Equi McCloskey with Sandy Polishuk, Interviews, May 1, 1971, and March 12, 1980, OHS ACC 28389—Equi.

2 "Aviatrix, 16, Qualifies," *Sunday Oregonian*, January 3, 1932, 27. Mary Equi McCloskey to Sandy Polishuk, Interview, May 1, 1971, ACC 28389—Equi.

3 "Margaret D." with Sandy Polishuk and Susan Dobrof, Interview, February 2, 1982, OHS ACC 28389—Equi.

4 Gay Walker, Reed College directory, correspondence with author, November 24, 2003; Mary Equi was listed in the class of 1936.

5 Mary Equi McCloskey with Sandy Polishuk, March 12, 1980, OHS ACC 28389—Equi; Marie Equi to Dr. Belle Ferguson, December 5, 1935, OHS ACC 28389—Equi.

6   Elizabeth Gurley Flynn to Mary Heaton Vorse, March 22, 1929, included in Baxandall, *Words on Fire*, 151–53.

7   Marie Equi to Hanna Sheehy-Skeffington, n. d. but probably 1928, Sheehy-Skeffington Collection; James Weldon Johnson for The American Fund for Public Service to Elizabeth Gurley Flynn, February 16, 1928, "Sojourn in West"; C. S. Smith to Fellow Worker, March 30, 1929; Norman Tallentire to Elizabeth Gurley Flynn, March 29, 1929; Elizabeth Gurley Flynn Papers, Tamiment Library.

8   Mary Equi McCloskey with Sandy Polishuk, May 1, 1971, OHS ACC 28389—Equi.

9   Marie Equi to Hanna Sheehy-Skeffington, February 20, 1928, and "white marriage" letter, n.d. but after 1927, perhaps Spring of 1928, Hanna Sheehy-Skeffington Collection, National Library of Ireland, Ms. 41, 177 (16), hereafter Sheehy-Skeffington Collection.

10 Mary Equi McCloskey with Sandy Polishuk, Interview, March 12, 1980, OHS ACC 28389—Equi. Historians have wondered if many of Flynn's personal papers from her years with Equi had been destroyed after being deposited with the Communist Party USA. Similar questions have been raised regarding possible lesbian relationships of Flynn's while she was imprisoned in the 1950s for two years in a federal prison camp near Alderson, West Virginia. She wrote a prison memoir, *The Alderson Story: My Life as a Political Prisoner*, but she mentions no lesbian relations of her own while there—or no account survived later editing. For a more indepth treatment of lesbians in the Communist Party—and specifically the fate of Elizabeth Gurley Flynn's papers—see Bettina Aptheker, "Keeping the Communist Party Straight, 1940s-1980s," *New Politics*, Vo. XII-1, # 45 (Summer 2008), http://newpol. org/content/keeping-communist-party-straight-1940s-1980s, accessed March 20, 2015.

11 Elizabeth Gurley Flynn to Mary Heaton Vorse, January and February 1930, as cited in Dorothy Gallagher, *All the Right Enemies: The Life and Murder of Carlo Tresca* (New Brunswick, New Jersey: Rutgers University Press, 1988), 118–21.

12 William G. Robbins, "Surviving the Great Depression: The New Deal in Oregon," *Oregon Historical Quarterly*, Vol. 109, No. 2, (Summer 2008), 311–17.

13 Probate #68335, Marie Equi, Office of County Clerk, Multnomah County, Oregon. Equi died intestate; once her probate was settled, her daughter became her only heir.

14 "Predicts Revolution Unless Aid Is Given to 5,000,000 Unemployed," *Boston Globe*, March 25, 1914.

15 Probate No. 28,462, Harriet F. Speckart, Circuit Court, Multnomah County, Oregon. The comparable value of Speckart's $28,000 nearly one hundred years later is about $366,000.

16 Ibid.

17 Kimberly Jensen, "Portland's 'Experimental' Woman Jury, Part 1, November 30, 1912, *Kimberly Jensen's Blog*, http://kimberlyjensenblog.blogspot.com/2011/05/portlands-experimental-woman-jury-part.html.

18 "Convict's Freedom Sought," *Oregonian*, February 23, 1929, 9; "Audience Demands Mooney's Release," *Oregonian*, February 25, 1929, 7.

19 Marie Equi to Hanna Sheehy-Skeffington, December 21, 1931, Sheehy-Skeffington Collection; Elizabeth Gurley Flynn to Alice Inglis, May 22, 1930, and July 11, 1934, Agnes Inglis Papers, Labadie Collection, University of Michigan.

20 Marie Equi to Hanna Sheehy-Skeffington, December 21, 1931, Sheehy-Skeffington Collection; Mary Equi McCloskey with Sandy Polishuk, Interview, March 12, 1980, OHS ACC 28389—Equi. Andre Ausplund, MD, had been convicted of manslaughter for the abortion-related death of a young woman in 1915. He was imprisoned and then resumed his abortion practice in Portland upon his release.

21 Marie Equi to Hanna Sheehy-Skeffington, February 14, 1930, Sheehy-Skeffington Collection.

22 Mary Equi McCloskey to Sandy Polishuk, Interview, May 1, 1971, OHS ACC 28389—Equi.

23 Dorothy Gallagher, *All the Right Enemies*, 123–25; Mary Equi McCloskey with Sandy Polishuk, May 1, 1971, Interview, Polishuk Collection; Elizabeth Gurley Flynn to Agnes

Inglis, September 10, 1936, Labadie Collection, University of Michigan; Elizabeth Gurley
Flynn to Kathy Flynn, August 6, 1955, Elizabeth Gurley Flynn Papers, Tamiment Library;
"Notes for Autobiography," as quoted in Camp, *Iron in Her Soul*, 130.

24 Julia Ruuttila with Sandy Polishuk, Interview, n.d., OHS ACC 28389—Equi.

25 Elizabeth Gurley Flynn and Bina Bobba, photograph, and concern about Equi in Dorothy
Gallagher, *All The Right Enemies*,119; Elizabeth Gurley Flynn to Alice Inglis, July 11, 1934,
Agnes Inglis Papers, Labadie Collection, University of Michigan.

26 Lillian Faderman, *Odd Girls and Twilight Lovers: A History of Lesbian Life in Twentieth-Century
America* (New York: Columbia University Press, 1991), 81–88, 99–105.

27 William G. Robbins, "Surviving the Great Depression: The New Deal in Oregon," *Oregon
Historical Quarterly*, Vol. 109, No. 2, (Summer, 2008), 311–17; Michael Munk, *The Portland
Red Guide: Sites and Stories of Our Radical Past* (Portland, Oregon: Ooligan Press, 2007)
96–98; "Negro Under Death Verdict Made Oregon Cause Celebre," *Oregonian*, May 3, 1934,
4. "Theodore Jordan Case, correspondence," International Labor Defense, AF/160955,
A2001-074, Portland Archives and Records Administration.

28 "Roosevelt Grants War Foes Amnesty," *New York Times*, December 25, 1933, 24; "1500 War
Opponents Freed of Taint, Civil Rights Restored by President," *Oregonian*, December 25,
1933, 1; Equi to Belle Cooper Ferguson, August 8, 1934, OHS ACC 28389—Equi; Equi to
Hanna Sheehy-Skeffington, April 1, 1938, Sheehy-Skeffington Collection.

29 William Bigelow and Norman Diamond. "Agitate, Educate, Organize: Portland, 1934,"
Oregon Historical Quarterly 89: 1 (Spring 1988), 4–29; Walter Gallenson, *The CIO Challenge
to the AF of L.* Cambridge, Mass., 1960, 602 as noted in David Robert Hardy, *The 1934
Portland Longshoreman's Strike*, thesis, Reed College, May 1971, 15.

30 Sandy Polishuk, *Sticking To The Union: An Oral History of the Life and Times of Julia Ruuttila*
(New York: Palgrave MacMillan, 2003), 45–50; Walter Gallenson, *The CIO Challenge to
the AF of L.*, 602 as noted in Hardy, *The 1934 Portland Longshoreman's Strike*, May 1971, 15;
"Gasoline Drought Becoming Acute," *Oregonian*, June 24, 1934, 1; Hardy, *The 1934 Portland
Longshoreman's Strike*, May 1971.

31 "A Friend for Labor," *The Hook, for Unity of Marine Crafts of the Pacific Coast*, the Official ILA
Bulletin, no. 11, vol. 11, July 11, 1937; Julia Ruuttila with Sandy Polishuk, Interview, June
6, 1981, OHS ACC 28389—Equi; "Veteran Labor Crusader Leaves Bed To Bring Check
for Strike Victims," *Portland Evening Telegram*, July 12, 1934, 1; Michael Munk, "Portland's
Silk Stocking Mob: The Citizens Emergency League in the 1934 Maritime Strike," *Pacific
Northwest Quarterly*, 91:3 (Summer 2000), 150–60.

32 "Long Dock Strike Becomes History," *Oregonian*, July 31, 1934, 1; Hardy, *The 1934 Portland
Longshoreman's Strike*, 134–37.

33 "Two Professional Women, Well-Known to Labor, Give July Messages," *Voice of Action*,
Seattle, July 5, 1935, 8.

34 Margaret D. with Sandy Polishuk and Susan Dobrof, Interview, February 2, 1982, OHS
ACC28389—Equi; Munk, *Portland Red Guide*, 91–93; Fred Leeson, *Rose City Justice: A
Legal History of Portland, Oregon* (Portland, Oregon: Oregon Historical Society Press, 1998),
127–33; *DeJonge v. Oregon*, 299 US 353 (1937); Munk, "Portland's 'Silk Stocking Mob'"
150–60.

35 Camp, *Iron in Her Soul*, 112–23. Camp wrote that the US Communist Party wanted to keep
Gurley Flynn's membership secret while she was also working for the International Labor
Defense.

36 Mary Equi McCloskey with Sandy Polishuk, Interview, March 12, 1980, OHS ACC
28389—Equi. Gallagher, *All the Right Enemies*, 125.

37 Elizabeth Gurley Flynn, "Sojourn in the West, 1927–1936," Series IV. EGF Papers, The
Tamiment Library and Robert F. Wagner Labor Archives, New York University; Baxandall,
Words on Fire, 30–34, including Elizabeth Gurley Flynn to Agnes Inglis, September 10,
1936, Labadie Collection; Baxandall, *Words on Fire*, 150–51; Camp, *Iron in Her Soul, 130*;
Elizabeth Gurley Flynn to Kathie Flynn, August 6, 1955, Elizabeth Gurley Flynn Papers,

Tamiment Library, as quoted in Baxandall, *Words on Fire*, 32. For Flynn's involvement with the Communist Party and her trial for charges under the Smith Act, see Camp, *Iron in Her Soul*, 197–220, 221–53.

38 Marie Equi to Dr. Belle Ferguson, April 6, 1936, OHS ACC 28389—Equi; "Margaret D." with Sandy Polishuk and Nancy Krieger, Interview, February 2, 1982, OHS ACC 28389—Equi; "Reed College Students Plan Dance," *Sunday Oregonian*, Section 3, 1; "Communist Party; Flyers, for Forums and discussions put on by Young Communist League," AF/160428, A2001-074 ("Red Squad" files), PARC.

CHAPTER 18

1 Stewart H. Holbrook, "Northwest Hysterias: Down With The Huns," *Sunday Oregonian*, April 4, 1937, 75; Marie Equi to Stewart Holbrook, April 23, 1937, Stewart Hall Holbrook Papers, 0701-0001, Box 5, Folder 19, University of Washington Libraries Special Collections. Holbrook intended for many years to write a biography of Equi, but he did not complete one.

2 Michael Munk, *The Portland Red Guide: Sites and Stories Of Our Radical Past* (Portland, Oregon: Ooligan Press, 2007), 226–29; Michael Munk, "Portland's Red Squad: A long and ongoing tradition, Part 1," November 2000, www.lclark.edu/~polyecon/reds1.htm accessed May 29, 2013; Murrell, "Hunting Reds," 374–401; John Terry, "Nobody in Oregon was above 'red squad' suspicion," *Oregonian*, February 5, 2006, B08; "Oregonians—and typical 'red squad' targets," *Oregonian*, February 12, 2006, www.oregonlive.com, accessed March 1, 2006; Julia Ruuttila with Sandy Polishuk and Nancy Krieger, Interview, June 6, 1981, OHS ACC 28389—Equi. Ruth Barnett as told to Doug Baker, *They Weep on My Doorstep* (Beaverton, Oregon: Halo Publishers Edition, January, 1969), 18–19.

3 Julia Ruuttila, memo on Francis J. Murnane, no date, OHS ACC 28389—Equi; Mary Equi McCloskey with Sandy Polishuk, Interview, May 1, 1971, OHS ACC 28389—Equi.

4 "'Liberals' Urged to Trim Martin," *Oregonian*, April 25, 1937, 14; Murrell, "Hunting Reds," 374–401; Monroe Sweetland to Marie Equi, August 21, 1937 and another of no date and Marie Equi to Monroe Sweetland, August 23, 1937, Oregon Commonwealth Federation Records, SCA Ms, Bx 033, Special Collections and University Archives, University of Oregon Libraries, Eugene, Oregon.

5 Julia Ruuttila memorandum to Sandy Polishuk, *research notes for Sticking to the Union*, n.d.; Marie Equi to Hanna Sheehy-Skeffington, March 24, 1938, Sheehy-Skeffington Collection.

6 Marie Equi to Hanna Sheehy-Skeffington, March 24, 1938, Sheehy-Skeffington Collection.

7 Marie Equi to Hanna Sheehy Skeffington, April 1, 1938, Sheehy-Skeffington Collection; Film File No. 42, Multnomah County Records Administration. Equi's registration is dated December 30, 1939.

8 Marie Equi to Hanna Sheehy-Skeffington, March 24, 1938, April 1, 1938, Sheehy-Skeffington Papers; Margaret D. with Sandy Polishuk and Susan Dobrof, Interview, February 2, 1982, OHS ACC 28389—Equi.

9 Marie Equi to Mary Equi Lukes, n.d., OHS ACC 28389—Equi.

10 Arthur Champlin Spencer, telephone conversation with the author, June 13, 2003.

11 Margaret D. with Sandy Polishuk and Susan Dobrof, Interview, February 2, 1982, OHS ACC 28389—Equi.

12 Marie Equi to Hanna Sheehy Skeffington, May 31, 1938, Sheehy Skeffington Papers; Obituary, Sophia Equi Gay, *New Bedford Standard Times*, May 22, 1942, 10; Marie Equi to Dr. Belle Ferguson, April 6, 1936, OHS ACC 28389—Equi. Tillicum refers to a variant of a native flower of the Pacific Northwest, the trillium.

13 Margaret Sanger Papers, Sophia Smith Collection, as noted in Chesler, *Woman of Valor*, 398, fn 572; also in same volume re: International Planned Parenthood Federation, 421–24; "Planned Parenthood Opening in Portland Far Cry from 1916 Battle," *Sunday Oregonian*, November 3, 1963, 35.

14 Julia Ruuttila to Nancy Clay, November 17, 1971, OHS ACC 28389—Equi; Stuart
    McElderry, "Building a West Coast Ghetto: African American Housing in Portland,
    1910–1960," *Pacific Northwest Quarterly*, 92:3, (Summer, 2001), 137–48; Dale Skovgaard,
    "Memories of the 1948 Vanport Flood," *Oregon Historical Quarterly*, 108:1, (Spring 2007),
    88–106.

15 "Hip Fractured," *Oregonian*, September 13, 1950, 19; Julia Ruuttila to Nancy Clay, Letter,
    November 17, 1971, OHS ACC 28389—Equi. Michael Munk, *The Portland Red Guide*
    (Portland, Oregon: Ooligan Press, 2011, Second edition), 25–26. Munk notes that
    longshoreman leader Francis Murnane asked Ruuttila to write the poem for Equi.

16 Equi was transferred to Fairlawn Hospital in Gresham, Oregon; the facility functioned as
    a nursing home. Standard Certificate of Death, State of Oregon, #8396, date received July
    29, 1952; Mary Equi McCloskey with Sandy Polishuk, Interview, May 1, 1971, OHS ACC
    28389—Equi. "Dr. Equi Services Set," *Oregon Daily Journal*, July 15, 1952, 7; Margaret D.
    with Sandy Polishuk, Interview, February 2, 1982, OHS ACC 28389—Equi. The Church of
    St. Michael the Archangel is located at 1701 SW Fourth Street, SW Fourth and SW Mill, in
    Portland.

17 Ralph Friedman, "Oregon's incurable case of compassion," *Northwest Magazine, Sunday
    Oregonian*, December 25, 1983; Mary Equi McCloskey with Sandy Polishuk, Interview, May
    1, 1971, OHS ACC 28389—Equi.

18 Equi and Speckart's vaults are located in the Harding Chamber, WH Section, Tier 7, Crypt
    Niche 1 at the Portland Memorial, 6705 SE Fourteenth Avenue. Probate No. 68335, Marie
    D. Equi, Multnomah County Circuit Court. "Divorce Granted," Oregonian, June 8, 1946,
    12. Mary Equi Lukes divorced her husband, Joseph, in 1946.

19 "Death Calls Dr. Marie Equi, Suffrage, Labor Champion," *Oregonian*, July 15, 1952;
    "Generous Dissenter, *Oregonian*, July 16, 1952, 16; "Dr. Marie Equi, World War I Crusader,
    Dies," *Oregon Daily Journal*, July 14, 1952; "Dr. Marie Equi Dies In Oregon," *New Bedford
    Standard-Times*, July 14, 1952; "Dr. Marie D. Equi," *New York Times*, July 15, 1952, 21;
    Several inaccuracies in the New Bedford obituary were repeated by other papers.

20 "Tribute Paid to Dr. Equi," *Oregonian*, August 16, 1952, 12.

21 Julia Ruuttila with Sandy Polishuk and Nancy Krieger, Interview, June 6, 1981 and Ruuttila
    to Sandy Polishuk, June 17, 1971, OHS ACC 28389—Equi.

Bibliography

ARCHIVAL COLLECTIONS

Archives of Office of Public Affairs, Federal Bureau of Prisons, Washington, DC.
Boucheron, Anthony (and Mary Ellen Parker White). White MSS., Lilly Library Manuscript
    Collections, Indiana University Libraries, Bloomington, Indiana.
California State Archives, Sacramento, California.
California State Prison Records, Sacramento, California.
Davis Phillips, Lucy I. Collection on Oregon Women Medical School Graduates. Accession
    2004-030. Historical Collections & Archives, Oregon Health & Science University,
    Portland, Oregon.
Duniway, Abigail Scott. Papers, MS 432. Oregon Historical Society Research Library, Portland,
    Oregon.
Duniway, Abigail Scott. Papers, 1852–1992, Special Collections and University Archives,
    University of Oregon Libraries, Eugene, Oregon.
Equi, Marie. Gay Lesbian Archives of the Pacific Northwest, GLAPN 2988-13, Oregon
    Historical Society Research Library, Portland, Oregon.
Elizabeth Gurley Flynn Papers, Tamiment Library & Robert F. Wagner Labor Archives, New
    York University, New York, New York.
Harriet F. Speckart v. Leopold F. Schmidt et. al., National Archives and Records Administration/San
    Bruno, Court Records, Record Group 21, Case 1908 U. Court of Appeals, Ninth Circuit,
    San Bruno, California.
Holbrook, Stewart Hall. Papers. Special Collections, University of Washington Libraries, Seattle,
    Washington.
Inglis, Agnes. Papers. Labadie Radical History Collection, University of Michigan, Ann Arbor,
    Michigan.
Marie Equi v. United States, Judgment Roll No. 8099, OR District Court 1919, National Archives
    and Records Administration/San Bruno, Records of District Court, San Bruno, California.
Massachusetts State Archives, Boston, Massachusetts.
Multnomah County Court Records, Portland, Oregon.
New Bedford Free Public Library, Special Collections, New Bedford, Massachusetts.
Northfield/Mount Hermon School, Dolben Library Archives, Northfield, Massachusetts.
Oregon Commonwealth Federation Records, 1936–1942, Special Collections and University
    Archives, University of Oregon Libraries, Eugene, Oregon.
Oregon Historical Society Research Library, Portland, Oregon, Accession 28389 "Materials
    relating to research on Dr. Marie Equi" and "Biography—Equi, Marie," Vertical File.
Pardee, George. Papers. Bancroft Library, BANC MSS C-B 400, Online Archive of California,
    http://ark/cdlib.org/ark:13030/hb7m3nb57x , accessed June 20, 1908.
Probate Case File 68335, Marie Equi, Date of Death: July 13, 1952, Multnomah County Circuit
    Court, Portland, Oregon.
Probate Case File 28462: Harriet Speckart, Date of Death: Mary 26, 1927, Multnomah County
    Circuit Court, Portland, Oregon.
Sanger, Margaret. Papers, 1900–1966. Library of Congress, Washington, DC.
Sanger, Margaret. Papers. Sophia Smith Collection, Smith College.
Sanger, Margaret. Margaret Sanger Papers Project, Department of History, New York University.
Skeffington, Hanna Sheehy. Collection, MS41, 177 (16). National Library of Ireland.

South Bristol Deeds, Registry of Deeds, New Bedford, Massachusetts.
United States Department of Justice. Mail and Files Division. "Department of Justice File on Dr. Marie Equi." Copies at Oregon Historical Society, Portland, Oregon and Lewis & Clark College Special Collections, Portland, Oregon.
Record Group: 60 "Central Files, Classified Subject Correspondence," File No. 9-19-1354-0 Bureau Papers Only & File 9-19-1354 parts 1–3. (Equi files, surveillance and correspondence).
United States Department of Justice files; National Archives, Civilian Records Unit (Archives II), Case File #9-19-1354-0 and Bureau Papers #9-19-1354, parts 1 and 2.
Vorse, Mary Heaton. Papers, Walter P. Reuther Library, Archives of Labor and Urban Affairs, Wayne State University, Detroit, Michigan.
Wellesley College Archives, Margaret Clapp Library, Wellesley, Massachusetts.
Wood, C. E. S. Collection. Huntington Library, Pasadena, California.

NEWSPAPERS AND JOURNALS

Boston Globe
Daily Olympian (Olympia, Washington)
East Oregonian (Pendleton, Oregon)
New Bedford Standard
New Bedford Times
New Bedford Standard-Times
New York Times
New York World
Northwest Medicine
Oregonian (Morning Oregonian)
Oregon Daily Journal
Oregon Historical Quarterly
Pacific Northwest Quarterly
Portland Evening Telegram
Portland News
Radical America
Republican Standard (New Bedford)
San Francisco Call
San Francisco Chronicle
San Francisco Examiner
Seattle Post-Intelligencer
The Dalles Chronicle
The Dalles Times-Mountaineer
The Dalles Weekly Chronicle
Western Historical Quarterly

JOURNAL ARTICLES

Allen, Douglas W. "Homesteading and Property Rights: Or, 'How the West Was Really Won.'" *Journal of Law and Economics* 34, no. 1 (1991).
Aptheker, Bettina. "Keeping the Communist Party Straight, 1940s–1980s," *New Politics*, Vol. XXI-1, #45, (Summer 2008) http://newpol.org/content/keeping-communist-party-straight-1940s-1980s.
Bergquist, James M. "The Oregon Donation Act and the National Land Policy." *Oregon Historical Quarterly* 58, no. 1 (1957).
Cook, Tom. "Radical Politics, Radical Love: The Life of Dr. Marie Equi." *Northwest Gay and Lesbian Historian* 1, no. 3 & 4 (1996).

Copeland, Tom. "Wesley Everest, IWW Martyr." *The Pacific Northwest Quarterly* 77, no. 4 (1986).

Dilg, Janice. "For Working Women in Oregon: Caroline Gleason/Sister Miriam Theresa and Oregon's Minimum Wage Law." *Oregon Historical Quarterly* 110, no. 1 (2012): 96–129.

Dubois, Ellen Carol. "Working Women, Class Relations, and Suffrage Militance: Harriet Stanton Blatch and the New York Women's Suffrage Movement, 1894–1909." *The Journal of American History* 74, no. 1 (1987): 34–58.

Hall, Greg. "The Fruits of Her Labor: Women, Children, and Progressive Era Reformers in the Pacific Northwest Canning Industry." *Oregon Historical Quarterly* 190, no. 2 (2008): 226–51.

Hallgarth, Susan A. "Women Settlers on the Frontier: Unwed, Unreluctant, Unrepentant." *Women's Studies Quarterly* 17, no. 3/4 (1989): 23–34.

Helquist, Michael. "Portland to the Rescue: The Rose City's Response to the 1906 San Francisco Earthquake and Fire." *Oregon Historical Quarterly* 108, no. 3 (2007): 474–86.

Helquist, Michael. "'Criminal Operations,' The First Fifty Years of Abortion Trials in Portland, Oregon," *Oregon Historical Quarterly*, 116:1, (Spring 2015): 6–39.

Hodges, Adam J. "At War over the Espionage Act in Portland." *Oregon Historical Quarterly* 108, no. 3 (2007): 474–86.

Hodges, Adam J. "Thinking Globally, Acting Locally: The Portland Soviet and the Emergence of American Communism, 1918–1920." *The Pacific Northwest Quarterly* 98, no. 3 (2007).

Hoffman, Dennis E., and Vincent Webb. "Police Response to Labor Radicalism in Portland and Seattle, 1913–1919." *Oregon Historical Quarterly* 87, no. 4 (1986): 341–66.

Jensen, Kimberly. "'Neither Head nor Tail to the Campaign': Esther Pohl Lovejoy and the Oregon Woman Suffrage Victory of 1912." *Oregon Historical Quarterly* 108, no. 3 (2007): 350–83.

Joffe, Carol. "Portraits of Three 'Physicians of Conscience': Abortion before Legalization in the United States." *Journal of the History of Sexuality* 2, no. 1 (1991): 46–67.

Johnston, Robert D. "The Myth of the Harmonious City: Will Daly, Lora Little, and the Hidden Face of Progressive-Era Portland." *Oregon Historical Quarterly* 99, no. 3 (1998): 248–97.

Kessler, Lauren. "The Ideas of Woman Suffrage and the Mainstream Press." *Oregon Historical Quarterly* 84, no. 3 (1983).

Krieger, Nancy. "Queen of the Bolsheviks: The Hidden History of Dr. Marie Equi." *Radical America* 17, no. 5 (1983): 55–71.

Lovejoy, Esther C. P. "My Medical School: 1890-1894." *Oregon Historical Quarterly* 75, no. 1 (1974): 7–36.

McCammon, Holly J., and Karen E. Campbell. "Winning the Vote in the West: The Political Successes of the Women's Suffrage Movements: 1866-1919." *Gender and Society* 15, no. 1 (2001): 55–82.

More, Ellen S. "'A Certain Restless Ambition': Women Physicians and World War I." *American Quarterly* 41, no. 4 (1989): 636–60.

Murrell, Gary. "Hunting Reds in Oregon, 1935–1939." *Oregon Historical Quarterly* 100, no. 4 (1999): 374–401.

Munk, Michael. "Portland's Silk Stocking Mob: The Citizens Emergency League in the 1934 Maritime Strike." *Pacific Northwest Quarterly* 91, no. 3 (2000): 150–60.

Palmateer, Dmitri. "Charity and the 'Tramp': Itinerancy, Unemployment, and Municipal Government from Coxey to the Unemployed League." *Oregon Historical Quarterly* 107, no. 2 (2006): 228–41.

Peterson, Karen Lea Anderson. "The Lucy Davis Phillips Collection: Finding the Lost Women Graduates of Oregon's Medical Schools." *Oregon Historical Quarterly* 113, no. 3 (2012): 430–43.

Rezneck, Samuel. "Unemployment, Unrest, and Relief in the United States During the Depression of 1893–1897." *Journal of Political Economy* 61, no. 4 (1953).

Rydell, Robert. "Visions of Empire: International Expositions in Portland and Seattle, 1905–1909." *Pacific Historical Review* 52, no. 1 (1983).

Schwantes, Carlos A. "Free Love and Free Speech on the Pacific Northwest Frontier." *Oregon Historical Quarterly* 82, no. 3 (1981): 271–93.

Smith, Sherry L. "Single Women Homesteaders: The Perplexing Case of Elinore Pruitt Stewart." *Western Historical Quarterly* 22, no. 2 (1991): 163–82.

Ward, Jean M. "'The Noble Representative Woman from Oregon': Dr. Mary Anna Cooke Thompson." *Oregon Historical Quarterly* 113, no. 3 (2012): 408–29.

Willingham, William F. "Family and Community on the Eastern Oregon Frontier." *Oregon Historical Quarterly* 95, no. 2 (1994).

Zenger, Susan. "She Didn't Raise Her Boy to Be a Slacker: Motherhood, Conscription, and the Culture of the First World War." *Feminist Studies* 22, no. 1 (1996).

THESIS

Adams, Sadie Ann. "'We Were Privileged in Oregon'": Jessie Laird Brodie and Reproductive Politics, Locally and Transnationally, 1915–1975." Master's Thesis, Portland State University, 2012.

Blankenship, Warren Marion. "Progressives and the Progressive Party in Oregon: 1906–1916." PhD Thesis, University of Oregon, 1966.

Hardy, David Robert. "The 1934 Portland Longshoreman's Strike." BA Thesis, Reed College, 1971.

Hodges, Adam. "The Industrial Workers of the World and the Oregon Packing Company Strike of July 1913." Masters Thesis, Portland State University, 1996.

Mottershead, Edi. "Florence Nightingale Ward, MD: Medical Sectarian or Medical Scientist?" Thesis, Mills College, Oakland, California, 2004.

Ruderman, David. "Petrel under Prosecution: Dr. Marie Equi and the Espionage Act of 1917." Undergraduate Thesis, Lewis & Clark College, 1997.

Zahnd, Elaine. "Protective Legislation and Women's Work: Oregon's Ten-Hour Law and the *Muller v. Oregon* Case, 1900–1913." PhD Dissertation, University of Oregon, 1982.

UNPUBLISHED PAPER

Polishuk, Sandy. "The Radicalization of Marie Equi," in "Biography—Equi, Marie," Vertical File, Research Library, Oregon Historical Society, 1971.

WEB PAGES

DaPrato, Norman Peter. "Descendants of Michele Antonio Equi, No Date." Norman Peter DaPrato Family Site, accessed November 22, 2004, myfamily.com.

Helquist, Michael. "Marie Equi (1872–1952)." Oregon Encyclopedia, accessed September 30, 2011, http://oregonencyclopedia.org/entry/view/equi_marie_1872_1952_/.

Helquist, Michael. "A Woman of Consequence: Dr. Marie Equi." Gay Lesbian Archives of the Pacific Northwest, accessed August 7, 2013, www.glapn.org/6050equi.html.

BOOKS

Abbott, Carl. *The Great Extravaganza: Portland and the Lewis and Clark Exposition.* Portland: Oregon Historical Society Press, 1981.

Abbott, Carl. *Portland: Planning, Politics, and Growth in a Twentieth-Century City.* Lincoln, Nebraska: University of Nebraska Press, 1983.

Adler, William M. *The Man Who Never Died: The Life, Times, and Legacy of Joe Hill, American Labor Icon.* New York: Bloomsbury, 2011.

Allen, Barbara. *Homesteading the High Desert.* Salt Lake City: University of Utah Press, 1987.

Avrich, Paul, and Karen Avrich. *Sasha and Emma: The Anarchist Odyssey of Alexander Berkman and Emma Goldman.* Cambridge, Massachusetts: Harvard University Press, 2012.

Baker, Jean H. *Sisters: The Lives of America's Suffragists*. First edition. New York: Hill and Wang, 2005.

Barnett, Ruth. *They Weep on My Doorstep*. Beaverton, Oregon: Halo Publishers Edition, 1969.

Boag, Peter. *Re-Dressing America's Frontier Past*. Berkeley: University of California Press, 2011.

Boag, Peter. *Same-Sex Affairs: Constructing and Controlling Homosexuality in the Pacific Northwest*. Berkeley: University of California Press, 2003.

Brechin, Gray. *Imperial San Francisco: Urban Power, Earthly Ruin*. Berkeley: University of California Press, 1999.

Browne, Sheri Bartlett. *Eva Emery Dye: Romance with the West*. First edition. Corvallis: Oregon State University Press, 2004.

Camp, Helen C. *Iron in Her Soul: Elizabeth Gurley Flynn and the American Left*. Pullman, Washington: Washington State University Press, 1995.

Capozzola, Christopher. *Uncle Sam Needs You: World War I and the Making of the Modern American Citizen*. New York: Oxford University Press, 2008.

Catt, Carrie Chapman, and Nettie Rogers Shuler. *Woman Suffrage and Politics: The Inner Story of the Suffrage Movement*. Americana Library, 12. Seattle: University of Washington Press, 1969.

Chace, James. *1912: Wilson, Roosevelt, Taft and Debs: The Election That Changed the Country*. New York: Simon & Schuster, 2004.

Chesler, Ellen. *Woman of Valor: Margaret Sanger and the Birth Control Movement in America*. New York: Simon & Schuster, 1992.

Coe, Urling C. *Frontier Doctor: Observations on Central Oregon and the Changing West*. Corvallis: Oregon State University Press, 1996.

Crosby, Alfred W. *America's Forgotten Pandemic: The Influenza of 1918*. Second edition. New York: Cambridge University Press, 2003.

Dawley, Alan. *Changing the World: American Progressives in War and Revolution*. Princeton, New Jersey: Princeton University Press, 2003.

D'Emilio, John, and Estelle B. Freedman. *Intimate Matters: A History of Sexuality in America*. New York: Harper & Row, 1988.

Duniway, Abigail. *Path Breaking: An Autobiographical History of the Equal Suffrage Movement in Pacific Coast States*. Second edition. Studies in the Life of Women. New York: Schocken Books, 1971.

Edwards, G. Thomas. *Sowing Good Seeds: The Northwest Suffrage Campaigns of Susan B. Anthony*. Portland: Oregon Historical Society Press, 1990.

Faderman, Lillian. *Surpassing the Love of Men: Romantic Friendship and Love between Women from the Renaissance to the Present*. New York: William Morrow and Company, 1981.

Faderman, Lillian. *To Believe in Women: What Lesbians Have Done for America—A History*. Boston: Houghton Mifflin, 1999.

Flynn, Elizabeth Gurley. *I Speak My Own Piece: Autobiography of "The Rebel Girl."* New York: Masses & Mainstream, 1955.

Flynn, Elizabeth Gurley, and Rosalyn Fraad Baxandall. *Words on Fire: The Life and Writing of Elizabeth Gurley Flynn*. The Douglass Series on Women's Lives and the Meaning of Gender. New Brunswick: Rutgers University Press, 1987.

Foner, Philip Sheldon. *Fellow Workers and Friends: I.W.W. Free Speech Fights as Told by Participants*, Contributions in American History No 92. Westport, Connecticut: Greenwood Press, 1981.

Fradkin, Philip L. *The Great Earthquake and Firestorms of 1906: How San Francisco Nearly Destroyed Itself*. Berkeley: University of California Press, 2005.

Franzen, Trisha. *Anna Howard Shaw: The Work of Woman Suffrage*. Urbana: University of Illinois Press, 2014.

Freedman, Estelle B. *Their Sisters' Keepers: Women's Prison Reform in America, 1830–1930*. Ann Arbor: The University of Michigan Press, 1981.

Fuller, Paul E. *Laura Clay and the Woman's Rights Movement*. Lexington: University of Kentucky Press, 1992.

Gerstle, Gary. *Working-Class Americanism: The Politics of Labor in a Textile City, 1914–1960*, Interdisciplinary Perspectives on Modern History. New York: Cambridge University Press, 1989.

Gordon, Linda. *The Moral Property of Women: A History of Birth Control Politics in America*. Urbana: University of Illinois Press, 2007.

Gunns, Albert F. *Civil Liberties in Crisis: The Pacific Northwest 1917–1940*. New York: Garland Publishers, 1983.

Haarsager, Sandra. *Organized Womanhood: Cultural Politics in the Pacific Northwest, 1840–1920*. Norman: University of Oklahoma Press, 1997.

Hamburger, Robert. *Two Rooms: The Life of Charles Erskine Scott Wood*. Lincoln: University of Nebraska Press, 1998.

Hareven, Tamara K., and Randolph Langenbach. *Amoskeag: Life and Work in an American Factory-City*. First edition. New York: Pantheon Books, 1978.

Harris, Katherine. *Long Vistas: Women and Families on Colorado Homesteads*. Niwot, Colorado: University Press of Colorado, 1993.

Hawley, Lowell S., and Ralph Bushnell Potts. *Counsel for the Damned: A Biography of George Francis Vanderveer*. First edition. Philadelphia: J.B. Lippincott Co., 1953.

Hoobler, Dorothy, and Thomas Hoobler. *The Irish American Family Album, American Family Albums*. New York: Oxford University Press, 1995.

Hunter Graham, Sara. *Woman Suffrage and the New Democracy*. New Haven, Connecticut: Yale University Press, 1996.

Jensen, Kimberly. *Mobilizing Minerva: American Women in the First World War*. Urbana: University of Illinois Press, 2008.

Jensen, Kimberly. *Oregon's Doctor to the World: Esther Pohl Lovejoy and a Life in Activism*. Seattle: University of Washington Press, 2012.

Johnston, Robert D. *The Radical Middle Class: Populist Democracy and the Question of Capitalism in Progressive Era Portland, Oregon*. Princeton, New Jersey: Princeton University Press, 2003.

Katz, Jonathan. *Gay American History: Lesbians and Gay Men in the U.S.A.: A Documentary History*. Revised edition. New York: Meridian, 1992.

Kennedy, David M. *Over Here: The First World War and American Society*. Twenty-fifth anniversary edition. New York: Oxford University Press, 2004.

Kennedy, Kathleen. *Disloyal Mothers and Scurrilous Citizens: Women and Subversion During World War I*. Bloomington: Indiana University Press, 1999.

Kissack, Terence S. *Free Comrades: Anarchism and Homosexuality in the United States, 1895–1917*. Oakland, California: AK Press, 2008.

Kohn, Stephen M. *American Political Prisoners: Prosecutions under the Espionage and Sedition Acts*. Westport, Connecticut: Praeger, 1994.

Kornbluth, Joyce L. *Rebel Voices: An IWW Anthology*. Chicago: Charles H. Kerr Publishing Company, 1988.

Kurzman, Dan. *Disaster!: The Great San Francisco Earthquake and Fire of 1906*. First edition. New York: W. Morrow, 2001.

Lansing, Jewel. *Portland: People, Politics, and Power, 1851–2001*. Corvallis: Oregon State University Press, 2005.

Larsell, Olof. *The Doctor in Oregon: A Medical History*. Portland: Binfords & Mort for the Oregon Historical Society, 1947.

Leeson, Fred. *Rose City Justice: A Legal History of Portland, Oregon*. First edition. Portland: Oregon Historical Society Press, Published in cooperation with the Oregon State Bar, 1998.

Levenson, Leah, and Jerry H. Natterstad. *Hanna Sheehy-Skeffington, Irish Feminist*. First edition, Irish Studies. Syracuse, N.Y.: Syracuse University Press, 1986.

Luchetti, Cathy. *Medicine Women: The Story of Early-American Women Doctors*. New York: Crown Publishers, 1998.

Lunardini, Christine A. *From Equal Suffrage to Equal Rights: Alice Paul and the National Woman's Party, 1910–1928*. University Park: Pennsylvania State University, 2011.

MacColl, E. Kimbark. *The Shaping of a City: Business and Politics in Portland, Oregon 1885–1915*. Portland, Oregon: The Georgian Press, 1976.

MacColl, E. Kimbark, and Harry H. Stein. *Merchants, Money, and Power: The Portland Establishment, 1843–1913*. Portland, Oregon: Georgian Press, 1988.

Mead, Rebecca J. *How the Vote Was Won: Woman Suffrage in the Western United States, 1868–1914*. New York: New York University Press, 2004.

Miller, Sally M. *From Prairie to Prison: The Life of Social Activist Kate Richards O'Hare, Missouri Biography Series*. Columbia: University of Missouri Press, 1993.

Morantz-Sanchez, Regina Markell. *Sympathy and Science: Women Physicians in American Medicine*. New York: Oxford University Press, 1985.

More, Ellen S. *Restoring the Balance: Women Physicians and the Profession of Medicine, 1850–1995*. Cambridge, Massachusetts: Harvard University Press, 1999.

Moynihan, Ruth Barnes. *Rebel for Rights: Abigail Scott Duniway*, Yale Historical Publications Miscellany. New Haven: Yale University Press, 1983.

Munk, Michael. *The Portland Red Guide: Sites & Stories of Our Radical Past*. Portland, Oregon: Ooligan Press, 2007.

Myers, Gloria E. *A Municipal Mother: Portland's Lola Greene Baldwin, America's First Policewoman*. Corvallis: Oregon State University Press, 1995.

O'Donnell, Terence, and Thomas Vaughan. *Portland: A Historical Sketch and Guide*. Portland: Oregon Historical Society, 1976.

Painter, George. *The Vice Clique: Portland's Great Sex Scandal*. Portland: Espresso Book Machine, 2013.

Polishuk, Sandy, and Julia Ruuttila. *Sticking to the Union: An Oral History of the Life and Times of Julia Ruuttila*. First edition, Palgrave Studies in Oral History. New York: Palgrave Macmillan, 2003.

Pratt, Alice Day. *A Homesteader's Portfolio*. Corvallis: Oregon State University Press, 1993.

Pratt, Laurence. *I Remember Portland 1899–1915*. Portland, Oregon: Metropolitan Printing Company, 1965.

Reagan, Leslie J. *When Abortion Was a Crime: Women, Medicine, and Law in the United States, 1867–1973*. Berkeley: University of California Press, 1997.

Richmond, Al. *Native Daughter: The Story of Anita Whitney*. San Francisco: Anita Whitney Seventy-Fifth Anniversary Committee, 1942.

Rosemont, Franklin. *Joe Hill: The IWW and the Making of a Revolutionary Workingclass Counterculture*. First edition. Chicago: Charles H. Kerr Publishing Company, 2003.

Sanger, Margaret. *An Autobiography*. New York: W. W. Norton, 1938.

Sanger, Margaret, Esther Katz, Cathy Moran Hajo, and Peter Engelman. *The Selected Papers of Margaret Sanger*. Urbana: University of Illinois Press, 2003.

Schlereth, Thomas J. *Victorian America: Transformations in Everyday Life, 1876–1915, The Everyday Life in America Series*. New York: HarperCollins Publishers, 1991.

Sinclair, Andrew. *The Better Half: The Emancipation of the American Woman*. First edition. New York: Harper & Row, 1965.

Solinger, Rickie. *The Abortionist: A Woman against the Law*. New York: Free Press, 1994.

Solinger, Rickie. *Reproductive Politics: What Everyone Needs to Know*. New York: Oxford University Press, 2013.

Starr, Paul. *The Social Transformation of American Medicine*. New York: Basic Books, 1982.

Stryker, Susan, and Jim Van Buskirk. *Gay by the Bay: A History of Queer Culture in the San Francisco Bay Area*. San Francisco: Chronicle Books, 1996.

Thomas, William H. *Unsafe for Democracy: World War I and the U.S. Justice Department's Covert Campaign to Suppress Dissent*. Studies in American Thought and Culture. edited by Paul S. Boyer. Madison: University of Wisconsin Press, 2008.

Tyler, Robert L. *Rebels of the Woods: The I.W.W. In the Pacific Northwest*. Eugene: University of Oregon Books, 1967.

Walsh, Mary Roth. *"Doctors Wanted: No Women Need Apply": Sexual Barriers in the Medical Profession, 1835–1975*. New Haven: Yale University Press, 1977.

Wheeler, Marjorie Spruill, ed. *One Woman, One Vote: Rediscovering the Woman Suffrage Movement*. Troutdale, Oregon: NewSage Press, 1995.

Winchester, Simon. *A Crack in the Edge of the World: America and the Great California Earthquake of 1906*. New York: HarperCollins, 2005

Index